Kant on Freedom, Law, and Happiness

PAUL GUYER

Florence R. C. Murray Professor in the Humanities
University of Pennsylvania

CAMBRIDGE
UNIVERSITY PRESS

PUBLISHED BY THE PRESS SYNDICATE OF THE UNIVERSITY OF CAMBRIDGE
The Pitt Building, Trumpington Street, Cambridge, United Kingdom

CAMBRIDGE UNIVERSITY PRESS
The Edinburgh Building, Cambridge CB2 2RU, UK   http://www.cup.cam.ac.uk
40 West 20th Street, New York, NY 10011–4211, USA   http://www.cup.org
10 Stamford Road, Oakleigh, Melbourne 3166, Australia
Ruiz de Alarcón 13, 28014 Madrid, Spain

© Paul Guyer 2000

First published 2000

Printed in the United States of America

Typeface Palatino 10.5/13 pt.   *System* QuarkXPress [AG]

A catalog record for this book is available from the British Library.

Library of Congress Cataloging in Publication data

Guyer, Paul, 1948–
Kant on freedom, law, and happiness / Paul Guyer.
p.   cm.
Includes index.
ISBN 0–521–65278–2 (hardcover). – ISBN 0–521–65421–1 (pbk.)
1. Kant, Immanuel, 1724–1804.– Contributions in ethics.   2. Ethics.
I. Title.
B2799.E8G89 2000
170′.92 – dc21   99–15853
                                                                        CIP

ISBN 0 521 65278 2 hardback
ISBN 0 521 65421 1 paperback

Contents

Acknowledgments   *page* vii
Note on Translations and Citations   xi

Introduction   1

Part I   Origins
1   Mendelssohn and Kant:
     One Source of the Critical Philosophy   17
2   The Unity of Reason: Pure Reason as
     Practical Reason in Kant's Early Conception
     of the Transcendental Dialectic   60
3   Freedom as the Inner Value of the World   96

Part II   Principles
4   Kant's Morality of Law and Morality
     of Freedom   129
5   The Possibility of the Categorical Imperative   172
6   The Strategy of Kant's *Groundwork*   207

Part III   Duties
7   Kantian Foundations for Liberalism   235
8   Life, Liberty, and Property: Rawls and Kant   262
9   Moral Worth, Virtue, and Merit   287

Contents

Part IV   *Hopes*

10   From a Practical Point of View:
      Kant's Conception of a Postulate
      of Pure Practical Reason   333
11   Nature, Freedom, and Happiness:
      The Third Proposition of Kant's
      Idea for a Universal History   372
12   Nature, Morality, and the Possibility of Peace   408

Index   435

Acknowledgments

The chapters that comprise this volume were written for diverse occasions over the past decade, and I have many conference organizers and editors to thank for their invitations. Chapter 1, "Mendelssohn and Kant: One Source of the Critical Philosophy," was written at the invitation of Christopher Hill for a special issue of *Philosophical Topics*, where it was published in volume 19 (1991): 119–52. Chapter 2, "The Unity of Reason," was first presented at a conference at the University of Chicago honoring the late Manley Thompson on the occasion of his retirement, and then published at the invitation of Henry Allison in a special issue of the *Monist*, which he edited, volume 72 (1989): 139–67. Chapter 3, "Freedom as the Inner Value of the World," was written at the invitation of Christel Fricke, Peter König, and Thomas Petersen for the Festschrift for Hans-Friedrich Fulda which they edited, *Das Recht der Vernunft: Kant und Hegel über Denken, Erkennen und Handeln* (Stuttgart–Bad Canstatt: Frommann-Holzboog, 1995), where it appeared in a superb translation by Thomas Petersen (pp. 232–62); this is its first publication in English. Chapter 4, "Kant's Morality of Law and Morality of Freedom," was written for a 1991 conference at Florida State University in honor of the late W. H. Werkmeister, organized by Russell M. Dancy, who then edited the volume in which it appeared, *Kant and Critique: New Essays in Honor of W. H. Werkmeister* (Dordrecht: Kluwer, 1993), pp. 43–89. Chapter 5, "The Possibility of the Categorical Imperative," was originally presented at Haverford College and, at the invitation of the late Marx Wartofsky, at

Baruch College of the City University of New York; it was then published in the *Philosophical Review* 104 (1995): 353–85. Chapter 6, "The Strategy of Kant's *Groundwork*," was written at the invitation of Marcelo Stamm for the Festschrift that he edited in honor of Dieter Henrich, *Philosophie in synthetischer Absicht* (Stuttgart: Klett-Cotta, 1998), pp. 271–98; the paper was also presented at the Second Brazilian Kant Congress (1997) at the invitation of Valerio Rhoden, Guido de Antônio Almeida, and Vera Cristina Bueno de Andrade. Chapter 7, "Kantian Foundations for Liberalism," was written at the invitation of Sharon Byrd, Joachim Hruschka, and Jan Joerden for a bicentennial conference on Kant's *Metaphysics of Morals* held at Smith College in 1996, and was then published under their editorship in *Jahrbuch für Recht und Ethik/Annual Review of Law and Ethics* 5 (1997): 121–40. Chapter 8, "Life, Liberty, and Property: Rawls and Kant," was written for a 1992 conference at the Philipps Universität, Marburg, organized by Burkhard Tuschling, and then published in the volume edited by Dieter Hüning and Tuschling, *Recht, Staat und Völkerrecht bei Immanuel Kant* (Berlin: Duncker and Humblot, 1998), pp. 273–91. Chapter 9, "Moral Worth, Virtue, and Merit," was written especially for this volume and appears here for the first time; I thank my longtime editor and friend Terence Moore for the encouragement to write this essay. Chapter 10, "From a Practical Point of View," was given as a lecture in 1995 at the Humboldt Universität zu Berlin, the Georg-August Universität, Göttingen, and the Ludwig Maximilians Universität, Munich, and then published at the invitation of Wilhelm Vossenkuhl in the *Philosophisches Jahrbuch* 104 (1997): 1–18. The paper appeared there in an abbreviated German translation, under the title "In praktischer Absicht: Kants Begriff eines Postulates der reinen praktischen Vernunft," which I prepared with help from Katerina Kaiser and Rolf-Peter Horstmannn; this is its first appearance in English. Chapter 11, "Nature, Freedom, and Happiness: The Third Proposition of Kant's *Idea for a Universal History*," is to appear in a French translation in L' *"Idee d'une histoire universelle du point de vue cosmopolitique" de Kant*, edited by Jean-Christophe Merle (Paris: Ophrys, forthcoming); this will be its first appearance in English. Finally, Chapter 12, "Nature, Morality, and the Possibility of Peace," was presented in 1995 at the

Eighth International Kant Congress in Memphis, at the invitation of the organizing committee, and published in the *Proceedings of the Eighth International Kant Congress*, edited by Hoke Robinson (Milwaukee: Marquette University Press, 1995), volume I, part 1, pp. 51–69; this chapter has been somewhat revised for this volume. Minor corrections and stylistic improvements have been silently made throughout; more significant departures from the previously printed versions of these chapters have been noted. I thank all of these editors and publishers for their original invitations as well as their permission to reprint these essays.

I hope that these chapters reflect the benefits I have received not only from the published works but also from the personal friendship and encouragement of such devoted and accomplished students of Kant and Kantian ethics as Henry Allison, Karl Ameriks, the late Lewis White Beck, Frederick C. Beiser, the late Mary Gregor, Dieter Henrich, Barbara Herman, Thomas E. Hill Jr., Rolf-Peter Horstmann, Christine Korsgaard, Onora O'Neill, Nelson Potter, John Rawls, J. B. Schneewind, Nancy Sherman, the late Manley Thompson, Allen Wood, and many, many others. These essays have also benefited from conversations with Samuel Freeman, R. Jay Wallace, and Juliet Floyd as well as the superb students who have worked on Kant's ethics with me in recent years, including Frederick Rauscher, Curtis Bowman, Josefine Nauckhoff, Jennifer Uleman, Cynthia Schossberger, Lucas Thorpe, and Julian Wuerth.

For their help in proofreading, I am grateful to Jennifer Dobe, Shane Duarte, Michael Felberbaum, Elizabeth Glazer, Scott Mann, Michael Rohlf, Jeffrey Scarborough, Laurie Siegel, Lucas Thorpe, Isabella Trautmansdorff, Ryan Vlasak, and Julian Wuerth.

Writing these acknowledgments, I have been reminded of the irreplaceable losses that students of Kant have suffered during the past decade. I would like to commemorate here the lives and works of not only Lewis White Beck, Mary Gregor, and Manley Thompson, but also John Atwell, Robert Butts, Eva Schaper, and J. Michael Young.

Note on Translations and Citations

All quotations from and references to passages in Kant's works are located by parenthetical citations of the volume and page number in *Kants gesammelte Schriften*, edited by the Royal Prussian (later German) Academy of Sciences (Berlin: Georg Reimer et al., later Walter de Gruyter, 1900–), except for citations from the *Critique of Pure Reason*, which are located by the customary use of the pagination of its first ("A") and second ("B") editions. Translations are based on the text of this edition, the so-called *Akademie* edition, unless otherwise indicated. The source of the translations in each chapter is indicated in a note in that chapter; most translations are my own, but where I have followed an existing translation, I have noted that. When I have cited the *Critique of Pure Reason*, I have not usually used any abbreviation for it, since the use of the "A" and "B" pagination will make the source clear. For other works, I have used the following abbreviations:

CJ	*Critique of Judgment*
CPracR	*Critique of Practical Reason*
G	*Groundwork for the Metaphysics of Morals*
IUH	*Idea for a Universal History from a Cosmopolitan Point of View*
JäL	*Jäsche Logic*
MM	*Metaphysics of Morals*
MM, DR	*Metaphysics of Morals*, Part I, "Doctrine of Right"
MM, DV	*Metaphysics of Morals*, Part II, "Doctrine of Virtue"

OPP	*Only Possible Basis for a Proof of the Existence of God*
OQ	*An Old Question Raised Again: Is the Human Race Constantly Progressing?* (*The Conflict of the Faculties,* Part II)
PP	*Toward Perpetual Peace*
R	*Reflexionen,* that is, the notes and fragments in Kant's *Handschriftliche Nachlaß* ("handwritten remains"), collected in volumes 14–19 of the *Akademie* edition.
Rel	*Religion within the Boundaries of Mere Reason*
RP	*What Real Progress Has Metaphysics Made since the Time of Leibniz and Wolff?*
TP	*On the Common Saying: That Might Be Right in Theory but Not in Practice*

Introduction

Immanuel Kant is the philosopher who brought to its culmination the eighteenth-century Enlightenment's argument for the freedom of human thought and action from the bonds of traditional political and theological autocracy. Yet Kant has also seemed to many to advocate an insistence upon obedience to law for its own sake, an insistence upon blind obedience to law that in the twentieth century just ended has been associated with the destruction of everything for which the Enlightenment stood. A profound paradox can be avoided only if it can be shown that Kant intended obedience to universal law to be mandatory solely as the necessary condition for the realization of human freedom and through that freedom a systematic and unselfish distribution of happiness among all persons seeking a systematic union of their purposes in a world both natural and moral in which each and every person is treated as an end and never merely as a means.[1] On this account, while all human beings must be treated as ends in themselves, the sheer fact of adherence to universal law is not an end in itself but is rather the means to the realization of the human potential for autonomy or freedom in both choice and action. In Kant's own words, "If only rational beings can be an end in themselves, this

[1] For the idea of a systematic union of purposes or a "whole of all ends in systematic interconnection," see G, 4:433; for the idea of a world that is both natural and yet moral, see the idea of "the world as it would be if it were in conformity with all moral laws" as a "moral world" at A 808/B 836; and for the idea of treating all persons as ends and never merely as means, see G, 4:429.

1

is not because they have reason but because they have freedom. Reason is merely a means."[2] Kant is the paradigmatic philosopher of the Enlightenment because he saw that the fundamental value of human freedom could be realized, preserved, and promoted only through laws, although not any laws handed down by political or religious tradition, but laws that human beings freely give to themselves through the use of their own reason, and that human happiness in turn could be valued not as the gift of a benevolent dictator, whether human or divine, but only as the product of human freedom itself.

Kant's practical philosophy – that is, his theory of the fundamental principles and conditions of the possibility of human action both moral and political – has of course always been recognized to revolve around the concepts of freedom, reason, law, and happiness. But the relationship among these concepts that the following essays propose – that freedom is our most fundamental value, that the law that we can formulate by means of our reason is valuable only as the means to freedom, and that a system of human happiness should be the outcome of the use of our freedom – has by no means been self-evident. The traditional approach to Kant's practical philosophy, certainly encouraged by much that Kant wrote in his two widely read masterworks of the 1780s, the *Groundwork for the Metaphysics of Morals* of 1785 and the *Critique of Practical Reason* of 1788, grounds Kant's moral philosophy on the fact of human freedom but not on its fundamental value. On such an approach, the relationship among the concepts of freedom, reason, law, can be described as follows. Freedom of the will is the fundamental characteristic of human beings as agents of actions, even though the thoroughgoing causal determinism of nature and all that it includes, even humans themselves as objects of knowledge, is the fundamental presupposition of all human cognition. (These two apparently incompatible suppositions are supposed to be reconciled by Kant's still controversial doctrine of "transcendental idealism.") The freedom of our capacity to choose among alternative principles and paths of conduct is accompanied by

---

[2] See Kant's lectures on natural law from the winter semester of 1784–85, *Naturrecht Feyerabend*, 27:1321.

reason, our capacity to formulate universally valid principles of both cognition and conduct, and we thus have the capacity to conform our freely chosen actions to universally valid principles. Indeed, we express our identity as rational beings only when we free our conduct from determination by merely natural factors such as inclinations and desires and instead determine our own conduct in accordance with universal laws furnished by our reason. Thus, as beings who are both blessed and cursed with freedom of the will, we have the freedom to choose whether or not to govern our actions by reason and its ideal of universal law, which, applied to the sphere of conduct, is the moral law; indeed, in order to live up to our potential as rational beings, we must govern our freedom by adherence to the moral law. Of course, we are not merely rational beings; as finite and mortal creatures in nature, we inevitably also have inclinations and desires, and the happiness of each of us lies in the fulfillment of the objectives suggested to us by such natural stimuli or incentives to action. But it is morally permissible for each of us to pursue our own happiness only within the bounds set by moral law as a limiting condition. Our complete good, or the ultimate objective of all our actions, is thus a composite good set for us by our dual nature: as rational beings, we aim to conform our freedom of choice and thus our principles of conduct to the moral law, and we see our virtue and any worthiness to be happy that we may achieve as consisting exclusively in our success in ruling our freedom through the moral law; as natural or, as Kant often says, animal creatures, we each aim to achieve happiness by fulfilling our naturally occurring desires; but as beings both rational and animal, we should always subordinate the latter goal to the former. We need not deny the permissibility of seeking our own happiness, but we must always seek virtue first and happiness only when the claims of virtue have been satisfied.[3]

---

[3] For an exemplar of the classical approach to Kant's ethics that is unparalleled in its economy and elegance, see J. B. Schneewind, "Autonomy, Obligation and Virtue: An Overview of Kant's Moral Philosophy," in Paul Guyer, ed., *The Cambridge Companion to Kant* (Cambridge: Cambridge University Press, 1992), pp. 309–41.

There is much that is intellectually admirable and morally uplifting in this understanding of Kant's austere and rigorous doctrine. Above all, at least for a certain kind of reader, Kant's idea that human morality is human autonomy, the governance of our freedom by a supreme principle of morality that we generate out of our own reason, is a welcome liberation from the idea that we can govern our behavior only by fear of punishment or hope of reward from a human or superhuman lawgiver. For Kant and those who see him as the paradigmatic philosopher of the Enlightenment, any idea of the latter sort, no matter how it is dressed up with the trappings of political prudence or religious piety, is a philosophy of human servitude, not of human freedom. At the same time, at least for philosophical sensibilities bred on Hume as well as Kant, there is something unsettling in this traditional approach to Kant's moral philosophy, particularly in its suggestion that our obligation and even our motivation to live up to the demands of the moral law follow simply and immediately from our identity as rational as well as natural beings. So understood, Kant's theory seems to pull a rabbit out of a hat or, in the terms made famous by Hume, to derive an *ought* from an *is*:[4] Kant seems to try to justify the most fundamental norm for our conduct, the indisputable principle of how we *should* act, which should surely be free from all the uncertainty of speculative metaphysics, precisely from a metaphysical characterization of our identity, which at best tells us how we *could* act, and which in any case seems far more controversial and dubious than the moral principle it is supposed to ground – one that Kant himself insists, in every one of his chief works in practical philosophy, is always accessible to untutored

---

[4] See David Hume, *A Treatise of Human Nature*, book III, part I, section I, in the edition by L. A. Selby Bigge (Oxford: Clarendon Press, 1888), 2 ed., rev. P. H. Nidditch (Oxford: Clarendon Press, 1975), pp. 469–70. While Kant is supposed to have been unable to read English, and thus unfamiliar with much in Hume's *Treatise*, which was not translated into German until 1791, after Kant had already written and published his major works in moral philosophy, Kant would have been well familiar with the basic character of Hume's argument from the latter's *Enquiry concerning the Principles of Morals*, published in 1751 and first translated into German as early as 1755 (see appendix I in the edition by L. A. Selby-Bigge, 3 ed., rev. P. H. Nidditch [Oxford: Clarendon Press, 1978], pp. 285–94).

human understanding and may need philosophical reflection to defend it from certain kinds of threats but certainly neither to discover nor to justify it.[5] But that Kant should attempt to derive a normative *ought* from a metaphysical *is* should seem strange not only in light of his own commitment to the immediate accessibility of the fundamental principle of morality to every normally reflective human being; it should also seem strange in light of the fact that the difference between the "theoretical" and the "practical" points of view – though also, to be sure, their ultimate compatibility – is one of the cornerstones of Kant's entire philosophical enterprise. As Kant famously put it in the preface to the second edition of the *Critique of Pure Reason* (1787), the point of his whole venture into the theory of human knowledge and its objects was to *limit* knowledge in order to leave room for faith and the moral insight that is the only possible basis for faith (B xxx), not to *ground* moral insight and faith in speculative metaphysical knowledge. If this is so, then Kant's moral philosophy must be founded on the recognition of the fundamental value of human freedom and not merely on the supposed fact of human freedom.

The essays collected in this book argue that the idea of freedom functions not just as Kant's fundamental metaphysical presupposition, in the form of freedom of the will, but also as his most fundamental normative presupposition: according to Kant, freedom of choice and its natural expression in action are what human beings value most, and the fundamental principle of morality and the rules for both political and personal conduct that follow from its application in both public and private spheres constitute the laws that we must adopt and adhere to in order to preserve and promote freedom itself as our most fundamental value. This is not to say that, as a systematic philosopher, Kant did not try to guarantee

---

[5] That the fundamental principle of morality is recognized by each and every one of us as soon as we reflect upon any example of human conduct is assumed by Kant in all of his writings on moral philosophy: for example, throughout the first section of the *Groundwork for the Metaphysics of Morals* (4:393–405), in the *Critique of Practical Reason* (e.g., §6, Problem II, 5:29–30), and in the *Religion within the Boundaries of Mere Reason* (Part I, 6:36–37). I discuss the implications of this assumption for the strategy and structure of the *Groundwork* and Kant's moral philosophy as a whole in Chapter 6.

that it is possible for us to realize the normative ideal of freedom and to live up to the laws necessary to achieve this end by solving the traditional metaphysical problem of the freedom of the will. Far from it; the problem of the freedom of the will was already a central issue in Kant's first purely philosophical publication, the *New Elucidation of the First Principles of Metaphysical Cognition* of 1755,[6] written long before (any of our evidence shows that) Kant had begun to think about the normative content of his eventual practical philosophy. But what Kant eventually came to argue is that, although purely theoretical philosophy can and indeed must make conceptual space for the *possibility* of the freedom of the human will, we can only infer the *actuality* of the freedom of our will from our consciousness of our obligation under the moral law, as the necessary presupposition of our ability to fulfill that obligation. This is the heart of Kant's argument in the *Critique of Practical Reason,* and the foundation for his view that we can act upon the basis of a faith for which the limits of knowledge can do no more than make room.[7] Thus Kant's mature view is that the metaphysical fact of our freedom can be established only upon the recognition of our moral obligations, and once the basis of our moral obligations themselves is seen to be nothing other than the fundamental value of freedom itself, the priority of his normative conception of freedom over his metaphysical conception of freedom becomes all the more apparent. For this reason, my primary

---

[6] In the *Akademie* edition, 1:385–416; in Immanuel Kant, *Theoretical Philosophy, 1755–1770,* ed. and trans. David Walford (Cambridge: Cambridge University Press, 1992), pp. 1–45. Kant's defense of a Leibnizian version of a compatibilist solution to the problem of free will, in which an action counts as free as long as it is a result of the internal cause of an agent's perception of the action undertaken as the best course of action open to him, even if that perception is fully determined by anything or everything in the agent's antecedent history, is found in the discussion of Proposition IX, 1:398–405. In this discussion Kant defends Leibniz's compatibilism against the radical indeterminism of the Pietist and anti–Leibnizo-Wolffian philosopher Christian August Crusius; Kant's later "transcendental idealist" solution to the problem of free will can be seen as his attempt to reconcile Leibniz and Crusius by combining a Leibnizian account of the phenomenal character of human actions with a Crusian account of their noumenal or "intelligible" character (see A 538–93/B 566–67).

[7] See *CPracR,* 5:29–30, 44–50, and many other passages.

concern in almost all of what follows is to document and to understand Kant's commitment to the normative thesis that freedom is our fundamental value, and I touch only occasionally upon his attempt to solve the metaphysical problem of the freedom of the will.[8]

The view that the preservation and promotion of freedom itself is the primary end of human action and that reason, thus the law that reason provides, is only the means did not spring full-blown from Kant's brow like Athena from the brow of Zeus. It emerged only gradually over the first three decades of Kant's philosophical career, from the commencement of his teaching and publishing activity in the middle of the 1750s to the publication of his mature masterpieces on morality and human history beginning in the middle of the 1780s. The three essays that form Part I of this collection under the title "Origins" focus on some moments in the long gestation of Kant's mature view. The first chapter, a study of Kant's early essay *An Inquiry concerning the Distinctness of the Principles of Natural Theology and Morality*, highlights some features of Kant's emerging conception of plausible methods for both theoretical and practical philosophy by contrasting Kant's essay with the elegant *Essay on Evidence* of Moses Mendelssohn, which the Berlin Academy of Science had actually selected over Kant's essay for the prize of fifty golden ducats offered in the academy's essay competition of 1762. (Although Kant did not share in the monetary award, which at that point in his life he could well have used, both essays were published together by the academy in 1764.) Like Kant's essay, this chapter is not devoted exclusively to moral philosophy; rather it places Kant's emerging moral philosophy in his emerging philosophy as a whole. But this should serve as a reminder that Kant's moral philosophy is always part of a larger philosophical enterprise, even if it is in many ways the driving force behind this enterprise; and throughout the chapters that follow, one feature of my approach is often to appeal to concepts and theses from all parts of Kant's philosophy to support my interpretation of his moral philosophy.

---

[8] My most extensive comments on the latter issue will be found in Chapter 10.

In this case, what we learn is this: the key issue of the essay as a whole is to argue, contrary to what Kant understands the assumption of Leibnizo-Wolffian rationalism to be, that knowledge in any area can never be derived from merely logical or "formal" principles, but always requires "material" or substantive premises about the objects of knowledge as well; the key insight for Kant's eventual practical philosophy contained in this work is then the idea that moral philosophy too must begin with a fundamental although indemonstrable material or substantive principle, a fundamental source of value, and cannot rely on any purely formal law alone: the rationalist idea that we must always strive to maximize perfection, for example, is useless without a substantive account of what human perfection is. At the time that Kant wrote this essay, to be sure, he did not yet have any clear idea of what the fundamental material principle of ethics could be, and he certainly did not yet have the idea that freedom itself could be our fundamental value, to be preserved and promoted by adherence to a formal law given by human reason; and many interpreters of Kant have surely thought that precisely because it was unclear what the source of a fundamental material principle for ethics could be, the key step in the development of Kant's ethics must have been nothing less than giving up the prize essay's view that morality requires a material principle and attempting to derive everything in morality from a purely formal law of reason instead. But my argument throughout the chapters in this book is that once Kant discovered that freedom itself could be seen as the basic human value that is preserved and promoted by adherence to universal law, he never had to surrender his initial insight that morality, like every other systematic product of the human intellect, requires a substantive or material as well as a formal principle: freedom itself is the substance for which the moral law provides the form.

In the remaining two chapters of Part I, I examine further steps toward his eventual practical philosophy that Kant undertook during the formative period of the 1770s – the so-called silent decade during which Kant in fact made enormous progress on both the theoretical and the practical philosophy that would be announced in his great works of the 1780s. In Chapter 2, on "The Unity of Reason," I consider the development of Kant's idea that the faculty of reason, or our tendency to seek completeness and systematicity in all forms of thought, leads to metaphysical illusion if taken as a basis for knowledge in the theoretical sphere but is salubrious and necessary in the practical sphere, or as a guide to conduct. This chapter draws especially on Kant's outlines for the emerging *Critique of Pure Reason* and its "Transcendental Dialectic" from the second half of the 1770s. In these materials, however, Kant leaves quite unclear *to what* the systematizing and totalizing tendencies of reason in what he will come to call its practical use are to be applied. In Kant's notes for his lectures on moral philosophy during this period, however, we can see him struggling with this issue, and these struggles are the topic of Chapter 3, on "Freedom as the Inner Value of the World." Here we see Kant gradually moving from the idea that reason is applied directly to our natural desires in order to produce a systematic form of happiness toward his ultimate view that reason should be applied to our freedom, because of the dignity of freedom, itself, in order to produce the possibility of a systematic exercise of freedom which, however, would have as its outcome, at least under ideal circumstances, a systematic form of happiness. Kant does not reach a systematic elaboration of this view in these materials, but he develops views about the value of freedom – as a self-sufficient source of happiness and as an intrinsic source of self-contentment – that point the way to the central ideas of his mature moral theory, that autonomy has a dignity that is incomparable to the value we place on any particular object of desire and yet itself sets an object for us, the highest good, which includes as an indispensable component the systematic happiness of mankind rather than the self-centered happiness of the individual.

The heart of Kant's mature view of the fundamental principle of morality, the idea that freedom itself is our most fundamental value and yet that freedom must have a systematic connection to human happiness, is the subject of the three essays included in Part II under the title of "Principles." In Chapter 4, "Kant's Morality of Law and Morality of Freedom," the traditional reading of Kant (for which there is, to be sure, much textual evidence), according to which his argument begins by simply assuming the necessity of a pure practical law and introduces any ends or objects of action only subsequently and only insofar as they are compatible with such a practical law, is contrasted with my approach, according to which Kant sees that moral reasoning must begin with the recognition of a morally necessary end, his candidate for which is the fundamental value of freedom itself, and then argues that conformity to universal law is the means to the preservation and promotion of freedom. Although I appeal to a variety of sources to defend this approach, the heart of my interpretation is an analysis of Section II of the seminal *Groundwork for the Metaphysics of Morals*, above all its crucial transition from the Formula of Universal Law to the Formula of Humanity as an End in Itself: it is precisely the capacity to set and consent to ends and the capacities necessary for us to pursue those ends in which humanity as Kant conceives it consists; the idea of humanity as an end in itself, in other words, is identical to the idea of the incomparable dignity of human autonomy or freedom governed by the law that we give to ourselves. This interpretation of Section II of the *Groundwork* is developed in more detail in Chapter 5, "The Possibility of the Categorical Imperative," where I present a fuller account of the relations among the various formulations of Kant's famous "categorical imperative," that is, the form in which the fundamental principle of morality presents itself to us as creatures who have inclinations as well as reason and the freedom to govern ourselves for the sake of that freedom itself. This chapter extends the arguments that freedom in the form of humanity is the fundamental aim and the condition of the possibility of the categorical imperative, that adherence to universal law is the means to this end, that recognition of the capacity for freedom in both oneself and others is the basis for applying this law to all, and finally that the kingdom of ends, which would be the result of universal adherence to this law under ideal circumstances, is in fact a condition under which every human being can freely pursue those of his or her ends that are maximally compatible with the rest of his or her own ends as well as with those of everyone else, thus the condition in which, ideally, the highest good would be realized.

Finally, Chapter 6, on "The Strategy of Kant's *Groundwork*," steps back from the details of Kant's argument to take a broader look at its method. Kant presupposes that both the foundation of morality in the fundamental value of freedom and the primary threats to this morality – namely, the popular philosophy that happiness is the object of morality on the one hand and the philosophy of determinism on the other, which can excuse us from the stringent demands of morality – are natural tendencies of ordinary human consciousness. This strategy imposes two tasks upon Kant: he must make plausible the idea that normal human consciousness immediately or at least readily recognizes the fundamental value of freedom itself; and he must also find a place for the ideas of both happiness and determinism within moral consciousness properly understood rather than allowing them simply to stand outside it. Thus, while Kant cannot allow untutored, individual conceptions of happiness to provide fundamental principles of morality, he can and must allow the idea of a rational and systematic conception of happiness, as the inevitable object of the free and systematic choices of human beings, to return into morality as the ultimate object of human action that is defined for it by the fundamental value of freedom – as the capacity, after all, to set ends – itself. This analysis thus shows that the doctrine of the highest good is not a causal addition to the fundamental principle of Kant's moral philosophy, the incomparable value of human freedom, but a direct consequence of it; this will be the indispensable premise for the Kantian theories of human hopes and human history to be investigated in Part IV of this volume.

Before I turn to Kant's analysis of human hopes, however, the essays in Part III, "Duties," explore the more immediate normative consequences of Kant's conception of freedom as the fundamental principle and object of morality. Chapters 7 and 8, "Kantian Foundations for Liberalism" and "Life, Liberty, and Property," explore Kant's reconciliation of the intrinsically coercive nature of government with the supreme value of human freedom. I defend Kant's assertion that coercion can indeed preserve freedom when it is properly threatened or used only as a hindrance to a hindrance to freedom, and then explore the restrictions on the use of governmental power that this justification of it implies. In particular, I argue that Kant's approach does not justify a libertarian or "night watchman" conception of the state as that is currently understood, but gives rise to a genuinely liberal conception of the state, according to which government, as the expression of the united will of the people, has a well-founded right to regulate the acquisition of property but no right to interfere with the free expression of the conscience and the beliefs of its citizenry. This argument is based on Kant's pathbreaking analysis of the difference between the institution of property, on the one hand, which is always a collective exercise of freedom of action and thus always indeed requires public regulation rather than merely permitting it, and on the other hand the freedom of thought and opinion, which is not an intrinsically collective exercise of freedom and thus does not legitimately invite public regulation. In Chapter 7 I analyze Kant's arguments for this position in some detail, and in Chapter 8 I suggest that John Rawls could have employed the details of Kant's political philosophy and not just Kant's general approach to moral philosophy in his own philosophical defense of liberalism.

In the last chapter in Part III, on "Moral Worth, Virtue, and Merit," I turn from Kant's analysis of those of our obligations that can be legitimately enforced by means of political and juridical coercion, what he calls the "duties of right," to his characterization of the much larger sphere of our duties for which coercive enforcement would be entirely inappropriate, what he calls "duties of virtue." Here I argue that the possibility of *self*-constraint out of respect for the value of freedom or autonomy is the thread that ties together everything that Kant calls virtuous, including both the morally praiseworthy motivation for fulfilling any duty, whether of right or of virtue, as well as the specific duties of virtue that enjoin upon us general ends or policies, such as those of developing our own talents and being beneficent to others, which cannot be mechanically translated into requirements to perform specific actions that would even be candidates for coercive enforcement. This chapter thus extends and completes the argument that Kantian duties are duties to preserve and promote human freedom.

Finally, the three essays in Part IV of the volume, under the title of "Hopes," return to the issue of the highest good and the conditions of the possibility of its realization within human history. I analyze Kant's conceptions of the postulates of pure practical reason, of progress in human history, and of perpetual peace, and show how all three depend on the recognition that the aim of systematic and unselfish human happiness that Kant includes alongside of virtue in his conception of the highest good cannot be understood as a merely natural end that is to be constrained by the requirements of morality; rather, the recognition that our own freedom of choice and action is the fundamental object of morality itself makes a systematic realization of happiness the ultimate object of morality, because freedom is, essentially, the capacity to set our own ends, and happiness is, essentially, the realization of our freely set ends. Chapter 10, "From a Practical Point of View," provides an interpretation of a postulate of pure practical reason as a subjectively valid representation of the existence of the conditions necessary to make the pursuit of such an end rational: in order for it to be rational for us to attempt to achieve a system of freely set and realized ends, we must have an at least subjectively compelling belief in the existence of the conditions of the possibility of such a goal, especially the authorship of nature, and I attempt to show how Kant could have countenanced such a subjectively compelling representation of these conditions within the bounds of his critique of traditional metaphysics and theology. The remaining two chapters in Part III, Chapter 11 on Kant's 1784 essay on universal history and Chapter 12 on his famous essay of 1795 *Toward Perpetual Peace,* argue that Kant's claim that a cosmopolitan world order is the inevitable end of history must be read within this same framework of practical postulates: this claim cannot be understood as a theoretical claim about what a natural science of history will some day conclusively demonstrate to be the inevitable outcome of natural forces, but is rather a view of history and the forces at work within it that we can and must freely adopt in order to pursue rationally the goals we freely set for ourselves in accordance with the fundamental principle of morality. In other words, we must understand Kant's teleological view of nature and the history of mankind within it as itself an expression of human freedom with the power to inspire us to work toward the realization of the conditions that could extend real political and moral freedom to every human being.

Part I
Origins

Chapter 1

Mendelssohn and Kant:
One Source of the Critical Philosophy

In June 1761 the Berlin Academy of Sciences announced an essay competition. The question, which was formulated by the Wolffian aesthetician and academy member Johann Georg Sulzer, asked:

> Whether metaphysical truths in general, and in particular the first principles of *Theologiae naturalis* and morals, are capable of the same clear proof as geometrical truths, and, if they are not capable of the said proof, then what is the real nature of their certainty, to what sort of degree can one bring their certainty, and whether this degree is sufficient for complete conviction? $(2:493)^1$

The deadline for the receipt of essays was 1 January 1763, and in May of that year the academy voted to award the prize (a commemorative gold medal worth fifty ducats) to an essay that turned out to be by Moses Mendelssohn and singled out for special commendation, as "most closely approaching the first in merit," a second essay, which turned out to be by Immanuel Kant. Apparently

---

This chapter originally appeared in *Philosophical Topics* 19 (1991): 119–52.

[1] All translations from Kant as well as Mendelssohn are my own. Citations from Mendelssohn's *Abhandlung über die Evidenz in Metaphysischen Wissenschaften* are drawn from Moses Mendelssohn, *Gesammelte Schriften: Jubiläumsausgabe,* vol. 2: *Schriften zur Philosophie und Ästhetik II,* ed. Fritz Bamberger and Leo Strauss (Berlin: Akademie-Verlag, 1931, reprint, Suttgart–Bad Canstatt: Friedrich Fromann Verlag [Günther Holzboog], 1972); parenthetical page numbers refer to this edition.

there was actually a tie between the two essays on the first two ballots that was broken only when Sulzer, who was presiding, cast his own vote in favor of Mendelssohn.[2] The following month Kant communicated to Samuel Formey, the secretary of the academy, his intention to add a supplement to his essay, which seems to have been written in haste shortly before the deadline;[3] but he apparently never supplied such a supplement, and the two essays were published together in Berlin the following year (1764) as originally submitted. Mendelssohn's piece was published under the title of an *Essay on the Evidence of Metaphysical Truths*,[4] Kant's under the title of an *An Inquiry concerning the Distinctness of the Principles of Natural Theology and Morality*.

Even apart from the Wolffian prejudices that prevailed at the academy, Mendelssohn's essay clearly deserved the prize. It is a masterly summary of the sophisticated synthesis of rationalism tempered by empiricism that had evolved from a century's work by Descartes, Leibniz, and Wolff, whereas Kant's contribution is a much less accomplished work, a statement of some of his grounds for rejecting the Wolffian synthesis, in terms drawn from the German Pietist anti-Wolffian Christian August Crusius as well as from the British moral sense philosophers, that gives only the most rudimentary indication that Kant was himself to develop a philosophical standpoint that would permanently destroy the reputation – if not entirely the influence – of Wolffianism. We have no

---

[2] See Alexander Altmann, *Moses Mendelssohn: A Biographical Study* (University: University of Alabama Press, 1973), p. 116.

[3] See his letter of 28 June 1763 (10:41–42). Kant's essay *Der einzig mögliche Beweisgrund zu einer Demonstration des Daseins Gottes* was published in the second half of December 1762, so he was still at work on that well into the fall of that year (2:470). He therefore could not have worked on the prize essay for more than a few weeks before the deadline for its submission. Some things about academic life remain constant.

[4] Brief discussions of the essay may be found in Lewis White Beck, *Early German Philosophy: Kant and His Predecessors* (Cambridge, Mass.: Harvard University Press, 1969), pp. 330–35, and Altmann, *Moses Mendelssohn*, pp. 112–30. Altman provided a much more detailed commentary in his *Moses Mendelssohns Frühschriften zur Metaphysik* (Tübingen: J. C. B. Mohr [Paul Siebeck]: 1969), pp. 253–391.

reason to believe that Kant felt any deep resentment at the academy's preference of Mendelssohn's work – correspondence between them three years later shows that Kant held Mendelssohn in high regard and was eager to get his opinion about his new work *Dreams of a Spritseer* (1766),[5] and their relations remained more than cordial until their last correspondence in October 1785, a few months before Mendelssohn's death. And when Kant did explicitly criticize Mendelssohn in his 1786 essay *What Is Orientation in Thinking?* he was responding to Mendelssohn's last work, the *Morgenstunden* of 1785, not the early prize essay. Nevertheless, we can look at some of the most distinctive theses of the critical philosophy that Kant was to evolve over the three decades after his loss to Mendelssohn as if they were designed precisely to refute the leading theses of Mendelssohn's essay and thereby show the academy the error of its judgment. This is undoubtedly due to the fact that Mendelssohn's essay did such a good job of summarizing the Leibnizo-Wolffian tradition that Kant was rejecting rather than to the direct influence of his essay itself on Kant's subsequent development. But in any case Mendelssohn's essay provides a useful lens for focusing on some of the most crucial aspects of the critical philosophy's rejection of the particular synthesis of rationalism and empiricism characteristic of the Wolffian tradition and its own quite different synthesis of rationalism and empiricism.

It is the purpose of the present chapter to use Mendelssohn's work as such a lens on the critical philosophy. The essay proceeds in three stages. First, I sketch the argument of Mendelssohn's prize essay. Next, I compare to that the main theses of Kant's prize essay, showing what differences there already were but also in what ways Kant still remained close to the Wolffian synthesis expounded by Mendelssohn. In the final part of the paper, I show how some of the most fundamental aspects of the critical philosophy can be understood as a rejection of the kind of view so elegantly represented by Mendelssohn as well as of views, including his original Crusian and intuitionist premises

---

[5] See his letters of 7 February 1766 and 8 April 1766, 10:67–68, 69–73.

for the rejection of Wolffianism, which had been earlier accepted by Kant himself.

I

The academy asked whether metaphysical truths, especially in natural theology and morality, could be as certain as mathematical truths. Both Mendelssohn and Kant responded by offering a theory of mathematical truth and then comparing the prospects for metaphysical truth with that. Mendelssohn argued that both mathematics and metaphysics consist of a body of analytical truths connected according to purely logical laws, which has to be tied down to reality at some point. In mathematics, it is the evidence of the senses that ultimately turns claims about possibilities into claims about reality, but claims about the senses that leave no room for skepticism. This is true in much of metaphysics and morality as well, he argues, and thus they too consist of a purely rationalistic analysis of concepts tied down to reality by certain fundamental judgments of experience, which are indubitable in the case of metaphysics but which are not all equally indubitable in the case of morality. But since metaphysics includes the ontological argument, which can infer from possibility to reality without the assistance of any sensory evidence at all, metaphysics is at least in part even more certain than mathematics. Kant hardly needed the stimulus of Mendelssohn's essay to turn against the ontological argument – he had already attacked it in his first philosophical work, the *New Exposition of the First Principles of Metaphysical Cognition* (*Nova Delucidatio*) of 1755 – but the centrality of it in Mendelssohn's defense of the rationalist program would certainly have given him impetus to continue the attack. But Kant's ultimate refutation of Mendelssohn will hardly be limited to the ontological argument: in the end, we shall see, the critical philosophy turns Mendelssohn's accounts of mathematics, metaphysics, and the fundamental principle of morality upon their heads – and while the critical philosophy, especially in the final form reached in the *Critique of Judgment*, concedes a large scope to empiricism in the discovery of particular laws of nature, we shall see that when it comes to fundamental principles it actually concedes less to empiricism than the form of Wolffianism represented by Mendelssohn.

Mathematics

Mendelssohn argues that mathematics, which includes the study of continuous as well as discrete quantities and intensive as well as extensive magnitudes, consists of a body of propositions derived entirely from the analysis of basic concepts in accordance with the logical law of noncontradiction where those basic concepts are themselves abstracted from sensory experience. "The certainty of mathematics is grounded on the general axiom, that nothing can both be and not be at the same time," or on the "principle of contradiction"; "and since the object of mathematics is in general *magnitude*, that of geometry in particular *extension*, one can say that in mathematics in general our concepts of magnitude, and in geometry in particular our concepts of extension, are developed and posited from one another." In the case of geometry in particular, "since there is nothing more at its base than the abstracted concept of extension, and from this source all its results are derived," one can say

> that everything which is asserted in it is necessarily connected with the original concept of extension through the principle of contradiction; so there can be no doubt that all geometrical truths must be found *enveloped* [*eingewickelt*] in the concept of extension which geometry then teaches us to *develop* [*entwickeln*]. (273)

For example, Mendelssohn claims, "the concept of extension contains the inner possibility that a space can be enclosed by three straight lines, [and] that two of them can enclose a right angle" (273–74). And, Mendelssohn continues, "whatever is inferred as a consequence" from such propositions or whatever "necessarily comes with them" is also to be understood as "originally and *implicite* to be found in the original concept of extension" (274): thus "the entire force of geometrical certainty rests on the necessary connection of concepts" (277).

Mendelssohn illustrates his claim by a reference to Plato's *Meno*:

21

what Socrates teaches the slave boy, he argues, is precisely how to analyze his "sensory impression of extension," although Plato had such a hard time admitting that so much truth can be contained in a sensory concept that he instead concocted his "strange idea" that the soul has already learned what it experiences in this life in some earlier condition and is merely stimulated to recall it by sensory impressions (275).[6] Mendelssohn's critique of Plato thus illustrates that what we might call his thoroughly rationalist theory of mathematical *proof* is to be accompanied by an equally empiricist theory of mathematical *truth*: the basic concepts from which all other mathematical results can be logically derived, such as the concept of extension, are themselves derived by abstraction from sensory impressions and describe actualities,[7] not mere possibilities, for that reason alone. As he puts it:

> The certainty of geometrical truths is supported only on the unalterable identity of an enveloped concept with the concepts derived [and] developed from it. This is the highest degree of certainty, which however is found only in pure theoretical mathematics. As soon as we want to make use of a geometrical truth in practice, that is, as soon as we want to make a transition from mere possibilities to actualities, then our ground must be an empirical proposition [*Erfahrungssatz*], which says that this or that figure, number, etc. is actually present. The entire domain of mathematics offers no example of an inference from merely possible concepts to the actuality of their object. (283)

---

[6] It seems incorrect to say that Mendelssohn agreed with Leibniz's unabashedly Platonic theory that "sensuous impressions are only the occasions for the soul to bring its innate representations to full consciousness" (Beck, *Early German Philosophy*, p. 332); as we will shortly see, Mendelssohn does believe that geometry's concept of extension is connected with the constitution of our own senses, but this does not mean that the senses merely stimulate the intellect to discover its innate ideas, as Leibniz believed.

[7] Mendelssohn's term is *Würklichkeit* (i.e., *Wirklichkeit*). I translate this as "actuality" in order to distinguish it from the Latinate *Realität*. I do not think there is any philosophical significance in Mendelssohn's (or, generally, Kant's) choice of a Latinate rather than Germanic word, but since Mendelssohn does at least once use the adjective *würklich* to modify the noun *Realitäten* (310, cited later in text), adopting this translation will save us from having to translate him as writing "real realities."

This empirical foundation for mathematics, Mendelssohn claims, does not detract from its "evidence." He argues that it would generally be absurd to demand of it "that it prove the *existence* of a quantity through the analysis of a merely possible concept," and argues that it is indeed only in metaphysics, and indeed even there only in a single case – that of the ontological argument – that there can be an inference from "a mere possibility to an actuality. In every other science, and thus also in mathematics, presence [*Vorhandenseyn*] can never be proved except through the senses" (284).

To conclude the first stage of his discussion, Mendelssohn then asks whether this account of "practical mathematics" does not leave it open to the "attacks of the doubters and idealists." His answer actually comes in two stages. The first is quite striking. He argues that even such opponents must admit that in "general illusion" there is a difference between *invariable* (*beständige*) and *variable* (*veränderliche*) appearances (*Erscheinungen*). The latter are occasioned by idiosyncratic and temporary conditions, "certain external contingencies," which can give unreliable results, such as a case of jaundice, which might disrupt the mechanism of color perception (285). Invariable appearances, however, "have their ground in the inner constitution of the human senses in general" (285), and because of this they "are connected with each other in a regular manner, so that one can never perceive one of them without being assured that one would be able to connect the others with it in an appropriate point of view." *And this is all the mathematician requires*, Mendelssohn claims: "the mathematician never concerns himself about the real existence of things" (284). Because the fundamental concepts of mathematics arise from the nature of human sensibility itself, there is no reason to fear that the results of correct mathematical analysis which arise from them necessarily rather than accidentally can ever be overturned: "We must . . . represent sensible things in this way and not otherwise, because our senses are constituted thus and not otherwise" (286). Since there is no alternative to representing things but as dictated by the fundamental constitution of our senses, the correspondence of the constitution of our senses to any independent constitution of things external to them does not need to be proved. The invariable constitution of our senses is itself an adequate empirical basis for the certainty of mathematics.

Later in the essay, in the discussion of natural theology, Mendelssohn reverts to the issue of the "properties of things external to us." He there argues in a more dogmatic fashion that "what does not pertain to the all-highest being cannot be a reality, since all possible realities pertain to him in the highest degree," and then infers that "extension" as well as "motion and color are mere appearances and not realities; for if they were realities they would have to be ascribed to the all-highest being" (309–10). He thus uses a theological premise to reach the Leibnizian conclusion that we must exclude "extension in general from the realities, and regard it as a mere phenomenon" (310).[8]

Kant's critical theory of mathematical knowledge will of course reject Mendelssohn's rationalist view that mathematical *proof* proceeds by logical inference alone. In spite of the Kantian sound of Mendelssohn's first thesis that mathematical *truth* is adequately grounded in the "inner constitution" of human senses in general, we shall see that here too Kant's position is significantly different from Mendelssohn's first position and indeed closer to his second. But although Kant actually repeats Mendelssohn's theological argument against the reality of space (and time) (B 71–72), his basic argument for this conclusion is quite different from anything offered by Mendelssohn. Before we can turn to Kant, however, we must consider the remainder of Mendelssohn's essay.

Metaphysics

Mendelssohn defines metaphysics as "*a rationally grounded cognition of qualities*"[9] as contrasted to quantities (286). As with "pure

---

[8] This argument is emphasized by Beck (*Early German Philosophy*, p. 333). In his brief treatment, he does not mention that it comes only twenty-five pages after Mendelssohn's first solution to the problem of the reality of our concept of extension and uses a theological premise which is not part of the first discussion. Altmann acknowledges that the issue is dealt with twice, but still writes as if the Leibnizian argument were an inevitable extension of the earlier discussion, which it is not because of the additional theological assumption (*Mendelssohns Frühschriften*, pp. 325–26).

[9] Mendelssohn uses the term *Beschaffenheiten* in this passage, but subsequently uses *Qualitäten* (pp. 287ff.).

theoretical mathematics," there is a part of metaphysics that "sets all actuality aside and merely develops our concepts of the qualities of things in order to understand their inner connection" (289). This analysis is harder in metaphysics than in mathematics because the former must employ arbitrary, merely verbal signs for its concepts, as opposed to the more revealing intuitive representations employed by the latter (290–92).[10] More importantly, however, metaphysics unlike mathematics cannot content itself with mere invariable appearances, but must "take the important step into the realm of actualities" (292). Metaphysics "is obliged to call the testimony of internal and external sense before its bench, and distinguish the true from the false, the certain from the uncertain; and if it will build upon the testimony of any sense then it must first place its reliability beyond doubt" (293). This requires establishing existence-claims, Mendelssohn holds: if metaphysics is to prove that the mind is distinct from the body, it is not enough to prove that the concept of thought excludes that of matter, and vice versa; it must also prove that we really have a body and that we really think. And it is not enough for metaphysics to prove that a necessary being must also be a "creator and preserver of all things," but also that such a necessary being exists. Thus metaphysics has a greater burden of proof than mathematics: the question of correspondence between our concepts and reality which mathematics can evade by appeal to the distinction between variable and invariable representations cannot be evaded in metaphysics.

"Nothing is harder for the understanding than the transition from concepts to actualities" (293), Mendelssohn says, but luckily

---

[10] The prize essays of both Mendelssohn and Kant compare not only the relative *certainty* but also the relative *ease of comprehension* (in Mendelssohn's term, *Faßlichkeit*) of mathematics and metaphysics, in terms of the distinction between intuitive and merely symbolic representation that had a long history in Wolffian philosophy (and which surfaces as late as Kant's discussion of the beautiful as the symbol of the morally good in §59 of the *Critique of Judgment*, as well as pervading Hegel's philosophy). I will not have space to pursue that issue here. It is the focus of Altmann's shorter treatment (*Moses Mendelssohn*, pp. 118–23), and receives considerable attention in his longer commentary as well (*Mendelssohns Frühschriften*, pp. 269–70, 283–94, 302–4).

metaphysics unlike mathematics has two points at which to successfully make this transition. Here Mendelssohn reveals the continuing influence of Descartes on the metaphysics of Wolff and himself: he argues that metaphysics can pin its analyses of the concepts of qualities through its proofs of the existence of the *self* and of *God*. As he says, "We have Descartes to thank for these two transitions from the possible to the actual" (294).[11]

Mendelssohn does not treat these two fundamental existential claims in the same way. In the case of the existence of the self, he asserts that we have not a "mere appearance" but an "inner conviction" or a "unique inner sensation" that "*I think*," "from which it can be inferred with certainty that *I therefore am*" (294). He says he will say more about this proof in the sequel, but in fact he does not do so, except to redescribe subsequently the proposition "I think" as an "undeniable intuitive proposition" (*unleugbares Anschaungssatz*). So we can assume not only that he believes the inference from "I think" to "I exist" to be one grounded by the fundamental law of noncontradiction, as in the case of mathematical inferences, but also that he belives that my "inner conviction" that I am thinking is not a mere appearance, not even an invariable appearance, but a form of empirical evidence – remember that he actually refers to the *cogito* as a "sensation" – which at the same time constitutes the reality it reports. An act of thought does not just report that I am thinking but itself makes it true that I am thinking: so there is no room for a gap between an appearance and reality in this case, and the empirical evidence that is the basis for my further, logically grounded inference is completely adequate to prove the actuality of my concept.[12]

---

[11] Altmann suggests that Mendelssohn concluded that metaphysics could not be as certain as mathematics because the arguments for the existence of self and God were not as secure as the basis of certainty in mathematics (*Moses Mendelssohn*, p. 122). I find no basis for this claim; indeed, Mendelssohn's final position on extension, that it is *only* an invariable appearance and not a reality, suggests that metaphysics delivers much stronger results than mathematics through the *cogito* and ontological argument.

[12] Beck writes as if Mendelssohn's argument about the self is an inference from the concept of a thinking thing to its existence, as the ontological argument is an inference from the concept of God to his existence (*Early German Philosophy*,

In the case of the argument for the existence of God, Mendelssohn makes no appeal to experience of any kind. In this case, "one goes with secure steps directly from the domain of possibility into the realm of actuality, and indeed that of the all-highest and most perfect reality that can be thought" (294). Mendelssohn considers the ontological argument at some length, and in a variety of forms, but basically he adopts the Leibnizian revision of Descartes' argument,[13] as he suggests with his opening statement that "just as in geometry the two propositions that an equilateral triangle has three equally large sides and an equilateral triangle has three equally large angles are inseparably connected, so firmly and indissolubly connected with each other are the two propositions that *the necessary being is possible* and *the necessary being is actual*" (294). Mendelssohn follows Leibniz's strategy of first showing that the concept of the most perfect being describes a possibility by arguing that it is the concept of the realization of all possible positive predicates, thus since positive predicates contain no negation there is no way for any of them to negate any other and thus give rise to any contradiction in the concept, and then arguing that this consistent concept of a most perfect being implies the existence of its object because the concept of necessary existence is more perfect than that of merely contingent existence and must therefore be included in the concept of the most perfect being. "The proposition that the most all-perfect being has a contingent existence contains an obvious contradiction. – The most all-perfect being is therefore either actual, or contains a contradiction"; but since it has already been shown not to be the latter, it must be the former (300–1).[14]

Given his concern with the comprehensibility as well as certainty

---

p. 334). This misses Mendelssohn's suggestion of the disanalogy between them and his emphasis on the indubitable *experience* of thought.

[13] This is stressed in the useful article by Alexander Altmann, "Moses Mendelssohn's Proofs for the Existence of God," in his *Die Trostvolle Aufklärung: Studien zur Metaphysik und politischen Theorie Moses Mendelssohns* (Stuttgart-Bad Canstatt: Fromann-Holzboog, 1982), pp. 135–51. See also *Mendelssohns Frühschriften*, pp. 310–16.

[14] It should be noted that Mendelssohn expounds the two steps in the opposite order from that I have just employed.

of metaphysics, Mendelssohn also suggests several other strategies for proving the existence of God: following the hint of Descartes's third meditation as developed by Wolff,[15] he argues that the certainty but contingency of my own existence – the latter illustrated by the fact of doubt itself – coupled with the principle of sufficient reason leads to the necessary existence of a more perfect being (299, 308–9), and he also employs a more Baumgartian argument from the idea that any particular being must be fully determinate and, again by the principle of sufficient reason, must have the ground of its determinacy in an existent being, which is the ground of all determinacy (302–3).[16] To maintain the logical model employed in the account of mathematical proof, he argues that the principle of sufficient reason itself has its ground in the principle of contradiction (304), and this leads him to a discussion and Leibnizian resolution of the possibility of "freely willed decisions in rational beings" (304), who are themselves created in accordance with the principle of sufficient reason. This largely completes his discussion of "evidence in the first principles of natural theology" properly so-called.

Mendelssohn argues for one further conclusion of great interest, however. Having demonstrated that the two objects that can be posited with certainty and thus be known with certainty to realize metaphysical concepts that would otherwise be merely possible are those of the *self* and *God*, he draws the inference that the only "qualities of things of that we can see with certainty that they are actual realities" are *mental qualities*, in particular qualities which can be conceived of either as "capacities of our [own] soul" or as corresponding qualities attributed to God (310; this is the context for his return to the issue of the reality of the concept of extension discussed earlier). His argument is a Cartesian[17] refutation of Spinozism, which was of course to become a burning issue for Mendelssohn's last years in the famous *Pantheismusstreit* initiated

---

[15] See Altman, *Moses Mendelssohn*, p. 124, and *Mendelssohns Frühschriften*, pp. 316–19.

[16] Altmann, *Moses Mendelssohn*, pp. 123–24.

[17] In fact, Descartes had already offered the argument, as if in anticipation of Spinoza; see *Principles of Philosophy*, Part I, §23.

by F. H. Jacobi.[18] He says that a skeptic may cause us to doubt the reality of external objects and their properties but not to doubt that we are thinking, indeed thinking of these properties; so we can doubt the reality of external objects and their qualities but not of thinking substance and its qualities (309). Indeed, we can conceive of the appearance (*Erscheinung*) of external objects and their properties as due to the *imperfections* of our cognitive faculties themselves: "An appearance is nothing but a concept the constitution of which must be partially explained by the incapacity of our cognition" (310). But we can only ascribe "realities" or real properties to the "all-highest being," so we cannot ascribe to him anything that we do not know to be a reality, *a fortiori* anything that we actually take to be the product of an *imperfection* in ourselves. Therefore we can ascribe mental predicates to God, but not predicates concerning extension, not even that of "the most perfect extension" or "infinite extension" (310). (Of course, the argument quantifies through an opaque context: our lack of knowledge that predicates of extension are "realities" should not lead us to *deny* them of God, but only to remain agnostic about them.) Mendelssohn also expresses his sympathies in Leibnizian and Wolffian terms: he argues that we can ascribe our perception of extension and its qualities to "limitations of our power of representation," but that we have such a power is itself not a limitation, and we can therefore conclude that it is "*the faculty of representation* that is only and alone known to us as realit[y]" (311).

Of course, Kant rejects the ontological argument in his mature work. But his eventual position on the representation of the *self*, or apperception, will constitute a new and complex element in his

---

[18] This arose from Jacobi's charge that Mendelssohn's lifelong friend Gotthold Ephraim Lessing had been and even admitted to being a Spinozist. For documents see Gérard Vallée, *The Spinoza Conversations between Lessing and Jacobi*, trans. G. Vallée, J. B. Lawson, and C. G. Chapple (Lanham, Md.: University Press of America, 1988), and, for the full text of Mendelssohn's reply to Jacobi, his *Morgenstunden, oder Vorlesungen über das Dasein Gottes* (1785), ed. Dominique Bourel (Stuttgart: Philipp Reclam Jun., 1979). For discussion, see Beck, *Early German Philosophy*, pp. 352–60, and Frederic C. Beiser, *The Fate of Reason: German Philosophy from Kant to Fichte* (Cambridge, Mass.: Harvard University Press, 1987), ch. 3, pp. 92–108.

thought that can certainly be seen as involving a rejection of Mendelssohn's dual use of the *cogito* to establish the certainty of an existential claim and the primary or even sole reality of mental as opposed to physical predicates: Kant will take pains to distinguish his own use of apperception from the Cartesian proof of the *existence* of the self, and his insistence that the mental predicates of self-knowledge can only be *used* in conjunction with spatial predicates for external objects, which can hardly be treated as mere imperfections, is of course one of the most central claims of the "Analytic of Principles" in the *Critique of Pure Reason*, especially its "Refutation of Idealism." We will be able to see much of that argumentation as a rejection of precisely the kind of view that Mendelssohn has here asserted.

Before we can consider that, however, we must complete the review of Mendelssohn's position by considering his views on the nature of certainty in morality.

Morality

Mendelssohn's outline of "the evidence of the first principles of moral theory" (*Anfangsgründen der Sittenlehre*, 315) once again shows his allegiance to Wolff but, like his treatments of mathematics and the existence of the self, also shows the intimate connection between the rationalist conception of the analysis of fundamental concepts and the empirical conditions for the application of this analysis.

The first stage of Mendelssohn's account states the first principle of morality and shows how its certainty may be demonstrated. The principle is a version of Wolff's perfectionist principle "Do what makes yourself and the condition of others more perfect, and omit what makes them more imperfect":[19] in Mendelssohn's words, "*Make the inner and outer condition, in appropriate proportion, of yourself and your fellow man as perfect as you can*" (317). Clarifying and amplifying Wolff's methodology, however, Mendelssohn argues that this principle can be reached in three distinct ways. First, one can follow the method of natural law reaching back to

---

[19] Christian Wolff, *Vernünfftigen Gedancken von des menschlichen Thun und Lassen* (Halle, 1720), §12. See also Altman, *Moses Mendelssohn*, p. 127.

the Stoics – Mendelssohn cites Marcus Aurelius – and "abstract out of the action and omission of men, their different inclinations and passions, sources of excitement and unrests, that in which they all agree, that disposition which is to be found throughout this great manifold"; when this is done, one discovers that all human actions "aim at the *preservation or improvement of the internal or external condition of ourself or of another creature*" (316). From this factual discovery Mendelssohn has no scruple about inferring the normative result,[20] the "universal practical maxim, the first law of nature" that everyone *ought* to so act (317). Second, Mendelssohn claims that "One can prove the same natural law *a priori* from the mere explanation of a being with free will" (*eines freywilligen Wesens*) (317). His argument here, supposedly based on conceptual analysis,[21] is that a being with free will always chooses among objects or representations that which pleases him, which will be nothing other than "the perfection, beauty, and order that he perceives or believes himself to perceive in the objects that present themselves to him" (318). One might take this to mean that a rational agent will always choose that which contributes to his *own* perfection, beauty, and order, but Mendelssohn seems simply to assume that perfection, beauty, and order *in general* present themselves as objects of rational choice to creatures whose actions are determined by their free will, and thus that "the free being is [naturally] obliged to bring forth as much perfection, beauty, and order in the world as is possible for him," from which the general maxim to make the inner and outer condition of "*yourself* and those nearest to you" as perfect as you can once again follows (318). Finally, Mendelssohn argues that we can reach the same result by

---

[20] As Beck stresses, no German philosopher before Kant appreciated Hume's problem about the inference from *is* to *ought* (*Early German Philosophy*, p. 330).

[21] Beck presents this argument as if it were simply the conclusion of the previous empirical argument (*Early German Philosophy*, p. 330), thus undermining Mendelssohn's argument for the allegedly parallel rôle of conceptual analysis in all three domains of mathematics, theology, and ethical theory. Altmann correctly recognizes that Mendelssohn intends to describe three different methods for reaching the principle of ethics, the first *a posteriori* and the second *a priori* (the third of course being theological) (*Moses Mendelssohn*, p. 127, and *Mendelssohns Frühschriften*, pp. 358–60).

conceiving of ourselves as the "property" or "servant" of God (319): since as such we are obliged to do what God wills, but, as the most perfect being, God can have no "other aim than the perfection of [his] creatures," therefore "I live in accord with the great final end of creation, I become an imitator of divinity, as often as I make any creature, myself or another, more perfect" (318). Like early Enlightenment thinkers such as Wolff and Shaftesbury but unlike earlier natural law theorists such as Pufendorf, Mendelssohn firmly believes that God commands us to do what is most perfect because it is most perfect, not that it is perfect just because he so commands it, and so the appeal to the commands of God simply ratifies what has already been established by the appeal to the natural consensus of mankind and the analysis of an agent with free will. And all of these arguments, he insists, yield the highest possible degree of certainty, or are "as binding as any geometrical proof" (319).

At the next stage of his argument, Mendelssohn considers how these general results are to be applied to particular circumstances. The three methods of proof can be taken to give rise to three general maxims for individual decision making – "(1) *Consider wherein the inclinations of all humans agree;* (2) *Know yourself as a being with free will;* (3) *Know yourself as the property of God*" – but all of these lead to the same conclusion, "*Make yourself and others perfect*" (321). However, he now adds that the determination of what will actually make ourselves and others more perfect, or the discovery of the "derivative natural laws, which prescribe to us what we should do and omit in particular cases" (323–24), is a complicated matter of empirical investigation. "The moral goodness of an action, the value or disvalue of our action and omission, depends not only on innumerable accompanying circumstances and contingencies but also on the consequences and effects of our actions, which cannot possibly be foreseen with certainty": we have to appeal to experience not only to figure out what changes that we can effect will best preserve or advance our own perfection or that of another, but also to figure out how we are most likely to succeed in bringing about such alterations, what our most probably successful means to these ends might be (323–24). In other words, Mendelssohn clearly recognizes that his perfectionism is a consequentialist doctrine, placing the value of an action in the contribution of its actual outcome to the perfection of the condition of particular persons.[22] From this it follows that even though the general principle of morality can be established by *a priori* conceptual analysis with utter certainty, particular prescriptions as well as evaluations of outcome are necessarily subject to the limits of empirical judgment.

Mendelssohn's conclusion is then that the general principles of morality can be reached by analyses that are just as certain as those of mathematics and metaphysics and that, like the principles of mathematics and the metaphysics of the self, they must be applied to reality by means of experience (the metaphysics of God or natural theology does not require any experiential input at all because of the ontological argument); but the empirical element in morality is not a few indubitable experiences that ground its fundamental concepts, like those of extension or thinking, but an indefinitely detailed array of empirical circumstances for the *application* of its principles in action. Thus the particular conclusions of morality cannot be as certain as theorems of mathematics and the metaphysics of the self. The latter requires only the constant appearance of objects due to the inner constitution of our senses or the self-evident intuition of our thought, and these, while empirical, leave no room for doubt; but the empirical judgments on which the application of the general principles of morality depends are neither so simple nor so certain, and particular or "derivative" moral laws can never be more than probable.

Mendelssohn's unflinching recognition of this consequence of his consequentialism must surely have been a stimulus for Kant's ultimate fundamental rejection of Wolffian perfectionism in moral philosophy. But before we can turn to Kant's mature position, we

---

22 Twenty years later, Mendelssohn based his argument in *Jerusalem* for the inadmissability of any coercive enforcement in religious matters on a clear distinction between the outward conformity of actions to requirements of duty and the motivation or disposition (*Gesinnung*) to such action, thus clearly introducing a nonconsequentialist element into his moral theory (*Jerusalem, or on Religious Power and Judaism*, trans. Allan Arkush [Hanover, N.H.: University Press of New England, 1983], p. 40) and perhaps preparing the way for Kant's *Groundwork for the Metaphysics of Morals* of two years later. But there is no trace of such nonconsequentialism in the *Essay on Evidence*.

must first consider his own prize essay of 1762. Here we will see that, although Kant was already working toward the rejection of a number of fundamental features of the Wolffian synthesis, his position on morality at this time was actually quite close to that described by Mendelssohn.

II

Kant's contribution to the academy's competition was, of course, composed without any knowledge of Mendelssohn's, and cannot be construed as a response to it. But there is much in it that is a response to the Wolffian tradition that Mendelssohn was summarizing. Yet there are also points of agreement, and Kant had a long way to go before reaching his mature position. Kant's critical philosophy of the 1780s will constitute a rejection of much in his own prize essay as well as much that is represented by Mendelssohn's.

Mathematics

In his prize essay, Mendelssohn argued for the fundamental identity of mathematical and metaphysical methods: except in the case of the ontological proof of the existence of God, which is entirely conceptual, they both depend on tying the results of purely logical analysis to reality by empirical judgments which are indubitable. Kant's prize essay, by contrast, is the first of his works that argue for a fundamental difference between the methods of mathematics and philosophy – indeed, he says, "nothing has been more damaging to philosophy than mathematics" (2:283). But the account of this difference that Kant gives in 1762 is by no means identical to that which he was to advance in the *Critique of Pure Reason*.

Kant begins by asserting that "One can arrive at any general concept in two ways, either through the *arbitrary connection* of concepts, or through *abstraction* from that sort of cognition which is made clear by analysis [*Zergliederung*]" (2:276). He then claims that mathematics always begins with general concepts reached by the first method: it arbitrarily forms a "definition" or "explanation" (*Erklärung*), such as the definition of a trapezoid as four straight

34

lines that enclose a plane surface where the opposite sides are not parallel, or of a cone as a right-angled triangle rotated on one of its sides. These definitions are constituted by a *synthesis* of the concepts of which they are composed (2:276). He then goes on to argue that one reaches further results by constructive manipulation of symbols for the concepts originally defined. In the case of arithmetic, one employs symbols for quantities, "together with special designations of their increase or decrease, their relations, etc.," and by means of "easy and certain rules" performs various operations of "substitution, connection, or subtraction" and so on to reach various results. In the case of geometry, one draws the figures originally defined, then adds to those figures a variety of further lines by means of which "relations are proved and the universal rule of the relations observed . . . *in concreto*" (2:278). Kant emphasizes that mathematical proofs are the products of active constructions, not inferences from definitions in accordance with the logical laws of identity and contradiction: "If the geometer wishes to prove e.g., that space is infinitely divisible, he takes some straight line standing vertically between two parallels, and from a point on one of these parallel lines draws others which intersect the [vertical] one. He cognizes from this symbol with the greatest certainty that this division must continue without end" (2:279). The mathematician constructs his definitions out of arbitrarily assumed concepts, then conducts his proof by providing symbols for the defined concepts and even more literally performing constructions upon them. Neither the definitions nor the subsequent proofs involve *analysis* as Mendelssohn had argued: the concepts are made, not analyzed, and the results constructed from them, not inferred.[23]

In the case of metaphysics, however, things are quite different. Here concepts of things are not arbitrarily defined but "already

---

[23] Some interpreters of the prize essay take Kant's insistence on the constructibility of mathematical concepts *in concreto* to be evidence of his assumption of an *empirical* foundation for them, which would thus imply at least a partial parallel with Mendelssohn's account (e.g., Beck, *Early German Philosophy*, p. 442; but cf. p. 448, where the arbitrariness of basic mathematical concepts is stressed). I do not see that Kant explicitly links his idea of constructibility with an idea of verification in experience.

given, although confused or not sufficiently determined," and the task of the philosopher is precisely to analyze these concepts, "comparing the separated marks with the given concepts in all kinds of cases" and by this means "making these abstract thoughts complete and determinate" (2:278). Thus, Kant stresses that while mathematics begins with definitions and literally constructs proofs on their basis, metaphysics reaches definitions only as the final result of a process of analysis of concepts that are given to it, but are given obscurely and incompletely and thus stand in need of intellectual analysis. Thus, whereas mathematics begins with definitions, metaphysics can reach definitions only at the end of a painstaking process of analysis:

> In mathematics I begin with the explanation of my object . . . in metaphysics I must never begin with that, and it is so far from being the case that the definition is the first thing which I cognize about an object that it is rather almost always the last. (2:283)

Kant's contrast between the constructive definition of mathematical definitions and proofs and the nonconstructive nature of philosophical methods was to survive into the "Doctrine of Method" of the *Critique of Pure Reason* (see A 727–38/B 755–66). However, there is a fundamental difference between Kant's theory of mathematics in the prize essay and in his mature philosophy. "In mathematics the definitions are the first thought which I can have of the thing to be explained, since my concept of the object first originates through the explanation, and it is therefore absurd to regard them as demonstrable [*erweislich*]" (2:281). The question of any proof or grounds for truth of the starting points of mathematical construction *simply does not arise*; we can explore any concepts we can construct, and if we can construct them, there is apparently no further question about their truth to be considered. Unlike Mendelssohn, who raises the question about the certainty of the basic concepts of mathematics and then resolves it, first by treating them as abstractions from invariable features of our sensory experience that are due to the inner constitution of human sensibility and thus as immune from any danger of revision whether or not they also correspond to real properties of external objects, then by the theological argument for the nonreality of extension, the Kant of 1762 takes no explicit stand on the question of truth and correspondence in mathematics. The mature Kant adopts quite a different position.

Metaphysics

On Kant's account in 1762, the task of metaphysics is to complete and clarify concepts and thus ultimately reach definitions. But the basic concepts in terms of which the analyses of others can be carried out are not arbitrarily constructed, but given to us, and in fact there is an innumerable number of these. Thus, many fundamental concepts such as "the concept of a *representation*," "*being next to* or *after one another*," "*space, time*," "the various *feelings* of the human soul," "the feeling of the *sublime*, of the *beautiful*, of the disgusting," "*desire* and *aversion*," "*appetite* and *abhorrence*" are basic to the analyses of other concepts but can themselves "never be afforded sufficient resolutions" (2:280). Further, metaphysics also involves an "immeasurable" number of "indemonstrable fundamental truths" or "propositions that constitute the foundation from which the definitions" philosophy seeks "can be discovered" (2:280). At this point, then, Kant considers neither a determinate method of discovery nor a method of proof to be available for the fundamental propositions of metaphysics. One can readily see why the Wolffian academy ultimately preferred Mendelssohn's more sanguine position.

But Kant does not conclude from this that there can be no certainty in metaphysics, for he does regard the fundamental propositions of metaphysics as in some sense self-evident and thus indubitable. In fact, Kant seems to extend the status that Mendelssohn reserved for the *cogito* to all fundamental metaphysical propositions:

> The genuine method of metaphysics is fundamentally identical with that which Newton introduced into natural science, and which had such useful results. There it is said that one should investigate the rules according to which certain appearances of nature proceed according to secure experience, especially with the help of geometry. Even when one has no insight into the basis of these in bodies, it is nevertheless certain that they act

according to these laws, and one explains complicated natural occurrences if one clearly shows how they are subsumed under these well-proven rules. Just so in metaphysics: through secure inner experience, i.e., an immediate self-evident [*augenschein-liches*] consciousness, one seeks those characteristics which certainly lie in the concept of some general quality [*Beschaffenheit*], and even if you do not know the entire essence of the thing, you can yet use this with security in order to derive much in the thing from it. (2:286)

Like Mendelssohn, Kant goes on to argue that philosophy is bedeviled by the fact that it must always deal with verbal rather than more intuitive symbols (2:291–92) but he nevertheless appears confident that it cannot be too hard to discover the self-evident fundamental propositions that will yield certainty in metaphysics. The source for these metaphysical concepts will be experience, as Mendelssohn may have suggested in the case of the self but certainly not in the case of God. But the kind of experience concerned seems more certain if not more clear than the "secure experiences" with which Newtonian science begins.[24]

In advocating this position Kant explicitly aligned himself with Crusius, which was tacitly to oppose himself to Wolff.[25] He quickly reiterates the argument of the *Nova delucidatio* that analysis always requires two logical principles, the law of identity for affirmative statements and the law of contradiction for negative statements (2:294; cf. *Nova delucidatio*, 1:389–90), not just one principle as Wolff

---

[24] The empirical basis of metaphysical analysis – in particular the analogy with Newton – is stressed in traditional accounts of the prize essay: see Max Wundt, *Kant as Metaphysiker: Ein Beitrag zur Geschichte der deutschen Philosophie im 18. Jahrhundert* (Stuttgart: Ferdinand Enke, 1924), pp. 132–33, and Herman-Jean de Vleeschauwer, *The Development of Kantian Thought: The History of a Doctrine*, trans. A. R. C. Duncan (London: Thos. Nelson and Sons, 1962), p. 33. But Kant's stress on the self-evident origin of metaphysical concepts in *inner* experience requires caution in their comparison with ordinary empirical evidence. Metaphysical concepts may have an origin in experience, but that need not imply the uncertainty and revisability which might ordinarily be associated with the idea of empirical evidence.

[25] The influence of Crusius in this period of Kant's development is persuasively argued by Wundt (*Kant als Metaphysiker*, pp. 128–29), and recognized by de Vleeschauwer (*The Development of Kantian Thought*, p. 35).

had supposed. He then expresses his fundamental agreement with Crusius that, even when so refined, the principles of philosophical analysis cannot yield any truths by themselves but can only be applied to fundamental propositions or "primary material principles of the human understanding" (2:295). Unlike Crusius, however, he does not think it does any good to attempt to lend an air of justification to these fundamental principles by subsuming them under an additional principle that "*what I cannot think of as other than true is true*"; this putative formal principle actually adds nothing to the fact that I think some particular material proposition is true,[26] and my metaphysical arguments must still be based on particular concepts and connections that I do not arbitrarily define as in mathematics but take to be self-evidently true and certain (2:296).

Kant will retain his claim that definitions come at the end rather than beginning of philosophical investigations, but of course he will radically revise his conception that metaphysics depends on an immeasurable number of fundamental concepts and propositions that are self-evident even though they cannot be discovered by any method. Key to this development will be his realization that the basic concepts of metaphysics are not due to *inner experience* but to the *conditions of the possibility of experience*, inner as well as outer. In this case, however, his eventual view will only take him further away from Mendelssohn, not closer to him.

Morality

Kant had less to say than Mendelssohn about the application of the method he proposed, and in the case of natural theology in particular he merely alluded to the argument, first suggested in the *Nova delucidatio* and then developed at length in the *Only Possible Basis for a Proof of the Existence of God* of 1762 (completed only weeks before the prize essay), that the existence of God cannot be demonstrated either from his own concept (ontological proof) or from the actual existence of other things (cosmological proof), but that it can be established as the necessary ground of even *possible* existence in

---

[26] Wundt only hints at this fundamental difference between Kant and Crusius; *Kant als Metaphysiker*, p. 134.

general (2:296–97).[27] But he did have some revealing things to say about the "primary grounds of morality" (2:298). His discussion begins with an anticipation of the idea most characteristic of his mature moral philosophy, that of the categorical imperative, but then follows a path otherwise very close to Mendelssohn's.

Kant begins by describing the twofold significance of assertions of obligation: they may assert that one thing ought to be done as a means to another, or that something ought to be one's purpose in acting "*immediately.*" Obligations of the first kind can be called "the necessity of the means (*necessitatem problematicam*)," those of the second kind "the necessity of the purpose [or "end": *Zweck*] (*necessitatem legalem*). Here it is interesting to note that his Latin expression suggests a necessity of *law* independent of all ends whatsoever, whereas both his German terminology and his argument itself imply that this form of obligation does not arise without any reference to an end but by reference to a *necessary end*: "Now since the use of means has no other necessity than that which pertains to the end, all actions that morality prescribes under the condition of certain ends are contingent and cannot be called obligations as long as they are not subordinated to an end that is necessary in itself" (2:298). The inescapable obligation of moral law appears to follow from the necessity rather than contingency of the fundamental end of morality.[28]

While Kant is clearly pointing the way toward his subsequent distinction between hypothetical imperatives and the categorical imperative, it may seem as if his assumption that the latter is dependent upon a necessary end rather than independent of all ends

---

[27] For discussion of this argument, see Allen W. Wood, *Kant's Rational Theology* (Ithaca: Cornell University Press, 1978), pp. 64–79.

[28] This is stressed in the interpretation of the moral theory of the prize essay offered by Josef Schmucker in *Die Ursprünge der Ethik Kants in seinen vorkritischen Schriften und Reflektionen* (Meisenheim am Glan: Verlag Anton Hain, 1961), especially, pp. 64–65. He argues persuasively against the interpretation of Paul A. Schilpp in *Kant's Pre-Critical Ethics*, 2d ed. (Evanston, Ill.: Northwestern University Press, 1960) that Kant's introduction of the categorical imperative in the prize essay is already evidence of pure formalism, or the derivation of the necessity of the end from the necessity of the law rather than vice versa; see *Ursprünge*, pp. 66–70.

whatever is later to be rejected. In subsequent chapters we will see that this is by no means true. For the moment, however, we must confine our attention to Kant's present conception of the necessary end that underlies *necessitatem legalem*. Here his position is both similar to yet significantly different from the Wolffian one. Kant suggests that the "end that is necessary in itself" might be either the "total greatest perfection" or "acting in accordance with the will of God," both Wolffian and Mendelssohnian formulas, especially if the will of God is thought to be determined by the total greatest perfection rather than vice versa (2:298). Kant clearly believes that the formula of perfection is fundamental, for he goes on to formulate the fundamental rule of morality in terms of it. In fact, in analogy to his argument that there is not one but two fundamental principles of truth, one for affirmative and one for negative truths, Kant states that there are two fundamental principles of morality: the primary *formal ground* of all obligation to *act*," namely, "Do the most perfect thing which is possible for you," and the basis for "the duty of *omission*," namely, "Omit that which would hinder the greatest perfection possible through you" (2:299). Thus far, Kant is in substantive agreement with Wolff and Mendelssohn; he signals his methodological disagreement, however, by insisting that such "immediate highest rule[s] of all obligation must be strictly indemonstrable." As with the most fundamental propositions of metaphysics, Kant argues that these principles cannot themselves be reached by analysis from anything more primitive. Mendelssohn's idea of deriving them from the analysis of the concept of an agent with free will is certainly not considered.

A similarity to Mendelssohn emerges at the next stage of Kant's argument, however. It will have been noted that Kant has characterized his principles of not injuring and advancing perfection as *formal* grounds of obligation; this is in contrast to *material* grounds, or actual information about what will in fact advance or injure the perfection of oneself and others affected by one's action. But no actual conclusions can be drawn from the formal principles without material principles as well: as Kant puts it, just as in the case of metaphysics

nothing flows from the primary formal principles of our judgment of the true where material first grounds are not given, so
no particular determinate obligation flows from these two rules
of the good if indemonstrable principles of practical cognition
are not connected to them. (2:299)

By calling the material first principles of obligation indemonstrable Kant means that they cannot be derived by analysis of
more primary concepts; but they do have a source of evidence,
namely *feeling*, in particular "an unanalyzable feeling of the good
(which is never to be found in a thing unconditionally, but always
in relation to a sensitive being)." Such a feeling is "entirely indemonstrable and is an immediate effect of the perception of the
object on the consciousness of the feeling of pleasure" (2:299). Kant
explicitly refers to Francis Hutcheson here (2:300), but his position
is fundamentally identical to that of Mendelssohn (who was also
well aware of the work of Hutcheson): the application of the general principle of morality is always dependent upon empirically
grounded judgments about what contributions to the abstract goal
of perfection can be made by particular objects in particular circumstances. For this reason Kant, like Mendelssohn, concludes
that certainty is more difficult to obtain in particular moral than
in particular theoretical judgments.

This is the conclusion of Kant's argument in his second-place
prize essay, but only the beginning of his evolution toward views
that would take him much further from the Wolffian synthesis
of rationalism and empiricism described in Mendelssohn's first-
place essay.

III

Kant's explicit references to Mendelssohn in his critical period are
limited. Aside from correspondence in which he expressed his ad-
miration for Mendelssohn's argument against state establishment
of religion in *Jerusalem* (16 August 1783, 10:344–47) and a refutation of the argument of Mendelssohn's *Phaedo, or the Immortality
of the Soul* (1767) in the second edition of the "Paralogisms of
Pure Reason" (B 413–15), his primary discussion of Mendelssohn

is contained in an article that the editor of the *Berlinische Monats-schrift* persuaded him to write on the great *Pantheismusstreit* between Mendelssohn and Jacobi on Spinozism and, in particular, the alleged Spinozism of Mendelssohn's lamented friend Lessing.[29] In this essay, *What Is Orientation in Thinking?* which was completed in August 1786, eight months after Mendelssohn's death, Kant sides with Mendelssohn against Jacobi in his insistence on rational argument rather than crude appeals to faith in metaphysics, but sternly criticizes Mendelssohn for failing to realize that arguments for the existence of a supersensible being that are based on the "felt *need*" of our own reason (8:139) can never lead to theoretical truth but only practical postulates. "Pure *rational belief* can never be transformed into *knowledge* by all natural data of reason and experience," he argues, so "the need of reason for a satisfactory *theoretical* employment can never be anything other than a pure *rational hypothesis* . . . but *rational faith*, which rests on the need of its employment with a *practical* aim, can be called a *postulate* of reason" (8:141). Kant thus takes the controversy surrounding Mendelssohn's last days as an occasion to reiterate the fundamental opposition of the critical philosophy to any attempt to revive rational theology as a theoretical discipline and to insist upon the centrality of the doctrine of the practical postulates.[30]

Perhaps these are the most fundamental lessons of Kant's own explicit critique of Mendelssohn, but in what follows I want to leave this broad issue aside and show how some of the most crucial aspects of Kant's more particular treatments of mathematics, metaphysics, and moral philosophy can be seen as a rejection of the Wolffian synthesis represented by Mendelssohn in 1762 as well as of Kant's own position of that time.[31]

---

[29] See note 18.

[30] See Chapter 10.

[31] Since my thesis is that much of the critical philosophy can be understood as if it were a refutation of Mendelssohn's *Essay on Evidence* as well as of Kant's own position in 1762, the description of Kant's mature views that must come next could easily exceed any reasonable bounds for a single essay. I therefore now have to proceed with less detail than before, although at several points I can introduce interpretations I have defended elsewhere into the present historical argument.

Mathematics

Mendelssohn had argued that mathematics constitutes a body of propositions derived by logical analysis from fundamental concepts abstracted from invariable appearances that reflect the inner constitution of human sensibility whether or not they also reflect the independent constitution of external objects, and had then appealed to theology in order to defend the Leibnizian view that extension is in fact only a phenomenal property, not a genuine reality. The Kant of 1762 had argued that mathematics consists of propositions reached by processes of active construction from completely arbitrary definitions as starting points. In his accounts of mathematics in 1770 and 1781 to 1787, Kant continued to insist that mathematical proofs are not purely analytical, grounded on principles of logic alone, but require nonlogical constructions (see B 15–16, B 40–41, A 47–48/B 64–65, A 734–35/B 762–63). In the theory of proof, then, his critical views were as opposed to Mendelssohn as was his argument of 1762. But Kant's mature theory of mathematical truth rejects his supposition of 1762 that the starting-points of mathematics are merely arbitrary constructions. His mature position may look like Mendelssohn's appeal to the inner constitution of human sensibility but is in fact fundamentally different from it on two crucial points. Kant's critical theory of mathematics therefore constitutes a rejection of both of the key claims of Mendelssohn's theory, its claims that mathematical proof is analytic and that mathematical truth is ultimately empirical.

The first similarity between Kant's mature theory of mathematical truth and Mendelssohn's is of course the claim, contrary to what Kant had earlier held, that the basic concepts of mathematics are not arbitrary but rooted in the pure forms of intuition – space and time – which constitute the special conditions of human sensibility. But once we get past this generality, there are two points of difference between Kant's theory and Mendelssohn's. First, Kant does not believe that our access to these basic sources of mathematical concepts is *empirical* but believes instead that it is pure, a claim for which he attempts to argue generally by proving that space "is not an empirical concept that has been derived from outer experience" (A 23/B 38) and time "not an empirical concept that has been derived from any experience" at all (A 30/B 46), and more specifically by holding that only *a priori* forms of intuition can explain the universality and necessity of mathematical propositions, for example, "the *possibility* of geometry as a body of *a priori* synthetic knowledge" (B 41). Thus, Kant rejects not only the rationalist aspect of Mendelssohn's theory, the view that propositions of pure mathematics can be reached by analysis alone, but even more emphatically the empiricist element of Mendelssohn's view, the supposition that it is empirical judgments of sense that tie the analytical structure of mathematics to reality.

Second, Kant rejects the indifference about the correspondence between our mathematical concepts and external reality that characterized the first stage of Mendelssohn's view but even more so his own early view. For now Kant does not just consider basic mathematical concepts to be arbitrary constructions; rather, he asserts that they reflect the subjective conditions of human sensibility *and nothing but those subjective conditions*: space and time, *a fortiori* the basic mathematical concepts grounded in their forms, represent "no property at all of things in themselves," "no determination of them that attaches to the objects themselves and which would remain even if one were to abstract from all subjective conditions of intuition" (A 26/B 42). Instead of simply ignoring the question of correspondence or raising it but leaving it undecided, Kant now decides it by denying that it is even possible for things in themselves as well our representations of them to have spatiotemporal form and thus for there to be any correspondence between the forms of things and the basic forms of our representations.

Views differ on why Kant makes this claim. As noted earlier, Kant does adopt, in fact adds to the second edition of the *Critique*, the argument asserted by Mendelssohn himself that extension and temporality (which Mendelssohn did not include, and to Kant's addition of which he violently objected)[32] cannot be real because then they would also be attributes of God. This argument flagrantly violates the strictures on the theoretical use of claims about the supersensible, which Kant had so eloquently defended in *What Is Orientation in Thinking?* so it is hard to understand why

---

[32] See his letter to Kant of 25 December 1770 (10:113–16).

he used it except perhaps as an ad hominem argument to divert Wolffians from other areas of disagreement, such as his view of the synthetic rather than analytic character of mathematical truth.[33] In any case it is hard to see this argument as basic to Kant's transcendental idealism. My own view is that his most basic argument is based on an assumed problem about necessity, which neither Leibniz nor Mendelssohn ever imagined: even if our representations are necessarily spatiotemporal, things in themselves could never be more than contingently spatiotemporal, so if we assume that both things and our representations of them are spatiotemporal, then our claims about space and time, both in mathematics and more generally in transcendental aesthetics itself, would be necessarily true only in part of their domain, not the whole of it (see especially A 48/B 65–66).[34] But whatever the reason, there is no doubt that in his mature philosophy of transcendental idealism Kant emphatically denies even the possibility of correspondence between our forms of intuition and thus the basic concepts of mathematics and any external reality.

Kant's rejection of Mendelssohn's philosophy of mathematics is thus complete in spite of the superficial similarity of their metaphysics of extension. Indeed, Kant's ultimate view, based on his concept of pure intuition and an assertion of the unconditionally necessary truth of claims about space and time, makes far less concession to empiricism than Mendelssohn's view, even if it is

---

[33] If this was his intent, it failed; see Henry E. Allison, *The Kant-Eberhard Controversy* (Baltimore: Johns Hopkins University Press, 1973). Hans Vaihinger argues that the addition of this passage to the second edition of the *Critique* is actually a response to Mendelssohn's argument in *Morgenstunden* that all thinking beings share the same mode of representation (*Commentar zu Kants Kritik der reinen Vernunft*, vol. 2 (Stuttgart, Berlin, Leipzig: Union Deutsche Verlagsgesellschaft, 1892), p. 510. He does not mention that the argument is largely identical to that which Mendelssohn had himself defended two decades before.

[34] I have expounded this interpretation at length in *Kant and the Claims of Knowledge* (Cambridge: Cambridge University Press, 1987), ch. 16, pp. 345–70, and "The Rehabilitation of Transcendental Idealism?" in Eva Schaper and Wilhelm Vossenkuhl, eds., *Reading Kant: New Perspectives on Transcendental Arguments and Critical Philosophy* (Oxford: Basil Blackwell, 1989), pp. 140–67. For a very different account, see Henry E. Allison, *Kant's Transcendental Idealism: An Interpretation and Defense* (New Haven: Yale University Press, 1983), ch. 5, pp. 81–114.

the latter that we might have been inclined to associate with traditional rationalism. Mathematics and the metaphysics of space and time are not where Kant is prepared to make his own accommodation with empiricism.

Metaphysics

Kant's doctrine of understanding is much more complicated than his doctrine of sensibility, but some of its most fundamental features can also be seen as a rejection of the Cartesian view that had been advocated by Mendelssohn. In fact, one could argue that the importance of refuting Mendelssohn grew as Kant approached the publication of the critical philosophy. In his earlier attempts to link a critique of metaphysics to the new doctrine of the *a priori* forms of sensibility and understanding that he was developing, Kant tended to focus on the cosmological disputes that he eventually described under the rubric of the "Antinomy of Pure Reason."[35] In the "Transcendental Dialectic" of the *Critique of Pure Reason*, however, the Antinomy was flanked by critiques of *a priori* arguments for the existence of a substantial self and the existence of God. The self and God were, as we saw, the twin pillars of Mendelssohn's reconstruction of Wolffian metaphysics.[36] A good part of Kant's effort in his critique of metaphysics is aimed at overturning precisely these twin pillars.

The comparisons between Mendelssohn's revival and Kant's rejection of rational theology are too obvious to need much discussion. Mendelssohn had defended the ontological argument

---

[35] See the inaugural dissertation, §§27–29 (2:414–17); for evidence and discussion of the evolution of Kant's views on this matter in the mid-1770s, see my "The Unity of Reason: Pure Reason as Practical Reason in Kant's Early Conception of the Transcendental Dialectic," *Monist* 72 (1989): 139–67; here, Chapter 2.

[36] Since Wolff and his more immediate expositors had always divided "special metaphysics" into the three topics of self, world, and God (rational psychology, cosmology, and theology), one cannot say that the tripartite organization of the "Transcendental Dialectic" was necessitated only by Mendelssohn's emphasis on the self and God. One might suppose, however, that even if Kant might have been tempted to present his critique of metaphysics exclusively as a critique of rational cosmology, Mendelssohn's revival of rational psychology and theology could have made this seem too restrictive.

above all, but also countenanced an argument to the necessary existence of God from the contingency of our own existence (e.g., 309) and an argument to the existence of God as the necessary condition of all determinacy (301–3); in addition, he had noted a considerable "power of persuasion" if not "demonstrative certainty" in versions of the argument from design (312). Kant agreed that the latter, which he called the physicotheological argument, had more intuitive appeal than any purely *a priori* argument for the existence of God (A 623/B 651), but criticized both that and the cosmological argument, his name for the argument from contingent to necessary existence, as resting on the ontological argument, toward which he maintained all of his earlier hostility. But in the *Critique* Kant also rejected his own earlier argument to the existence of God as the ground of all possibility. This represented his last chance ever to infer from mere possibility to actual existence or reality. Since such an inference was precisely what Mendelssohn thought rational theology alone offered metaphysics, Kant's mature critique of rational theology thus completely rejected Mendelssohn's hope for this discipline, and in *What Is Orientation in Thinking?* he explicitly claimed that rational theology could be reconstructed only as a practical rather than theoretical discipline.

Kant's mature position on self-knowledge is vastly more complicated than his critique of theology, and is less obviously directed against Mendelssohn. But even the few points that can be mentioned here will demonstrate its radical opposition to the Cartesian theory Mendelssohn had asserted in 1762. In the "Paralogisms of Pure Reason" Kant rejected any attempt to affirm metaphysical propositions about the real nature of the self on the basis of formal or logical features of our representation of it (see, e.g., A 346/B 404), undercutting the entire idea that metaphysical claims about the soul can be reached by analysis. In the second-edition version of the "Paralogisms," he explicitly rejects the Cartesian *cogito* which had been so explicitly revived by Mendelssohn. Like Mendelssohn, Kant does hold that "the I think is . . . an empirical proposition." In contrast to what he takes to be the theory of Descartes, he holds that the further proposition that I exist is contained in it, not inferred from it by subsumption under a major premise of the form "Everything that thinks exists," because he thinks that would convert the existence of any thinking thing into necessary existence (B 422n).[37] What differentiates his position from Mendelssohn's, however, is his insistence that the empirical proposition that I think "expresses an *indeterminate* empirical intuition." For this can be taken to imply two conclusions, both of which are fundamentally opposed to the kind of view suggested by Mendelssohn.

First, Kant clearly wants to argue that the entirely indeterminate experience of thinking itself, because it "here signifies only something real, that is given, but only to thought in general, therefore neither as appearance nor as thing in itself (*Noumenon*) but only as something which in fact exists" (B 422n), conveys no metaphysical information about the real nature of the self. It therefore cannot be viewed, as Mendelssohn had viewed it, as the single experience we need in order to prove the reality of a particular metaphysical conception of the self which is otherwise reached solely by analysis. Mendelssohn had argued that we could prove by conceptual analysis that the self is distinct from body, and only needed to appeal to the self-evident experience of thinking to prove that we have such an immaterial self; Kant rejects this assumption by insisting that neither the mere experience of thinking nor the formal concept of the self as subject can decide in favor of either materialism or spiritualism (see, e.g., B 420).

Second, Kant also wants to use the indeterminacy of the experience of thought to oppose Mendelssohn's Cartesian position that we can make judgments applying mental predicates to the self without also using physical predicates of it. Kant claims that the indeterminate experience that I think "precedes the experience that should determine the object of perception in time through the

---

[37] His criticism is obviously fallacious: The major premise "Everything that thinks exists" and the minor premise" I think" do not imply that I necessarily exist, but at most that it is necessary that if I think then I exist. Only if a minor premise of the form "I necessarily think" is subsumed under the major premise might one get anything suggesting the conclusion "I necessarily exist." Kant might have supposed Descartes meant to assert such a premise in his doctrine that my *essence* is to think and thus that I necessarily think *when* I exist; but Descartes's emphasis on the contingency of human existence in Meditation III is surely incompatible with such a supposition.

category" (B 422n), or that it does not itself give any determinate knowledge of the empirical self. This refers back to the extended argument alluded to in the second edition of the transcendental deduction and developed in the "Analytic of Principles," especially the "Refutation of Idealism," which is precisely that determinate judgment about the temporal relations of states of the self is possible only if these states are connected to representations of spatial relations which can only be interpreted as relations of objects external to and distinct from the self (see especially B 156 and B 275–78). Kant's argument is thus that in order to make any determinate use of the indeterminate experience of thought we have to employ predicates for physical or material as well as mental entities.[38] This is a rejection of Mendelssohn's Cartesian conception of the independence and priority of mental over physical predicates.

Kant's theory of empirical self-consciousness is thus a decisive rejection of Mendelssohn's Cartesian mentalism. At the same time, Kant's more general employment of the concept of transcendental apperception for the deduction of the categories of pure understanding constitutes a rejection of his own earlier conception of metaphysical *method*. But this rejection of his earlier view involves no *rapprochement* with Mendelssohn. In 1762, Kant had held that there was no particular method for the discovery of the indemonstrable basic concepts and propositions of metaphysics and that no determinate table could be drawn up of these potentially innumerable concepts (2:281). In the *Critique*, he rejects both of these views, and tries to base his rejection of them in the concept of transcendental apperception. He argues that a determinate table of fundamental concepts of objects in general can be derived from the logically possible forms of judgment, and then argues that these functions of judgment are also the forms adopted by the synthesis of individual representations, which are necessary in order to obtain a unitary representation of the self (e.g., B 143). But, it is

---

[38] For an extended interpretation of Kant's "Refutation of Idealism" along these lines, see *Kant and the Claims of Knowledge*, part IV, pp. 279–329, or its predecessor, "Kant's Intentions in the Refutation of Idealism," *Philosophical Review* 92 (1983): 329–83.

crucial to note, these categories are not especially *mentalistic* categories, but *concepts of objects in general*, whether mental, physical, or anything else; and in fact Kant attempts to argue that the unity of apperception requires the use of these general concepts of objects for the representation of objects contrasted to the self as well as for the representation of the self itself (see especially B 140–42). They are thus not concepts drawn from inner experience in particular, in spite of their connection to apperception, but conditions of the possibility of experience in general. Kant's arguments for this thesis are not clear nor obviously successful, but there can be no doubt that his general theory of apperception involves not only the rejection of his earlier view that the fundamental propositions of metaphysics are indenumerable as well as indemonstrable deliverances from inner experience, but also a rejection at an even more general level than previously described of Mendelssohn's Cartesian separation of mental from physical predicates. On Kant's account, the categories connected with pure apperception are neither mental nor physical predicates, but the general forms for conceiving of any objects; and when they are used to make the indeterminate experience of thinking into determinate empirical self-consciousness, they must be used in application to the essential form of outer as well as inner experience.

I must leave these claims about Kant's rejection of Mendelssohn's metaphysics at this programmatic level in order to now turn to his rejection of the account of first principles of morality that he and Mendelssohn had largely shared in 1762.

Morality

Again, my discussion must be confined to a few points of the greatest generality. Perhaps the most obvious point is that Kant's critical moral theory fundamentally rejects the perfectionism common to both Mendelssohn's and his own earlier view, for precisely the reason so clearly brought out in Mendelssohn's exposition: the principle to preserve and enhance the perfection of oneself and others may be sufficiently clear and distinct, but the judgments about the consequences of particular paths of actions which it requires are always empirical and therefore uncertain. In fact, Kant has two objections. He argues that the concept of perfection is little more than a disguised concept of the conditions supposed to be necessary for human happiness, and all judgments about happiness, since they rest on "data of experience," are "very changeable" and can thus "yield *general* but never *universal* rules" (*CPracR*, 5:36). But even more importantly, although Mendelssohn had stressed that what will best contribute to human perfection and thus what ought to be done in a particular action is dependent upon the circumstances, Kant argues that the human capacities and talents as well as external conditions, gifts of nature and gifts of fortune, which actually constitute the Wolffian concept of perfection, essentially depend upon a *moral* condition for their worth: they are morally valuable if put in the service of a good will, but reprehensible if not (*G*, 4:393). The moral value of human perfection thus depends upon the moral value of the good will and cannot itself be used to define moral value. In Kant's mature view, therefore, the problem with the concept of perfection is not merely that is indeterminate and can only be applied through uncertain empirical judgments, but more fundamentally that it is essentially amoral, and needs to be grounded in a more fundamental concept of moral value.

This much is obvious. On further points, however, the comparison between Kant and Mendelssohn becomes more complex. Mendelssohn, it will be recalled, had argued that the fundamental principle of morality could be discovered both by examining what is common to the inclinations of all men and also by analyzing the concept of a being with free will. There are similarities yet also crucial differences between these claims and the methodological assumptions of Kant's mature practical philosophy. On the first issue, Kant does present the argument of the *Groundwork* as commencing from "common moral rational knowledge" (*G*, 4:392), and maintains that he is only systematizing the moral beliefs of everyman. Thus he turns the tables on a critic who had accused him of merely formulating a new principle of morality in the *Groundwork* by asking, "Who would want to introduce a new principle of all morality and, as it were, first invent it? as if the entire world before him did not know what was duty" (*CPracR*,

5:8n).[39] But, one must keep in mind, he does not appeal to a consensus in the actual *inclinations* of all humans, as Mendelssohn had, but to a convergence in the *moral judgments* of ordinary and untutored persons.[40] In their *inclinations*, Kant argues, all people agree in seeking happiness, indeed first and foremost their own happiness, but they land in irresolvable conflicts if they merely follow those inclinations: "without regard to duty, all humans already have of itself the most powerful and inmost inclination to happiness, precisely because all inclinations are united into a sum in this idea" (*G*, 4:399). But what "the moral cognition of common human reason" exacts from all humans is precisely their recognition of the principle that they must constrain their pursuit of happiness by the principle of the "possible universal legislation" of their maxims; and what Kant takes himself to have to supply is indeed only the proper formulation of this common recognition: common human reason "to be sure does not abstractly consider [its principle] in such a universal form, but always has it before its eyes and makes it the measure of its judging [*Beurtheilung*]" in all particular moral judgments (*G*, 4:403). Thus Kant does not simply appeal to the actual *behavior* of ordinary persons in order to derive a principle of morality, as Mendelssohn did, but appeals specifically to their *moral judgments*. He takes it that common human reason recognizes the difference between inclination and morality from the outset and tries to confirm his own account of the principle of morality by appeal to this distinction. Mendelssohn's appeal to universal consensus is firmly in the natural law tradition, and tries to ground morality in the natural law of human behavior; Kant argues that the difference between natural and moral law is itself a fundamental part of human moral sense, and thus uses the appeal to a universal consensus to do nothing less than reject the entire approach summed up by Mendelssohn's first method.

Mendelssohn's second claim was that the principle to preserve and enhance perfection could be derived from an analysis of the concept of a being with free will. Here it may seem as if Kant's

---

[39] Kant was referring to Gottlob August Tittel, *Über Herrn Kants Moralreform* (Frankfurt and Leipzig: Gebrüder Pfähler, 1786). See 5:506.
[40] For further discussion of this issue, see Chapter 6.

mature method in ethics follows Mendelssohn's model, for much of the argumentation in both the *Groundwork* and the *Critique of Practical Reason* seems designed to demonstrate precisely that the fundamental principle of morality can be derived from an analysis of the concept of the freedom of the will, and that we need to appeal to a fact of reason (as the *Critique of Practical Reason* puts it) in addition to this mere concept only in order to establish the synthetic proposition that we *have* free will. This would seem to parallel closely Mendelssohn's method of transforming possibility into actuality by tying the results of analysis to a fundamental empirical proposition.

There can be no doubt that Kant does employ this method at some of the most prominent points in both the *Groundwork* and the second *Critique*. The second section of the *Groundwork* asserts that "since moral laws are to be valid for every rational being in general, they must therefore be derived from the universal concept of a rational being in general," and then goes on to define a rational being precisely as a being with "the capacity to act according to the *representation* of laws, i.e. according to principles, or a *will*" (4:412). Kant then advances his argument by tacitly redefining the concept of a rational being as one who determines its will by reason *alone*, independently of inclination (4:412–13), and thus by a completely universal law, which of course turns out to be the categorical imperative: "in a will that is necessarily in accord of itself with reason, as its principle, the [imperative] is *categorical* (4:414). The argument of the third section of the *Groundwork* then appears to be designed to demonstrate that *we* are indeed beings who possess a free will governed by reason and are therefore obliged by the categorical imperative. Kant does not attempt to do this by an empirical claim, of course, but by a metaphysical argument: he argues that we are forced to conceive of ourselves as things in themselves as well as appearances, that since it is reason that distinguishes us from all other things we must assign reason to the intelligible realm, and that by so doing we prove that our will is governed "under laws, which, independent of nature, are not empirical but grounded in reason alone" (4:452). Unfortunately, the argument is doubly fallacious: first it conflates reason as that which *empirically* distinguishes us from other creatures, for example, rats and pigeons, with that which makes the *transcendental* distinction between ourselves as appearances and as noumena; second, it violates the *Critique of Pure Reason*'s distinction between the *negative* and *positive* senses of the concept of noumenon (B 307, added after the publication of the *Groundwork*, but similar in spirit to A 252) by treating our real nature not as *unknown* but precisely as *intelligible*, that is, as *known* to be governed by reason alone. This makes the argument circular: proving that we have a foot in the noumenal world proves that we have a free will governed by reason alone because the noumenal world is conceived on the model of reason from the outset.[41]

As if to correct these problems, Kant replaces the metaphysical argument of the Third Section of the *Groundwork* by the bare appeal to the "fact of reason" as an indubitable recognition of our ability to live up to the dictates of the moral law in the *Critique of Practical Reason* (see especially 5:30).[42] But if, as he puts it, it is "experience [that] confirms this order of concepts in us" (5:30), then this only seems to bring him closer to Mendelssohn's methodology, for it must then seem as if it is experience that confirms the application to our own case of the preceding analysis of the concept of the freedom of the will as implying the moral law. In any event, there can be little doubt that the preceding argument is meant to be such an analysis: in §§5 and 6 of the second *Critique*

---

[41] For further discussion of the problems with *Groundwork* III, see Dieter Henrich, "Die Deduktion des Sittengesetztes," in Alexander Schwann, ed., *Denken im Schatten des Nihilismus* (Darmstadt: Wissenschaftliche Buchgesellschaft, 1975), pp. 55–112, and Karl Ameriks, *Kant's Theory of Mind: An Analysis of the Paralogisms of Pure Reason* (Oxford: Clarendon Press, 1982), ch. 6, pp. 189–233.

[42] What Kant means by the "fact of reason" is actually obscure: at 5:31, for instance, he suggests that the fact of reason is simply our consciousness of the moral law itself, not consciousness of our ability to act in accordance with it as at 5:30. But if the larger structure of the argument parallels that of the *Groundwork* in seeking to transform analytic propositions into synthetic ones then it requires that we take the interpretation suggested by 5:30 as fundamental. For further discussion of this issue and references to additional literature, see Henry E. Allison, *Kant's Theory of Freedom* (Cambridge: Cambridge University Press, 1990), ch. 13, pp. 230–49.

Kant presents what has come to be known as his reciprocity thesis[43] precisely in the form of a conceptual analysis. First, he argues that the purely legislative form of the maxims required by the categorical imperative requires a free will, because only a free will could be determined to act by a purely formal feature of a maxim rather than a material interest in its outcome (5:28–29); next he argues that, conversely, a free will must necessarily act on the moral law because it can act only on a formal rather than material ground (5:29). Thus the central argument of Kant's mature moral philosophy seems not to reject Mendelssohn's approach but to adopt his idea of discovering the fundamental principle of morality by an analysis of the concept of the freedom of the will.

There is, however, a fatal flaw in Kant's argument: a free will is not *logically* or analytically compelled to act only on moral rather than material considerations, but rather must do so only if it is to *maintain* or *preserve* its freedom. There is no logical contradiction in freely choosing to give in to inclination or even to undercut the possibility of subsequent free actions – as indeed Kant's later interpretation of radical evil as a freely chosen adherence to evil maxims in the *Religion within the Boundaries of Mere Reason* (6:35–39) clearly implies. Rather, conformity to the law of reason is necessary in order to preserve or enhance one's freedom of action on all possible future occasions – as Kant's analysis of the examples in the *Groundwork* implies. The connection between the freedom of the will and the categorical imperative is thus not logical but substantive: a free will is logically free to destroy its own freedom, but a free will that does not will to do so needs to abide by the moral law.

I would contend that Kant recognized this fact at some level, and that his Mendelssohnian analysis of the concept of a free will was therefore accompanied by an alternative approach that is based upon the fundamental recognition of the intrinsic value of freedom itself and the realization that action in accordance with the moral law preserves and enhances this value. Here, as in the prize essay, the assumption is that absolute obligation, "*necessitas*

---

[43] See Henry E. Allison, "Morality and Freedom: Kant's Reciprocity Thesis," *Philosophical Review* 95 (1986): 393–425.

legaḷ*s*," must be derived from a *necessary end*, although now the necessary end is freedom rather than perfection. On this approach, freedom is not merely a necessary end or even the instrument for the realization of human perfection, as it is on Mendelssohn's analysis, but it is itself the fundamental value or perfection of human beings.

This approach is clearly evident in Kant's *Lectures on Ethics*, delivered at the outset of the critical period, where he writes that "The inherent value of the world, the *summum bonum*, is freedom in accordance with a will that is not necessitated to action. Freedom is thus the inner value of the world."[44] But, I would suggest, it is also present in the *Groundwork* itself. For in introducing the Formula of Humanity as an End in Itself after the Formula of Universal Law, Kant argues that the existence of something "with absolute worth" is necessary as "the ground of a possible categorical imperative," and then introduces "humanity and all rational being in general" as that which possesses absolute worth and is thus the ground of a possible categorical imperative (4:428). This seems to imply that something that is a necessary end because it has absolute worth gives rise to the categorical imperative, not vice versa. In particular, Kant's argument is that we treat humanity as an end in itself by recognizing that the patients of our actions affecting other human beings are also themselves agents who are capable of and must be allowed to determine their own ends – that is, are beings capable of free action who must be allowed to exercise their own freedom. The value of freedom itself seems to determine the value of humanity, and to impose the constraints on the actions of any individual that are reflected in the universalizability requirement of the categorical imperative. Kant claims that "if there is to be a highest practical principle and a categorical imperative in regard to human will, it must be something that constitutes an *objective* principle of willing out of that which is necessarily an end for everyone because *it is an end in itself*" (4:428): and nothing less than the freedom of human action itself seems to be this end in itself and is thus the necessary end that is to be preserved or advanced by action in accordance with the categorical imperative.

[44] *Lectures on Ethics*, trans. Louis Infield (London: Methuen, 1930), p. 122.

If this interpretation of Kant's deepest level of argument in moral philosophy is correct, then there is a radical difference between Kant's methodology and Mendelssohn's but also a deeper similarity between Kant's critical approach and his original position of 1762 than at first appeared. In contrast to Mendelssohn, Kant's argument does not depend on analysis of the concept of the freedom of the will but on the substantive claim that freedom of the will is the sole unconditional source of moral value. Yet this substantive claim, precisely because it is a claim about absolute value, cannot itself be reached by any method of analysis: it cannot be derived from any theoretical construct nor from any more elementary moral concept[45] but must somehow simply be accepted and recognized as the only appropriate basis for moral theory. In this sense, the fundamental proposition of morality and the ground of the possibility of the categorical imperative is itself indemonstrable – precisely as Kant maintained in 1762 when he said that "the immediate ultimate rule of all obligation must be absolutely unprovable" (2:299). Only now Wolff's and Mendelssohn's conception of human perfection as a goal to be reached through the instrument of human freedom has been replaced with the idea that human freedom is the perfection of human being itself.

This only scratches the surface of the difference between Kant's moral theory and the tradition summed up by Mendelssohn. As in the case of theoretical philosophy, Kant's theory is in a way even more rationalist or at least aprioristic than Mendelssohn's: instead of arguing that conceptual analysis must always be tied down to reality by experience (except in the case of the ontological argument), Kant postulates that in both theoretical and practical reasoning we approach reality with forms of intuition, categories, and ultimate values of completely nonempirical origin. His accommodation with empiricism takes a different form: experience does not justify our most fundamental principles, but provides an infinitely rich field for their application, a field so inexhaustible that the idea of either a scientific or a moral system can only be a regulative idea asymptotically approached, never something ac-

---

[45] See Schmucker, *Die Ursprünge der Ethik Kants,* p. 68.

tually achieved. But that is a story for another occasion.[46] Here I can only hope to have succeeded in using the device of contrasting the evolution of Kant's critical philosophy to the views espoused by his early competitor Moses Mendelssohn in order to show the distance Kant travelled from the leading philosophy of his own place and time.

---

[46] I have made a start on this story in "Reason and Reflective Judgment: Kant on the Significance of Systematicity," *Nous* 24 (1990): 17–43, and "Kant's Conception of Empirical Law," *Proceedings of the Aristotelian Society*, suppl. 67 (1990): 221–42. See also my "Los principios del juicio reflexivo," *Diánoia: Anuario de Filosofía* 17 (1996): 1–59.

Chapter 2

The Unity of Reason: Pure Reason as Practical Reason in Kant's Early Conception of the Transcendental Dialectic

I

Understanding provides one form of unity in our experience – let us say, at least for the sake of illustration, that form of unity constituted by the capacity to assign any given experiences a uniquely determined place relative to any other given experiences in the ideal chronology of our experience as a whole. But the unity of experience does not, as Kant sees things, exhaust the forms of unity we must seek among our representations. In addition to the unity of experience sought by understanding, Kant suggests, the faculty of reason aims at "the unity of reason" (A 302/B 359).[1] But what might Kant mean by the unity of reason? Two ways to interpret this phrase readily come to mind. First, we might take it to imply that reason has a single domain of application: there is only one species of pure reason. Second, we might take it to connote the uniqueness of the way in which pure reason functions or the product it aims to yield: pure reason aims to introduce a single special sort of unity into whatever it is to which it is appropriately applied.

Neither of these propositions would initially appear to capture Kant's conception of pure reason. First, Kant seems to suppose, at least in the *Critique of Pure Reason,* that pure reason can be both theoretical and practical; while there must obviously be some

This chapter originally appeared in the *Monist* 72 (1989): 139–67.
[1] All translations from Kant's German texts are my own.

connection between theoretical and practical reason, pure reason apparently cannot be described as having a unique domain of application. Second, Kant in fact seems to ascribe two different products to pure reason, not just one, or to see it as functioning in two distinguishable ways. Some pages after introducing the phrase "unity of reason" in the *Critique of Pure Reason,* Kant says that pure reason can "serve the understanding as a canon for its extended and harmonious [*ausgebreiteten und einhelligen*] employment, by means of which the understanding does not, to be sure, come to know any object beyond what it would know according to its own concepts, but is led better and further in this knowledge" (A 329/ B 385). In a note written a few years before the publication of the *Critique,* Kant wrote that "Reason serves to give necessity to understanding and to circumscribe and give unity [*Umfang und Einheit zu geben*] to the sphere of its employment" (R 5553, 18:225). Such remarks suggest two different ways in which pure reason can aim to improve upon what is already accomplished by the understanding. First, reason can aim to *extend* the use of understanding beyond the limits to which it is ordinarily confined, which, since the ordinary limit of understanding, set by the forms of sensibility, is precisely to remain indefinitely extendable, would consist in nothing other than circumscribing its sphere – making *complete* and *unconditioned* knowledge that is left incomplete and conditional by understanding alone. Second, reason can aim to *harmonize* or to make *consistent* or *systematic* knowledge that need not be such in order to satisfy the requirements of understanding alone. On their face, these two aims – let us call them *completeness* and *systematicity* – are not obviously identical. Completeness most naturally seems to characterize the set of the *objects* of knowledge, or the extension of our knowledge, as Kant's own term implies: it suggests that the objects of a certain form of knowledge constitute a totality of some kind, a group that is in some particular way complete and self-contained, thus to which nothing further can be added. Systematicity might instead seem to imply some kind of organization of the *representations,* the concepts, judgments or principles that constitute knowledge, rather than any property, distributive or collective, of the objects of knowledge themselves: it suggests that our concepts or laws about objects, rather than (or, perhaps one should say, in addition to) the objects themselves, are organized in a certain, perhaps hierarchical way. Thus, insofar as pure reason is both theoretical and practical it seems to have not one but two spheres of employment; and insofar as it aims to complete and circumscribe as well as to harmonize subordinate forms of cognition it seems to have a dual function or manner of use.

Fond of dualities as Kant is, however, such a conclusion would miss the underlying unity of his conception of reason. In what follows I attempt to lay at least the historical foundations for an approach to Kant's conception of pure reason on which it is, after all, fair to speak of the "unity of reason" in the two senses initially suggested. That is, one conclusion I should like to reach is that the underlying assumption of the critical philosophy is that pure reason has a positive and constructive use only as practical reason, and that any attempted theoretical application of pure reason leads only to what Kant comes to call "transcendental illusion." As Kant sometimes puts it, the theoretical use of reason is entirely dialectical or negative (see *R* 5647, 18:25–26), and only its practical use is positive. As Kant wrote in a note from about 1785, or right in the middle of the critical period,

> in addition to sensibility and understanding (both *a priori*) the faculty of reason also contains principles for the employment of both [of the others], and indeed limits the concepts of understanding to experience and those of sensibility also to the same, so that their condition will not be extended to things in themselves, God and spirit. At the same time therefore to give to reason freedom to think of something beyond experience, which is to be sure necessary for the completion of our use of understanding but which can never be thought by means of theoretical concepts except negatively, [and] which can be thought positively by moral concepts alone and which contains the totality of conditions for all. (*R* 5649, 18:297)

The second conclusion I would like to reach is that the two conceptions of unity I have characterized, completeness on the one hand and systematicity on the other, should not be thought of as competing conceptions of the unity of reason but rather as, at least in the end, two aspects of the unity of reason, or two criteria both of which must be satisfied if any body of thought is ultimately to satisfy the claims of reason. Understanding may have to be satisfied with what Kant calls the exposition of appearances, which we may think of as an indefinitely extendable process of simply ordering appearances relative to each other, but reason is satisfied only when its objects can be seen as constituting a complete and systematic whole. Kant may not always make both of these aspects of unity equally prominent. In particular, the dialectical delusions of reason detailed in the "Antinomy of Pure Reason" arise from unjustified postulations of completeness in series of objects or their conditions without apparent reference to systematicity, which seems to come forth as a quite independent and indeed legitimate goal of theoretical reason in Kant's theory of regulative ideals. But precisely where Kant allows pure reason a positive role, namely in the sphere of the practical, his ultimate aim is to show how the requirements of both systematicity and completeness must be conjointly satisfied. As Kant sees it, the fundamental law of morality essentially requires nothing but systematicity – of purpose – itself; but reason also requires that the world of purposes be completed as well as systematic. This is what, at least at the deepest level of Kant's thought, generates the conception of the highest good.

The historical picture into which these conclusions would fit is this. Prior to the critical revolution, Kant assumed that the ultimate object of knowledge is an objective world, where the two essential characteristics of a world were, on the one hand, "FORM, which consists in the coordination of substances," and, on the other, "ENTIRETY, which is the *absolute* allness of its component parts"[2] – in other words, systematicity and completeness. After the critical turn, Kant realized that the ontological ideal of a world had to be transformed into a subjective ideal of the unity of knowledge: we could strive for unity as systematicity and completeness in our representation of the world without ascribing it to the world as it is independent of our representation of it, and indeed we could only regard unity as a subjective ideal of knowledge. But

---

[2] *On the Form and Principles of the Sensible and Intelligible World*, §2, 2:390, 391; translation from George Kerferd and David Walford, *Kant: Selected Pre-Critical Writings* (Manchester: Manchester University Press, 1968), pp. 51, 53.

Kant also realized that what had to be reduced to a subjective ideal in the case of knowledge could remain an objective ideal in the case of practice, for in the case of practice we must not strive to confine our concepts to the limits of the perceptible world (which are nothing other than its indefiniteness or incompleteness), but must instead strive to make the world fit our own concept – of a systematic whole of human purposes. To be sure, we cannot ourselves guarantee that the natural world will fully reflect the unity we strive for, but we can make sure that our own intended purposes are fully systematic and can also hope for God to complete the system of our intentions by realizing the highest good. Thus, the ideal of unity, which reason must subjectivize in the case of theoretical reason, can be retained in the case of practical reason precisely because there the subjective is also objective; and Kant is in a sense able to retain his original conception of reason precisely by equating pure reason with practical reason.

There are a number of distinct way stations in the evolution of this view. It is by no means fully developed in the *Critique of Pure Reason*, for while Kant there denies pure theoretical or speculative reason the power to complete knowledge by terminating series of conditions, he still assigns it the task of systematizing knowledge by means of the regulative ideals of hierarchy in laws and continuity in forms and species as well as by means of the teleological conception of the natural world as a system in service of God's purposes (see A 686/B 714 ff.). Yet even these regulative rather than constitutive ideals of speculative reason are reassigned in the *Critique of Judgment:* the regulative ideals of systematicity in general are assigned to the newly introduced faculty of reflective judgment, and the teleological conception of the world as a system subordinated to an ultimate purpose is reassigned to reflective judgment working in conjunction with practical reason as the source of the idea of human freedom as the only purpose that is an end in itself.[3] One can suggest that theoretical reason's positive even if only regulative ideal of systematicity is reassigned to reflective judgment precisely to preserve the critical thesis that it is only as practical reason that pure reason has a positive function.

---

[3] See *CJ*, §84.

Telling this whole story would go well beyond what can be done here. This chapter is confined to the origins of Kant's critical conception of the unity of reason. Its first part considers Kant's original exposition of the transcendental dialectic in the mid-1770s. Here we see how Kant transforms his original, ontological conception of a world into the subjective conception of the unity of knowledge and see the emergence of Kant's thesis that pure reason has a positive or constructive role only as practical reason, producing nothing but illusion if given an objective theoretical role. Its last part sketches Kant's preliminary conception of practical reason. Here I show how Kant thinks that pure reason strives to produce systematicity by enjoining us to seek a system of purposes in ourselves and others and strives to complete this system of purposes by postulating ideas of reason. In particular, I try to show that Kant does not conceive of systematicity and completeness as two alternative aims of practical reason but attempts to link them in a single conception of the unity of reason. Thus, in the end, Kant attempts to find the unity of reason in a conception of the unified function of practical reason. As the *Critique of Pure Reason* itself suggests, what pure reason strives to produce above all is the "necessary unity of all possible ends" (A 328/B 385).

II

In the *Critique of Pure Reason*, Kant does not suggest an entirely uniform approach to the three forms of dialectical inference which he there recognizes. In his treatment of rational psychology, the "Paralogisms of Pure Reason," and of rational theology, the "Ideal of Pure Reason," Kant treats the speculative claims of pure reason as entirely unfounded because they depend on strictly fallacious inferences. In these inferences, reason "stretches its wings in vain in attempting to get beyond the world of sense by the mere power of speculation" (A 591/B 619). But in his treatment of rational cosmology in the "Antinomy of Pure Reason," Kant seems to allow for a more positive role for speculative reason: in the antinomies reason generates competing pairs of arguments each member of which is supposed to be valid, and which could even be seen as sound if true premises were available; and, he argues, although

65

there is no true premise underlying the first two, "mathematical" antinomies, concerning the extent and composition of the world in space in time, in the case of the second two, "dynamical" antinomies, concerning the world's dependence on a first and necessary cause, it is at least possible that the premises that would transform both sides of the arguments into theoretically sound inferences are true. In the mid-1770s, however, Kant presented a different picture. On the one hand, at least before about 1778, Kant seemed to think of the dialectic as concerning only the cosmological antinomies and had not yet connected his earlier critique of arguments for the existence of God to the dialectic nor invented the critique of rational psychology presented under the rubric of the "Paralogism." On the other hand, Kant's treatment of the antinomies in this period seemed to deny that reason was capable of any valid speculative arguments at all, and instead to conclude that the appearance of insuperable contradiction in theoretical philosophy could be entirely avoided by what might be called a purely methodological precaution, the recognition that reason provides subjectively valid ideals for the unification of our knowledge without ascribing any properties to objects whatsoever. In fact, at one point Kant goes so far as to say that since the "transcendental synthesis is unconditional, but also proceeds by means of purely intellectual concepts, there is really no antinomy" (*R* 4760, 17:711), and at another he calls the "rationalizing principles" (*vernünftelnde principien*) of the dialectic "transcendental paralogisms," that is, implies that they are *all* fallacious (*R* 5596, 18:245). At the same time, however, Kant constantly suggests that the faculty of pure reason that only misguidedly attempts speculative and dogmatic claims in theoretical philosophy has a clearly constructive, even dogmatic function in the sphere of the practical.

The following reflection, from the period 1776–78, gives a good idea of the conception of the proper function and application of pure reason that Kant entertained in much of the decade preceding the publication of the *Critique of Pure Reason*:

The purpose of metaphysics: 1. To make out the origin of synthetic *a priori* knowledge. 2. To obtain insight into the restricting conditions of the empirical use of our reason. 3. To show the independence of our reason from these conditions, thus the possibility of its absolute use. 4. By that means to extend our use of reason beyond the bounds of the sensible world, although only negatively, that is, to do away with the hindrance which reason makes itself (from principles of its empirical use). 5. To show the condition of the absolute unity of reason, by means of which it can be a complete *principium* of practical unity, that is, of the concordance of the sum of all purposes.

(These same principles of extension [*Erweiterung*] are again negative in regard to their empirical employment, where nothing but nature is valid.)

The dogmatic use of our reason beyond the bounds of (possible) experience cannot be objectively determining, and no new synthesis takes place; rather it is only a harmony of theoretical with practical unity, since the practical employment is led beyond the bounds of the pragmatic, thus beyond the present world, according to the analogy of empirical employment, but in relation to the conditions of a complete unity, and thereby our business of reason *a parte priori* and *posteriori* is completed.

(Freeing the unity of reason from the limits of its empirical employment makes its transcendental employment possible.)

Since the extension of reason is here only negative, yet the absolute unity of the knowledge of objects in general and of all their purposes (free of all restrictions of sensibility) is requisite for the absolute spontaneity of reason, so is the extension practically necessary.

Reason is the faculty of the absolute unity of our knowledge.

The principles of the completion of our knowledge, that is of the (absolute unity of the employment of reason [or]) the absolute whole thereof are the *synthesis* of reason.

They contain conditions of wisdom, that is of the harmony of the sum of all our purposes. (*R* 4849, 18:5–6)

This series of remarks asserts most of the theses we will be considering. First, Kant asserts that metaphysics has the constructive task of explaining the origin of synthetic *a priori* knowledge – this is the task of a transcendental aesthetic and analytic (and is not discussed here). Second, metaphysics must determine the limits of empirical knowledge, so as to demonstrate how interference with the proper role of reason may be avoided; however, this function is entirely negative and, in particular, requires that reason be prevented from interfering with itself. This last requirement can only be understood as the requirement that the practical function of reason not be undermined by the inevitable collapse of the presumption that reason has a positive theoretical function. Finally, reason's positive function is practical, and it accomplishes this function by providing a principle for the "sum of all purposes." That is, the essence of practical reasoning is to provide a method for the harmonization of possible purposes (of the relevant agents).

All of these assertions require elaboration, of course. I begin with some of Kant's most general remarks about the nature of dialectical inference, for these most directly reflect Kant's new recognition that his previous ontological characterization of the systematicity and completeness of a world must be transformed into a subjective ideal that can become objective only in the sphere of practice. A number of the marginalia Kant entered in his copy of Baumgarten's *Metaphysica* around 1776 make clear the basic diagnosis that illusion, or at least confusion, arises from mistaking subjectively valid principles for the organization of thought itself for objectively valid principles postulating and describing certain objects of experience or properties thereof. Thus, one reflection remarks that "it is often found that others take the maxims of reason as axioms of reason and the rules of method as principles of theory (doctrine), similarly the limits of judgment are taken for limits of objects" (*R* 4971, 18:45). A note Kant made ten pages further on again stresses the danger of confusing subjective features of knowledge with features of objects:

> In all judgments illusion rests on the confusion of the subjective with the objective. Especially in the case of principles of reason, where *a priori* subjective grounds can also be [mistaken for] objective grounds.
>
> In transcendental science everything must be derived from the subject, [but] only some of that is related to objects. (*R* 5058, 18:75)

Comments of this sort are immediately conjoined with remarks indicating the underlying practical use of pure reason. Thus, *R* 4971 is followed by this:

> In the world of sense we follow the principles of empirical knowledge, in the world of understanding the principles of pure knowledge of understanding. The latter however have no relation to the exposition of the appearances with which we are affected, but rather only to that which is given through the understanding (pure employment of freedom), or morality. Here the necessary presupposition is that there is a God. A belief. (R 4972, 18:45)

Although Kant does not here make a clear terminological distinction between what he eventually came to distinguish as understanding and reason, the import of the remark is clear: the only two varieties of constructive principles of thought are principles of empirical knowledge for the exposition of appearance on the one hand and principles of practical reason, for the "pure employment of freedom," on the other. The paradigmatic speculative postulation of God, which might be thought to belong to pure theoretical reason, is in fact a presupposition of morality only. Two pages later, Kant again makes clear the primacy of practical reason: "The foremost of all sciences of reason are metaphysics and morals, but the former for the sake of the latter. Its use is dialectical; insofar as reason opposes something to the dogmatic objections of reason, then the grounds of [the] moral are without hindrance" (R 4982, 18:50).

A group of five loose sheets (R 5756 to 5760), which Erich Adickes ascribed to the period 1775–77 and which constitute Kant's first sketches of the transcendental dialectic (in fact, the first of them, R 5756, seems to constitute Kant's first surviving outline for the whole *Critique of Pure Reason*), expand upon the theory of dialectical illusion and, at least a bit, on the purely practical role of pure reason. I can only highlight the following salient points in these notes. First, Kant stresses that reason strives to introduce unity and completeness into our knowledge. Second, he makes clear his view that an interpretation of such unity and completeness as theoretically objective characteristics of objects (the world) would overstep the bounds of what can be given by sense and thus be confirmed in experience – this limitation of the claims of reason by the claims of sensibility, rather than vice versa, being the mark of the revolution in Kant's thought since 1770. Third, he asserts, although without much explanation, that the proper application of reason's ideal of unity and completeness is in the sphere of practice rather than theory.

All of these themes are evident in *R* 4757. Kant begins this discussion by contrasting "immanent principles of the empirical employment of the understanding," which are "both principles of the possibility of experience (of distributive unity) as well as of the possibility of the objects of experience," with "transcendent principles of the pure employment of the understanding," which are not "conditions of appearance"; under these rubrics, he then lays out a version of the antinomy of pure reason:

> Immanent principles (space and time are conditions of appearance) or transcendent principles (they are not).
>
> The former of the empirical, the latter of the pure employment of understanding. The agreement of reason with itself in the whole.
>
> The former needs no first *a priori*, rather *a posteriori* and from these *progressus* or *regressus in infinitum*.
>
> Immanent principles of the empirical employment of understanding:
>
> 1. There is no boundary to the composition and decomposition of appearances.
>
> 2. There is no first ground or first beginning.
>
> 3. Everything is mutable and variable, therefore empirically contingent, since time in itself is necessary, but nothing is necessarily fixed to time.
>
> Transcendent principles of the pure employment of understanding:
>
> 1. There is a first part, namely the simple as the *principium* of composition, and there are limits to all appearances together.
>
> 2. There is an absolute spontaneity, transcendental freedom.
>
> 3. Something is necessary in itself, namely the unity of the highest reality, wherein all manifoldness of possibilities can be determined through limits. . . .
>
> Since space and time are only conditions of appearance, there must be [a] *principium* of the unity of pure reason, through which knowledge is determined without regard to appearance.

Here Kant generates the antinomies under three rather than four headings, but in fact the same four oppositions are described as in the subsequent *Critique*. As far as empirical knowledge is concerned, there is no limit or boundary to composition or extension in space and time, no limit or simple to be reached in the decomposition of empirical objects into their spatiotemporal parts, no first cause that is not itself the effect of some antecedent, and no absolutely necessary condition of the contingent existents encountered in experience. Pure reason, on the other hand, proposes that there is a determinate limit to the composition of objects, that there are simples to be reached in the decomposition of objects, that there is a spontaneous cause of existence not itself dependent on any antecedent, and that there is an absolutely necessary existence at the ground of all contingents. Kant's next step, however, is not to describe these opposed sets of assertions as the products of equally valid inferences, each performed by pure reason itself. Instead, he contrasts the immanent principles of empirical knowledge, which are principles of the possibility of objects, with the principles of pure reason, which have an apparently subjective significance only – except for their application in practical reason, hinted at in passing. And because the principles of reason are of merely subjective or internal significance, Kant suggests, there is no genuine contradiction between the principles of empirical knowledge and of pure reason but only an "apparent antinomy":

Ground of the Antithetic
or of the apparent Antinomy of Pure Reason

The former are principles of the exposition of experience, the latter of the spontaneity of *pure reason*. Harmonies with itself in the whole, therefore also of morality.

We must have principles of the original unity or the systematic unity of our cognitions, that is of the spontaneity thereof, insofar as we act independently and will practically [and] *originarie* determine the appearances or ourselves among the appearances.

They are principles of the self-determination of reason
or of the unity of the whole of our determinations of reason.

All possible cognitions constitute a whole for reason, therefore the synthesis of absolute unity is the condition of reason.

Here Kant suggests that there is really no antinomy of pure reason at all, because the postulations of pure reason that appear to be opposed to the theses asserting the limitations of empirical knowledge are not themselves competing principles for the "exposition of appearance," but are instead internal principles for the unification of knowledge or for the agreement or harmony of knowledge with itself. In fact, here Kant suggests that the unity he has in mind concerns both the origin or starting point and the systematicity or organization of knowledge – he refers to both "original" and "systematic" unity. Further, Kant again suggests a link to practical reason. What the connection is he hardly makes clear, but there is at least a suggestion that the unity of some form of our cognitions, where that unity may concern both origins and systematicity, is a necessary condition of practical and not just theoretical reasoning.

Further exploration of this suggestion is required, but Kant does not provide it here. Instead, he now concludes by giving his methodological solution to the "apparent antinomy": even the appearance of antinomy can be avoided by following certain rules for the correct use of both sense and reason:

Dialectic.
Rules.

1. Not to judge according to rules of appearance that which does not belong to appearances at all, e.g., God with [rules for] space and time.

2. Not to subject to its conditions that which does not belong to external appearance, e.g., spirit [*Geist*].

3. Not to hold as impossible what cannot be conceived (and what cannot be represented in intuition): the totality of the infinite or infinite division. The infinitude of the series, the finitude of that which is derivative without the *substratum originarium*.

Further, not to confuse the principles of the absolute unity of reason with those of empirical unity.

a. Simplicity of the thinking subject.

b. Freedom as the condition of rational actions.

c. *Ens originarium* as the *substratum* of all connection of its representations in a whole.

d. [Not to] confuse the restriction of the world concerning origin and content with limitation.

Principles of reason are those which are the conditions of the unity of our knowledge, insofar as it is determinable *a priori*, consequently only those which contain the completeness of speculative knowledge *a priori*, which is in agreement with the ideas of practical [knowledge(?)] *a priori*. (*R* 4757, 17:703–5)

These concluding comments are as suggestive as what went before. First, Kant clearly implies that the appearance of antinomy or "antithetic" can be avoided entirely by the use of certain rules for avoiding confusion between the conditions of experience and the conditions of pure reason. The rules Kant actually offers might seem to look back to the approach to "subreptic axioms" taken in the inaugural dissertation, where Kant's methodological solution to apparent antinomies was to ensure that unjustifiable demands for sensible verification not improperly hinder metaphysical speculation – there Kant wrote that "great care must be taken *lest the domestic principles of sensitive cognition transgress their boundaries and affect things intellectual.*"[4] But here Kant does suggest that it is at least as important not to infect the "empirical unity" of knowledge with rules of "absolute unity" as the other way around, and in this he transforms the standpoint of 1770. Following this suggestion, he then in fact introduces references to all three of the topics of the mature dialectic, implying that it would be improper to interpret as rules of "empirical unity" pure reason's absolutistic conceptions of the simplicity of the thinking subject and of the *ens originarium* as well as its supposition that the world must have a determinate origin and extent (*Einschrankung der Welt dem Ursprung und Inhalt nach*). Finally, he again tantalizingly alludes to a connection between the "absolute unity of reason" and "freedom as the condition of rational actions," once more hinting that a principle of unity is the key to practical reason.

The next reflection, *R* 4758, goes over much the same terrain,

---

[4] *The Forms and Principles of the Sensible and Intellectual World*, §24, 2:411; Kerferd and Walford, *Selected Pre-Critical Writings*, p. 81.

although it includes the particularly nice remark that "The transcendent principles are principles of the subjective unity of knowledge through reason, that is, of the harmony of reason with itself" (*R* 4758, 17:706). But *R* 4759 is of greater importance. Here Kant first lays out clearly the quadripartite structure of the mature "Antinomy of Pure Reason." At the same time, he also makes it very clear that this set of four theses and antitheses represents not two sets of equally valid inferences of pure reason, but rather independent principles for the unity or exposition of appearances, or experience, on the one hand, and merely subjective principles for the unity of reason, on the other. Again, he suggests that the principles of the unity of reason are of purely practical significance: "The principles of absolute *synthesis* are rational and conditions of practical knowledge *a priori.* " In addition, this note also introduces Kant's mature tripartite division between sensibility, understanding, and reason, perhaps for the first time:

> 1. Principles of intuition. That conditions of intuition are not the things [themselves] [*Sachen*].
> 2. Of the understanding, e.g., *principium rationis.*
> 3. Of reason.

But because of the length of this note, I only show how its presentation of the antinomy is flanked by assertions of the purely practical use of pure reason:

> Reason goes from the universal to the particular, understanding from the particular to the universal. The universal [in the case of] the latter is only *secundum quid* and belongs to the empirical or physical use of reason. The former is absolute and belongs to the free use or the metaphysical. Likewise to the moral [use].
> (Exposition and rationality.)
> (To appearances.) (Unity of experience and unity of reason.)
> Principles of the exposition of appearances presuppose these as *conditioned* throughout, thus nothing posited absolutely.
> 1. No absolute totality (*totalitas secundum quid*) of composition, thus infinite *progressus*. . . .
> 2. No absolute totality of decomposition, thus nothing unconditionally simple. (*non simplicitas absoluta.*)

74

(Infinite progression cannot be conceived and the unconditional cannot be made intuitable.)

3. No absolute totality of the series of generation, no absolute spontaneity. (*non causalitas absoluta.*)

4. No unconditional necessity. All things can be taken out of
time and space. (*non necessitas absoluta.*)

(The world in a physical understanding.

The simple -- - -------- --------------

spontaneitas -- - -------- --------------

necessitas -- - -------- --------------)

As principles of empirical employment all of these propositions are (objectively) certain, but contrary to reason.

(To things in general)

Principles of rationality or comprehension (thereof). From
the universal to the particular: absolute synthesis.

1. Unconditional all of the (dependent) whole. World-origin.
(*in mundo noumeno datur universitas.*)

2. Unconditionally simple. (*monas.*)

3. Unconditional spontaneity of action. (*Libertas transscen-
dentalis.*)

4. Unconditionally necessary being. (*necessitas absoluta originaria.*)

(The world in a metaphysical understanding.

The simple -- - -------- --------------)

These propositions are subjectively necessary as principles of
the employment of reason in the whole of knowledge: unity of
the whole of the manifold of knowledge of the understanding.
They are practically necessary in regard to . . . [*breaks off*].

There must be principles of the self-determination of reason
that are distinct from those where reason is determined through
appearances and their conditions. These are principles of the
unity of knowledge in the whole, thus not partial but total unity.
(*R* 4759, 17:708–11)

The abrupt end to Kant's incomplete thought in the penultimate
paragraph quoted is symbolic: Kant does not actually spell out how
pure reason's interest in unconditional unity is to be the key to
practical reason. But the rest of Kant's conception of the antinomy

at this stage is fairly clear. The unity of experience is always conditional, because those items which are to be unified in experience – namely, intuitions or appearances – are themselves always conditional. Kant makes this premise plain in the next reflection: "For all appearance is possible only in space and time. Time (and space) is only determinable through appearance. But it is however without any first [member]" (*R* 4760, 17:713). Thus, there can be no limit to the extent of the world in space and time, for beyond any limit there must lie more space and time; there can be no simple part in the decomposition of empirical objects, for within any part there must lie another; there can be no first member in any series of causes, for any member must itself have a cause; and there can be no necessity in any such series that is not itself dependent on something else. To these limitations on the unity of experience reason opposes its demand that these conditions be removed: there must be some unconditional limit to the whole of the world, there must be unconditionally simple substances that cannot be further divided – indeed, monads; there must be an origin, at least of actions, that is not itself the effect of something prior; and something must be unconditionally necessary. But these propositions postulating the completeness of the world which is the object of our knowledge are only subjective necessities of thought: they describe how we must unify our experience but are not themselves valid for the exposition of the appearances of objects. But they do have a (to be sure unexplained) practical significance.

Throughout these sketches of the antinomy, reason's demand for unity is understood as a demand for an end to iterated conditions, that is, as a demand for completeness or closure in the set of the objects of knowledge. Systematicity, as a special form of the internal organization of knowledge, does not seem to be at issue, in spite of Kant's repeated suggestion that the principles of reason are rules for the unity of knowledge itself. This is particularly evident in the last of this group of sketches, *R* 4760, from which Kant's remark that the "antinomy of reason" is "really no antinomy" has already been quoted. Here Kant does say that the "ground" of the principles of reason is the "unity of the entire employment of reason, by means of which it has collective unity"; this certainly sounds as if pure reason strives for systematicity. But the conflict he actually describes is again that between the conditioned and the unconditioned, the incomplete and the complete. Thus, that "all empirical *synthesis* is conditioned" implies that there is "No simple, no bound to magnitude, no first ground, no necessary being," whereas the "unconditioned" but "purely intellectual" synthesis of reason asserts that "The world is limited. It consists of the simple. There is freedom. There is a necessary being" (*R* 4760, 17: 711). This is even plainer at the end of this reflection, where Kant explicitly equates the demand for unity with a demand for a first or unconditioned member in all of the syntheses of reason. On the side of appearances, Kant writes, "There is a *regressus in infinitum* (from the empirical *termino* on) of dimension, division, generation, and dependence." This is because "With experiences we always remain in the chain of appearances." But, Kant continues,

> Insofar as we take the things lying at the ground of appearances, which can consequently be thought only through concepts of the understanding, the unity of their synthesis requires an absolute first (of the inner state of reason) (that is an unconditioned) in origin, in composition, in action, in existence in general. These are the conditions of the (subjective) unity in the employment of reason in regard to appearances, as the former are the principles of the manifold. In those uniformity of condition, but in these unconditional unity. (*R* 4760, 17:713)

Reason's requirement for unity seems to be equivalent to its requirement for the termination of syntheses, but this requirement is of purely subjective significance and cannot be carried over into the exposition of appearances or experience.

At this point, reason's role or function may well seem unitary – it serves to terminate otherwise interminable syntheses – but the link that Kant envisages between reason so conceived and the sphere of the practical must seem more obscure than ever. Before we turn to that link, however, I consider several sketches Kant left showing how he transformed the antinomy of reason as thus far developed into the tripartite dialectic that was expounded in the *Critique of Pure Reason,* for these show in more detail how Kant thought that dialectical illusion arose from transforming a subjectively valid ideal for the unity of knowledge itself into an ontological conception of the world. Once we have seen that Kant originally conceived of all three elements of the dialectic while still maintaining his purely negative conception of pure theoretical reason, we will then be ready to consider the clues to his conception of practical reason.

III

Four loose sheets (*R* 5552 to 5555) assigned to 1778–79 offer Kant's earliest surviving sketches of the whole, tripartite dialectic. As in the published "Transcendental Dialectic," Kant provides several explanations for the generations of the paralogism, antinomy, and ideal of pure reason that are not obviously identical. Thus, *R* 5553, the most elaborate of these sketches, begins with the suggestion that reason is essentially a faculty of inference that reaches pure ideas by envisioning the iteration of a series of inferences the premises of which are always conditional until an unconditional premise is reached:

> As the senses are related to the understanding, so is the understanding related to reason. The appearances of the first acquire from the second the unity of understanding through concepts and concepts acquire in the third faculty the unity of reason through ideas (through prosyllogisms a higher subject is always found, until finally nothing further can be found, of which the former would be the predicate . . .). (*R* 5553, 18:221–22)

This parallels the argument by means of which Kant introduces the "Transcendental Ideas" in the published "Transcendental Dialectic," which also describes reason as both generating a series of inferences but then seeking to put a stop to it by the introduction of an object that has no further conditions, that is, is unconditioned. In particular, the *Critique* explicitly argues that the forms of inference at issue are generated by the relational categories, so that reason's series of prosyllogisms generates three forms of dialectical inference from the three categories of relation.[5] But there

[5] As Kant puts it,
> There will be as many pure concepts of reason as there are species of relations which the understanding represents by means of categories; and

are many puzzles about this way of generating the dialectic. First, two quite different activities seem to be ascribed to a single faculty of reason – reiterating forms of inference on the one hand and trying to put a stop to such iterated inference on the other – which seem as if they should be ascribed to two different faculties of mind. Second, if reason seeks to stop an otherwise endless iteration of inferences by introducing the idea of an unconditioned or complete object of thought, it is not clear why such an attempt should be confined to the case of the relational categories alone; completeness also seems an intelligible goal in the case of the thought of quantity, quality, and relation. And in fact it is quite clear that the quadripartite structures of the antinomy and the paralogism, if not of the ideal of pure reason, are supposed to be generated by combining the idea of an unconditioned subject of thought on the one hand and an unconditioned object of appearance on the other with the four headings of the categories, quantity, quality, relation and modality. Kant indicates as much when he notes: "System of transcendental ideas. 1. There are 3 titles according to the three kinds of inferences of reason; there are 4 dialectical inferences according to the 4 categories" (*R* 5553, 18:223). Finally, there is a special puzzle in the case of the paralogisms as to why the unconditioned which is introduced should be the idea of an unconditioned subject *of thought* rather than an unconditioned substance of accidents more generally, pure substance rather than pure subject.

In fact, the theory of prosyllogisms or, as Kant also calls them, "episyllogisms" (*R* 5553, 18:227), seems to be something of an epicycle, and the original sketches of the dialectic make it plain that Kant often ignored it and simply suggested that reason directly introduces the idea of a completely total or unconditioned

> there will therefore be sought *first, an unconditioned of categorical* synthesis in one *subject, second,* of *hypothetical* synthesis of the members of a *series, third,* of *disjunctive* synthesis of the members of a *system.*
>
> There are therefore exactly so many kinds of inferences of reason, each of which progresses to the unconditioned by means of prosyllogisms: the one to a subject which is not itself a predicate; the next to the presupposition which itself presupposes nothing further; and the third to an aggregate of the members of the division to which nothing further is requisite in order to complete the division of a concept. (A 323/B 379–80)

instantiation of certain forms of thought, which may then be used to generate inferences of reason without having been reached by any series of inferences. Even when Kant dispensed with the theory of iterated prosyllogisms, however, he remained ambivalent about what reason's demand for the unconditioned is applied to in order to generate the three main forms of ideas of reason. Some comments suggest that the three ideas of reason are generated simply by making the three categories of relation, namely substance, causation, and disjunction, complete or unconditional. But other passages suggest that what reason represents as unconditioned is nothing other than the three basic constituents of knowledge in general – namely, the subject, appearance, and the object – or even the three *faculties* of knowledge – namely, apperception, sensibility, and concepts of objects. In attempting to show that the transcendental illusions are generated from the representation of the faculties of knowledge as themselves unconditioned, Kant sustains his underlying insight that such illusion arises from confusing the subjective unity of knowledge with a special unity in the objects of knowledge.

The first of these accounts is suggested in one passage in *R* 5553, where Kant simply enumerates "1. The unconditioned of inherence (or of the aggregate). 2. That of dependence or the series. 3. That of the concurrence of all possibilities to one and of one to all," and then characterizes these ideas as ideas of the totality of conditions realized in objects: "Just as the inferences of reason determine a judgment in general through subsumption, so reason determines the objects in the totality of conditions" (*R* 5553, 18:228). But this same reflection explores at greater length the idea that what reason treats as unconditional or completed is three ideas connected with the structure of thought itself. At one place he characterizes the "threefold forms of transcendental illusion" thus:

> The first illusion is that where the unity of apperception, which is subjective, is taken for the unity of the subject as a thing. The second: where the subjective determination of sensibility and its condition is taken for an object. The third: where the universality of thought by reason is taken for a thought of a totality [*All*] of the possibilities of things. (*R* 5553, 18:224)

Here the idea is simply that reason mistakes the purely formal unity of apperception for a conception of a unified subject underlying all of one's thoughts, that it imports an illicit conception of completeness into our conception of the forms of intuition, and that it imports the idea of a total determination of all possibilities – an ideal of pure reason – into the purely formal requirements for thought of an object.

The same line of thought is expounded at greater length as the reflection continues. First, Kant directly characterizes reason's role as that of introducing unconditional unity into our thought:

> In the understanding concepts are directed toward possible experience, but for reason possible experience is directed according to concepts, just as in the exercise of all virtue it must be directed according to concepts and is only possible thereby, even though it never attains the concepts. In the *regressus* to its conditions possible experience is directed according to the concepts of reason or transcendental ideas. The business of reason consists in creating unconditional unity in the greatest manifold in the employment of the understanding. That concept of reason which connects the greatest particular unity with this universal [unity (?)] accords with possible experience and is in so far a correct rule. But a concept which is not in relation to possible experience cannot be objectively valid. . . .
>
> Reason serves to give necessity to understanding and to circumscribe and give unity [*Umfang und Einheit zu geben*] to the sphere of its employment.
>
> The manner of regarding the particular as a determination of the universal (the true universal, which is not drawn from the particular by induction) is an *a priori* unity, which is quite distinct from the unity of experience. (*R* 5553, 18:225)

The first of these paragraphs suggests that unconditional unity is simply the intrinsic goal of reason, by means of which it attempts to direct the theoretical use of the understanding, although illegitimately, in precisely the same way in which it employs this idea to direct the exercise of virtue, although there quite legitimately. The third paragraph contrasts true universality with merely inductive generalization, intimating that any claim to unconditioned totality in the use of any concept must be ascribed to reason rather than understanding. The second paragraph might be taken to be another echo of Kant's underlying idea that reason aims at both completeness (*Umfang*) and systematicity (*Einheit*).

The next page of the reflection then moves on to suggest that reason simply demands such true rather than comparative totality of conditions, or unconditionality, with respect to the general concepts of the subjective conditions of thought themselves, namely the ideas of the thinking subject, appearances, and objects in general:

> The system of dialectical inferences rests on the unity of them in one inference of reason, wherein [there is] 1. subjective unity of all representations, that is, unity of the subject, second synthetic unity of the object or of appearance, this either of appearances: collectively, or of the thought of objects in general: distributively (disjunctively). . . .
>
> 1. Note. In the inferences of reason, if the *major* is an empirical proposition (all men are mortal), then it is still a universal concept. But since it is only from induction, it is yet not knowledge from concepts. Therefore such is required in the end from reason, in order for true universality to arise; for from this alone will reason hold something as determined and necessary in itself.
>
> 2. The analytical inferences are to be sure from concepts; but their *major* is a universal identical judgment, which does not express unity of that which is distinct. . . .
>
> The unconditional subjective conditions of thought.
>
> The unconditional (objective) condition of appearances.
>
> The unconditional objective condition of all objects in general.
>
> I understand by an idea a concept which is sufficiently grounded in reason but for which no object can be given in any possible experience.
>
> Whereto then does the idea go and why is it grounded in reason, in order to relate itself to objects. The idea of the soul is grounded in the fact that the understanding must relate all thoughts and inner perceptions to the I and regard this as the only constant subject, in order that the most complete unity of self-knowledge may result.
>
> The idea of the unconditioned for all conditions of appear-

ance is grounded in reason as a prescription to seek the completeness of all knowledge of the understanding in subordination [i.e. series].

The idea of the unconditional unity of all objects of thought in one *ens entium* is necessary in order to seek affinity among all that is possible and thereby also thoroughgoing connection as unity of principle.

In right mere concepts of reason are necessary, but in morality ideas. The former can be given a congruent object in experience, but the latter not, since they contain the highest unity of reason of freedom which is concordant with oneself and all purposes of its determination. (*R* 5553, 18:225–26)

Again the tantalizing reference to the unity of purposes is quoted only to be put aside. The main point is that reason simply seeks completeness in its thought of the thinking subject, its thought of the series of appearances, and in the thought of the connections among objects in general; but in so doing it gives rise to purely dialectical inferences to a unitary self, a completed series of appearances, or an *ens entium* or *realissimum*. This explanation of the origin of transcendental illusion does not attempt to suggest that the transcendental ideas automatically arise from any series of ordinary inferences, but instead recognizes that the idea of unconditional universality is imported into the work of the understanding by pure reason, although misguided understanding may then attempt to conduct its ordinary inferential business under the aegis of these illegitimate ideas. Nor does this explanation begin with any exploitation of the three specifically relational categories; it thus leaves open the possibility that each of its three ideas – the soul, the cosmos, and the *ens realissimum* – may be further characterized by all four sorts of categories if appropriate. Instead, reason creates the ideas of the unconditional unity of the self, of appearances, and of the possibilities for objects in general, and can then further differentiate these ideas in terms of unconditional quantity, quality, relation, and modality. Kant suggests that the four types of categories will give rise to four paralogisms about the soul in this remark: "In transcendental psychology the unitariness, simplicity and modality of passive existence flow from the one concept of substance" (*R* 5553, 18:228). More generally, that crossbreeding the four kinds of categories with the three basic aspects of thought – subject, appearance, and object in general – will provide the armature for the dialectic as a whole is exactly what Kant implies in concluding *R* 5553:

> The unconditional unity (of the synthesis) of the subject. 2. The unconditional unity of the synthesis of conditions in appearance. 3. The unconditional unity of the synthesis of thought in general. All by means of the four categories, so far as they indicate unconditional unity.

Kant then goes on to make explicit that the transcendental ideas arise from reason applying its quest for the unconditioned to the basic components of knowledge itself, and, finally, to remind us again that reason's conception of the subjective unity of knowledge itself has no objective validity:

> The transcendental idea can have nothing as its object but the faculties of knowledge [*Erkenntniskräfte*] or representations in general in relation to them. Therefore 1. apperception, second the apprehension of appearance, 3. the concept of the understanding in general. The first is the concept of reason of the subject, the second of the object, insofar as it is given, the third of the object of thought in general.
>
> That pure reason has no objective content for its dialectical inferences. (*R* 5553, 18:229)

In this way Kant attempts to link the several divisions of the mature dialectic to his original claim that reason was concerned with the subjective unity of knowledge itself, and to reiterate his distinction between the latter and any objectively valid quality of the objects of knowledge.

IV

At this point I turn to the issue of Kant's early conception of practical reason. On the one hand, we obviously find confirmation for Kant's thesis that it is only as practical reason that pure reason can be permitted a constructive role at all. On the other hand, we here find the problem that in the sphere of practical reason pure reason seems to have two distinct functions, employing the idea of systematicity to give the content of moral principles but, apparently, independently employing the completeness function of reason to yield God, freedom, and immortality as the presuppositions of morality or, as he later called them, practical postulates. I will conclude this part of the discussion by examining one way Kant suggests to unify these two apparently diverse functions of pure practical reason.

One gnomic utterance from about 1778 juxtaposes most of the key concepts underlying Kant's practical philosophy:

> In the world of understanding [*Verstandeswelt*] the *substratum* is intelligence; action and cause, freedom; the community, happiness from freedom; the primordial being [*Urwesen*], an intelligence through idea; the form, morality; the *nexus* , a *nexus* of purposes. This world of understanding lies at the ground of the sensible world and is that which is truly self-sufficient [*das wahre selbststandige*]. (*R* 5086, 18:83)

Unpacking this note would require a whole interpretation of Kant's moral philosophy; here I must confine myself to asking what Kant means by his suggestion that the characteristic form for the synthesis or connection of objects in a moral world is a "*nexus* of purposes." What I suggest is that Kant means little more than he says, or little more than he suggests in similar phrases we have already encountered, such as his remarks already quoted that "the complete *principium* of practical unity" is the "harmony of all purposes in a sum" or that "the conditions of wisdom" are simply those for the "harmony of all our purposes in a sum" (*R* 4849, 18:6). That is, a nexus of purposes is simply a group of purposes, which, although their actual content must remain unspecified because, as the *Critique* says, we are dealing with the unity of *possible* purposes, must nevertheless be made conjointly compatible or able to constitute a systematic whole as opposed to a mere aggregate, which might coexist in thought but not in realization. In other words, morality does not constrain our purposes except by requiring them to be systematic – where that, of course, means that each agent's purposes, both known and as yet unknown, must be able to constitute such a systematic sum and that all agents' purposes, again both known and as yet unknown, must be able to constitute such a sum. Morality sets us no more specific purpose than that all purposes be able to constitute a sum – or a unity of reason; a conceptually simple aim, though it may require both principles and subtlety of judgment in order to apply it in practice, because we are then dealing with particular purposes most of which are at any given time merely possible and barely foreseeable.

Some of Kant's references to "necessary" ends make it sound as if morality sets out to impose ends more specific than this. Without going to the *Metaphysics of Morals*, we can find such language in several reflections also from the period around 1776:

> Moral laws do not arise from reason, but are rather those that contain the conditions by means of which alone it is possible for free actions to be determined and known according to rules of reason. This however happens when we make the universally valid purpose the ground of [our] actions. Thereby particular purposes accord with those which one can regard as if all things were possible through them.
>
> The morally good requires complete unity of the ground of action before reason, consequently that it be derived from the *idea archetypa*, which is the purpose of the whole world.
>
> That which is in accord with the conditions under which everything happens according to *a priori* rules necessarily pleases. For it brings forth harmony with the whole nature. and therefore a consciousness of the harmony of actions with oneself and with all others. (R 5445, 18:184)

And likewise,

> Moral laws are those that contain the conditions through which free actions are in accord with the universally valid purpose, therefore the private will with the original and highest will. Either with the universal purpose of nature or of freely acting beings. The will is therefore considered according to the unity of the ground, insofar namely as all wills lie in one will. . . . (R 5446, 18:184)

The reference to a grammatically singular "universally valid will" in these remarks makes it sound as if morality postulates some single, special object of the will or purpose which all agents must have, and to which they must subordinate their other, and otherwise indifferent, private purposes. But many of Kant's other remarks make it plain that there is no such special purpose, or rather that such a purpose is just the unity of the other possible purposes of ourselves and other agents. Reason has unity, in the sense of systematicity, as its special object, and practical reason, therefore, the unity or systematicity of purposes; but more specific purposes are no more given by reason itself than, say, intuitions are given by understanding.

Among the sketches of the transcendental dialectic we have been considering, this point of view may be expressed most clearly in Kant's comment that "ideas are necessary in morality" because "it contains the highest unity of reason of freedom agreeing with oneself and all the purposes of one's determination" (*R* 5553, 18:226). Although unduly condensed, this remark suggests that the essence of morality is the possibility of agreement among the purposes one freely determines to pursue – there is no hint that there is any specific purpose to be pursued by the moral agent, but rather consistency among purposes, whatever they may be determined to be. Some of Kant's contemporaneous reflections on moral philosophy[6] make the point even more clearly by stating that what morality requires is consistency or "universality" among purposes, the direct object of which is the *happiness* of oneself or other agents. The following notes are particularly illustrative:

> Moral philosophy is the science of purposes, so far as they are determined by pure reason. Or of the unity of all purposes (where they do not contradict themselves) of rational beings. The matter of the good is empirical, the form given *a priori*. Morality is the good out of principles of spontaneity. Thus of the universality of the good. (*R* 6820, 19:172)

Here Kant quite specifically suggests that (i) the purposes that practical reason unifies are themselves "empirical," or not given by reason; (ii) the purposes that must be unified are not just one's own, but those of rational beings generally, oneself of course included;

---

[6] I.e., marginalia in his copy of Baumgarten's *Initia Philosophia Practicae Primae.*

and (iii) the unity of such purposes to be attained consists simply in their compatibility, or the avoidance of contradictions among them. A note a few paragraphs on makes the first of these points even more obvious by specifically naming happiness as the object of individual actions and thus implying that the unity of reason in actions is nothing other than the unity of actions individually aimed at happiness:

> Everything that makes [one] skilled is practical; what makes [one] clever, pragmatic; what makes [one] wise, moral. The first concerns merely the form of action, the second, the general purpose of action, [namely] happiness; the third, the idea of the unity of the harmony of these purposes with themselves. (*R* 6823, 19:172–73)

Again the idea is that the only requirement that morality, or practical reason, adds to the goals set by the individual aims of happiness and the technical requirements for pursuing happiness is that one pursue only such particular aims of happiness as are compatible with other aims of one's own and other agents. Kant makes the same idea clear some pages later when, in contrast to the "*principium* of the necessary unity of our actions," he says that "from self-inclination arise actions that do not have necessary unity among themselves and others" (*R* 6843, 19:177); again the idea is that all that morality requires is the unity of reason among one's own actions and between one's own and others'. The dual requirement that one act so as to ensure harmony both among one's own possible purposes and between one's own and others' purposes, finally, is emphasized in this remark:

> If your will is to agree with all of your inclinations through universally valid conditions, then it must agree with that to which they are all related, namely yourself, i.e., [your] personality. Duties to oneself.
>
> Your actions should agree with your freedom and (with the universal) [in] your inclinations, with the freedom of others and [with the universal] in their inclinations.
>
> (With your inclination and the inclination of others, with your freedom and the freedom of others.) (*R* 6851, 19:179)

Again, what pure reason requires is simply consistency within your own freely chosen purposes and between yours and those of others, where, as long as this requirement of consistency is satisfied, inclination seems to be a perfectly legitimate source of the purposes to be made consistent, if not in fact the only source of such purposes – it is in any case the only such source that is mentioned. The unity of practical reason simply requires that empirically given purposes – which are, of course, like anything else empirical, never fully given at a single time and thus specificable only indeterminately as the possible purposes of oneself and others – be made compossible.

This is by no means yet an adequate account of how morality's requirement of universalizability is to be derived from the fundamental notion of the unity of reason. In particular, Kant has not yet seen how to reconcile his insights of 1762 that morality must involve both a formal principle and a necessary end. Only when he begins to realize that freedom itself can be regarded as a necessary end that also imposes an organizing principle on our contingent, particular ends will he be ready to begin developing his mature moral philosophy. We will consider Kant's further preliminary steps in this direction in the next chapter, and then see how this idea of freedom as itself both the matter and form of practical reason becomes central to his mature moral philosophy in the next part of this book. In the remainder of this chapter, I offer an abbreviated discussion of Kant's conception of the postulates of pure practical reason, the purpose of which is limited to showing the connection of this aspect of Kant's moral philosophy to the underlying idea of the unity of reason. We shall return to a fuller discussion of these postulates and their implications for Kant's view of nature and history in the final part of this volume.

Kant sometimes writes as if the postulates of freedom, the existence of God, and the immortality of the soul all have the same status and are reached in the same way, in the first instance by simply leaving reason's tendency to postulate the completeness of a series of conditions unhindered in the sphere of the practical by the requirement of sensible confirmation that hinders it in the realm of theory. Thus, we saw that R 4757 simply presented the "simplicity of the thinking subject" (which was traditionally taken to imply its immortality), "freedom as the condition of rational actions," and an *"ens originarium* as the *substratum* of all connection of representations in a whole" as "principles of the absolute unity of reason," which could be maintained at least as "ideas of practical *a priori"* reason as long as they were not judged according to the "rules of appearance" (17:704–5). Another passage from a few years later also suggests that pure reason, seeking completeness as contrasted to systematicity, postulates God, freedom, and immortality as the completions of the ideas of necessity, causality, and substance simply because there is no reason not to in the sphere of practice rather than theory:

> we must subordinate a schema to all of our pure concepts of understanding, a way of combining the manifold in space and time. – Since this schema exists only in the sensible representation of the subject, we therefore 1. know only objects of the senses, thus do not attain to the supersensible. (Geometry.) 2. But the concepts can be extended to all objects of thought in general. However, they yield no extension of theoretical knowledge. In a practical respect, however, where freedom is the condition of its use, practical-dogmatic knowledge can occur – God, freedom, and immortality (spiritual nature).
>
> In nature however, that is, in space and time, nothing unconditional can be met with, and yet reason demands that as the totality of conditions, while it will make the object itself. . . .
>
> Three forms of [something] intellectual (intelligible) (*noumenon*) contain the unconditioned, and one can have knowledge of freedom and its laws and thereby prove the objective reality of mankind as *noumenon* in the midst of its mechanism as *phaenomenon*. – God as the unconditionally necessary substance. Freedom as unconditioned causality and immortality as personality (spirit), which is independent of *commercio* with the body (as its condition).
>
> The categories applied to the intelligible can ground practical-dogmatic knowledge, namely when they are directed to freedom and determine the subject thereof only in relation to that; for then we know God only according to the analogy of subsistence (duration), freedom according to the analogy of causality in the

connection of force with effects in the succession of time, immortality according to the analogy of the connection of everything at one time. . . . [*breaks off*]. (R 5552, 18:220–21)

The details of Kant's treatment vary – thus the last paragraph of R 5552 generates the ideas of God, freedom, and immortality from the three relational categories of substance, causation, and interaction rather than from the more general ideas of quality, relation, and modality, which Kant employs elsewhere; and the analogies to which reason is supposed to appeal are hardly very clear. But the general idea again seems to be simply that in the sphere of practice rather than theory there is no bar to reason's postulation of the unconditioned or that which is complete.

In each of his three published critiques, we will see, Kant attempts to provide more direct arguments that the nature of practical reasoning actually presupposes the postulation of God, freedom, and immortality, and he also will differentiate between the postulation of freedom on the one hand and the postulations of God and immortality on the other: freedom is a necessary presupposition of action according to a law of reason at all, whereas God and immortality are required only for the more specific purpose of allowing rational action to be directed at the attainment of the highest good. The early remarks on the conception of pure practical reason which we have been considering have little to say about the latter issue, but do make it clear that the presupposition of freedom does stand in a separate position from the postulation of God and immortality; for they do include explicit assertions of the claim, to become familiar in the *Groundwork* of 1785, that freedom is a presupposition of action directed by the conception of a rule or law, quite apart from any further specification of the object of such action. Perhaps the clearest of these remarks is this:

> Transcendent freedom is the necessary hypothesis of all rules,*
> thus of all use of the understanding. One should think so and
> so, etc. Consequently this action must be free, that is not already
> determined (subjectively) of itself, but rather have only an objective ground of determination.
>
> *(It is the property of beings for whom the consciousness of
> a rule is the ground of their actions.) (R 4904, 18:24)

The idea is simply that if we are to make the consciousness of a rule – for that matter, a rule for thought as well as a rule for action – the ground of our decision, then we must be free to make our thought or action comply with the rule independently of antecedent conditions within or without ourselves. There is no way we can think of the rule rather than antecedent conditions as the determining factor in our action unless we conceive of ourselves as free to act according to the rule rather than the antecedent conditions. To be sure, Kant stresses that the necessity of such a presupposition is not equivalent to an explanation of its possibility:

> The practical concept of freedom is that which suffices in order to perform actions according to rules of reason, which therefore gives reason's imperatives their power; the speculative or rationalizing [*vernünftelnde*] concept of freedom is that which suffices to explain free actions according to reason. The latter is impossible. . . . (R 4725, 17:688)

Freedom remains a necessary presupposition of action which the agent conceives to be determined by a rule of any sort, a presupposition that cannot be explained by speculative reason but cannot be precluded either. The presupposition of freedom thus need not be directly connected to reason's postulation of the unconditioned, though obviously Kant thinks the idea can be reached in that way as well.

Are we then left with the idea that God and immortality are postulates of practical reason simply because outside the sphere of theory there is nothing to hinder reason's postulation of the unconditioned, and thus with the idea that there is no connection between pure practical reason's concern for systematicity – which does of course presuppose freedom – and its postulation of the other transcendental ideas, God and immortality? I cannot here discuss Kant's published argument for the two remaining practical postulates; I will only draw your attention to several suggestions that God, at least, must be presupposed as the cause of the realization of the system of purposes, the ideal of which furnishes the content of the principle of morality itself (and remember that in R 4972 Kant referred to the concept of God alone as the presupposition of morality). In these remarks, Kant suggests that what pure reason ultimately postulates in virtue of its freedom from the limits of empirical knowledge is the *complete* or *unconditioned realization of systematicity* in the purposes of rational agents. One note is also found in Kant's copy of Baumgarten's ethics, although it is apparently later than the ones quoted before, coming from around 1783–84:

> The pragmatic interest from the principle of happiness as a subjectively universal purpose only makes belief in God a hypothesis; the moral interest from the principle of the system of all purposes as an objectively necessary final purpose [*Endzweck*] of rational beings makes it a postulate, that is, a strictly necessary presupposition of pure reason. God as the highest self-sufficient good, in which alone morality as the highest formal good can have reality, that is a ground of the existence of an intelligible world, that is a realm of ends. . . . (R 6111, 18:458)

Here the idea is not that belief in the existence of God as an ultimate arbiter of rewards is justified by one's private interest in happiness, or even, presumably, by one's private interest in happiness in proportion to one's moral worth; instead, Kant suggests that we must believe in the reality of God in order to believe in the possibility of the realization of the system of ends that is our idea in any moral motivation. We will see later how important this idea becomes to Kant.

The emerging importance of the idea of the highest good is also visible in Kant's metaphysics lectures from around 1778. Here Kant does introduce the concept of the highest good, as in his published treatment of the postulates of practical reason, and leaves us with the impression that the highest good is itself the ultimate form of systematicity, a systematic harmony between all intended purposes on the one hand and all outcomes of action of the other. Pure reason then satisfies its interest in completeness by postulating the realization of such systematicity and its necessary presupposition, namely a cause sufficient to realize it:

> What now is the *summum bonum?* It is the *unification of the greatest happiness with the greatest degree of capacity to be worthy of this*

happiness. If there is to be a highest good, then happiness and the worthiness thereof must be combined. Now in what does this *worthiness* consist? In the practical agreement of our actions *with the idea* of universal happiness. If we conduct ourselves in such a way that, if everyone else so conducted themselves, the greatest happiness would arise; then we have *so* conducted ourselves as to be worthy of happiness. The happiness of a creature can only take place insofar as his actions are derived from the idea of universal happiness and are in harmony with universal happiness. The divine will is of such a kind that it is in harmony with the idea of universal happiness; thus it will apportion happiness to each insofar as his actions agree with that, and insofar as he has made himself worthy of that. Now if conduct agrees with the idea of universal happiness, then it also agrees with the highest divine will. Good conduct is therefore the condition of universal happiness, and only he is worthy of happiness whose conduct agrees with the idea of universal happiness. Since God wills universal happiness, the conduct of such a person agrees with the divine will. This is the highest point and the ground of all morality. God is the highest principle of all such happiness according to the worthiness of the person. That there is such a being is to be sure not proven from the moral principle dogmatically, but is demonstrated as a necessary hypothesis of our practical actions according to laws of morality. (*Metaphysik L1*, 28:337)

This, then, is Kant's underlying idea of the unity of reason: practical reason aims at the greatest possible happiness, which, of course, since happiness simply consists in the attainment of purposes or objectives, can be nothing but the result of the attainment of the (or a) maximally consistent system of purposes. The object or content of morality is thus derived from practical reason's interest in systematicity, although of course we must keep in mind that it must be under the description of rational systematicity per se rather than systematic *happiness* that this interest furnishes morally worthy motivation. Unhindered by the limits of sensibility that govern the theoretical or speculative use of reason, practical reason is also free to postulate the realization or completion of this ideal, which is understood to require a degree of power exceeding that available to ourselves. Thus the practical postulation at least of God is necessary for the postulation of completed systematicity in the sphere of practice. It is this vision of completed systematicity in practice, ultimately, that Kant wishes to preserve from the misplaced postulation of the unity of reason in theory.

Chapter 3

Freedom as the
Inner Value of the World

Throughout the critical decade of the 1780s, from the early *Lectures on Ethics* to the two main works, the *Groundwork for the Metaphysics of Morals* and the *Critique of Practical Reason*, Kant constantly reiterates that *freedom* or *autonomy* and not *happiness* is the fundamental ground of moral value and object of moral endeavor, "the inner value of the world." As the *Lectures on Ethics* put it:

> Freedom is a part of the capacity which gives all others their infinite usefulness, it is the highest degree of life, it is the property that is a necessary condition at the basis of all perfections. . . . if all creatures had a faculty of choice bound to sensuous drives, the world would have no value; the inner value of the world, the *summum bonum*, is the freedom to act in accordance with a faculty of choice that is not necessitated. Freedom is therefore the inner value of the world. (27:1482)[1]

A German translation of this chapter was originally published as "Freiheit als 'der innere Werth der Welt,'" in Christel Fricke, Peter König, and Thomas Petersen, eds., *Das Recht Der Vernunft: Kant und Hegel über Denken, Erkennen und Handeln* (Stuttgart-Bad Canstatt: Frommann-Holzboog, 1995), pp. 231–62. The English version appears here for the first time.

[1] This citation is to a passage from the lecture transcription known as the *Moral Mrongovius*, which seems identical to the text edited by Paul Menzer in 1924, *Eine Vorlesung Kants über Ethik*, and translated into English by Louis Infield as Kant's *Lectures on Ethics* (London: Methuen, 1930). For the most part, the text of the *Moral Mrongovius* is identical to the *Moral Collins* which J. B. Schneewind and Peter Heath have translated in their recent edition of Kant's *Lectures on*

And as the *Groundwork* says, "The legislation itself which determines all value must for that reason have a dignity, i.e., an unconditioned, incomparable value. . . . *Autonomy* is therefore the ground of the dignity of human and of every rational nature" (4:436). These claims raise two great puzzles. First, if the value of freedom has nothing to do with happiness, what is the source of its value? Second, Kant also constantly asserts that *virtue* is equivalent to *worthiness to be happy* – this assumption is, of course, especially prominent in Kant's introduction of the concept of the highest good in the *Critique of Practical Reason*, where he writes "virtue (as the worthiness to be happy) [is] the *supreme condition* of everything that may even seem desirable to us, consequently also of all our striving for happiness," and thus that "*happiness* is requisite" for our "entire and complete good," so that "to be in need of happiness and also to be worthy of it, yet not to participate in it, can never be in accord with the perfect will of a rational being" (5:110). Yet if freedom or autonomy has nothing to do with happiness at all, why should virtue be equated with the worthiness to be happy, and why should it seem unacceptable to a rational being to see virtue unaccompanied with happiness? Why should happiness, as the object of a desire that is merely natural to every finite yet rational creature (5:25–26), have anything to do with virtue at all?

In the present chapter I do not discuss all the difficulties of reconciling these claims with Kant's published moral philosophy of the 1780s but instead show that in the course of the development of his ethical theory, as documented above all in the notes and fragments on moral philosophy preserved in volume 19 of the *Akademie* edition,[2] Kant did suggest several key connections between freedom, happiness, and the worthiness to be happy, connections

Ethics (Cambridge: Cambridge University Press, 1997), although they also include a portion of the *Moral Mrongovius* that does not overlap *Moral Collins*.

[2] *Kant's handschriftlicher Nachlaß, Vol. 6: Moralphilosophie, Rechtsphilosophie und Religionsphilosophie*, ed. Friedrich Berger (Berlin: de Gruyter, 1934). Berger edited volume 19 on the basis of material left after his death by Erich Adickes, who had edited the previous volumes 14 through 18 of Kant's notes. The dating of the material in volume 19 had apparently been established by Adickes, so I will refer to the conjectures about the dates as his.

that could go a long way to answering these two questions without undermining his most basic goal of finding the moral law in a pure and *a priori* principle of practical reason. Specifically, I argue that notes deriving mostly but not exclusively from the 1770s suggest the following propositions:

1. The value of freedom is not unconnected to happiness; rather, while happiness is the natural end of human beings, the *systematic distribution* of happiness, both in one's own life as a whole and in the whole community of human beings, thus the maximization of happiness, can be expected only if human actions are conducted in accordance with an ideal of reason that is a product of human freedom rather than a mere law of nature; moral law thus requires an *a priori* concept of the universality of happiness and can never be grounded merely on empirically given ends, but it does not require a disregard of the goal of happiness altogether and, indeed, makes no sense without reference to happiness.

2. We may also take a special satisfaction in seeing ourselves as active rather than passive creatures and thus take an additional pleasure in seeing our happiness as the result of our own efforts, the product of our freedom rather than of nature; the fact that we have this special source of satisfaction may be distinct from the fact that it is only through our own freedom rather than nature that we may systematize and thereby maximize human happiness, but the former is hardly incompatible with the latter.

3. There are two direct connections between virtue and the *worthiness* to be happy: (i) worthiness to be happy, as opposed to mere happiness, must be a consequence of the *merit* of an agent, which in turn entails a free act of the agent, as expressed in virtue; and (ii) our conception of an agent's worthiness to be happy reflects the agent's *entitlement* to happiness as depending upon her willing participation in a system for the universal distribution of happiness as the object of her free self-governance by the law of reason rather than by merely natural circumstances. The second of these connections makes sense only in light of the fact that the value of freedom is not unconnected to happiness, but rather consists at least in part in the fact that it is only through the exercise of our freedom that we can produce a *system* of happiness.

The primary task for the present chapter is to present and separate the evidence for these three conclusions, all of which are intertwined in a note like this one:

> There is no determinate rule of ends except the universal validity of the ends of nature and the ends of human beings, i.e., from the whole of nature and the ends of human beings. Thereby the relations to happiness in the individual actions of humans are brought under determinate principles with regard to nature as well as with regard to each other. He is worthy of happiness whose free actions are directed to harmony with the universal grounds of that, who is therefore capable of that from his own action. From the idea of the whole the happiness of each part is here determined. (*R* 7058, 19:237; 1776–78)

After the previous chapter, we should not be entirely surprised that Kant began by equating the object of morality with the systematization or universalization *of happiness,* and therefore saw the use of reason and thus freedom for the regulation of particular inclinations with this larger end in mind as the basis of moral value. In section I of this chapter, I review the ample evidence that Kant held this view during his formative years. Although I do not have room to analyze Kant's arguments against happiness as a possible ground of the moral law in the *Groundwork* and second *Critique,* I argue in this section that Kant's notes also make a contrast between the idea of a system of happiness and the empirical origin of particular inclinations in a way that shows that the former is *a priori* and thus a possible ground of a principle of pure practical reason. Thus these notes show that the rigid separation between morality and all considerations of happiness that is apparently required by the opening demand for such a principle in the *Critique of Practical Reason* – but which then makes its later doctrine of the highest good virtually unintelligible – is not in fact necessary. In section II, however, I show how Kant also began to formulate a conception of the value of freedom that does not depend solely upon seeing it as necessary for a maximal systematization of happiness, although it is also not inconsistent with such a role; while in the materials we consider here Kant certainly did not yet reach his mature conception of the incomparable dignity of autonomy as the foundation of his moral philosophy, he was clearly taking steps in that direction. In section III, finally, I show how Kant's original thought that morality requires the free use of reason for the system – that is, the systematic distribution – of happiness is essential to the equation between virtue and the worthiness to be happy that he takes for granted in his mature writings and employs as the premise for the postulates of practical reason.

I FREEDOM AND THE
SYSTEM OF HAPPINESS

In many notes from the 1770s, Kant hardly separates morality and happiness, but instead argues for two theses: (i) morality requires the use of reason precisely in order to systematize and thereby maximize happiness, not just for oneself but for all, which in turn requires freedom because such systematization would not be the natural outcome of following inclination; but (ii) this does not make morality dependent on a merely empirical concept or rule, because while individual inclinations, or the "matter" of desire, may be entirely empirical, the concept of a *whole* or *system* of satisfactions is not itself an empirical concept but a formal concept which is *a priori*, just like the concepts of a system of spatial locations or a system of natural laws, which subsume empirical intuitions under *a priori* forms. In the previous two chapters, we have seen evidence for this theory in Kant's early publications and in his earliest complete outlines for the emerging *Critique of Pure Reason*. Here we examine the evidence for it that is to be found in Kant's early notes for his lectures on ethics.

(i) Many texts demonstrate Kant's recognition that the essence of morality is nothing other than the use of reason to systematize happiness, that is, to regulate our attempts to satisfy our inclinations so that we satisfy only those which fit into an intra- and interpersonal system of happiness. We might take as a motto for all of Kant's remarks along these lines this sentence: "*The conformity of an action with a necessary and universal rule of satisfaction* [Wohlgefallens] *is morality*" (R 6805, 19:167; 1773–75). Many further passages make the same point that the use of moral law restricts the pursuit of one's own individual inclinations, but in behalf of the more systematic satisfaction of one's own ends and those of others, thus not in opposition to the pursuit of happiness in any sense at all but rather in behalf of the systematic and therefore maximal happiness of all. Here are a few examples, first from the mid-1770s and then from the early 1780s as well.

The following notes are from the period 1776–78. The first is of great interest, because, although it is similar to the famous argument of the *Groundwork* in insisting that we be governed by reason rather than instinct (see 4:395), it does not infer from this that reason is not connected to happiness at all but rather infers that the free use of reason is the necessary condition for the universalization of happiness:

> Our actions must not be subjected to the incentives and allurements or deterrences of sensibility, since these always have a private relationship to what is useful. The rule of actions whereby, if everyone acted in accordance with them, nature and choice among men would be universally harmonious for happiness, is a law of reason and thus signifies morality.
>
> If reason merely provided service to the senses, for executing their demands, we would be placed in a greater contradiction with ourselves and with others than even the animals, who are ruled through instinct, which is in accord with their needs. . . . Now since morality is grounded on the idea of universal happiness from free conduct, we are necessitated to conceive of even the cause and government of the world in accordance with an idea, namely that which makes everything harmonious or is concerned with happiness itself through harmonious efforts; for otherwise the moral idea would have no reality in expectation and would be a merely sophistical concept. (*R* 6958, 19:213–14; 1776–78)

I do not comment here on Kant's suggestion that the idea of morality is merely sophistical unless we have some expectation of its realization, for that raises issues beyond the scope of this chapter;[3] here I emphasize only Kant's suggestion that morality is grounded on the idea of universal happiness from free conduct.

---

[3] This issue will be pursued further in Chapter 10.

His assumption seems clear that the instinctive pursuit of the gratification of any particular momentary demand of sense may contradict either the more enduring happiness of the individual or the more universal happiness of all, and that free conduct in accord with the law of reason is designed precisely to avoid this unfortunate outcome and thereby maximize the happiness of both oneself and others. There is no suggestion at all that the function of reason and freedom is to bring about some end that has no connection with universal happiness whatever.

There are many other similar passages that could be adduced,[4] but I content myself with quoting one passage, apparently from the early 1780s and thus written closer in time to the *Groundwork*, which like *R* 6958 uses the later work's contrast between instinct and reason to emphasize that reason's function is to seek a universal and systematic distribution of happiness rather than to aim at some other end altogether. This extensive, freestanding draft is entitled *On Practical Philosophy*. These are its crucial claims in the present context:

> The first and most important observation that the human being makes for himself is that he is determined by nature to be himself the author of his happiness and even of his own inclinations and skills, which make possible this happiness. From this he infers that he has to order his actions not in accordance with instincts but in accordance with concepts of his happiness which he himself makes. . . . He will therefore have as his foremost object himself as a freely acting being in accordance with this independence and self-mastery, so that his desires will harmonize among themselves with his concept of happiness and not with instincts, and in this form consists the conduct that is appropriate to the freedom of a rational being. His action must first be instituted in accord with the universal end of mankind in his own person, and therefore in accordance with concepts and not instincts, so that these may harmonize with each other, since they harmonize with what is universal, namely nature. It

---

[4] Some examples are *R* 6950, 19:212; 6977, 19:218; 7021, 19:228–29; 7197, 19:270–71; 7211, 19:286. Some of these will be cited further in section III of the present chapter.

is therefore not empirical self-love that should be the motivating ground of a rational being, for this goes from one to all, but the rational [self-love], which derives its rule for the individual from the universal. In the same way he will become aware that his happiness depends on the freedom of other rational beings, and if everyone merely had himself for his object, this would not agree with self-love, [thus] that he must restrict his own happiness by concepts and even by the condition that he be the author of universal happiness or at least not contradict others as the authors of their own.

Morality consists in the laws of the generation of true happiness from freedom in general. (*R* 7199, 19:272–73)

What is particularly striking about this note is that it clearly links morality not only to the production of "true happiness" but even to rational self-love, where that is understood, however, as the desire to achieve happiness for oneself not just as an individual but as part of the larger collectivity of mankind in general. There may be a hint of a merely prudential argument here, that is, an argument that one need attend to the happiness of others because they may be in a position to advance one's own, which they will not do for free but only in exchange for an equal concern with theirs; but this does not seem the predominant claim of the note. Instead, Kant's thought seems to be that happiness is the universal end of mankind, and out of a recognition of the validity of this end one will rationally govern one's instincts so as to maximize the realization of this end both in oneself and in others. Such a universal happiness, a whole from which one's own share must be derived, seems to be the "true happiness" that is the object of the law of morality, by no means something incompatible with it or even merely externally connected with it. Morality requires a rule of reason, generated from freedom and not natural instinct, not in order to achieve some other end than happiness but in order to pursue a universal happiness, in which one's own long-term happiness is not sacrificed to any particular inclination and the happiness of all is not sacrificed to the happiness of any one person, but in which the satisfaction of individual inclinations is permitted to the extent that this is compatible with one's own long-range happiness and the equal satisfaction of others.

(ii) In the *Critique of Practical Reason* particularly, Kant appears to separate happiness from morality altogether because morality demands an *a priori* principle and happiness seems to be a merely empirical concept (e.g., §2, 5:21). But his earlier notes forestall any such simplistic argument by making it clear that, although particular inclinations, which furnish the "matter" of desires and thus of happiness, are only given empirically, the concept of universal happiness is not itself an empirical concept but a concept of "form" that is given *a priori* just like any other concept of a form. This is clearly stated both early and late in Kant's reflections. Thus, R 6820, conjectured to date to 1776–78, states:

> Moral philosophy is the science of ends so far as they are determined through pure reason. Or of the unity of all ends (since they do not contradict themselves) of rational beings. The matter [*materie*] of the good is empirical, the form given *a priori*. Morality is the good from principles of spontaneity, hence the universality of the good. (19:172)

Here Kant suggests that although the matter of the good is given empirically, presumably because it is inclination that sets individual ends, this matter is not replaced but determined by pure reason, precisely by being regulated by an *a priori* formal concept, namely that of universality. The mere empirical occurrence of inclinations or desires does not itself suffice to give them form, that is, to systematize them and allow for their universally acceptable satisfaction; for that an *a priori* concept of reason is required; but this *a priori* concept of reason, in turn, functions precisely to determine its empirical matter, not to reject it altogether.[5] This last point is even more clearly stated in this striking note:

> We do not understand anything of merely moral happiness or blessedness. If all materials that the senses afford our will were canceled, what would remain of righteousness [*Rechtschaffenheit*], goodness, self-mastery, which are only forms for ordering these materials in oneself? Since we have insight into happiness

---

[5] A similar point was observed, although this passage was not cited, by Keith Ward in *The Development of Kant's View of Ethics* (Oxford: Basil Blackwell, 1972), p. 56.

and the true good only in this world, we must believe that we overstep the boundaries of our reason if it paints new and even higher forms of perfection for us. (*R* 6883, 19:191; 1776–78, 1769?)

Here Kant clearly says that morality does not furnish any perfection or happiness of a special kind, but consists in nothing less and nothing more than ordering "the materials the senses afford our will." To think anything other than this is like metaphysical error, overstepping "the boundaries of our reason."

Sometimes Kant does seem to say that reason produces an entirely *a priori* satisfaction, but in such passages it is nevertheless clear that what he means is that reason supplies not a nonempirical form of happiness but an *a priori* concept of systematic or universal happiness that has to be applied to empirically given ends. The following note makes this plain by stating that reason itself does not give ends before introducing the idea of an "*a priori* delight":

> Reason alone can give no end, thus no incentive; it is reason, however, that so restricts all ends without distinction that they must stand under a single common rule. It alone determines the conditions under which free choice stands under a self-sufficient rule. For the drives, taste, the inclinations have no harmony [*Einstimmungen*] and need a rule.
>
> Reason here creates an *a priori* delight, i.e., one that takes place even when the object is not compared with my inclination or satisfaction of my drives, for then my inclinations in general are nevertheless contained under the universal [ones]. That this consideration of delight *a priori* or in general has precedence rests on the fact that the *principium* of order and form is essentially necessary and precedes, without which there would be no concordance [*Zusammenhang*] in my private enjoyment or between this and that of others. The regulative precedes, and nothing must conflict with that; otherwise there is no concordance among the manifold, no security. Everything would be tumultuous. The *a priori* delight subsists with that which brings order to whatever may happen, through which it makes it into a whole. (*R* 7029, 19:230–31; sometime between 1771 and 1778?)

Throughout this passage Kant makes it clear that even while particular ends can only be given empirically the principle of their order can only be given *a priori*. Although the first sentence of the second paragraph taken by itself might suggest that morality is concerned with a special *a priori* kind of delight, the continuation of that paragraph explains that what Kant means is only that morality supplies an *a priori* principle for the universalization and systematization of happiness, that is, a principle that dictates that one satisfy only those of one's inclinations which are compatible with satisfaction of a systematic set of one's own preferences and with a system in which others' preferences may be satisfied as well as one's own. Thus, whereas the matter of happiness – the inclinations that present themselves to any one individual at any one time – cannot furnish a principle of morality, the concept of the systematization and universalization of happiness is *a priori* and can serve as such a principle.

Finally, although the context is much more complicated, and suggests other themes as well, Kant clearly makes this point in the most extensive of all of his unpublished notes on ethics, the crucial *R* 7202. Although this note apparently stems from the 1780s, it uses much the same language as the notes from the preceding decade. Its second paragraph reads:

> The matter of happiness is sensuous, but its form is intellectual: now this is not possible otherwise than as freedom under *a priori* laws of its agreement with itself, and this not to make happiness actual but for its possibility and its idea. For happiness consists in well-being [*Wohlbefinden*] insofar as this is not externally contingent, also not empirically dependent, but rests on our own choice. This must determine, and not depend on the determination of nature. This, however, is nothing other than well-ordered freedom. (19:276)

The same theme is sounded two paragraphs later:

> The function of the *a priori* unity of all elements of happiness is the necessary condition of its possibility and its essence. The *a priori* unity, however, is freedom under universal laws of choice, i.e., morality. That makes happiness as such possible and does not depend on it as the end and is itself the original form of happiness. (19:277)

This paragraph too clearly assumes that the individual elements of happiness can be and are only given empirically, but that its "unity" and "original form" are *a priori* and thus can satisfy the demand for an *a priori* principle of morality.

In the passages we have considered thus far, the ultimate locus of value seems to be universal happiness itself, as the maximal realization of a natural human end, and the law of reason, together with the freedom from which it arises, seems to be valuable primarily as the necessary condition for the realization of this universal happiness. In other words, the value of reason and freedom seems to be instrumental or external to the realization of such happiness, not intrinsic to it. However, Kant also begins to characterize a form of value that is intrinsic to reason and freedom and often even suggests that its intrinsic value outweighs its instrumental value. We will now look at Kant's efforts to characterize such an intrinsic value of freedom; but, as we do so, let us not forget that finding such a value will not in itself require rejecting the supposition that reason and freedom do have instrumental value as the necessary condition for realizing the *a priori* concept of universal happiness, for there is no reason why freedom cannot be the source of two distinct but compatible satisfactions.

II THE INTRINSIC VALUE OF FREEDOM

The second and new idea to be found in Kant's reflections is that we value the fact of our independence from nature, our possibility of self-governance, for its own sake. It is not always easy to separate this idea from the thought that we can use our freedom to modify our desires and thereby connect our happiness to the realization of conditions under our own control rather than to natural conditions, the occurrence of which is contingent or mere luck as far as we are concerned – in other words, that we can use our freedom to make happiness not only more systematic and therefore extensive than it would otherwise be, but also more *secure* (an idea, of course, already familiar to the ancients). This would be another reason to ascribe *instrumental* value to freedom. Many passages do not clearly separate the ideas that freedom can be used to make happiness more systematic and secure from each other (e.g., *R* 6621, 19:114–15) or from the idea that it also is an intrinsic source of satisfaction – and since these ideas are not ultimately incompatible, perhaps Kant initially had no great incentive to separate them. But in at least some passages Kant did suggest that we take a unique and indeed higher satisfaction in the fact of our freedom itself than in any of the products of this freedom, a thesis that may have been transformed in his published writings into the idea that the value of autonomy has nothing to do with happiness in the ordinary sense at all.[6]

In a number of notes, Kant seems to argue only that we can use our freedom to make our happiness more secure, which is just another argument for the instrumental value of freedom. One of the clearest such notes is this early one from 1769–70:

> Contentment from liberation from pain is welfare [*Wohlfahrt*].
> Contentment from the satisfaction of inclinations is happiness.
> Contentment [*crossed out*: from the self-sufficiency of enjoyment is blessedness] from a possession of well-being that is independent of external things is self-contentment. Self-contentment, for which the world contains no external addition, is blessedness. (*R* 6616, 19:111)

Here what Kant stresses is simply the independence of contentment from external things, that is, presumably, conditions beyond our control, and the only reason suggested for calling such contentment blessedness rather than mere happiness seems to be its obviously greater security and endurance.

---

6 Ward does not seem to notice that the idea of morality as an intrinsic source of a special satisfaction is present in the *Reflexionen* alongside the idea of morality as providing the *a priori* form for the empirical matter of happiness (*Development*, p. 57). This makes the transition from Kant's writings of the 1770s to those of the 1780s even more of a mystery than it needs to be; seeing that Kant's two ideas of the connection of morality to happiness actually coexisted during the 1770s also helps us see that they are not actually incompatible, and thus that the published writings drive more of a wedge between morality and happiness than is necessary for Kant's own purposes. Schmucker also fails to draw a distinction between Kant's two conceptions of happiness in these materials, see Joset Schmucker, *Die Ursprünge der Ethik Kants in seinen vorkritischen Schriften und Reflektionen* (Meisenheim am Glan: Verlag Anton Hain, 1961), pp. 314–15.

From the middle of the 1770s, we can also find passages that suggest that the value of freedom is special because it puts us in control of the sources of happiness ourselves. For example,

> Since, however, self-contentment elevates the soul and holds it blameless from many sensuous gratifications, which in its eyes rightly count for little, since one can overwhelm them with stronger ones, it is thus a greater and the greatest motivating ground of reason to make happiness into a product of spontaneity independent of the senses. (*R* 6892, 19:196)

Here again the decisive contrast seems to be between happiness that is a product of our own spontaneity and happiness that is of the qualitatively same kind but simply less reliably produced by the senses because of their dependence on external circumstances.

Finally, from the 1780s, at least one paragraph of the seminal *R* 7202 seems to place the special value of freedom in its ability to provide a more secure and certain foundation for happiness than mere nature:

> For the senses no complete satisfaction can be found – it cannot even be determined with certainty and universally what will be in accord with their needs; they are always raising their expectation and are unsatisfied without being able to say what would be enough for them. The possession of this enjoyment is even less secured on account of the changeability of luck and the contingency of favorable circumstances and the shortness of life. But that disposition which instructed through reason in how to make good and harmonious use of the materials for well-being [is] certain *a priori*, can be completely known, and belongs to ourselves. (19:277)

Here again it seems that the basis of the value of freedom is that it allows us to modify our desires in such a way as to make their satisfaction independent of luck and contingent circumstances.

Other notes, however, begin to conjoin this quite traditional idea that we maximize the certainty of attaining happiness by setting our happiness in conditions under our own control with the distinct idea that we take a separate form of pleasure in the fact of our freedom itself. This striking note from the mid-1770s weaves these different ideas together:

The *principium* of morality is autocracy of freedom with regard to all happiness or the epigenesis of happiness in accordance with universal laws of freedom. Happiness has no self-sufficient value insofar as it is the gift of nature or luck. Its origin from freedom is what constitutes its self-sufficiency and concordance [*Zusammenstimmung*]. Good conduct, therefore, i.e., the use of freedom according to rules in accordance with which happiness is the self-creation of good or regular choice, has an absolute status [*Bestand*], and the worthiness to be happy is the agreement with the highest good through nothing other than the completion [*Ergänzung*] of the faculty of free choice, insofar as it agrees with the universal rules of happiness in the whole. The moral feeling here pertains to the unity of the ground and the self-possession of the sources of happiness in rational creatures, to which all judgment of value must be related. The good use of freedom is of more value than contingent happiness. It has a necessary inner value. Hence the virtuous person possesses in himself happiness (*in receptivitate*) however bad the circumstances may be. He has in himself (as much as it is in him) the *principium* of the *epigenesis* of happiness. (*R* 6767, 19:186; 1776–78)

Kant's claims that happiness has no *self-sufficient* value if it is the gift of luck, that the use of freedom is of more value than *contingent* freedom, and that virtue offers a source of happiness *however bad the circumstances may be* all continue to suggest the idea that by the use of our freedom to determine what we will set our happiness in, we can make our happiness more secure, and thus that the value of freedom is essentially instrumental. Here, however, Kant also says that the good use of freedom has a value that is not only necessary but also *inner*, and that it is a condition of the value of any other form of happiness or at least of the worthiness to be happy. This suggests that we have an intrinsic satisfaction in the fact of our freedom that is not only more secure but also more important than any other form of satisfaction, although why such a form of satisfaction should be a condition of worthiness to enjoy any other is a separate claim that is not explained here.

Sometime in the 1780s Kant wrote another note that also juxtaposes the distinct ideas of the intrinsic value of freedom and of its instrumental value as a more secure source of happiness than mere nature, although in this case Kant clearly recognizes that these are two separate ideas: "Freedom has dignity on account of its independence; it also has a high price since we thereby become the author of the good in accordance with our own concepts, which we can extend and multiply far beyond the natural instincts of animals" (*R* 7248, 19:294). Here, using language familiar from the *Groundwork* (4:434–35), Kant suggests that our freedom allows us to secure and maximize the good in ways that merely following our instincts does not; but since the good at issue appears to be one that can be produced at least to some extent by instinct, it would seem that he must have happiness in mind. He also suggests that the fact of independence itself is a source of a special dignity, although he does not explain what this is.

Finally, however, a number of other notes do not refer to the instrumental value of freedom for securing happiness at all but instead suggest that freedom is the source of an entirely different kind of contentment, beside which ordinary happiness, the satisfaction of desires, even if secure, necessarily pales. There are several different ways, however, in which Kant characterizes this deeper contentment, and their explanation is not obvious.

One way Kant characterizes the special contentment we take in the fact of our freedom itself rests on the distinction between the active and the passive. Without explanation, he simply says that we have an intellectual rather than sensuous pleasure in that with regard to which we are active rather than passive: "With regard to ourselves we have a sensuous pleasure with regard to that which we suffer, and an intellectual one with regard to what we do (but not on account of an inclination), thus with what we do in accordance with an idea either of the original or of the universal human preference" (*R* 6974, 19:218; 1776–78?). The same unexplained postulation of an additional kind of pleasure in the fact of our own activity also reappears in *R* 7202, although there it is not simply contrasted to the sensuous pleasure that can be more effectively and extensively ensured through the instrument of our freedom but is instead added to it:

It is true that virtue has the advantage that from that which nature offers it can bring about the greatest welfare. But that it, as it were, serves as a means is not what its higher value consists in. That it is we ourselves who bring it forth as its author without regard to empirical conditions (which can only yield particular rules of life), that it brings *self-contentment* along with it, that is its inner value. (19:277)

Here Kant does not deny that freedom has an instrumental value as the most secure source of happiness, but just adds that we take an additional – and even greater – pleasure in the thought that we are the authors of our happiness by our own actions. But why this thought should be so satisfying, let alone outweigh the satisfaction of the very happiness in the ordinary sense that we produce by means of our own activity, is not explained.

Other passages associate a special form of happiness with our membership in an intellectual rather than sensible world. Paradigmatic among these passages is this one:

Happiness is twofold: either that which is an effect of the free choice of rational beings in themselves, or that which is only a contingent and external effect dependent on nature. Rational beings can make the true happiness, which is independent of everything in nature, for themselves through actions that are directed to themselves and reciprocally to each other. And without this, further, nature cannot afford genuine happiness. This is the happiness of the intelligible world [*Verstandeswelt*]. . . . I must seek on my part to attain the example of perfection in a possible good world.

That is good in itself, which does not depend merely on contingent conditions, but on my will. (*R* 6907, 19:202–3)

The last line seems once again to break down the distinction between the intrinsic and instrumental value of freedom; but what precedes it suggests that there is a distinctive form of happiness that is associated with our potential for membership in an intellectual rather than merely sensible world. Another note a few entries later suggests the same thought, while also linking up to the idea that we take pleasure in activity:

Happiness *a priori* cannot be set on any other basis [*Grund*] than the rule of the harmony of free choice. This is a ground of happiness prior to all knowledge of means through experience and a condition of its possibility in all cases. Through it the world pleases the understanding; it is the creator of happiness and not its *usurpateur*. (*R* 6911, 19:203–4)

Yet another note also suggests that we take pleasure in conceiving of ourselves as members of an intellectual rather than sensible world, which world we enter by freely willing in accord with moral law:

The principle of unity of freedom under laws establishes an *analogon* with that which we call nature, and also an inner source of happiness that nature cannot give and of which we ourselves are the author. We then find ourselves in an intellectual world bound in accordance with particular laws, which are moral. And we are pleased therein.

The unity of the intelligible world in accordance with practical principles, like that of the sensible world in accordance with physical laws. (*R* 7260, 19:296–97)[7]

But what none of these notes explain is *why* it is so pleasing to us to conceive of ourselves as members of an intellectual rather than sensible world – *a fortiori* why the freedom by means of which we can conceive of ourselves as members of such a world is the source of a satisfaction that is greater than the happiness in the sensible world to which it is added and which it can even replace.

However, a few remarkable notes suggest what might underlie these unexplained assertions. The last few notes we have quoted suggest a peculiar sort of Platonism, on which it seems that we take a special satisfaction in being transported from the sensible into an intellectual world – as if what we enjoyed was leaving the sensible world behind, or being freed *from* the sensible world. But the notes I now cite suggest that the source of our special and deepest satisfaction in the exercise of our freedom is not our escape from the sensible world but the very fact of our *unification* of our desires and conduct *in* the sensible world, or our transformation of the sensible world *into* a rational world, something that we ultimately enjoy simply because it is our vocation to be rational,

[7] Adickes could not decide whether this note was from the 1780s or mid-1770s.

but which we can achieve only by the free exercise of our capacity to be rational, and not if we merely remain the passive subject of our inclinations. Thus, in the mid-1770s, Kant wrote that:

> The first ought [*das erste Sollen*] is a condition, under which alone freedom becomes a faculty in accordance with constant rules, which determine *a priori*. This lawfulness is a necessary need [*Bedürfnis*] of reason in regard to a faculty, which dynamically determines *a priori*.
>
> The will that is restricted to no object, which is thus pure, must above all not contradict itself, and freedom as the condition of the intellectual world and of its *commercii* must have unity.
>
> The independence of freedom from sensibility presupposes its dependence on the universal condition that it agree with itself. (*R* 6850, 19:178)[8]

Here Kant claims that it is simply a demand of reason that we use our freedom in a constant, consistent, or harmonious way, and that such unification is itself a "dynamical" condition, that is, presumably, something that itself can result only from the exercise of our own agency, not anything we can reasonably expect to result from a passive attitude toward our own sensibility and its inclinations. He does not explicitly say that being rational in this way must please us, but it does not seem farfetched to assume that he thought that the satisfaction of a "necessary need" should be more satisfying than the satisfaction of any merely contingent need, such as the needs of mere sensibility.

In the next decade, Kant states that disunity or contradiction within the will is displeasing to us in the highest degree, which naturally enough suggests that the achievement of unity or harmony in our willing is, conversely, our deepest source of satisfaction. Once again from the extraordinarily rich note *R* 7202:

> Now this unrestraint, through which I can will what is contradictory to my will itself . . . must be displeasing to me in the highest degree, and a law in accordance with which freedom is restricted to conditions under which it (the will) agrees with itself must be recognized as necessary *a priori*. I cannot renounce

---

[8] See also *R* 6854, 19:180, especially lines 15–17.

this law without contradicting my will, which alone can establish practical unity of the will in accordance with principles.
These laws determine a will, which one can call the pure will,
which precedes everything empirical, and determines a pure
practical good, which is the highest although only formal good,
since it must be created by ourselves, hence is in our power, and
also makes possible [of] everything empirical, so far as it is in
our power, a unity in regard to the complete good, namely a pure
happiness. (19:281)

These lines clearly suggest that some form of systematicity or
self-consistency, "practical unity," is both the source of our highest
pleasure, a "pure happiness," and can be created only by ourselves,
or by the exercise of our active power rather than passivity. Freedom is thus the source of our highest satisfaction precisely as our
power to satisfy our need for rationality itself. Kant brings all
these thoughts together in a lapidary statement apparently written
right over *R* 6850, although it is not clear whether it was written
shortly afterward, that is, still in the mid-1770s, or in the next
decade, that is, in the same period as *R* 7202. Here Kant says:
"The apperception of sensation is substance, that of self-activity
is the person. The value of the person rests on freedom that is
harmonious with itself in accordance with original rules" (*R* 6861,
19:183).[9] In other words, moral personality as the unified exercise
of freedom is analogous to the unity of apperception itself as the
product of the exercise of our cognitive spontaneity, and is maximally pleasing as answering what is our most fundamental need
of all, our need for unity itself. Indeed, seeing that our pleasure in
unity itself is the ultimate source of moral value not only ties together Kant's epistemology and ethics, but ties them both to his
aesthetics as well, where our satisfaction in the unification of the
manifold of representation is also the ultimate explanation of our
pleasure in aesthetic response.[10]
Kant suggests this last connection in several further notes in

---

[9] For another comparison between the unity of the will and the unity of apperception, see also *R* 7204, 19:283–84; again, Adickes could not determine
whether this was written in the mid-1770s or in the 1780s.

[10] See above all *CJ*, Introduction, §VI, 5:187–88.

which he argues that there is pleasure associated with each experience of life, but maximal pleasure in the experience of a *unified* life, where individual experiences do not cancel each other out; moreover, the *unity* of a life cannot be seen as a product of mere nature but can only be seen as a product of our free and active intellect. Thus the note immediately following that last cited says:

> In the end everything comes down to life; what enlivens (or the feeling of the advancement of life) is pleasant. Life is unity; hence all taste has as its *principio* the unity of enlivening sensations.
>
> Freedom is the original life and in its connection the condition of the agreement of all life; hence that which advances the feeling of universal life, or the feeling of the advancement of universal life, causes a pleasure. But do we feel well in universal life? The universality makes all our feelings concordant, although this universality is not a particular kind of sensation. It is the form of *consensus*. (*R* 6862, 19:183)[11]

In these notes, there certainly does not seem to be any *opposition* between the pleasures of the sensible and intelligible worlds. Rather, what Kant appears to be arguing is that although our pleasures considered separately are merely natural, the principle of their unity is intellectual, therefore a product of freedom rather than nature, but also itself a source of pleasure even greater than that of our particular sensory gratifications. Kant does not, after all, think that we enjoy living in an intelligible world as contrasted to living in a sensible world; rather, he argues that we can most fully enjoy living in a sensible world through a power to unify that we possess only as creatures with a free intellectual capacity. This thought also runs through this entry:

> There is only one principle of life and therefore only one *principium* of the feeling of pleasure and displeasure, which now can be aroused through reason. . . . the free use of the powers and freedom in general is that which is most important and most noble, [but], if it is *lawless* [*regellos*] and not unifiable with itself, then it must displease every rational being. (*R* 6871; 19:187)

---

[11] See also *R* 6870, 19:187.

Freedom is the source of our most important and noble satisfaction because it is only through the free use of the intellect that we can unify our lives.

This line of thought naturally raises the question whether the distinction between instrumental and intrinsic accounts of the value of freedom does not in the end collapse, that is, whether freedom does not turn out to be of value as the necessary condition for the satisfaction of the maximally consistent set of desires in oneself and others after all. This conclusion should be resisted: although Kant has argued that we do maximize the satisfaction of desires by systematizing them through the free use of reason, he also clearly sees the free use of reason to achieve systematic unity as the source of a profound pleasure in unity itself regardless of the fact that it is desires that are being systematically satisfied. At the same time, however, the two sources of satisfaction are hardly mutually exclusive but are instead thoroughly compatible. So while our special satisfaction in the highest practical good of unity, which must be achieved "dynamically," and the maximal intra- and interpersonal satisfaction of our sensory inclinations, or our collective material good, are not conceptually identical, neither are they unrelated to each other, and Kant's conception of the highest good is no miscegenation. In this chapter, however, I can consider only one puzzle about the highest good.

III VIRTUE AS THE WORTHINESS TO BE HAPPY

As I said at the outset, beyond his claim that freedom is the inner value of the world the other profound mystery in Kant's ethics is his frequently reiterated characterization of virtue as the worthiness to be happy. If virtue and happiness had no connection at all, their connection through the idea of worthiness would seem utterly inexplicable. As we have just seen, however, there are many places where Kant does not completely oppose virtue and happiness but rather connects the *a priori* principle of morality to the genuinely *a priori* concept of a systematic whole of intra- and interpersonal happiness. This might explain why virtue should *produce* happiness, at least under ideal circumstances of individual and collective compliance with the principle of virtue. But this still does not explain why virtue should be construed as *worthiness* to be happy. Where does the element of *desert* that it seems natural to associate with the idea of worthiness come from?

In Kant's most prominent deployment of this connection, in the introduction of the concept of the highest good in the *Critique of Practical Reason,* he first proceeds as if virtue and happiness are two entirely separate goods connected only by what has recently come to be called a "reactive attitude":[12] his idea seems to be that although there is no intrinsic connection between the moral good of virtue and the natural good of happiness, it would nevertheless pain an impartial rational observer to see someone who is successful in striving after the moral good of virtue nevertheless be frustrated in her independent but acceptable natural desire for happiness (5:110). As Kant continues his exposition, he does introduce an "analogue of happiness that must necessarily accompany the consciousness of virtue," which, using a term we have encountered in several *Reflexionen,* he calls "*self-satisfaction*" and a "negative delight" (5:117). Although Kant now calls this state merely an "analogue" of happiness rather than a pure and most noble form of happiness itself, it clearly seems to be an heir to the satisfaction with freedom we have just been describing and to be immediately connected to virtue itself. Such a connection would certainly explain why virtue should be connected to this special feeling, although since such a connection seems to be immediate, it would not obviously require the thought of any sort of divine intervention to make it intelligible and would, therefore, actually undermine Kant's inference from the moral necessity of the highest good to the practical postulation of the existence of God. That argument seems to require that virtue be considered worthiness to be happy in the ordinary, natural sense of happiness, something that is not an immediate consequence of virtue but needs to be connected to it by an extra step. But if happiness in that sense

---

[12] The term was introduced by Sir Peter Strawson in his famous article "Freedom and Resentment," reprinted in his *Freedom and Resentment and Other Essays* (London: Methuen, 1974), pp. 1–25, and given its most extensive examination in R. Jay Wallace, *Responsibility and the Moral Sentiments* (Cambridge, Mass.: Harvard University Press, 1994).

simply has no connection with virtue, then it is hard to see why the two should be connected in the sentiments of any rational observer at all.

Several of Kant's notes, however, suggest two ideas that seem to have supported the equation of virtue with the worthiness to be happy, which by the time of his published writings had come to seem so obvious to him as to need no real explanation. The first – which does not actually presuppose any particular conception of the relation between virtue and happiness – is the general claim that worthiness to enjoy a good, whether natural or otherwise, presupposes that one *merits* it, or has earned the right to it *by one's own actions*, and that as the product of our only genuine *free* actions, or, in other words, as one of the two possible outcomes of our only genuine *actions* at all, virtue is the only ground for any merit at all. The second, however, is that since universal happiness or a system of happiness is not a merely natural good or a product of merely natural behavior but something that even under the best of circumstances would be produced only by virtuous action, enjoyment of one's own share of universal happiness is the *appropriate* reward for genuine merit – payment in kind, as it were. This argument does presuppose that a system of happiness in the ordinary sense, rather than that special form of self-satisfaction that may be connected to consciousness of virtue immediately, is an end that may seem natural but which in fact can only be conceived and achieved through the exercise of freedom governed by moral law.

Both of these assumptions are expressed in a reflection that has already been quoted in its entirety, so here only part of it need be repeated: "He is worthy of happiness, whose free actions are directed to agreement with its universal ground, who is therefore capable of it from his own action. From the idea of the whole the happiness of each part is here determined" (R 7058, 19:237). The first of these sentences stresses that it is from an agent's *free actions* that his entitlement to happiness arises, where, of course, freedom of action is a necessary condition of virtue. The second stresses that the reason why virtue should be rewarded with happiness is simply that one's own happiness need not be willed as a merely natural, selfish goal, antithetical to morality, but can also be willed as one's own part of the whole that virtuous action aims to produce, namely a universal system of happiness. It is in that case the appropriate consequence of virtue because it would be an inevitable consequence of virtue under ideal circumstances – that is, if virtuous action necessarily had its intended effect.

Another passage from the middle of the 1770s also emphasizes the two themes that universal happiness is possible only as a result of free action and that only one's own free action makes one worthy of one's share in that happiness:

> Happiness, which is only possible from the relation of all in the world to the private will of the person, is also only possible in a whole according to an idea. In that, however, everyone's private will must also be contained, consequently a universally valid will only can yield the ground of the assurance of happiness; thus we can either not hope to be happy at all, or we must bring our actions into harmony with the universally valid will. For then alone are we capable of happiness in accord with the idea, i.e., with the representation of the whole, and since this capability is a consequence of our free will, also worthy of happiness. (*R* 6971, 19:216–17)

The first part of this note argues both that happiness in accordance with an idea, or a shared system of happiness, is the only end of human activity that can assure the happiness of the individual, and also, by emphasizing that such universal happiness can only be produced in accordance with an idea, implies that it can only be a product of human freedom, not nature. The conclusion of the last sentence quoted stresses that only insofar as our own happiness as part of this larger whole is a product of our own free will do we in any sense deserve it.

Several other notes separate the two assumptions I have ascribed to Kant. Kant's discussions of imputation frequently stress that freedom of action is a necessary condition of moral *blame* or disapprobation, but few discussions seem expressly intended to make explicit that it is also a necessary condition of *merit*. A draft of a "catechism," although only from the 1790s, does make precisely this point. Here Kant shows the questions that the moral trainee must be asked and how they must be answered:

5) What does one call the condition in which all the wishes of a human being . . . are satisfied? – I don't know. – Happiness, because everything like that rests on luck.[13]

6) Could you then be happy in the highest degree but yet dissatisfied with yourself in the highest degree, and why? [No.] Because you are conscious and say to yourself that you are not worthy of this happiness.

7) Can another who makes you happy also make you worthy of happiness, or must it be yourself whose conduct makes you worthy? – I must do it myself.

8) What then must be the first of all your wishes, to be happy or to be worthy of happiness? To be worthy, i.e., to so act that at least I am not unworthy of it. – Since you must do it yourself, thus you are free. (*R* 7315, 19:312)

Question (7) makes it plain that worthiness is only earned or merited by one's own action, not by the action of another; question (8) implies that such an action must be a free action. Kant does not spell out his reasoning for affirming (8) as well as (7), but his formulation of his conclusion seems to imply that he is making the same assumption that underlies his famous inference from obligation to freedom in the *Critique of Practical Reason*: just as there his argument is that our knowledge of our obligation under the moral law implies our freedom to comply with it even when everything we know about our own past behavior suggests we would not, and thus implies our freedom to do otherwise than what a merely deterministic extrapolation from our past behavior would entail (5:30), so here he seems to assume that what makes you worthy of happiness is that you choose to act in a certain way even when you could have done otherwise. Merit depends on one's own action, and on one's free action; so *worthiness* to be happy can stem only from one's own free action.

Of course, the exercise of one's freedom can result in evil as well as virtue, so the fact of one's freedom itself is a necessary, not a sufficient condition of meriting happiness. One must use one's freedom to achieve virtue in order to merit any positive reward.

---

[13] Here, of course, Kant is emphasizing the presence of the word *Glück* (luck) in *Glückseligkeit* (happiness).

But why is it that the reward that is earned by virtue is happiness in particular? Many passages suggest that the answer to this is the second assumption I have ascribed to Kant, namely that the reason why virtue is equated with the worthiness *to be happy* is not that one's own happiness is a merely natural desire, which might be gratified by the performance of some unconnected obligation, as a child might be rewarded with a treat because she did well on a test, but rather nothing less than one's own proper share of the good that virtuous action is directly aimed to produce, namely the universal system of happiness.

One of the bluntest of these passages says:

> The worthiness to be happy consists in the merit, which actions in behalf of happiness have which, so far as lies in freedom, would, if they were universal, really make oneself as well as others happy. One says: a human being deserves to eat who grows his own bread or also cares for the bread of others. (*R* 6857, 19:181, 1776–78)

Just as the production of bread for both oneself and others both entitles one to eat and also naturally tends toward actually producing that desired outcome, so virtuous action entitles one to happiness as one's own share in its outcome, which would be inevitable under ideal circumstances – that is, if our own freedom ("so far as lies in freedom") were the sole factor determining the outcome. Of course, no individual agent's own actions are actually a sufficient condition for the realization of the system of happiness – the actions of others and nonhuman natural forces can and often do intervene between one's intention and the intended outcome. That is why the virtue of any particular agent can *at most* produce *worthiness* to be happy.

Another note from the same period puts the same point in more formal terms:

> The concept of morality [*Sittlichkeit*] consists in the worthiness to be happy (the satisfaction of one's will in general). This worthiness rests on agreement with the laws under which, if they were universally observed, everyone would participate in happiness in the highest degree, as can happen only through freedom. But why must one conduct oneself so as to be worthy of happiness?

1. This agreement with universally valid laws of choice is, in accordance with reason, a necessary ground of our self-approval and satisfaction with ourselves, whatever others may do. (*R* 6892, 19:195–96)[14]

This passage intimates that merit is indeed connected to a "reactive attitude," although above all to that of self-approval rather than the approval of others, and thus that compliance with the demands of morality is a necessary condition of worthiness to be happy because that is a reward; but it also suggests that the compliance with the moral law is specifically linked with happiness as its reward because the moral law is precisely a law dictating universal participation in happiness. Freedom figures as the necessary condition for the worthiness to be happy because it is the necessary condition for both merit and universal happiness.

Numerous other passages confirm the view that virtue is worthiness to be happy precisely because virtue concerns the universal distribution of a good in which one is then entitled to one's own fair share. One last citation exhibiting this point will have to stand in for many others:

Do the good gladly. Seek your happiness [*crossed out*: through freedom] under its universally valid conditions [*crossed out*: of freedom), i.e., conditions that are valid for everyone's happiness and for everyone's freedom to create it for himself, and also for the essential ends of nature. . . .

Seek your happiness under the condition of a universally valid will (for yourself as well as for others, and for the inclination as well as the choice of others). This rule does not show the way to happiness, but limits the efforts in its behalf to conditions that make them worthy of it, insofar as it makes them harmonious with the universal system. (*R* 6989, 19:221; 1776–78; see also *R* 7049, 19:235; *R* 7197, 19:270–71; *R* 7202, 19:279, lines 12–20)

This passage sums up many of Kant's key points. Morality cannot be a set of *a priori* rules for achieving happiness, because only

---

[14] The final paragraph of this note, however, associates self-satisfaction with that other form of happiness that comes from independence from the senses altogether; this paragraph was quoted in the second section.

empirical knowledge can furnish the particular objects of happiness for both oneself and others; and because of this, other persons in particular must always be left free to pursue their own happiness after their own conception of it.[15] But morality does furnish the *a priori* idea of a universally valid system of happiness, or of a universal distribution of happiness; and it is reasonable for this idea to function as a necessary condition of any particular agent's entitlement to happiness: restricting one's own pursuit of happiness to conditions compatible with a universal system of happiness and making one's own happiness one's object only as part of that system are necessary and sufficient conditions for one to earn the right to one's own fair share in that system. Of course, satisfaction of these requirements is not a sufficient condition for actually receiving that share – although it is a sufficient condition for experiencing the other form of happiness, the special self-contentment of virtue.

During the development of his ethical theory Kant repeatedly asserted the following propositions: (1) the free use of reason in accordance with an *a priori* idea of the universal form or system of happiness is a necessary condition for maximizing happiness; (2) only the free use of reason can produce a system of happiness that satisfies our fundamental desire for unity itself and thus pleases us independently of the fact that it is happiness that is in this case maximized by such a system; and (3) only our free use of reason to produce such a system satisfies our reasonable view that we are entitled to our own happiness only as part of such a system, and only our own exercise of freedom in behalf of such a system of happiness satisfies our underlying supposition that we only merit any reward at all as a result of our own freely chosen actions. Perhaps none of these ideas was yet identical with what seems to be the leading idea of Kant's mature practical philosophy, the idea that freedom is the inner value of the world, or, in the terms in which he was to put it in the *Groundwork*, that our autonomy

---

[15] This point, of course, was stressed in Kant's writings of the 1790s, above all in the *Metaphysics of Morals* (6:388). The relationship between that work's claim that the happiness of *others* is an end that is also a duty of virtue and the earlier claim that a *universal system* of happiness, including one's own, is the object of virtue, is complex and cannot be discussed here.

has a dignity that is beyond all mere price (G, 4:435–36). How Kant managed to develop the latter idea without jettisoning the insight into the connections between freedom, reason, and a system of happiness that he had achieved in the jottings we have studied here will be a recurring issue in many of the following chapters.

Part II
Principles

Chapter 4

Kant's Morality of Law and Morality of Freedom

Kant's comments on moral philosophy prior to the *Groundwork for the Metaphysics of Morals* of 1785 include two striking claims. The first is the substantive claim that freedom is the source of all value – that it is intrinsically valuable, and that other valuable things must not merely be compatible with freedom but actually derive their value from the value of freedom. Kant made this claim in the lectures on ethics that he gave in the early 1780s:

> Freedom is, on the one hand, that faculty which gives unlimited usefulness to all the other faculties. It is the highest order of life, which serves as the foundation of all perfections and is their necessary condition. All animals have the faculty of using their powers according to will. But this will is not free. It is necessitated through the incitement of *stimuli*, and the actions of animals involve a *bruta necessitas*. If the will of all beings were so bound to sensuous impulse, the world would possess no value. The inherent value of the world, the *summum bonum*, is freedom in accordance with a will that is not necessitated to action. Freedom is thus the inner value of the world.[1]

This chapter originally appeared in R. M. Dancy, ed., *Kant and Critique: New Essays in Honor of W. H. Werkmeister* (Dordrecht: Kluwer, 1993), pp. 43–89.

[1] Immanuel Kant, *Lectures on Ethics*, translated by Louis Infield (London: Methuen, 1930), pp. 121–22. See *Kant's Vorlesungen, Moralphilosophie Collins*, 27:344, and *Moral Mrongovius*, 27:1482. Infield's translation was based on *Eine Vorlesung über Kants Ethik*, ed. Paul Menzer (Berlin, 1924). Menzer used a manuscript (*Brauer*) that was later lost. However, his text is virtually identical to that of *Collins*. Since

Kant's claim is that human beings differ from other animals in virtue of their possession of a will that is not necessarily determined by mere inclinations, and that this fact about them is the ultimate source of value for anything in this world.

Kant's second claim is methodological and had been made many years before these lectures, in the first work in which he publicly addressed issues of moral philosophy, *An Inquiry concerning the Distinctness of the Principles of Natural Theology and Morality*, which he wrote at the end of 1762 for a Berlin Academy essay competition and which the academy published as the runner-up in 1764.[2] Here Kant argued that the fundamental principles of morality[3] are indemonstrable. They cannot be derived from any theoretical principles because of the essential difference between knowledge and feeling, or truth and goodness, and they cannot be derived from any other practical principles because then they would no longer be fundamental. Here is how he put it:

> Only in our own times has it begun to be understood that the faculty for representing the *true* is *cognition*, but that for sensing the *good* is *feeling*, and that these must not be confused with each other. Now just as there are unanalyzable concepts of the true, i.e., of that which is to be found in the objects of cognition considered in themselves, so there is also an unanalyzable feeling of the good. . . . It is a job for the understanding to analyze and make clear the composite and confused concept of the good by showing how it arises from simpler sensations of the good. But if this [good] is simple, then the judgment: this is good, is fully indemonstrable, and is an immediate effect of the consciousness of the feeling of pleasure with the representations of the

the time when this chapter was originally written, a complete translation of *Collins*, a partial translation of *Mrongovius*, and a complete translation of *Metaphysik der Sitten Vigilantius* (see note 7) have become available in Peter Heath and J. B. Schneewind, eds., *Lectures on Ethics* (Cambridge: Cambridge University Press, 1997).

2 Kant's essay lost out to one by Moses Mendelssohn. For discussion and comparison of the two essays, see Chapter 1 in this volume.

3 At this stage he treated the fundamental principles of *commission* and of *omission* as separate principles, thus ascribing to morality two fundamental principles rather than a single one.

object. . . . Thus, if an action is immediately represented as good, without containing in a hidden manner a certain other good that can be recognized in it by analysis and on account of which it is called perfect, then the necessity of this action is an in-demonstrable material principle of obligation. (2:299–300)

Kant's account here stresses the difference between feeling and knowledge, because at this stage, under the influence of British moral sense theorists, especially Francis Hutcheson, he was con-tent to interpret the ultimate source of value as a feeling of pleas-ure in an object or action. This view certainly changed when he identified freedom as the ultimate source of value in his lectures. But the premise of Kant's argument is not affected by this change: an ultimate value cannot be derived from any merely theoretical proposition, but neither can it be derived from any other value, so at some point any theory of value must come to one or more in-demonstrable assertions of ultimate value.

These two claims may seem distant from the derivation of the categorical imperative that is usually taken to be the heart of Kant's mature moral theory. I would like to argue, however, that the fun-damental but indemonstrable value of freedom itself is the heart of Kant's moral theory, not only in the *Groundwork for the Meta-physics of Morals* but even, contrary to all appearances, in the *Critique of Practical Reason* of 1788. Kant does not argue that the categorical imperative obligates us independently of its subordi-nation to any fundamental value, but rather that it is the principle we must follow in order to give our unique freedom full expres-sion in the phenomenal sphere, where the effects of our choice take place. At the noumenal level, the freedom of our will may be a given although inscrutable fact, but in the phenomenal world steps must be taken to preserve our potential for free choice and action and to enhance the conditions under which we exercise our agency, and it is the function of the principle of morality to direct us to take such steps for the expression of our freedom.

I

This interpretation cuts against the grain of the standard approach to Kant's ethics. On standard accounts, moral theories are divided between teleological theories, which derive principles of right and obligation from an antecedent conception of what is fundamentally good or valuable, and deontological theories, which do not define the right on the basis of an antecedent definition of the good but either define or at least constrain the good by an antecedent determination of what is right or obligatory. Indeed, the distinction itself is taken to have been originated by Kant, and his own theory is taken to be a paradigmatic instance of a deontological theory.[4] The paradoxical but fundamental fact about the method of a critique of practical reason, he claims, is *"that the concept of good and evil must not be determined prior to the moral law (for which, by all appearance, it would have to serve as the ground) but rather (as also happens here* [in his own theory]*) it must be determined after the moral law and through it"* (CPracR, 5:62–63). The reason for this, Kant argues, is that if good and evil were defined antecedently to the moral law, then they could only be determined on the basis of pleasure and pain, in which case the determination of good and evil, as well as any moral law derived from them, would necessarily be empirical and contingent rather than pure and universal and necessary:

> the concept of the good as of an object does not determine and make possible the moral law, but on the contrary the moral law first determines and makes possible the concept of the good insofar as it deserves this name.
>
> This remark, which concerns merely the method of the highest moral inquiries, is of importance. It explains at once the ground responsible for all confusions of philosophers in regard to the highest principle of morals. For they sought for an object of the will in order to make it into the matter and ground of a law (which would then be the determining ground of the will not immediately but only mediately through the object that is brought to the feeling of pleasure or displeasure), when they

---

[4] It is not, however, the only instance of a deontological theory he recognizes: a divine command theory of morality, such as that advocated by the influential Pietist philosopher Christian August Crusius, is also a deontological theory, although in Kant's view it is "heteronomous" rather than "autonomous" because it places the fundamental source of obligation outside of rather than inside ourselves (see *CPracR*, 5:41).

should have first sought for a law that would determine the will immediately and an object only in accordance with this law. Now whether they placed this object of pleasure, which was to yield the highest concept of the good, in happiness, in perfection, in moral feeling, or in the will of God, their principle was always heteronomy, and they must unavoidably have stumbled into empirical conditions for a moral law. (*CPracR*, 5:64)

Only if the moral law is defined before rather than after the concept of the good, Kant holds, can this lapse into empiricism be avoided.

Kant's argument for a deontological rather than teleological approach to the highest principles of morality rests on two assumptions. First, it assumes that the fundamental principle of morality must be universal and necessary. Second, it assumes that any determination of the good independently of the moral law could only be grounded in the feeling of pleasure and would therefore be empirical, thus not necessary and universal but contingent and idiosyncratic. Kant certainly never surrenders the first of these assumptions. If he could locate a fundamental source of value in something other than pleasure and not merely empirical like pleasure, however, then he could derive the moral law from an antecedent conception of fundamental value without lapsing into empiricism after all. I argue that in the *Groundwork*, and ultimately even if only grudgingly in the *Critique of Practical Reason*, this is precisely what Kant accomplishes by means of a conception of the intrinsic value of the freedom of rational agency. If this were to mean that Kant's theory turns out to be teleological rather than deontological, that would be no objection, for Kant's stated reason for insisting on a deontological rather than teleological theory, the assumption that pleasure is the only source of value alternative to the moral law itself, will also have been rejected. In the end, however, it is probably better to say Kant's theory undercuts the traditional distinction: his final view is surely that the freedom that is intrinsically valuable is freedom that governs itself by law, or autonomy, and this conception incorporates ideas of both value and duty in itself. No end that is not licensed by the unconditional constraint of the moral law can be good, but the unconditional constraint furnished by the moral law is in turn the condition necessary to preserve and enhance the unconditional value of freedom itself. The moral law is not only a constraint on our pursuit of contingent ends; it is also the expression of a necessary end.

Most of the exposition in the *Critique of Practical Reason*, to be sure, employs the purely deontological method on which Kant there insists and makes no reference to the fundamental value of freedom. Kant begins this work by defining "practical laws" as those which "are valid for the will of every rational being" and by assuming that if pure reason is capable of being practical by determining the will, then "there must be practical laws" (*CPracR*, 5:19). The main argument is then confined to two aims: first, to prove that the categorical imperative, which licenses maxims of action on the basis of their universalizability alone, is the only practical law valid for the will of every rational being (although it would not present itself to less conflicted creatures than ourselves in the form of an imperative); and, second, to prove that we have the free will necessary for us to be capable of acting in accordance with such a purely formal law.

The argument is straightforward. First, Kant maintains that the desire for any particular object or "matter" of the senses is idiosyncratic rather than valid for all rational beings, and thus cannot give rise to a practical law (*CPracR*, §2, 5:21), and that this holds for the generic end of happiness as well. Even though happiness seems to be a general concept and all agents appear to agree in striving for it, in fact each agent's conception of happiness is nothing but the conception of the satisfaction of all of her various individual desires, and because of the natural conflicts of desires there are inevitably conflicts within any one individual's conception of happiness as well as among several individuals' conceptions of happiness. Such conflicts prevent the general idea of happiness from serving as a universal and necessary goal and source of practical law (*CPracR*, §3, 5:25–26; §4, 5:27–28).

Since this argument precludes all particular objects of desire from grounding the moral law, Kant concludes that the only alternative is that the moral law be nothing other than "the mere *form* of a universal legislation": a rational being must infer that its subjective principles of intention, what Kant calls "maxims," can serve as practical laws "only through their mere form, which *makes them fit for universal legislation*" (*CPracR*, §4, 5:27). That is, whatever one's particular object in adopting some maxim might be, action in accordance with that maxim is permissible only if it could be universally accepted as a principle of action.

The next stage of Kant's argument is then to maintain that only a will that is not determined by the objects or matter of desire, but is rather "entirely independent of the natural law of appearances, namely the law of causality," is capable of being determined by the mere legislative form or universality of its own maxims. So if we are capable of acting in accordance with the fundamental, purely formal practical law, then we must have a will that is free in "the strictest, i.e., transcendental sense" (*CPracR*, §5, 5:29).[5]

Kant then concludes by insisting that we are all conscious of this moral law and that we all recognize that we are unconditionally bound by it, as we prove by holding up all of our actions to it independent of any empirically grounded reasons for so doing (*CPracR*, §7, 5:31), indeed even when empirical circumstances provide strong arguments *against* so doing, as in the case of someone threatened with death if he stands by the moral law. And because it is a fact that we recognize our obligation under the moral law, we can infer that we are free to fulfill this obligation: "one therefore judges that he can do something because he is conscious that he ought to, and he cognizes freedom in himself, which without the moral law might otherwise remain unknown" (*CPracR*, §6, 5:30). This consciousness of our obligation under the purely formal

---

5 Space does not allow a discussion of the converse of this claim, which Kant also holds to be true, namely, that a free will necessarily acts in accordance with the moral law because it has no motive to do otherwise (*CPracR*, §6, 5:29). Although this claim is widely accepted, and Kant's two theorems are canonized as his "reciprocity" thesis (see Henry E. Allison, *Kant's Theory of Freedom* [Cambridge: Cambridge University Press, 1990], pp. 201–13), the second claim is obviously false and leads directly to Henry Sidgwick's objection to Kant: if a free will necessarily acted in accord with the moral law, then anyone who violated the moral law would prove by that fact alone that he lacked a free will (and was therefore not responsible for his criminal action). Freedom of the will does not *logically* imply conformity to the moral law; rather, it must be shown that conformity to the moral law is *substantively* necessary to preserve freedom of the will. This is assumed in what follows.

law of practical reason, from which the freedom of our will may be inferred, is what Kant calls the "fact of reason."[6]

Kant follows this basic argument with a theory of the "incentives" (*Triebfedern*) of pure practical reason. Here he holds that "the incentive of the human will (and that of every other created rational being) can never be anything other than the moral law, thus the objective determining ground must also always and entirely alone be the subjective determining ground of the action, if this is not merely to contain the letter of the law without its *spirit*" (*CPracR*, 5:72).[7] This is a position related to what has come to be known as "internalism" in recent discussions, the view that the principle that determines which actions morality requires must itself also provide the *motive* for being moral.[8] Kant has two reasons for his insistence that only the moral law itself can be the – morally praiseworthy – incentive for duty. First, it is based in his conception of the moral estimation of individual character: there is nothing praiseworthy in doing any action, even one in outward conformity with the moral law, out of any sort of self-interest or inclination, so the only morally praiseworthy type of action is one motivated by the prospect of conformity to the law itself. This is what he means by saying that only action in which the objective law is also the subjective determining ground is in conformity with the spirit as well as the letter of the law:

[6] At *CPracR*, §7, 5:31, line 25, Kant calls the "consciousness of this fundamental law" the "fact of reason"; however, he cannot mean that the fact of reason is merely the consciousness of the content of the law, for nothing about our ability to comply with it and thus about our freedom would follow from the mere *content* of the law; these would follow only from the fact that we are bound by the law and must be capable of complying with it. For further discussion, see Lewis White Beck, *A Commentary to Kant's Critique of Practical Reason* (Chicago: University of Chicago Press, 1960), pp. 166–70, and Allison, *Kant's Theory of Freedom*, p. 213, where a similar conclusion to mine is reached.

[7] See also *Metaphysik der Sitten Vigilantius* (1793–94), 27:487–88.

[8] Although some recent discussions of Kant take for granted that this is his position, it should be noted that it was not always his view; see *Lectures on Ethics*, p. 39 (*Moralphilosophie Collins*, 27:274–75, and *Moral Mrongovius*, 27:1422–23). This makes it important to consider Kant's reasons for his own assertion of internalism.

> The essence of all moral worth of actions lies in their being *immediately determined by the moral law*. If the determination of the will took place in *accordance* with the moral law, but only by means of a feeling, of whatever sort . . . thus not *for the sake of the law*: then the action would certainly contain *legality* but not *morality*. (*CPracR*, 5:71)

But, second, that the moral law itself can be an adequate motive for acting dutifully is also required in order to guarantee that it is always possible for us to act even in mere conformity to the moral law: because a formal law does not represent anything particular as an object of desire, there cannot be any guarantee that we can always act in conformity to it if our action is necessarily dependent on any desire. It must therefore be possible for us to be motivated independently of desire, which Kant takes to mean that we must be able to be motivated by the moral law itself. As Kant puts it in his lectures from the 1790s, "the categorical imperative contains an unconditioned moral necessitation, without having [the] purpose and aim of the action as its ground: there therefore remains only the *form of lawfulness*, which is the determining ground of free action."[9]

For the sake of his account of moral worth and for the possibility of acting independently of any inclination, then, Kant argues that it must be possible for us to be motivated by the moral law alone. Yet he also insists that this does not constitute any *explanation* of the possibility of such motivation, and indeed that moral theory *cannot* provide any such explanation. "For how a law can be the determining ground of the will for itself and immediately (which is yet the essence of all morality) is an unsolvable problem for human reason and identical with the problem of how a free will is possible" (*CPracR*, 5:72). Kant's position throughout the *Critique of Practical Reason* is that theoretical philosophy is incapable of explaining the possibility of freedom of the will and that practical philosophy does not explain anything at all, although it can prove that we *have* free will; thus the possibility of our being motivated by the purely formal law of morality is certain but

---

[9] *Metaphysik der Sitten Vigilantius*, 27:495.

inexplicable. All that can be explained, Kant holds, is how the free determination of the will by the formal law of morality affects our feelings and inclinations. Here is where Kant introduces his famous theory of the moral feeling of respect: he argues that anything that checks inclinations, no matter how, must produce a feeling of pain; that the determination of our will by the moral law (at least often) constitutes a check to our inclinations, and so must produce pain; but that precisely by reining in self-conceit this determination of the will also produces a positive effect on our feelings, which can be called respect (*CPracR*, 5:73).

The theory of respect therefore traces out the psychological effect of our being motivated to act by the moral law alone, but cannot explain how the moral law itself motivates us to comply with it. That it does is what Kant called the fact of reason, but the fact is also a mystery. And this is what remains profoundly unsatisfying about the argument of the *Critique of Practical Reason*: it assumes that a practical law must be necessary and universal, infers from this that it must be entirely formal, and just insists that we are capable of acting not only in accordance with it but even entirely out of respect for it without explaining in what sense we have any *reason* to do such a thing. The theory of respect only adds that, if we are motivated to act in accordance with the moral law, that motivation will generate a psychological feeling to compete with the feelings of self-love and inclination, but provides no basic explanation of how the moral law can motivate us by providing a reason for adherence to it in the first place.[10]

II

It can easily appear that the same pattern of argument is adopted for the derivation of the categorical imperative in the *Groundwork for the Metaphysics of Morals*.

The preface to this work derives the necessity of a pure moral

[10] The literature on Kant's theory of respect is vast. For some further discussion, see Karl Ameriks, "The Hegelian Critique of Kantian Morality," in Bernard den Ouden and Marcia Moen, eds., *New Essays on Kant* (New York: Peter Lang, 1987), pp. 179–212, and chapter 10 of my *Kant and the Experience of Freedom* (Cambridge: Cambridge University Press, 1993), particularly pp. 356–68.

philosophy from the "common idea of duty and moral law," which is taken to imply that any moral law must contain "absolute necessity" for all rational beings and therefore exclude any empirical grounds from the basis of morality (*G*, 4:389); and it intimates both of Kant's grounds for internalism by arguing that any motivation other than that *for the sake of* the moral law itself would leave even mere conformity to the requirements of the moral law contingent as well as *mißlich*, which means disagreeable or morally contemptible as well as merely precarious or contingent.

The body of the work is then divided into three sections, which Kant labels the "Transition from the common moral rational knowledge to the philosophical"; the "Transition from the popular moral philosophy [*Weltweisheit*] to the metaphysics of morals"; and finally the "Transition from the metaphysics of morals to the critique of practical reason." On a superficial reading, the contents of the three parts are as follows. In the first section, Kant starts off with the intuitive recognition that a good will is the only thing of absolute value because the value of any other kind of good, whether of nature or fortune, depends on being put to use by a good will (*G*, 4:393); links this with an equally intuitive recognition that a good will is one that acts for the sake of duty alone (*G*, 4:397); and then argues that a will that acts for the sake of duty alone must be one that acts on the purely formal principle of the "universal lawfulness of actions in general" for the simple reason that it has been "robbed" of any incentives and objects based in inclination (*G*, 4:402). This first section thus clearly derives the moral law from an antecedent conception of the intrinsic value of the good will, contrary to the argument that any conception of value must be derived from an antecedent recognition of the law. However, Section II appears to replace this teleological argument from common sense with an argument that, like that of the *Critique of Practical Reason*, derives the formula for the moral law from an analysis of the concept of a practical law and its application to human beings in the form of a categorical imperative itself. The transition from this philosophical analysis of the moral law to a "metaphysics of morals" then appears to consist in Kant's confirmation of the correctness of his formulation of the moral law by the demonstration that it gives rise to an acceptable systematization of our duties – which is after all what Kant was to publish under the title of a *Metaphysics of Morals* a dozen years later. Finally, Section III effects the transition from this metaphysics of morals to a critique of practical reason by providing the proof that we are beings with a free will capable of acting in accordance with the moral law as analyzed in Section II – it thus adds the synthetic *a priori* proposition that it is actually possible for us to act on the moral law to the *a priori* analysis of the content of the moral law that preceded it.[11]

Central to this superficial interpretation of the structure of the *Groundwork* is the supposition that Section I contains only a popular appeal to common sense, to be superseded by Kant's more properly philosophical formulation of the moral law in Section II.[12] On such an account, the key argument of the work would be the opening argument of Section II, which closely parallels the opening argument of the *Critique of Practical Reason*.

This argument contains three essential steps. First, it begins with the assumption that the moral law must hold universally and necessarily for all rational beings – the moral law "is of such extensive significance that it must be valid not merely for humans but for all *rational beings in general*, not merely under contingent conditions and with exceptions but *absolutely necessarily*" (*G*, 4:408) – although to imperfectly rational creatures like ourselves such a purely rational law would present itself in the form of an unconditional *constraint* or categorical *imperative* (*G*, 4:413–14). Second, the argument again points out that, although happiness can be assumed to be the general end of at least beings like ourselves who are both sensuous as well as rational, it is at best a necessary end of nature, not reason, and is in any case too indeterminate and inconsistent an end to give rise to any genuinely universal law. Thus,

[11] Chapter 5 will explore in much greater detail issues surrounding Kant's conception of a "metaphysics of morals." Chapter 6 will present a more extensive account of the argumentative strategy of the *Groundwork* as a whole.
[12] In Chapter 6, I argue that Kant intends the appeal to common knowledge in Section I of the *Groundwork* to be refined and defended in the subsequent sections, but never to be superseded.

It is a misfortune that the concept of happiness is such an inde-terminate concept that although every human being wishes to achieve it he can never determinately and self-consistently say what it is he really wishes and wills. The cause of this is that all the elements that belong to the concept of happiness are empirical,

from which it follows that

no imperative in regard to happiness is possible which would in the strictest sense command to do that which makes [for] hap-piness, because happiness is not an ideal of reason but of imag-ination, which rests merely on empirical grounds. (*G*, 4:418)

Finally, the argument again concludes with an inference to the only alternative: because the object of happiness has been excluded from the possible objects of a moral law, but because all particu-lar actions aim at some objects presumed to be a part of someone's happiness, there can be no other basis for the moral law than the conformity of one's maxims in such actions to the idea of law as such, or their universalizability. In Kant's words,

If I think of a *hypothetical* imperative in general, then I cannot know in advance what it contains until the condition is given to me. But if I think of a *categorical* imperative, then I immedi-ately know what it contains. For since besides the law the im-perative contains only the necessity of the maxims being in ac-cord with this law, but the law contains no condition to which it is limited, there remains nothing but the universality of a law in general to which the maxims of the action should accord, and which accord alone the imperative really represents as neces-sary. (*G*, 4:420–21)

As in the *Critique of Practical Reason*, the essence of the argument consists in its initial assumption that a moral law must be entirely universal and necessary, its disqualification of any principle aim-ing at happiness from this role, and its final inference that the categorical imperative can therefore require nothing but the pos-sibility of the universalizability of our maxims as conformity to the idea of lawfulness as such.

On this account, Section II of the *Groundwork* would add only two points to this purely formal deduction of the moral law: first, *confirmation* of this analysis of the moral law by showing that it does indeed give rise to an acceptable system of duties – Kant's famous four examples of the wrongs inherent in suicide, deceitful promising, neglect of talents, and the refusal of beneficence (*G*, 4:421–23, 429–30); second, the *reformulation* of the categorical imperative into versions that, as Kant says at one point, can bring this very abstract "idea of reason closer to intuition (by means of a certain analogy) and thereby to feeling" (*G*, 4:436). In contrast to the original formulation of the categorical imperative, *"Act only in accord with those maxims through which you can at the same time will that they should be a universal law"* (*G*, 4:421), which can be called the Formula of Universal Law, these more "intuitive" formulations are the Formula of Humanity as an End in Itself, *"So act that you always at the same time use humanity in your own person as well as in the person of every other as an end, never merely as a means"* (*G*, 4:429), and the Formula of the Realm of Ends (*Reich der Zwecke*) (*G*, 4:433), which requires *"that the will be able to regard itself as through its maxims at the same time universally legislating"* for a realm of equally qualified colegislators (*G*, 4:434).[13] But these formulations are not supposed to add anything essential to the original formulation of the categorical imperative, merely to help it "gain entry" because they are in some sense closer to feeling (*G*, 4:437).

Like the argument of the *Critique of Practical Reason*, however,

---

[13] Kant's expression *Reich der Zwecke* is frequently translated as "kingdom" rather than "realm" of ends. It seems to me that nothing could be more misleading, since the idea of a kingdom implies that there is one agent free to give laws to others who are not equally free. In fact, the best translation of the expression would probably be a "republic of ends." (H. J. Paton defends the translation as "kingdom" on the ground that the alternative "realm" is only the anglicization of the French word for kingdom, *royaume* [*The Categorical Imperative: A Study in Kant's Moral Philosophy* (London: Hutchinson, 1947), pp. 187–88]; but this is clearly irrelevant, since German, not French, is being translated, and the German word for "kingdom" is *Königtum*). Even if *Reich* were translated as "empire" that would be better than "kingdom," for it would at least imply that there is a class of rulers who have the sovereignty to legislate even if they are also answerable on some matters to an emperor.

this argument would leave the underlying motivation for adhering to the moral law a mystery: it explains why the empirical goal of happiness cannot be a universal and necessary basis for the adoption of any law, but otherwise seems simply to assume that we are motivated to adhere to the moral law and can be motivated to do so apart from any end without explaining how such a thing is possible. In the *Groundwork*, however, this argument seems to be afflicted with another problem as well. Its introduction of the idea of humanity as an end in itself appears to rest on a fallacy.

As usually read, Kant's transition from the Formula of Universal Law to that of Humanity as an End in Itself begins with the assumption that every act of rational willing must have some end or object at which it is aimed, an "objective ground of its self-determination" in the sense of an external state of affairs which the use of the will is designed to bring about (*G*, 4:427). Such an end may in principle be given by inclination, in which case it is valid only for the individual, or by reason, in which case it would be valid for all rational beings. Likewise, the internal state that moves an individual to adopt an end may be merely a "subjective ground of desire," or "incentive" (*Triebfeder*), in which case it is again valid only for the individual who has that desire, or it may be an "objective ground of the will" or "motivating ground" (*Bewegungsgrund*) that would be valid for all rational beings. Next Kant seems to assume that if there can be an objective law to which human beings can conform their behavior, there must also be an objective ground of the will and likewise an objective end that is valid for all rational beings. "Otherwise the ends that a rational being would propose to itself as the *effects* of its action on the basis of preference (material ends) would be entirely relative; for only their relation to a faculty of desire in the subject constituted in a particular way would give them value, which could therefore not yield any principles valid and necessary for all rational beings and not just for that [particular] will" (*G*, 4:427–28). Such an objective and necessary end must be seen as something that has value for all rational beings, not just some. The only candidate for such an object with absolute value is "the human being and in general every rational being" as an "end in itself" (*G*, 4:428).

Kant has been widely taken to be making such an argument.[14] But although many commentators let it pass, such an argument would be fallacious.[15] For if it were assumed that all agents were already bound by the moral law independently of their adoption of any end at all, then, even if every particular action of each agent would have to aim at some end or other, there would be no obvious reason why they must all aim at some single, necessary end. They might simply apply the moral law as a supreme constraint to their various individual ends in order to determine which are permitted by morality and which are not (as indeed the "categorical imperative procedure," as it is called by Rawls and others, is generally understood),[16] without having any common, let alone necessary end. Thus, even when several drivers are all obeying the speed limit, it hardly follows that they have any common aim in driving or any common reason for driving no faster than the speed limit: some may be driving to get home to their families,

[14] He even more clearly seems to make such an argument in the later *Metaphysics of Morals*: "An *end* is an *object* of free choice, the representation of which determines the latter to an action (through which the former is to be brought about). Thus every action has its end. . . . But since this act, which determines an end, is a practical principle, which does not provide the means (thus is not conditioned) but the end itself (consequently unconditioned), thus it is a categorical imperative of pure practical reason. . . . Now there must be such an end and a categorical imperative corresponding to it. For since there are free actions, there must also be ends to which these are directed as objects. Among these ends there must be some that are at the same time (i.e., according to their concepts) duties. – For if there were none of this sort, then, since no action can be without an end, all ends for practical reason would only be means to other ends, and a *categorical* imperative would be impossible" (6:384–85).

[15] The argument is accepted without demur by Paton, *The Categorical Imperative*, p. 168, and more recently by Christine M. Korsgaard, "Kant's Formula of Humanity," *Kant-Studien* 77 (1986): 183–202, at p. 186 (this article is reprinted in her *Creating the Kingdom of Ends* [Cambridge: Cambridge University Press, 1996], chap. 4, pp. 106–32). She argues there that if there is a necessary end, there must be a categorical imperative, and if there is a categorical imperative, there must be a necessary end. What I am about to argue is precisely that although the latter is not obviously true, the former is and is indeed the fundamental basis of Kant's derivation of the categorical imperative itself.

[16] See John Rawls, "Themes in Kant's Moral Philosophy," in Eckart Förster, ed., *Kant's Transcendental Deductions: The Three Critiques and the Opus postumum* (Stanford: Stanford University Press, 1989), pp. 81–113, especially pp. 82–83.

others to get away from their families, and some may be conforming to the speed limit out of respect for the law or concern for other drivers but others only because they are afraid of the consequences of a ticket or an accident. Conformity to a common law does not by itself imply the existence, let alone necessity of any common end.

Kant is not, however, making such a fallacious inference. In fact, he is not taking the validity of the categorical imperative for granted, as he does in the *Critique of Practical Reason*, but is instead arguing precisely that only if we can find an objective and thus universally compelling end that can give rise to a universal law can we explain why rational beings should be bound by such a law in the first place. Indeed, Kant introduces the discussion of rational being as an end in itself by saying that it is still a *question* whether "it is a necessary law *for all rational creatures* always to evaluate their actions according to maxims that these could always themselves will to serve as universal laws" and that "one must, however much he resists it, take a step into metaphysics" in order to answer it (G, 4:426). The question that must now be answered is just *what sort of end, if not the end of happiness, could possibly motivate us to act on the basis of such a law,* and the step into metaphysics – practical not theoretical metaphysics, as Kant says – that must be taken in order to answer this question requires nothing less than the *discovery* of something with absolute value for all rational beings that could give any rational being a reason to adhere to the principle of morality. Kant is not looking for an end that the antecedent adoption of the principle of morality could force a rational being to adopt, but for an end the intrinsic and absolute value of which would compel any rational being to adopt the principle of morality. Something with absolute value must be found in order to explain our adherence to an unconditional law:

> But if it were supposed that there is something *whose existence in itself* has absolute value, which as an *end in itself* could be the ground of determinate laws, then in it and in it alone would lie the ground of a possible categorical imperative, i.e., practical law. (G, 4:428)

Rational being as an end in itself is introduced in order to provide an end with absolute value for the sake of which any rational being would see fit to adopt the moral law.[17]

In summary, then, Kant's argument is that an agent would have no reason to adhere to a principle unless it advanced an end, and no reason to adhere to an unconditional law unless it advanced an end with absolute value; but the ordinary objects of actions, that is objects of inclination, have only "conditional worth," and cannot furnish an end with absolute value that would justify adherence to an unconditional law; so "*objective ends*, i.e., things whose existence is an end in itself" must be recognized "because without them nothing of *absolute value* would be found; but if all value were conditioned, thus contingent, no highest practical principle for reason in general could be found" (*G*, 4:428). "If therefore there is to be a highest practical principle and in regard to the human will a categorical imperative, it must be one that forms an objective principle of the will out of the representation of that which is necessarily an end for everyone because it *is an end in itself*," and this necessary end and thus ground for a categorical imperative can be nothing other than "*rational nature exist[ing] as an end in itself*" (*G*, 4:428–29).

We must obviously ask what the idea of rational being as an end in itself means, why it has absolute value, and how it gives rise to the moral law. But first we may observe that this interpretation of Kant's intentions at this juncture in the *Groundwork* gives rise to a picture of the organization of the work that is different from the standard view. Remember that both the first and second sections of the *Groundwork* are described as "transitions," the first from the "common moral rational knowledge to the philosophical" and the second from "popular moral philosophy [*Weltweisheit*] to the metaphysics of morals." These titles might be taken to connote a *single* transition from Section I to II, thus implying that the argument of Section I simply gives way before the argument of Section II, with the properly philosophical treatment of morality

---

[17] The argument of this paragraph is developed more fully in Chapter 5, section III.

beginning only with the derivation of the formulation of the categorical imperative from the mere concept of it at the outset of Section II. However, Section II is not called a transition from "common moral rational knowledge" to the metaphysics of morals, but rather a transition from "popular moral philosophy" to the metaphysics of morals, where popular moral philosophy is characterized with the old-fashioned term *Weltweisheit*, which Kant does not use to describe his own views and which may even have a pejorative connotation.

What these titles really mean, I suggest, is that popular moral philosophy is nothing other than the formalistic deduction of the categorical imperative from the mere concept of a practical law itself, and that *this* argument is to be, if not entirely replaced, then at least supported by a genuine metaphysics of morals when the moral law is derived from an underlying ground in absolute value rather than simply assumed – the precise point in his argument where, Kant says, we must take a step into metaphysics however reluctantly. And if this is so, then the initial, clearly teleological derivation of the moral law from the unconditional value of the good will in Section I is itself not replaced by the analysis of the concept of a universal practical law in Section II, but is rather only refined and defended in the metaphysics of morals to which that mere analysis itself gives way.[18] In both Sections I and II, that is, it is ultimately agreed that an unconditional law can only be derived from something with absolute value, and all that is happening is that the intuitive conception of the good will is being replaced with the more abstract notion of rational being as an end in itself. Indeed, only such an interpretation would explain why Kant uses the profoundly *respectful* term "common moral rational knowledge" to characterize the starting point of Section I: the initial insight into absolute value is never superseded but is only refined by Kant's own "philosophical" theory. It is thus by means of the replacement of popular moral philosophy with the metaphysics of morals that the transition from common to philosophical moral rational knowledge is completed.

[18] Again, see Chapter 6.

III

We can now turn to the substantive questions about Kant's conception of rational being as an end in itself. We must naturally begin with the question of what Kant means by the requirement that rational being be treated, as he puts it, always as an end and never *"merely as a means* for the arbitrary use of this or that will" (*G*, 4: 428). Kant's renewed discussion of the four examples of duty certainly makes much of his meaning clear: it shows that by a rational being Kant means an agent capable of setting its own ends by means of its reason, and that by treating a rational being always as an end and never merely as a means Kant has in mind, in the first instance, treating such a being as one who must be able to assent to actions affecting him because or at least as if they also serve ends that he as a rational agent sets for himself. This is perhaps clearest in Kant's treatment of the prohibition against deceitful promises: what is wrong with such an act is that "he whom I would use for my own ends through such a promise cannot possibly agree with my mode of proceeding against him and therefore contain the end of this action in himself" (*G*, 4:429–30); by contrast, "to value a rational being as always at the same time an end" is precisely to treat him "as one who must always be able to contain the end of one's action in himself as well" (*G*, 4:430). The first step toward treating another as an end, then, is treating him as one who must always be able to consent freely to one's treatment of him as compatible with the ends he himself adopts as a rational agent.

This is not the whole of what is involved in treating rational beings as ends in themselves, however. Kant's examples also make clear that the required treatment of those who are agents capable of setting and pursuing ends also requires taking steps to enhance their prospects for the successful exercise of their agency by improving the circumstances under which ends they freely set can be pursued and even by directly assisting such agents in their pursuit of those ends. Thus, in the case of the duty to develop one's own talents, one's duty consists in doing what one can to ensure that the agency of both oneself and others can successfully be used in the pursuit of particular ends; and in the case of the duty of beneficence, Kant maintains that one has a duty, "so far as he can, to advance the ends of others" (*G*, 4:430).

Thus, there are two components to Kant's conception of treating rational beings as ends in themselves. As he puts it, the first step must certainly always be to *preserve* rational agency in oneself or others as the condition of the possibility of setting ends: this requires that one not act against the specific ends of others, but also more generally that one not injure or destroy rational being in oneself or others. Freedom may be given and perhaps in the noumenal realm it cannot even be destroyed (perhaps this is an implication of Kant's postulate of immortality); but the empirical or phenomenal manifestations of free agency can certainly be injured or destroyed, and our first duty is to avoid this. This requires that one not act against the specific ends of others, but also more generally that one not injure or destroy free rational agency in oneself or in others. This duty is thus the source of the prohibition of suicide and murder, which destroy the underlying agency as such, as well as of such specific prohibitions as that against deceitful promises, which limit without completely destroying the rational agency of another. These two kinds of prohibitions are what Kant calls perfect duties. But beyond this, one also has a duty to do what one can to *advance* the successful exercise of rational agency in oneself and others: this is the source of the imperfect duties requiring policies of developing one's own talents and practicing beneficence: as Kant says, "neglecting these might well be compatible with the *preservation* of humanity as an end in itself but not with the *advancement* of this end" (*G*, 4:430). Finally, Kant clearly believes that these two requirements are lexically ordered, thus that our first duty must always be to preserve rational agency free of injury before we can consider enhancing its exercise. The *Groundwork* does not make an explicit argument for this assumption, however.

If we accept this account of what treating rational agents as ends in themselves consists in,[19] our next question must obviously

---

[19] What Kant is advocating is clearly coherent. It is sometimes objected that the idea of treating humanity or the rational being therein as an end is incoherent because an end is something to be brought into existence by an action yet the

be why this capacity of rational agency in human or other rational beings is in fact an end in itself with absolute value. Why should an agent's capacity to set its own ends make that agent itself an object of absolute value to be respected under all circumstances? Here is where Kant's intentions become more obscure.

One suggestion has been that the idea of rational agency as the capacity to set ends solves Kant's problem of value precisely by locating the source of all conditional values in the rational agent's capacity *to create values*. On this account, Kant's problem is taken to be that of stopping an infinite regress from objects of merely conditional value to yet other objects of always merely conditional value, and the way to stop this regress is by supposing that rational choice itself confers value on its objects. That is, rational agency itself is supposed to solve the problem of providing a basis for merely conditional values because rational agency itself is nothing less than the power to *create* values *ex nihilo* by making objects into ends. As Christine Korsgaard writes, "Kant's answer . . . is that what makes the object of your rational choice good is that it *is* the object of a rational choice. . . . His idea is that rational choice has . . . a value-conferring status."[20] Or as Leslie Mulholland proposes, "a rational being is related to moral values of any sort (good and evil) . . . not as a means but as the subject that produces those values by its relation to the law of its willing. . . . the rational being is the ground of the categorical imperative, not

other persons who are the objects of one's actions already exist, except in the case of procreation – which can hardly be the sole object of our moral duty. (See Robert Paul Wolff, *The Autonomy of Reason: A Commentary on Kant's Groundwork of the Metaphysic of Morals* [New York: Harper and Row, 1973], p. 175. For a rejection of this sort of approach, as if in anticipation of Wolff's objection, see Paton, *The Categorical Imperative*, p. 169.) Obviously this is a superficial grammatical objection: although it may not be grammatical to speak of *making persons my end*, it is certainly grammatical to speak of *making it the end of my actions* always to treat myself and others as beings capable of setting their own ends, in particular by always preserving their capacity to set ends and its preconditions and by advancing or enhancing that capacity as the occasion allows or requires. There is no room for mystery as to Kant's meaning. See also Chapter 5, note 17.

[20] "Kant's Formula of Humanity," p. 196.

through its being an end of moral (or nonmoral) value, but through its autonomously producing the moral law."[21]

The problem with this proposal, however, is that although it may put a stop to the alleged infinite regress of merely conditional value, it does not appear to place any particular *constraint* on the creative value setting of the agent, that is, to explain why any such agent should set values only in a way that is compatible with other agents' creation of values, unless it does so by begging the question, that is, precisely by using an already *moral* conception of rational agency and thus simply assuming that a rational agent is one who adheres to the moral law of universalizability and so will not create any nonuniversalizable assignment of values. Without that assumption, it is not clear why any agent should respect the ends of any other agent in creating his own values *ex nihilo*. But that restriction is what the idea of rational agency as an end in itself is supposed to explain, not assume. Mulholland recognizes this problem, but tries to resolve it by treating the idea of the rational agent as a theoretical rather than moral concept, that is, as a concept of one who adheres to a universal law, as it were, as a matter of definition rather than moral value. But that will not do, for a mere definition always leaves open the question why any actual agent should define himself as a rational agent in this sense, that is, believe that his behavior *ought* to be conformed to the requirement of a mere definition.[22]

However, Kant does not try to sidestep the problem of the absolute value of rational agency as an end in itself in this way. Instead, he attempts to confront it head-on by explicitly assigning absolute moral value to a property of rational agency from the outset. How he does this is suggested by the passage from his lectures with which we began: he sees our capacity to set and pursue ends of our own choice as a fundamental manifestation of our freedom and sees freedom itself as possessing absolute value. The categorical imperative then becomes an unconditional law because

---

[21] Leslie A. Mulholland, *Kant's System of Rights* (New York: Columbia University Press, 1990), pp. 108, 110.

[22] See ibid., pp. 108, 111.

compliance with it is what is necessary to preserve and enhance the existence and exercise of freedom itself.

Kant makes the structure of such an argument plain in the introduction to another series of lectures from the early 1780s, in this case lectures on natural law that were given during the very months in 1784 when he was writing the *Groundwork*.[23] Here Kant begins by arguing that nonrational things must be used as means by rational beings in order to have any value, and then continues that in order for anything in the world to have value as an end, there must be something that is an end in itself.[24] Then Kant explicitly adds that in order for something to be the source of value for conditionally valuable things it must itself be intrinsically valuable:

> That the existence of something must be an end in itself, and not all things can be merely means, is just as necessary in the system of ends as an *Ens a se* is in the existence of efficient causes. A thing that is an end in itself is a *Bonum a se*. What can be considered merely a means has its value as a means only when it is used as such. There must therefore be a being that is an end in itself. A thing in nature is a means for another; that goes on forever, and it is necessary at last to think of a thing that is itself an end, otherwise the series would come to no conclusion.[25]

So something must put an end to the infinite regress in the means-end series, but if that thing is to make the members of this series conditionally valuable then it must itself be unconditionally good, a *bonum a se*. Thus Kant denies that anything that is itself value-neutral can create value *ex nihilo*.

Kant's next step is to assert that man himself is this necessary end, but also that he enjoys such a status specifically on account of his freedom:

> Man namely is an end in himself, he can therefore have only an inner value, i.e., dignity, on which no equivalence can be set. . . .

[23] See 4:627, where letters by various correspondents from March, April, and May 1784, stating that Kant was working on his "*Prodromus zur Moral*," are reported.
[24] *Naturrecht Feyerabend*, 27:1319.
[25] Ibid., 27:1321.

The inner value of man rests on his freedom, that he has his own
will. Since he is to be the final end, his will must not depend on
anything else. Animals have a will, but they do not have their
own will, but the will of nature. The freedom of humans is the
condition under which the human being can be an end himself.[26]

Here Kant not only explicitly asserts that freedom is the basis for
the human being's status as an end in itself, but also ventures an
explanation for this claim that may not seem entirely dissimilar to
the account we rejected earlier: the free will of human beings can
put an end to the infinite regress of conditional value precisely
because it is itself not dependent on anything else. But here Kant
has explicitly asserted that this as it were theoretical fact does not
suffice to explain unconditional value, and that freedom can play
this role only if it is recognized to be a *bonum a se*.

The structure of Kant's argument is not so clear in the *Groundwork*, but its character becomes clear when the initial intuitive idea
of the absolute value of the good will is refined into the notion of
the incomparable *dignity* of *autonomy*, the property of being governed by a law but only a law that one has freely chosen for oneself. Kant stresses this point at several key places in Section II.
"Reason relates every maxim of the will as universally legislative
to every other will and to every action toward itself," he says, not
because of "feelings, impulses, and inclinations," or "on account
of other practical motivating grounds or further advantage, but
rather out of the idea of the *dignity* [*Würde*] of a rational being
who obeys no other law than that which he at the same time gives"
(*G*, 4:434). He claims that there is a unique dignity, not to be traded
off against any mere "market price" (*G*, 4:434), in being "free in
regard to all laws of nature, obeying only those which one gives
oneself and in accordance with which one's maxims can belong to
a universal legislation (to which one at the same time subjects oneself)" (*G*, 4:435–36). Indeed, Kant pulls out all the stops by characterizing our autonomy as "sublime":

Only the dignity of humanity as rational nature without any
purpose or advantage to be obtained, thus respect for a mere

[26] Ibid., 27:1319–20.

153

idea should nevertheless serve as an exceptionless precept for the will, and in just this independence of the maxims from all such incentives [does] its sublimity consist and the dignity of every rational subject [as] a legislative member in the realm of ends. (*G*, 4:439)

Kant's claim is that there is an unparalleled dignity in elevating ourselves above the mere laws of nature by the free exercise of rational agency, and that this unparalleled dignity can serve as the source of the absolute value necessary to explain the rationality of our adherence to the categorical imperative: it is a value that any rational being would find compelling.

Finally, in spite of its avowedly deontological rather than teleological method, the argument of *Critique of Practical Reason* ultimately culminates in the same assertion of the absolute value of the freedom of rational agency. Although, as we saw, its discussion of incentives begins by saying that there can be no explanation of our underlying motivation to obey the moral law, only a description of its psychological manifestation in the feeling of respect, it concludes with an account of the absolute value of freedom that is essentially identical to that of the *Groundwork*. This extraordinary passage must be quoted at length:

> *Duty!* you, sublime, tremendous name . . . what is worthy of your origin, and what is the root of your noble descent, which proudly rejects all relation to inclinations, and from what root is to be derived the indispensable condition of that value which humans can alone give to themselves?
>
> It can be nothing less than that which elevates men above themselves (as part of the sensible world), which connects them to an order of things, which only the understanding can think. . . . This is nothing other than *personality*, i.e., the freedom and independence of the mechanism of nature in its entirety, considered as the capacity of a being which is subject to special laws of pure practical reason, namely those given by its own reason, so that the person, as belonging to the sensible world, is subject to its own personality insofar as it also belongs to the intelligible world; for it is then not to be wondered at that the human being, as belonging to two worlds, cannot contemplate his own

essence in relation to his second and higher vocation except with reverence, and its laws with the highest respect. (*CPracR*, 5:86)

Even in the *Critique of Practical Reason*, then, there can be little doubt that the foundation of Kant's entire moral philosophy is his belief in the absolute value of the freedom of rational beings. The moral law is a categorical imperative for us precisely because it is the law by means of conformity to which this intrinsically valuable freedom can be preserved and enhanced.

IV

Before we can consider whether Kant can justify such an unabashed assertion of the intrinsic value of freedom, we must ask whether this account of absolute value is not liable to the same kind of objection that I brought against the account of rational agency as value setting *ex nihilo*: doesn't Kant's account of the dignity of autonomy beg the question of motivating adherence to the moral law by assigning value only to freedom that already acknowledges this law? As I see it, Kant tried out two different approaches to this problem. One is that which is perhaps implicit in the passages just cited from the *Groundwork* and *Critique of Practical Reason*, in which it is clearly supposed that what is sublime above all else is nothing less than *autonomy* in the strong sense, that is, freedom that is expressed in or even achieved by adherence to a law other than the law of nature, which is therefore (by elimination) identical to the moral law. On this account, to be sure, the value of adherence to the moral law may be assumed, but at least there is no pretense that this is not a fundamental moral value from the outset. Moreover, adherence to the moral law by itself is not seen as valuable; rather the freedom expressed in and achieved by adherence to the moral law is intrinsically valuable. Thus, on this account, freedom is at least a necessary condition of the value of adherence to the moral law. One might put this point by emphasizing that what is sublime is not mere conformity to the moral law for any reason whatsoever, but *freely chosen* adherence to the moral law – freedom without adherence to the moral law may not be intrinsically valuable, but adherence to the moral law without freedom would also lack any absolute value. So even if the value of allegiance to universal law is being assumed, it is also clear that no account of absolute value can be complete without recognition of the intrinsic dignity of free choice. On this approach, the distinction between teleology and deontology ultimately collapses.

Sometimes, however, Kant attempts an alternative and more purely teleological solution to this problem. On this approach there is no initial assumption of the moral value of adherence to the moral law for its own sake; rather, freedom per se is intrinsically valuable, but the introduction of consistency both within one's own choices of ends and among the ends of oneself and others by means of compliance with the requirement of universalizability is argued to be necessary in order to maximize the exercise of this freedom and thus maximally realize its potential intrinsic value. On this account, freedom itself is the absolute value and adherence to the law is the condition necessary for the maximal realization of this value rather than a part of its very concept. In Kantian terminology, the connection between freedom and the moral law is synthetic rather than analytic.

Kant's 1784 lectures on natural law suggest such an approach. As we saw, Kant begins these lectures by arguing that something which is good in itself, a *bonum a se*, is necessary in order to put a stop to the infinite regress of merely conditionally valuable things, and that human freedom itself is this intrinsically valuable good. He continues his argument by explicitly asserting that it is freedom alone and not the rationality of the use of freedom that is the source of its value: as he puts it,

> If only rational beings can be ends in themselves, they cannot be such because they have reason but because they have freedom. The reason is merely a means. . . . Without reason a being cannot be an end in itself; for it cannot be conscious of its existence, nor reflect on it. But reason is not the cause of man's being an end in himself with a dignity that can be replaced by no equivalent. Reason does not give us the dignity. Freedom, only freedom, makes us ends in ourselves. Here we have the capacity to act according to our own will. If our reason were disposed according to universal laws, our will would not be our own, but

the will of nature. – If the actions of man lay in the mechanism of nature, then their ground would not be in himself, but outside him. – I must presuppose the freedom of the being when he is to be an end for himself. Such a being must therefore have freedom of the will.[27]

In other words, if we were merely to conform to a universal law, that would confer no special dignity upon us; what confers this dignity upon us is precisely that we freely choose to act, even when we choose to act in accordance with a law.

Finally, Kant tries to explain how our status as ends in ourselves, although not analytically equivalent to our self-governance by a universal law of reason, gives rise to such a law: precisely because each rational being, therefore each human being, is an end in himself, he ought never to be used merely as a means, and each ought to restrict the freedom of his own agency by respecting the value of the agency of everyone else. Thus Kant says:

> Man is an end, it is therefore contradictory that he should merely be a means. . . . The human will is therefore restricted to the condition of universal agreement with the will of others. – If there is to be a system of ends, then the end and will of a rational being must agree with that of [every] other. The will of a human is not limited by all of nature . . . except by the will of other humans.[28]

Human beings are ends in themselves solely because they are free – "Freedom is not only the highest but also the sufficient condition" for being an end in oneself.[29] But because each is free and thus possesses the intrinsic dignity of an end in himself, anyone acting against the freedom of others would realize the value in his own freedom only by destroying the same value in another's freedom. Thus, no free being should act against the freedom of any other, for that only diminishes the total amount of freedom. It is therefore necessary for men to form a system of ends, a condition in which the use of the freedom of each is restricted by the possibility of the

[27] Ibid., 27:1321–22.
[28] Ibid., 27:1319.
[29] Ibid., 27:1322.

freedom of all precisely so that none need lose his freedom. This is the origin of the categorical imperative. The constraint of freedom by law is not part of what makes freedom itself valuable but rather the condition under which the intrinsically valuable freedom of all can be realized.

A similar strategy, though with a more general account of the ultimate necessity of constraining our freedom by laws, is inherent in the lectures on ethics from which we quoted at the outset. Kant follows his initial statement there that freedom is the intrinsic value of the world with the claim that "freedom unrestrained by rules of its conditional employment is the most terrible of all things."[30] His explanation of why freedom must be restrained by rule may seem ambiguous. At first, he suggests that freedom must conform to the "essential ends of humanity," as if these defined some antecedent notion of absolute value, thus as if freedom alone were not the sole source of unconditional value but as if some other moral notion were also assumed. But, as he continues, Kant makes it clear that freedom must be restricted only for the sake of freedom itself: "It must therefore be restricted, though not by other properties or faculties, but by itself." Because Kant is explicitly discussing duties to oneself here, he illustrates his claim by representing intrapersonal consistency as the necessary condition for the maximization of one's own freedom:

> The supreme rule is that in all the actions that affect himself a man should so conduct himself that every exercise of his power is compatible with the fullest employment of them. . . . That freedom, the principle of the highest order of life, should annul itself and abrogate the use of itself conflicts with the fullest use of freedom. But freedom can only be in harmony with itself under certain conditions; otherwise it comes into collision with itself.[31]

But the principle applies in interpersonal cases as well: what is terrible about the violation of lawfulness is that it uses freedom to destroy freedom, whether in one's own case or that of another. A

---

[30] *Lectures on Ethics*, p. 122; *Moralphilosophie Collins*, 27:344; *Moral Mrongovius*, 27:1482.
[31] *Lectures on Ethics*, p. 123; *Moralphilosophie Collins*, 27:346; *Moral Mrongovius*, 27:1483–84.

free but lawless act now may undermine my own freedom on some subsequent occasion, as in the case of drunkenness, or on all subsequent occasions, as in the case of suicide, or it may undermine the freedom of another on some occasion, as in the case of a deceitful promise, or in all cases, as in murder. In any event, the point is that freedom must be subjected to law, not because subjection to law represents an antecedent source of value, but in order to maximize the preservation and exercise of freedom itself.

By means of this argument Kant could justify adherence to the moral law on the basis of the absolute value of freedom itself without begging the question of the antecedent validity of that law. In his published works he preferred to speak of the dignity of autonomy, building conformity to the law into the conception of that which has ultimate value rather than deriving it from it. Perhaps he preferred to do that to save himself from having to spell out to his readers the argument that he spelled out to his students, or perhaps this preference has a closer connection to his underlying justification of the absolute value of freedom. We must now turn to that question, but before we do so I will briefly consider the implications of my argument thus far concerning the relationship among the three formulations of the fundamental principle of morality.

V

As noted earlier, Kant himself recognizes three versions of the principle: the Formula of Universal Law, the Formula of Humanity as an End in Itself, and the Formula of the Realm of Ends. He makes two observations about the relations among these three formulations. First, he claims that the Formula of Universal Law is the "strict method" preferable for "moral judging [*sittliche Beurteilung*]," but that the other formulations bring the moral law "closer to intuition." Second, he claims that the first formulation concerns the *form* of moral maxims, "which consists in universality," while the Formula of the End in Itself concerns their *matter*, namely an end, while the Formula of the Realm of Ends provides a "*complete determination* of all maxims" (*G*, 4:436–37). It is easy to interpret the claim that the first formula is the "strict method" whereas the others bring it "closer to intuition" to mean that the proper *deduction* of the categorical imperative leads directly to the Formula of Universal Law whereas the others are only aids to comprehension for the less abstractly minded. However, Kant's reference to intuition should not be dismissed lightly, for of course it is one of his most profound principles throughout his work that there can be no proof of the reality of any concept without an intuition,[32] and when he suggests that the formulas of the End in Itself and the Realm of Ends bring the moral law closer to intuition he may well be intimating that these formulas are necessary to prove the reality of the moral law itself. And when he says that the Formula of the End in Itself provides the *matter* of morality and the Formula of Universal Law its *form*, he may also be suggesting that the introduction of the end in itself with absolute value is the primary step in the proof of the moral law, for a form without matter constitutes only a possibility, not reality.[33]

If this is correct, then we should interpret the relation among the three formulations of the moral law in the following way. The Formula of the End in Itself displays the objects of our action in moral behavior, namely ourselves and other human beings, in light of their intrinsic value as free rational agents, and thus provides the fundamental end and motive for our adherence to the moral law. The Formula of the Realm of Ends describes in objective terms the state of affairs that would be brought about by compliance with the moral law: each rational being would be treated as an end in himself who must be able to subscribe freely to the principles by which all are treated and would treat all others only according to the same principles; thus each member of such a realm could be regarded as freely legislating universal law along with all the others. Each rational agent would be both subject and sovereign in such a realm – which is, of course, only an ideal since it would actually be brought about only under conditions of perfect compliance with the moral law by each of its members (*G*, 4:433). Finally, the Formula of Uni-

---

[32] He explicitly applies this to the case of moral concepts at *Critique of Judgment*, §59, 5:351.

[33] This proposal is developed at greater length in Chapter 5.

versal Law would function as the decision procedure by which any agent would test his proposed maxims of action to see if they do in fact imply the treatment of others only as ends and never as means and could thus serve as the legislation for a realm of ends. This would be the sense in which the first formula would provide the "strict method" for "moral evaluation": it would not provide the strict method for the *deduction* of the moral law but rather for its *application*. The Formula of the End in Itself, as both closer to intuition and providing the matter of moral maxims, would be the real basis for the *deduction* of the moral law.[34]

---

[34] This approach to the relation of the three formulas may be contrasted to two others in the recent literature. Onora O'Neill has argued that the first and second formulas are extensionally equivalent because they merely describe the same mode of behavior from two different points of view: the first formula describes moral behavior from the point of view of the rule that the agent should follow, while the second formula describes it in terms of the objects of the agent's actions, namely other rational beings as ends in themselves (see "Universal Laws and Ends-in-Themselves," in her *Constructions of Reason: Explorations of Kant's Practical Philosophy* [Cambridge: Cambridge University Press, 1990], pp. 126–44, especially pp. 141–42). This is implied by my account, but my account gives the Formula of the End in Itself priority in Kant's actual deduction of the moral law, which O'Neill's does not.

Thomas W. Pogge has argued that the Formula of the End in Itself provides a more complete moral law than the Formula of Universal Law, first, because the first principle gives rise only to a requirement to universalize one's maxims across an ill-defined class of beings who may be affected by one's actions, whereas only the second principle gives rise to the requirement to include all persons among the class on whom the effects of one's actions are to be considered, and, second, because the first formula only gives rise to perfect duties not to injure rational agents, and only the second formula gives rise to the imperfect duties actually to advance or enhance the conditions for the exercise of their agency ("The Categorical Imperative," in *Grundlegung zur Metaphysik der Sitten: Ein Kooperativer Kommentar*, ed. Ottfried Höffe [Frankfurt am Main: Vittorio Klostermann, 1989], pp. 172–93, especially pp. 176–77, 182–83). Both of these claims are debatable; but in any case, Pogge notes only in passing that it is the second formula that provides the rationale for the first (p. 182) and does not adequately explain the primacy of the Formula of the End in Itself in Kant's ultimate deduction of the moral law.

Again, these issues will be pursued further in Chapter 5.

VI

We can now finally turn to the question of Kant's ultimate justification for the ascription of absolute value to the freedom of rational agents.

We can begin by dismissing out of hand two arguments that are sometimes interpreted as if they were supposed to justify the ascription of absolute value to the freedom of rational agency. First, immediately after claiming that a supreme practical principle can only be derived from a conception of that which is necessarily an end in itself (*G*, 4:438), Kant states:

> The ground of this principle is: *rational nature exists as an end in itself*. Man necessarily represents his own existence thus; in this way it is therefore a *subjective* principle of human action. But every other rational being represents his existence according to this same rational ground, which also holds for me; it is therefore at the same time an *objective* principle, from which as a highest practical ground all laws of the will must be able to be derived. (*G*, 4:429)

This statement has been interpreted to argue that since *each* human being represents *his own* rational agency as possessing unconditional value, each person has a reason to value the rational agency *of every other* agent in the same way. However, this is obviously fallacious.[35] Even if I value my own freedom of agency above all else and you value yours in precisely the same way, it does not follow automatically that *I* have a reason to value *your* agency (I may love my wife and you your husband – it certainly does not follow from that alone that I should love your husband). But I do not think that Kant means to make such an argument. Rather, he is only saying that it is true as a subjective – or psychological – fact about *all* human beings that they recognize the unconditional value of the

---

[35] Paton imputes such an argument to Kant, admitting that it "looks like a fallacy," and then proposes a reinterpretation of it on which it is not, namely, that each man values his own agency only because of the general value of rational agency that it represents (*The Categorical Imperative*, p. 176). My only objection to this is that I do not believe that Kant meant to make the fallacious argument in the first place.

freedom of rational agency in general, not just their own freedom, and that they can also recognize that all rational agents would place equal value on this end, therefore that is an unconditional end for all rational agents that complies with the original requirement that the moral law and thus its source be valid for all rational beings. This is not a fallacy, although of course it still leaves the unconditional value of such freedom unexplained – as indeed Kant clearly acknowledges when he adds to this very claim that all rational beings recognize that rational nature is an end in itself a footnote that states that "I adduce this proposition here as a postulate" (*G*, 4:429n).

The second claim that could only incorrectly be interpreted as a justification of the fundamental principle of absolute value comes after Kant reviews the relation among all three formulations of the moral law, where he says:

> We can now end where we began, namely with the concept of an unconditionally good will. That *will* is *absolutely* good which cannot be evil, thus whose maxims if they are made into a universal law never contradict themselves. (*G*, 4:437)

This does make clear that the thesis that rational being is an end in itself is meant to be the development of the original claim of the absolute value of the good will. It could be taken as an argument that a will that adheres to the moral law is necessarily or "absolutely" good precisely because, since it always adheres to this law, it cannot ever do wrong. But, of course, this is a tautology and does not explain why it is good to adhere to the moral law in the first place. It may explain the goodness of a good will in terms of its unwavering commitment to the moral law, but the goodness of the absolute value which that commitment itself serves needs to be separately explained. Explaining why the good will is *absolutely* (*schlechterdings*) good because it never wavers from the law is not the same as explaining why commitment to that law is *unconditionally* (*unbedingt*) good in the first place, that is, has a goodness that is not merely a means to something else.

So we are still left with the underlying issue of justifying the ascription of unconditional value to freedom. Let us now turn to several thoughts that Kant does seem to have intended at various times as justifications of this conception of the nature of absolute value. The first of these is what we might think of as a Stoic argument for freedom: freedom is unconditionally good because it frees us from dependence on nature and therefore from the contingency that affects any other kind of good. Kant suggests such an argument in one of his notes (*R* 7202), which has already been cited several times in Chapter 3:

> A certain basis (fount, foundation) of satisfaction is necessary, which no one must lack, and without which no happiness is possible, the rest are accidents. . . . This basis is self-satisfaction (as it were *apperceptio iucunda primitiva*). It must depend neither on the gift of nature nor on luck and accident, since these need not accord of themselves with our essential and highest ends. Since the satisfaction must be connected with its source necessarily and universally, thus *a priori* and not merely according to empirical laws, which are never apodictically certain, it must 1. depend on the free will, which we can ourselves make in accordance with the idea of the highest good. 2. this freedom must to be sure be independence from all sensuous necessitation, but yet not altogether without law.[36]

Almost a decade after the *Groundwork*, in the essay on *Theory and Practice*, Kant seems to suggest a similar point by arguing that freedom is central to virtue because virtue "is that which nobody but man himself can give to or take away from himself," and therefore something that can never depend upon nature.[37]

As we saw, in Chapter 3, although Kant tries out such an argument in numerous notes from the 1770s, its connection to happiness is too simple for it to be the basis of Kant's view in the *Groundwork*. The *Groundwork* denies that absolute value can ever

---

[36] *R* 7202 (*Duisburg Nachlass* 6), 19:278. The *Akademie* edition, that is, Erich Adickes, assigned this to the 1780s without finer discrimination. A translation of it is also provided in Paul Arthur Schilpp, *Kant's Pre-Critical Ethics*, 2d ed. (Evanston, Ill.: Northwestern University Press, 1960), pp. 127–30. Schilpp, following Paul Menzer, dated it to 1775 but gave no argument for so doing. Schilpp's translation of the paragraph I have quoted is radically misleading, translating *Selbstzufriedenheit* as "self-sufficiency" rather than "self-satisfaction" and thus masking the problem I am about to point out.

[37] *On the Common Saying: That Might Be Right in Theory but Not in Practice*, 8:283n.

be found in happiness, whereas the argument of *R 7202* and others of the preceding decade seem to consist just in the assertion that our own free will is a *more reliable source* of happiness – "satisfaction" or "self-satisfaction," as Kant says – than any external object of nature. To be sure, the argument against the moral significance of happiness in both the *Groundwork* and *Critique of Practical Reason* turns at least in part on the premise that what will constitute the happiness of any individual is uncertain and contingent, and setting one's happiness in one's own freedom may obviate this problem to some degree. But even so, if freedom is seen as a reliable condition for happiness, then that will yield only a reason for valuing *one's own* freedom, not freedom in *general*. So it seems most unlikely that this Stoic argument for the independence of happiness which is rooted in freedom from the vagaries of nature could be Kant's main argument in his mature writings.

And indeed, although Kant may appear to reproduce this kind of argument in the *Critique of Practical Reason*, in fact its meaning is subtly changed:

> Does one not have a word that designates not a pleasure [*Genuß*] like that of happiness but yet a delight in one's own existence, an analog of happiness, which must necessarily accompany the consciousness of virtue? Yes! this word is *self-contentment*. . . . Freedom and the consciousness of it as a capacity to follow the moral law with an overpowering disposition is *independence from inclinations*, at least as determining (if not *affecting*) grounds of our desire, and, so far as I am conscious of it in following my moral maxims, the sole source of an unalterable contentment connected with it and resting on no particular feeling. (*CPracR*, 5:117–18)

Here Kant does not suggest that freedom is morally valuable because it can produce a kind of contentment that is independent of the vagaries of happiness dependent on nature; on the contrary, he suggests that freedom produces such a happiness because of our consciousness of its moral significance. This argument presupposes, rather than providing a moral account of, the absolute value of freedom.

Kant does, however, suggest another argument for the absolute value of the freedom of rational agency – the teleological argument that freedom or autonomy rather than mere happiness is the ultimate end of nature and our own ultimate end because nature somehow makes it so.

As is well known, Kant employs a teleological argument for the absolute value of the good will in Section I of the *Groundwork*. Here he argues that because nature gives us nothing without purpose but obviously did not give us the faculty of reason for the pursuit of happiness, since reason is not particularly effective at achieving that end, it must have given us reason for the sake of the development of the good will instead (*G*, 4:395–96). Because this argument occurs in the allegedly merely intuitive exposition of the first section, it is usually dismissed as not entirely serious.

However, Kant hints at the same sort of argument about the purpose of freedom itself in any number of key passages that cannot be so lightly dismissed. For instance, Kant summarizes his discussion of humanity as an end in itself in the second section of the *Groundwork* thus:

> Now when we look back over all previous efforts that have been undertaken to discover the principle of morality, it is no wonder that they must have failed. One saw the human being bound to law through his duty, but it did not occur to one that he is subject *only to his own yet universal legislation*, and that he is bound to act only in accordance with his own will, which is yet, in accord with the end of nature [*dem Naturzwecke nach*], a universally legislative will. (*G*, 4:432)

Here Kant suggests that the autonomous will freely legislating universal laws for itself is itself the end of nature. Although he does not explicitly say that freedom itself is the end of nature and intrinsically valuable for that reason, it is hard to see how it could only be the universal legislation and not also the freedom in so legislating which is the end of nature.

The same sort of teleological argument, though put in terms of good and evil instead of universal law, also occurs in the *Critique of Practical Reason*, only a page before Kant's argument for the deontological rather than teleological method in ethics:

> [The human being] is yet not so completely an animal as to be indifferent to everything that reason says for itself and to use it merely as an instrument for the satisfaction of his needs as a sensuous being. For the fact that he has reason would not elevate him in value above mere animality at all if he used reason only for the sake of that which instinct accomplishes in animals: it would then only be a particular way that nature had made use of in order to equip man for the same end which it had made the vocation of animals, without giving him a higher end for his vocation. Given his natural constitution, he no doubt needs reason in order to take account of his weal and woe, but he also has it for a higher purpose, not merely to take into consideration what is in itself good and evil, about which pure, not sensuously interested reason alone can judge, but rather to distinguish entirely the judgment of reason [from that of sensuous interest] and to make it the highest condition of the latter. (*CPracR*, 5:61–62)

Here again the argument is that nature cannot have given man reason for the same purpose as animal instinct, yet it has not given him reason without any purpose, so its purpose must be morality itself. And here Kant stresses in addition that, although the fundamental purpose of reason must be given to us by nature, its intrinsic value consists in nothing less than the fact that it elevates us above mere nature.

A teleological argument for the ultimate value of autonomy is intimated in other writings from the same period as the *Groundwork* as well. For example, it is the key to Kant's argument for natural evolution toward political and international constitutionalism in the essay *Idea for a Universal History from a Cosmopolitan Point of View*, where it is presented as Kant's Third Thesis:

> Nature has willed: that human kind should bring forth entirely out of itself everything that goes beyond the mechanical arrangement of his animal existence, and that he should partake of no other happiness or perfection than that which he creates for himself through his own reason free of instinct. (8:19)

Here the purpose of man's nature is described as nothing less than man's free use of his own reason to produce everything that elevates him above the level of animal existence. Even where what might be thought of as the normal material ends of human action are concerned, namely happiness and perfection, Kant stresses that there is an extra requirement that these be produced out of our own freedom, and that it is our end to so produce them because it is nature's end for us. Our conception of absolute value seems to derive from that of nature.[38]

Finally, the completion of Kant's critical philosophy in the *Critique of Judgment* culminates with nothing less than the statement that humanity is the ultimate end of nature as a system of purposes precisely because of its capacity for freely setting its own ends.[39] In his discussion of teleological judgment, Kant argues that individual organisms may be seen as systems in virtue of the relations among their parts, and groups of organisms as systems insofar as some of them serve purposes of the others; but nature as a whole can be seen as a system only if the whole of it can be seen as in the service of something that is an end in itself (§82). Such an end can be found in man, Kant argues, but not in the end of his happiness, which is obviously not a particular end of nature at all: as regards happiness, "nature is so far from having selected man as its special favorite and favored him with well-being above all other animals that it has on the contrary spared him as little as every other animal from destructive effects, in pestilence, hunger, danger of flood, frost, attack from other animals large and small, and so on" (§83, 5:430). Apparently the only thing that nature has given to man that is different from what it has given to everything else is freedom itself:

> There remains among all of his purposes in nature as that which can be regarded as the final end which lies outside of it and which can therefore be regarded as its ultimate end only [humanity's] formal, subjective condition, namely its aptitude for setting ends in general for itself and (independent of nature in its determination of ends) employing nature as a means appropriate to the maxims of its free ends in general. (§83, 5:431)

---

[38] For further discussion of the Third Thesis of the essay on history, see Chapter 11.

[39] That it will culminate here is suggested in the Introduction to the *Critique of Judgment*, 5:195–96.

The ultimate end of nature can be nothing less than the freedom by means of which mankind alone can step outside of or beyond nature and freely put nature to use for purposes of its own choosing. The only natural capacity unique to humankind is its potential to free itself from mere nature by the exercise of its freedom.

This teleological argument for human freedom as the ultimate end of nature undoubtedly attracted Kant from an early stage. But it should also be clear that, by ultimately positioning this argument in the *Critique of Judgment*, Kant was explicitly acknowledging that it cannot be given the force of a constitutive proof of theoretical or practical reason, but is only a regulative principle for the conduct of our own faculty of judgment: "The faculty of judgment's concept of a finality of nature is to be counted among concepts of nature, but only as a regulative principle of the cognitive faculty" (5:197). As a regulative ideal, the conception of the absolute value of freedom can serve to motivate our practical behavior and guide it toward rational coherence, just as the regulative ideal of the systematicity of natural laws can serve to guide as well as motivate our theoretical inquiry. But no more than it can be transcendentally deduced that nature is intrinsically systematic can it be proved that nature really has this purpose apart from our own judgment. This purpose is ultimately a conception by means of which we ourselves can make sense of our own nature, not something that nature imposes upon us.[40] By seeing our freedom as the ultimate end of nature, we can give ourselves a dignity that we lack as mere organisms of nature, or elevate ourselves above nature, but nature itself cannot force us to dignify ourselves in this way, nor can any theoretical proposition about nature force us to see ourselves in this way.

Indeed, if any natural fact could force us into the dignity of freedom, that dignity would thereby be undermined: in Kant's view freedom is intrinsically valuable because it is ultimately by our freedom that we distinguish ourselves from the rest of nature,

---

[40] Christine Korsgaard appeals to the *Critique of Judgment*'s discussion of the ultimate end of nature to confirm the significance of earlier expressions of teleology in Kant's ethical writings as well ("Kant's Formula of Humanity," p. 202). She does not observe the radical implications of this context, however.

which merely seeks contentment or happiness. Kant makes this point, no doubt obscurely enough, by saying that we may be the *ultimate* end (*letzter Zweck*) of nature in virtue of our freedom, but that our freedom is the *final* end (*Endzweck*) of ourselves. What he means by an ultimate end is simply that to which everything else in nature is merely a means, and that can itself be something in nature; but what he means by a final end is "an end that needs no other as the condition of its possibility," which is thus not dependent on nature or "an end that nature itself is sufficient to effect and bring forth in accord with its idea, because it is unconditioned."[41] This is to say that human freedom cannot itself be brought forth by nature, although it may be the only thing that lends any value to nature; and if human freedom cannot itself be brought about by nature, it is hard to suppose that its value can be imposed on us by nature. Although nature may somehow point us in this direction, it can only be we ourselves who place absolute value in our freedom and bring this value to nature. Thus we can never simply appeal to the ends of nature to prove the unconditional value of freedom. The *Critique of Judgment* is not a simple reassertion of the teleological argument but rather a sorrowful good-bye to it.[42]

At the very outset of his career we saw that Kant declared that the fundamental principle of morality must be indemonstrable.[43] Even after he shifted the basis of value from feeling to freedom, he was forced to the same conclusion. Indeed, it seems clear that he knew this all along – in the lectures of natural law from 1784 he had plainly stated that "The freedom of the [human] being must be presupposed if it is to be an end in itself. Such a being must therefore have freedom of the will. How I am to comprehend it, I do not know; yet it is a necessary hypothesis if I am to think

---

[41] *CJ*, §84, 5:434–35.

[42] The issues raised in the past several paragraphs are further discussed in my article "The Unity of Nature and Freedom: Kant's Conception of the System of Philosophy," in Sally S. Sedgwick, ed., *Systematicity in Kant and German Idealism* (Cambridge: Cambridge University Press, forthcoming).

[43] See Chapter 1.

of rational beings as ends in themselves."[44] Only by seeing ourselves as free can we import a source of unconditional value into
the world or, in Kant's obviously deeply felt way of putting it, elevate ourselves above the level of mere animal existence. But no
argument can prove to us that we must look at ourselves in this
way: we cannot derive this self-conception from some more fundamental value; we cannot really prove that it is the ultimate purpose of nature; even if we could, no acknowledgment of a fundamental value as the ultimate principle of our behavior could be
forced upon us by a mere theoretical fact anyway; and if our freedom could be forced upon us by any theoretical fact about nature,
then it would not be freedom and would lose its absolute value
after all. But the regulative ideal of the intrinsic value of our freedom may nevertheless be the most coherent basis for all of our
judgments of value.

[44] *Naturrecht Feyerabend,* 27:1322.

Chapter 5
The Possibility of the Categorical Imperative

I THE FORMULATIONS OF THE CATEGORICAL IMPERATIVE AND THEIR PROBLEMS

In spite of two centuries of study and many fine commentaries, Kant's *Groundwork for the Metaphysics of Morals*[1] remains a deeply perplexing book. Several of its most vexing difficulties concern Kant's intentions in its second part. Here Kant indicates that he takes himself to be offering three different formulations of the fundamental principle of morality – a principle that we human beings call the "categorical imperative" (CI) because it presents itself as an obligatory constraint to creatures like us, whose will, because of our liability to inclination, is not necessarily determined by the pure principle of morality (*G*, 4:413). But there are many questions about these three formulations of CI – about which ones they are,

---

This chapter originally appeared in *Philosophical Review* 104 (1995): 353–85.

[1] Translations are my own, although many are influenced by those of H. J. Paton, *Immanuel Kant: Groundwork of the Metaphysics of Morals* (New York: Harper and Row, 1964), originally entitled *The Moral Law* (London: Hutchinson, 1948). I comment on my divergences from Paton only where I think his version is actually misleading. I like Paton's translation of Kant's title because it preserves the sense of active effort implied by Kant's gerundive *"Grundlegung"* better than such passive translations as *Fundamental Principles of the Metaphysics of Morals* (T. K. Abbott) or *Foundations of the Metaphysics of Morals* (Lewis White Beck), without employing Ellington's neologism "grounding."

about the relationships that Kant intended to establish among them, about the basis from which he thought he could derive them and the manner in which he intended them to be derived from this basis, and about the relationship between the argument for and about the three formulations of CI in *Groundwork* II and the argument of the remainder of the book, especially the argument of *Groundwork* III.

The first difficulty is the question of just *which* statements of CI Kant takes to be its three primary formulations. In his initial enumeration of the formulations, Kant suggests that the three fundamental formulations are what have come to be known as the Formula of Universal Law (FUL), "*Act only on that maxim through which you can at the same time will that it should become a universal law*" (*G*, 4:421), the Formula of Humanity as an End in Itself (FHE), "*Act so that you always use humanity, in your own person as well as in the person of every other, never merely as a means, but at the same time as an end*" (*G*, 4:429), and the Formula of Autonomy (FA), which Kant does not initially state in the grammatical form of an imperative but rather in the form of "the Idea *of the will of every rational being as a universally legislating will*" (*G*, 4:431). In introducing this third formula, Kant explicitly calls it "the third practical principle of the will, as the supreme condition of the conformity of the will with universal practical reason" (*G*, 4:431), and on the next page he reiterates his designation of it as the "present third formulation of the principle" of morality (*G*, 4:432). However, after next stating that "[t]he concept of every rational being, that it must consider itself as universally legislating through all the maxims of its will, . . . leads to a very fruitful concept which depends on it, namely that of *a kingdom of ends*" (*G*, 4:433), Kant adds a review of "the three ways that have been adduced of representing the principle of morality" in which what he treats as the third formulation of CI is not the Formula of Autonomy that he originally so classified but rather a principle employing the idea of a kingdom of ends that he has just said is derived from the Formula of Autonomy, namely the principle "[t]hat all maxims from our own legislation ought to harmonize into a possible kingdom of ends, as a kingdom of nature" (*G*, 4:436), which we can call the Formula of the Kingdom of

Ends (FKE).[2] So what are the three main formulations of CI according to Kant himself – FUL, FHE, and FA, as he says at *G*, 4: 431–32, or FUL, FHE, and FKE, as he says at *G*, 4:436? And is this a significant question, or is the difference between FA and FKE insignificant?[3]

[2] Note that here Kant does formulate his principle in something approximating the grammatical form of an imperative, which he did not do in the introduction of FA. Note that here there is also some significance to my departure in several particulars from Paton, who writes, "All maxims as proceeding from our own making of law ought to harmonize with a possible kingdom of ends as a kingdom of nature." First, in agreement with Thomas Pogge, I translate Kant's *zu* more literally as "into" rather than as "with" in order to convey the idea that the kingdom of ends is an ideal we strive to bring about through our actions, not a preexisting reality with which we merely attempt to comply; see his "The Categorical Imperative," in *Grundlegung der Metaphysik der Sitten: Ein kooperativer Kommentar*, ed. Ottfried Höffe (Frankfurt: Klostermann, 1989), pp. 172–93, at p. 186. Second, I preserve Kant's comma between "kingdom of ends" and "kingdom of nature," in order to preserve the appearance that the latter phrase is in apposition to the former, not introducing any fundamentally new requirement in addition to the idea of a kingdom of ends itself but rather suggesting that our aim from the outset is always to *realize* the ideal of a kingdom of ends in our actual actions, that is, in the kingdom of nature.

[3] In suggesting that there are *four* formulations of CI the relationships among which must be understood, I would appear to be ignoring the well-known position of H. J. Paton that there are *five* different formulations: in addition to the four I have listed (which he called formulae I [FUL], II [FHE], III [FA], and IIIa [FKE]), Paton also considered as a distinct formulation (Ia) what he called the Formula of the Law of Nature, "Act as if the maxim of your action were to become through your will a *universal law of nature*" (*G*, 4:421). Paton thought that formula Ia added an indispensably teleological conception of nature and thus of the *natural* purposes of humans to the purely formal requirement of universalizability in formula I (see *The Categorical Imperative: A Study in Kant's Moral Philosophy* [London: Hutchinson, 1947], pp. 149–52). But Kant himself does not refer to this as a separate formulation of CI in his catalogs at *G*, 4:431–32 or 436. This is because, as Philip Stratton-Lake has most recently argued, on Kant's own view formula Ia does not add any teleological assumptions not included in formula I, but merely expresses the "typic" or condition of the possibility of its application: that is, in considering whether a law is universalizable, the task set for us by formula I, we do not need to refer to any ends actually set by nature, human or otherwise, but only to consider whether the world that would be defined by the universalization of the maxim being tested by FUL would actually be consistent with the realization of the end for the sake of which the adoption of that maxim is being considered. See Stratton-Lake, "Formulating

The next question that arises is, whatever precisely Kant thinks that the three main formulations of CI are, how in his view are they related? Kant's own explicit statement on this issue is doubly confusing. First, he claims that FUL, FHE, and FKE are "merely so many formulations of precisely the same law," differing only in that the latter two "bring an idea of reason nearer to intuition" (*G*, 4:436) and thus help "secure acceptance for the moral law" (*G*, 4:437), whereas the first furnishes the "strict method" most useful for actual "moral *judgment*" or decision making (*G*, 4:436). On this account, the three formulas would seem to be equivalent in their theoretical significance, although they would apparently have different roles in moral judgment, where FUL would dominate, and in moral education, where it looks as if FHE and FA and/or FKE should have the more significant role. However, Kant immediately follows this denial of a significant theoretical difference among the three formulations with the suggestion that they do play theoretically distinct and irreducible roles in the elucidation of the principle of morality: he says that FUL specifies the *"form"* of morally appropriate maxims, "which consists in their universality"; FHE specifies their *"matter* – that is, an end" to be achieved through the adoption of moral maxims; and only FKE offers "a *complete determination* of all maxims" by completing the "progression . . . through the categories of the *unity* of the form of will (its universality), of the *multiplicity* of its matter (of its objects, i.e., its ends), and of the *allness* or totality of the system thereof" (*G*, 4:436). But since Kant uses the contrast between "form" and "matter" in so many different ways throughout his corpus, and since he makes clear elsewhere what he means by the complete determination of a *concept of an object* but not what he might mean by the complete determination of a *principle* (or even that there

Categorical Imperatives," *Kant-Studien* 84 (1993): 316–40, at pp. 322–23; also, Bruce Aune had earlier argued (in *Kant's Theory of Morals* [Princeton: Princeton University Press, 1979], pp. 111–16) that Ia is merely the "typic" of I. This argument clearly holds in those cases where the universalization of a proposed maxim would lead to what Kant calls a contradiction in conception, or a self-contradiction (*G*, 4:424); it may not hold in the case of a contradiction in willing, where the universalization of a maxim is not obviously self-contradictory but would undercut ends that every rational will is assumed to have.

could be any such thing),[4] it is not at all clear what actually is meant by this explanation of the theoretically distinct contributions of the three formulations to our understanding of the fundamental principle of morality.

But our problems in understanding the argument of *Groundwork* II only begin with this obscure statement. Further problems are raised by some of Kant's other statements about the character of his argument in *Groundwork* II and its relation to the argument of *Groundwork* III.

Early in the argument of *Groundwork* II, Kant states that he intends to ground the principle of morality in the concept of rational being in general and not in any specific features of human nature (*G*, 4:412). Still early in his exposition, after he has introduced the contrast between hypothetical and categorical imperatives but before he begins the series of formulations of CI, Kant indicates that there are two different questions about the possibility of CI that he will need to solve. He writes:

> The question now arises: how are all these imperatives possible? This question does not demand to know how the execution of the action that the imperative commands can be conceived, but rather merely how the necessitation of the will can be conceived which the imperative expresses in the task [which it sets]. (*G*, 4:417)

I take this to be a reference to the difference between the tasks Kant assigns to the Second and Third Parts of the *Groundwork: Groundwork* III will be concerned with the question of how it is possible for *us human beings* actually to execute CI, that is, act in compliance with it; but before that question can be reached there is a more general question about how it is possible for *any rational being* to will to act in compliance with CI that must be answered – only this brief remark does not make very clear exactly what this preliminary question is.

Likewise, in the transition from discussing FUL to discussing FHE and then again in the transition from FHE to FA and FKE, Kant each time suggests that there is a question about the possi-

[4] See *Critique of Pure Reason*, A 133/B 172.

bility of a categorical imperative that needs to be resolved within *Groundwork* II and its discussion of rational being in general, thus prior to the argument of *Groundwork* III that we are beings to whom this concept of rational being does apply. Kant concludes his discussion of FUL and his presentation of the four examples of the kinds of duties that arise from it by saying:

> We have thus at least shown that if duty is a concept which is to have meaning and real legislation for our actions, this can be expressed only in categorical imperatives, by no means in hypothetical ones. . . . But we have still not come so far as to prove *a priori* that there actually is an imperative of this kind. . . . (*G*, 4:425)

Considered by itself, this might be taken as an allusion to the issue that remains to be settled in *Groundwork* III; but a page later Kant says:

> The question is therefore this: is it a necessary law *for all rational beings* always to judge their actions in accordance with maxims they themselves can will that they should serve as universal laws? If there is such a law, it must already be connected (entirely *a priori*) with the concept of the will of a rational being in general. But in order to discover this connection one must, however much one may bristle, take a step beyond it, namely, into metaphysics, although into a region of it that is different from speculative philosophy, namely, into the metaphysics of morals. (*G*, 4:426)

The second remark suggests that there is a fundamental question about the possibility of *any* rational being willing to adopt FUL that must be answered within the confines of *Groundwork* II and its metaphysics of morals[5] before we reach the question of whether

---

[5] Note that the "Transition from Popular Moral Philosophy to a Metaphysics of Morals" takes place in *Groundwork* II (*G*, 4:406), whereas *Groundwork* III contains the "Transition from a Metaphysics of Morals to a Critique of Pure Practical Reason" (*G*, 4:446). Like the subsequent *Critique of Practical Reason* of 1788 (which supersedes it), the transition to a critique of pure practical reason in *Groundwork* III concerns not the content of the principle of morality but the fact of our own freedom to act in accordance with the canon of rationality which

we are rational beings bound by CI. Kant then immediately proceeds to the discussion of FHE, thereby suggesting that the introduction of the idea of an end in itself is a necessary step in the demonstration of the very *possibility* of any rational agent, not just us, being bound and moved by CI. Again, however, it remains unclear just *what* question about the possibility of any rational being acting in accord with CI Kant is raising.

Similarly, Kant's transition to FA after his second discussion of his four examples following his statement of FHE also suggests that there is an outstanding question about the possibility of the principle of morality for any rational being that must be answered within *Groundwork* II rather than within *Groundwork* III. Kant's characterization of FA as the "supreme condition" of the conformity of the will with universal practical reason (*G*, 4:431) suggests that now this third principle adds another essential condition of the *possibility* of any rational being actually willing in accord with CI that must be in hand before it can be demonstrated that we ourselves are rational beings subject to the moral law and capable of complying with it. Kant amplifies this suggestion when he says:

> Imperatives as previously represented, namely that of the universal lawfulness of actions similar to *an order of nature*,[6] [and] that of the universal *supremacy as ends* of rational beings in themselves, did, just insofar as they were represented as categorical, exclude from their proper authority every mixture of interest as an incentive;[7] they were, however, merely *assumed* to

that principle expresses. As Kant's remarks at *G*, 4:426–27, indicate, a metaphysics of morals is metaphysical because it shows a moral *principle* to be *a priori* rather than empirical, not because it adduces a metaphysical conception of the moral *agent*. The transition to a metaphysics of morals in *Groundwork* II thus concerns the content of the principle of morality, and the present remarks thus suggest that there is a question about the possibility of CI that needs to be answered by a synthetic proposition about rational beings in general, not the synthetic proposition about ourselves that is to be demonstrated in *Groundwork* III.

6 This sentence provides additional evidence for the view that Paton's formula Ia is not meant to be essentially distinct from formula I: the order of nature is only an analogy for the order of universal law, not anything additional to it.

7 *Triebfeder*. Paton translates this here as "motive," although he elsewhere translates it as "incentive" which connotes a motive based in sensuous inclination.

be categorical. . . . But that there were practical propositions, which commanded categorically, could not itself be proved, any more than it can be proved in this chapter generally; but one thing could have been done, namely, to show that the renunciation of all interest in willing from duty, as the specific mark distinguishing a categorical from a hypothetical imperative, was expressed in the imperative itself by means of some determination that it contains, and this is what is done in the present third formulation of the principle. (*G*, 4:431–32)

Here Kant suggests that a critical condition for understanding the possibility of any rational being acting in accord with CI that is not addressed in either its first formulation as FUL or its second formulation as FHE, namely the possibility of any such being acting in accord with CI in spite of the renunciation of interest that CI demands, must be added as part of the metaphysics of morals of *Groundwork* II before he can proceed to the critique of practical reason and its proof of our own freedom in *Groundwork* III. Is this the question about the possibility of CI he has been referring to since *G*, 4:417, and is it the only such question?

Just as he suggests that there are two different questions about possibility that are to be answered in *Groundwork* II and III respectively, Kant also suggests that there are two different synthetic *a priori* propositions to be demonstrated in these two parts of the work. Thus, at the outset of *Groundwork* II, Kant suggests not only that the argument of this chapter must concern rational being in general rather than specific features of human nature, but also that this argument is to be entirely *analytical*, thus that all of the formulations of CI are to be derived from the *analysis of the concept* of a rational being in general: "since moral laws are to hold for every rational being in general, they are already to be derived from the universal concept of a rational being in general" (*G*, 4:412). This

---

But "motive" should be reserved for Kant's more general term *Bewegungsgrund* (literally, moving or motivating ground), of which a sensuous inclination is only one kind, and a ground originating in reason another. If *Triebfeder* is translated as "motive," then Kant's theory will end up implying that moral action has no motive, which he does not mean; what he means is that the motive of moral action must be rational rather than sensuous, that is, not a *Triebfeder*.

naturally suggests that it is only in *Groundwork* III that any synthetic, let alone synthetic *a priori*, proposition is to be proved; thus, *Groundwork* II seems to be intended to derive its several formulations of CI from an analysis of a concept of a rational being, and *Groundwork* III to prove that CI in its several formulations is binding *for us* by a proof of the synthetic proposition that *we are* rational beings who instantiate the concept that was analyzed in the preceding section. Yet in spite of Kant's claims that the argument of *Groundwork* II is entirely analytical and that a *"possible synthetic use of pure practical reason"* remains to be demonstrated in *Groundwork* III in order to demonstrate that "morality is something and not merely a chimerical idea without truth" (*G*, 4:445), there are also several passages in which he clearly suggests that there is a synthetic *a priori* proposition connected to CI that must be proved *within Groundwork* II. Thus, immediately preceding his formal introduction of FUL Kant says that "with the categorical imperative" we have "a synthetic-practical proposition *a priori*," a claim he explains by saying that in the categorical imperative, "without a presupposed condition from any inclination, I connect the deed with the will *a priori*, thus necessarily (although only objectively, i.e., under the idea of a reason which has full power over all subjective motivating causes)" (*G*, 4:420 and 420n). This statement suggests that the connection of the categorical imperative to the will of *any* rational being is synthetic rather than analytic, and that the synthetic proposition asserting the connection of the categorical imperative to the will of any rational being is not identical to the synthetic proposition to be demonstrated in *Groundwork* III that we humans are rational beings. But how can an analysis of a concept of rational being in general yield a synthetic connection between its will and CI?

We now see that we need to answer both a substantive question of *what* conditions of the possibility of action in accord with CI Kant believes are added to FUL by FHE and FA and/or FKE, and a technical question about *how* an analysis of the concept of rational being in general can yield a synthetic *a priori* connection between that concept and the categorical imperative. I use an analogy to the distinction between "logical" and "real" possibility in Kant's theoretical philosophy to frame my answer to these questions. According to this distinction, which Kant first used at the outset of his polemic with rationalism two decades before the publication of the *Critique of Pure Reason*,[8] the requirement that a concept satisfy the logical condition that it contain no self-contradiction is only one necessary condition for judging that it represents even a possible object; to determine that the object conceived by a concept is a real possibility also requires two other conditions: that it be conceived in accordance with the pure concepts of the understanding necessary to formulate the concept of an object of judgment (the categories), and that it be conceived in accordance with the forms of intuition through which any empirical intuition that could confirm the reality of such a concept would have to be given. As Kant puts his point in the first *Critique*'s "Postulates of Empirical Thought," where he is showing how the pure concepts of possibility, actuality, and necessity are to be schematized, or put into empirically applicable form,[9] the requirement that in a concept of anything as possible "there must be contained no contradiction is, to be sure, a necessary logical condition, but far from enough for the objective reality of the concept, i.e., the possibility of such an object as is thought through the concept" (A 220/B 267–68); instead, if the concept of possibility "is not to have a merely logical significance and express the form of *thought* analytically, but is to concern *things* and their possibility . . . , [it] must reach possible experience and its synthetic unity, in which alone objects of cognition are given" (A 219/B 267). Of course, the theoretical requirement that the concept of an empirically possible object must satisfy all the constraints imposed by the categories and the principles of judgment derived from them, as well as those derived from the forms of intuition, cannot be carried over without modification into practical philosophy, for it is no part of

[8] See *The Only Possible Argument in Support of a Demonstration of the Existence of God*, 2:77–78, in Immanuel Kant, *Theoretical Philosophy, 1755–1770*, ed. David Walford (Cambridge: Cambridge University Press, 1992), pp. 122–23.
[9] For an explanation of this interpretation of Kant's notion of schematism, see my *Kant and the Claims of Knowledge* (Cambridge: Cambridge University Press, 1987), pp. 157–72.

Kant's thought that we need to prove the empirical possibility of pure morality.[10] Rather, the analogy that I intend is that while Kant's initial formulation of CI as FUL states a purely formal constraint on practical reasoning, which we can compare with the logical constraint of noncontradiction in theoretical reasoning, and which may even suffice as a rule for moral judgment (as Kant suggests at *G*, 4:437), the further formulations of CI state conditions that are also necessary to make intelligible how the adoption of FUL by *any* rational agent can be possible in both of two different ways bearing a loose analogy to the two different ways in which the categories and the forms of intuition are conditions for the real possibility of a theoretical concept. These conditions of possibility must be specified before it is proved in *Groundwork* III that we ourselves are rational beings – a further step that would be analogous to proving the objective reality of a theoretical concept after it has been shown to define a real rather than merely logical possibility. Of course, in theoretical philosophy that further step would consist in adducing or constructing an actual intuition for the concept, whereas the proof of the reality of human freedom does not involve any appeal to intuition.

The two stages in the proof of the real possibility of CI for any rational being may be conceived in the following way. First, we may take Kant to be making tacit appeal to a concept of rational being from which it follows that any action of such a being must have not only a *form* or *rule* but also an *end* or *object* and also an *incentive* or *motive*, although of course not an empirical end or motive. Thus, while FUL may be seen as being derived from an analysis of the specific concept of a *moral* or *practical law*, Kant's argument for FHE presupposes an analysis of the broader concept of a *rational being* that states that a rational being never acts without an

[10] Here I have in mind, of course, Kant's famous claim, "It is absolutely impossible to establish through experience a single case with complete certainty where the maxims of an otherwise dutiful action have rested solely on moral grounds and on the representation of one's duty" (*G*, 4:407). And it is equally obvious that subjection to the universal law of causation, which is a necessary condition of the real possibility of empirical objects, is not going to be a necessary condition of the real possibility of action in accord with CI, but is instead in Kant's view incompatible with the latter.

end, or a goal to be achieved by its action, even where the action is one of adopting a principle, so that a rational being never adopts a principle without it being possible to characterize an end that is realized in or through that principle;[11] and his argument for FA turns on the need to specify a motive that can make it rational for such a being to adopt FUL. Thus, the very action of adopting FUL itself cannot be shown to be rational unless an end valid for rational being as such that can be realized both in and through compliance with FUL and a motive that can be satisfied by this compliance can be identified – a task quite distinct from showing that we human beings with all our sensuous inclinations are actually capable of complying with CI (the issue in *Groundwork* III and the *Critique of Practical Reason*). However, to make sense of Kant's claim that the connection of CI to the will of any rational being is synthetic, we need to assume that while an analysis of the concept of rational being is supposed to reveal the *need* for such an objective end and motive, Kant's designation of rationality (in the form of humanity) as the only end in itself that can give a reason for any rational being to accept FUL and his account of the dignity of autonomy as the basis of any rational being's interest in adopting FUL are intended to be seen as synthetic rather than analytic claims (even though his brief arguments for FHE and FA may leave obscure just *why* their conclusions should be synthetic rather than analytic). On this account, the synthetic *a priori* proposition demonstrated in *Groundwork* II – that any rational being has a ground to will to act in accord with FUL – would be a *different* synthetic *a priori* proposition from the proposition that is to be proved in *Groundwork* III – that we human beings *are* rational

---

[11] The phrase "in or through" is meant to suggest that the relationship between the adoption of the principle and the realization of an end need not be merely *instrumental*, in the sense that the adoption of the principle is merely a causally efficacious but logically independent means to the realization of the end, which might at least in principle be reached through other means; it might be *constitutive*, in the sense that the end is already attained in acting on the principle itself, and there is also no other way to attain the end. I subsequently argue that the end connected with the formal principle of universalizability is related to it in *both* of these ways. (I owe this way of putting my point to R. Jay Wallace.)

beings who are bound to act in accord with CI and are capable of doing so.

Second, I argue that Kant's discussion of FKE makes a further contribution to establishing the real possibility of action in accord with FUL for any rational being, analogous to showing that a theoretical concept is compatible with the forms of intuition or is schematizable. Although FA may provide an account of how any one rational being can have an interest in acting in accord with FUL, and thus adds to the account, begun in the discussion of FHE, of what it is that makes it rational for any being to adopt CI, it does not yet show that the formal requirement of universalizability and the end of respecting rational being as an end in itself are realizable in a domain consisting of a *manifold* of moral agents. What has to be shown here is that a multitude of agents always can find a single maxim of action acceptable to all in spite of whatever empirical interests may separate them. By postulating "the systematic combination of different rational beings through common laws," a "whole of all ends (of rational beings as ends in themselves) as well as of the individual ends that each may set for himself," which requires abstraction "from all personal differences of rational beings as well as all content of their private ends" (*G*, 4:433), FKE expresses the further assumption that must be made in order to ensure that a multitude of agents can actually formulate a universally acceptable maxim of actions, and thus that FUL can actually be applied to a domain of multiple agents. (This is again a theoretical question distinct from the factual question of whether we human beings with our divergent inclinations can actually comply with CI.)

Thus, FHE and FA on the one hand, and FKE on the other, describe two different essential conditions for the possibility of adopting FUL. My argument is thus that only the four formulations of CI taken together display all the conditions necessary to show that action in accord with CI is a real possibility for any rational agent, *a fortiori* a real possibility for ourselves if we are or are capable of acting as rational agents. In other words, my claim is that while FUL alone may suffice to define the *form* of CI, only FUL, FHE, FA, and FKE taken together suffice to conceive of the possibility of a realm of rational agents acting in compliance with CI, or to conceive of a possible object for the concept of CI.

This chapter is hardly intended to provide a complete assessment of Kant's arguments for his four formulations of CI and their plausibility, but only to provide an account of the relationship among these formulations that could serve as a framework for such an assessment.[12]

II THE FORMULA OF UNIVERSAL LAW

In particular, my interpretation does not claim anything novel about FUL itself, so here I make only two points necessary for my subsequent argument.

[12] This chapter further develops the approach to Kant's ethics suggested in Chapter, 4, while going beyond the interpretation of the relationship among the three formulations of CI sketched there. That chapter was written before I had seen "Leaving Deontology Behind," the final chapter of Barbara Herman's *The Practice of Moral Judgment* (Cambridge, Mass.: Harvard University Press, 1993), pp. 208–40. Both my earlier essay and this one share Herman's views (1) that "[f]or the alignment of morality with rationality to enable us to understand the special demands of morality . . . it must reveal the sense in which rationality as a regulative norm represents a distinctive conception of value" (p. 213), and (2) that both FHE and FA add to FUL conditions under which it is possible for CI to "'connect' substantive requirements on willings with the concept of the will of a rational being as such." Beyond my appeal to Kant's distinction between logical and real possibility for a framework for my interpretation, however, there will be another difference between Herman's account and mine. According to Herman, Kant's "successive formulations [of CI] interpret the arguments of the CI procedure in terms that reveal the aspects of rational agency that generate contradictions under universalization," thereby showing "*how* content is derived from the constraints of universal form for willing" (pp. 237–38). On this account, the several formulations of CI all analyze the same concept, but substantive information necessary for the successful use or application of the "CI procedure" is introduced only successively. I will not take a position here on whether the succession of formulations is necessary in order to derive substantive moral rules from the idea of CI. But I will argue that Kant progresses from an analysis of the concept of a moral law to an analysis of the concept of rational agency; that his argument is not exclusively analytic, but also includes a specification of the end for any rational agent that can be considered synthetic; and that both phases of this extended argument are necessary in order to explain the possibility of action in accord with CI, whatever substantive moral rules that entails, both for individual rational agents and for any community of rational agents.

185

There is no doubt that FUL is supposed to be reached by a strictly analytical argument, but there is room for question about what concept it is that the argument is supposed to analyze. However, we should notice that although Kant begins the argument of *Groundwork* II as a whole by saying that "moral principles" must be derived from the "concept of a rational being in general" (*G*, 4: 412), he introduces his first explicit statement of FUL by stating that "the formula . . . that contains the only proposition that can be a categorical imperative" can be derived analytically from the "mere concept of a categorical imperative" (*G*, 4:420), or of a moral law. His argument is that since the very idea of a CI excludes the possibility that the validity of its command is conditional upon any contingently occurring particular desire for an end, only the universal validity of an agent's maxim, as a purely formal feature of it, remains as that which can be commanded by the imperative:

> For since besides the law this imperative contains only the necessity of the maxim to conform to this law, but the law contains no condition to which it is limited, there is nothing left but the universality of a law in general to which the maxim ought to conform, which conformity alone the imperative properly represents as necessary. (*G*, 4:420–21)

This analysis turns on the prior definition of a categorical imperative as "one that would represent an action as objectively necessary for itself, without relation to another end" (*G*, 4:414). This argument itself can be seen as deriving from a prior stipulation that any genuine moral law must hold for all rational beings:

> If one does not wish to deny to the concept of morality all truth and all relation to any possible object, then one cannot dispute that its law is of such widespread significance that it must hold not merely for men but for all *rational beings in general*, not merely under contingent conditions and exceptions, but *absolutely necessarily*. (*G*, 4:408)

This suggests that FUL is reached by a two-staged analysis: first, the concept of morality entails the validity of its fundamental principle for all rational beings; then the argument continues that a principle valid for all rational beings cannot depend on any empirical condition, so an imperative that cannot depend upon any empirical condition can only command conformity to the idea of the universality of maxims as such.

On this account, the analysis of the concept of *morality* or *moral law* would stipulate the validity of a moral law for all rational beings, but would not itself require a complete analysis of the more complex concept of *rational being*. Thus, while Kant's argument seems simply to assume that any rational being should adopt the requirement of universality without mentioning an end that is served by so doing, this is not an objection to it, because the analysis of the concept of rational being itself that stipulates that a rational being must always have an end and a motive for its action has not yet been introduced. Only when this analysis has been broached does Kant need to introduce FHE and FA in order to explain the rationality of adopting FUL itself.

But before we can consider how FHE is introduced into Kant's argument, we need to consider whether Kant's analytical argument for FUL will *preclude* his subsequent argument for FHE. In the analysis thus far considered, Kant is clearly claiming that the idea of acting for any empirically given reason – thus, acting to bring about any *empirically given* end or objective – is incompatible with the idea of the universality of moral law. But he also seems to suggest that CI commands action without regard to *any* end at all, or that the requirement (established in *Groundwork* I) that the goodness of virtuous action lie within the action itself and its relation to CI as its principle means that its goodness is not connected to *any* end intended to be achieved by such action. The following seems to preclude a virtuous action's being a means to any end:

> All imperatives are formulas for the determination of an action that is necessary in accord with the principle of a will that is in some way good. Now if the action would be good merely *for something else* as a means, the imperative is *hypothetical*; if it is represented as good *in itself*, thus as necessary in a will that is in itself in accord with reason, as the principle thereof, then it is *categorical*. (G, 4:414)

And so does this claim, that a CI

[d]oes not concern the matter of action and that which should result from it, but rather the form and the principle from which it itself flows, and the essentially good in it consists in the disposition, let its consequence be what it may. (*G*, 4:416)

Such remarks seem to assert that a rational being acts without any regard to ends at all, and that the goodness of its actions is entirely independent of any end that may be achieved through them, arising instead solely from the kind of principle that is the motivation for them. In fact, however, the idea that a rational being wills in the absence of any end whatever is not only incompatible with the fuller analysis of the idea of rational agency Kant is going to introduce, but is also *not* implied by the analysis that has led to FUL.

First, the argument by which Kant reaches FUL actually excludes from the grounds for adopting a fundamental principle of morality only *empirically given* ends, not any sort of end altogether, for the obvious reason that a maxim adopted only in order to attain a particular empirically given end would be contingently rather than universally and necessarily valid.[13] What the concept of a CI excludes is not purpose as such, but any *arbitrary* purpose:

That which it is necessary to do in order merely for the attainment of an arbitrary aim [*einer beliebigen Absicht*] can itself be considered as contingent, and we can always free ourselves from the precept by giving up the aim; the unconditional command, on the contrary, leaves the will no arbitrary choice [*Belieben*] in regard to the opposite, thus it alone brings with it that necessity which we demand for a law. (*G*, 4:420)

Kant will make exactly this point when he subsequently introduces FHE: "The ends that a rational agent arbitrarily [*nach Belieben*] sets as *effects* of his action (material ends) are all only relative; for only their relation to a faculty of desire in a subject which is determined in a particular way gives them their value" (*G*, 4:427). Thus

---

[13] In other words, the argument for FUL is an attack upon *empiricism* in practical philosophy, parallel to Kant's attack on empiricism in theoretical philosophy, not an argument for the rationality of action without any end.

what needs to be excluded by CI is not all ends whatsoever, but only ends that agents arbitrarily adopt because of their contingent desires.[14]

The same pattern of argumentation is found in the *Critique of Practical Reason*, where Kant begins with the assumption that a practical principle must be universally valid (§1, 5:19), asserts that "[a]ll practical principles that presuppose an *object* (matter) of the faculty of desire as their determining ground are empirical" (§2, 5:21), and from that infers that a proper practical principle must determine the will through its form rather than its matter (§4, 5:27). Again, what is excluded is not the idea of an end as such – here Kant does not even use the word *Absicht* or *Zweck* – but only matter or object of the *faculty of desire*. In all of these passages, then, the logic of Kant's analysis entails only the independence of the principle of morality from any contingent and empirically given end, not the exclusion of any concept of end as such.

Kant's initial contrast between hypothetical and categorical imperatives may not make this point clear. Here he states that while hypothetical imperatives "represent the practical necessity of a possible action as a means to something else, whatever it may be," a CI represents "an action as objectively necessary for itself, without relation to another end" (*G*, 4:414), and that while a hypothetical imperative says "that an action is good for some *possible* or *actual* aim," a CI "declares the action as objectively necessary without relation to any aim, i.e., even without any other end" (*G*, 4:414–15). These statements seem to suggest that CI commands obedience from rational beings without reference to any end at all. But even in these statements, what Kant twice excludes is relation to *another* end, an end to which the action commanded would be a *mere* means. This leaves open the possibility that there may be an end achieved *in* the adoption of CI itself.

Likewise, a number of Kant's comments after his initial introduction of FUL make it clear that he does not mean CI to be adopted without any motivation whatsoever, but only without

---

[14] Cf. Herman's remark, "Purely formal principles do not have *no* content; they have *noncontingent* content" (*The Practice of Moral Judgment*, p. 217).

any contingent desire for an end as the motive for its adoption. Thus, after the derivation of his four examples of duty from FUL (*G*, 4:422–24), Kant claims to have shown only that if *duty* is a meaningful and authoritative concept, then it can be expressed only in categorical imperatives, but that it remains to be proved *a priori* "that there actually is an imperative of this kind." To prove that there actually is a CI, he says, requires showing "that there is a practical law which by itself commands absolutely and without all incentives [*Triebfedern*]" (*G*, 4:425). In the next three paragraphs, however, he makes clear, by saying it no fewer than ten times, that what he means by requiring that the practical law command without "all incentives" is that it command without any merely *empirical* and *contingent* incentives: feelings (*Gefühle*), propensities (*Hange*), inclination (*Neigung*), subjective causes (*subjektiven Ursachen*), and so on – in a word, without reference to the *special characteristic of human nature* (*G*, 4:425). All of these are empirical feelings directed to objects of contingent desire. What is required instead is that "if there is such" a law, it "be connected (entirely *a priori*) with the concept of a will of a rational being in general" (*G*, 4:426). To do this requires precisely that a *nonempirical* end be supplied through which a rational being in general could be moved to adopt CI or to connect the law to its will, a noncontingent end that could be the object of a nonempirical motive. Kant states that "if *reason for itself alone* determines conduct (the possibility of which we will now investigate)," then "everything related to the empirical of itself falls away" (*G*, 4:427). I suggest we read this to mean that all empirical ends fall away when reason supplies a nonempirical end through which FUL can be connected to the will of a rational being.

Finally, the same point emerges at the outset of Kant's introduction of FHE. Here Kant says, "Practical principles are *formal* if they abstract from all subjective ends; they are, however, *material* if they are grounded on the latter, thus on certain incentives" (*G*, 4:427). This implies that a formal principle such as FUL does not have to be adopted without regard to all ends whatsoever, but only without regard to "subjective" ends, that is, those set by merely empirical incentives.

III THE FORMULA OF HUMANITY
AS AN END IN ITSELF

My next claim is that Kant's discussion of FHE represents the first step beyond FUL into the metaphysics of morals announced at G, 4:426, or, better, a two-step, in which he first asserts that a fuller analysis of the concept of the will of a rational being in general than has yielded FUL shows the necessity of a nonempirical concept of an end for a rational being as such, produced out of the resources of reason alone, and then, in a move that is intended to yield a synthetic proposition, argues that rational being itself is the only such nonempirical end. The provision of this end thus supplies a further necessary condition for the rationality of any agent's adoption of CI, or for the real possibility of CI.

Kant makes it plain at the outset of his discussion of FHE that his analysis of rational agency is more complex than has been revealed by FUL. He first characterizes the will, "a faculty to be encountered only in rational beings," as the faculty "of determining oneself to action in accord with *the representation of certain laws*" – which may be taken to sum up FUL – but then adds that there must also be an end, "which serves the will as the objective[15] ground of its self-determination" (G, 4:427). A rational will does not act on a law without any end in sight – that would be the paradigm of irrationality. If CI were already connected to the will of a rational being, then any end *compatible* with it might suffice for rational action; but if CI itself remains to be connected to rational willing, then what is needed is an end that can itself make acceptance of this law reasonable for any rational being. Thus, if there is to be a universally valid practical law, there must be an end that is universally valid, and such an end must be given by reason itself. Such an end would have "an absolute value" or be an "end

---

[15] Paton proposes that "objective" be replaced by "subjective," meaning roughly "in the subject" rather than having a ground in objects, which sense he claims is "rare" in Kant (*Groundwork*, 94 n. 63.2). But this would destroy the sense of Kant's argument, which is that if it is to be rational for any agent to determine its will in accord with an objective law such as FUL, then there must be an objectively valid end that can serve as its reason for so doing.

in itself" in that its value would not derive from any subjective, arbitrary, or material desire. And, Kant plainly states, "in it and it alone would lie the ground of a possible categorical imperative" (*G*, 4:428). Without the existence of such an objectively and universally valid end it would not be possible, on an analysis of a rational agent as one that both conforms its will to a law and has an objectively valid end, for such a being to adopt CI, in the sense that it would not be intelligible why such a being should do so. Thus the provision of an objectively valid end is a necessary condition of the real possibility of action on CI.

Kant characterizes in at least four different ways the objective end of reason he now introduces: "man and in general every rational being"; "rational beings that can be called *persons*" (both *G*, 4:428); "*rational nature*"; and "*humanity in your own person as well as in the person of everyone else.*" "Rational nature" is the fundamental characterization, and the other formulations are derivative from this: a being is a person insofar as it has rational nature, and "humanity" here connotes not the properties essential to humans as members of a biological species but rather the rationality that makes biological humans persons.[16] Thus, Kant's claim is that rationality itself is the end for rational willing in general, objective in the two distinct senses of describing an end for action and being universally valid, which makes it possible for a rational being to adopt CI as its maxim. For the purposes of this chapter, I assume without further argument that making rational being an end in itself requires the preservation and promotion of freedom, and that the realization of this end is achieved (at least in part) through the adoption of FUL, whose requirement of universal acceptability preserves the possibility of *consent* on the part of all agents affected by any agent's proposed maxim.[17] Here the only issue I

---

[16] Thus, "humanity" and "personality," which are distinguished in the *Religion* to connote self-love and rationality respectively (6:27), are here used synonymously to connote rationality only.

[17] For discussion of the normative implications of Kant's conception of rational being as an end in itself, see especially Thomas E. Hill Jr., "Humanity as an End in Itself," *Ethics* 91 (1980): 84–90, reprinted in his *Dignity and Practical Reason in Kant's Moral Theory* (Ithaca: Cornell University Press, 1992), pp. 38–57, and see also Chapter 4 in this volume. In the most general terms, Kant's conception

can discuss is how we are to understand the way in which Kant introduces this claim into the argument of *Groundwork* II. Kant introduces FHE by blandly stating, "Now I say: man and in general every rational being *exists* as end in itself" (*G*, 4:427). But what is the status of this assertion?

of rational being as an end in itself requires that we *preserve* rational being, both by avoiding the destruction of the *existence* of rational beings (whether ourselves or others) and by preserving the possibility of the *exercise* of rational agency in the form of *consent* to our actions (*G*, 4:429–30), but also that we go beyond these essentially negative duties by *promoting* the development of rational nature *in* rational beings, that is, doing what we can to advance the development of both our own and others' *capacity to act rationally* (see *MM*, 6:427) – in our own case, for example, by developing talents that will allow us to satisfy rationality's demand that we develop the means that will allow us to attain our morally permissible ends, whatever they may turn out to be.

FHE is sometimes taken to entail only that the *existence* of rational being is never to be acted against, which would furnish us with a *constraint* on our permissible actions but would not supply any positive goal that could itself be an end of rational agency instead of or in addition to ends determined by naturally occurring desires. In support of such an interpretation, H. J. Paton appeals to a passage in which Kant says, in Paton's translation (p. 105), that "the end must here be conceived, not as an end to be produced, *but as a self-existent end.* It must therefore be conceived only negatively – that is, as an end against which we should never act" (*G*, 4:437). Paton interprets this to mean that "[a]n objective and absolute end could not be a product of our will; for no mere product of our will can have absolute value. An end in itself must therefore be a self-existent end, not something to be produced by us." (Paton, *The Categorical Imperative*, p. 168; see also Bruce Aune, *Kant's Theory of Morals*, p. 76). What we can do with respect to such a self-existent end, however, since we cannot bring it into existence, is just to refrain from damaging or destroying its existence. Thus Paton interprets FHE as implying only a limitation on our actions, not as itself giving us a positive goal for action, and thus as not advancing Kant's argument past FUL (*The Categorical Imperative*, p. 178).

But this interpretation – although it explains why Paton thinks that Kant must rely on a teleological conception of natural ends in order to introduce any positive rather than merely negative duties (i.e., why he thinks there is a difference between his formula Ia and formula I) – rests on a misleading translation and on taking Kant's remark out of context. First, the sentence I have quoted is preceded by this: "In the idea of a will which is absolutely good without any limiting condition (of the attainment of this or that end) there must be abstraction from all ends *to be effected* [*zu bewirkenden Zwecke*] (as would make every will only relatively good" (p. 437). This should again be read to exclude only particular, contingently good ends, which would make the will to produce

Kant might seem to be reaching this assertion by an argument by elimination, in which case his procedure in arguing for FHE would be analogous to his method of argument for FUL. Just as there the formal requirement of universalizability was reached by the exclusion of all empirical maxims, so here the idea that reason itself is the end of reason could be seen as being reached by the exclusion of everything else as an end for universally valid willing simply on the ground that any other end would be empirically given and therefore not universally valid. This might look like another merely analytical argument, yielding a merely analytical conclusion rather than a synthetic connection between FUL and the will of any rational being. However, we must be intended to see the proposition that rational being is an end in itself as a fundamental synthetic *a priori* proposition, which could give rise to the further synthetic *a priori* proposition that the adoption of FUL is rational for any rational being, because FUL gives the form of the law that must be adhered to if the end of preserving and promoting rational being is to be attained, but that cannot itself be deduced by any antecedent argument. There are two ways in which we might be supposed to be intended to see this proposition as synthetic *a priori*. On the one hand, Kant's method in the *Groundwork* might be intended to be analogous to his method in the *Pro-*

them merely relatively rather than absolutely good. Second, what Kant actually writes in the sentence at issue is not that the end of an absolutely good will is *self-existent* but that it is *selbstständig*, that is, *self-sufficient* or *independent*. (The latter is Lewis White Beck's translation; see *The Foundations of the Metaphysics of Morals* [Indianapolis: Bobbs-Merrill, 1959], p. 56). This again suggests that Kant's claim is that the value of the good will is independent of particular, contingent ends, not that it is the kind of thing that cannot be brought into existence by our own action. Thus, Kant's remark that the end of moral action has to be conceived "negatively" as something that is not to be "acted against" has to be interpreted in the context of his aim in the whole paragraph, which is to show that FHE and FUL specify coextensive sets of duties. Kant has already clearly admitted positive duties to improve and promote the conditions of rational willing as well as negative duties not to destroy instances of rational nature. Thus he must mean here only that both the negative and positive duties entailed by FHE are negative or not to be acted against in the sense that they limit or constrain the pursuit of any merely subjective or personal ends. There is thus no suggestion that a supreme *limiting* condition consists of merely *negative* duties.

legomena to Any Future Metaphysics of two years before, in which he assumes the synthetic *a priori* status of propositions of mathematics and pure natural science in order to prove the existence of *a priori* forms of intuition, but does not attempt to give a transcendental deduction of the former propositions themselves. On this account, we would just have to see that the proposition is synthetic *a priori*. Alternatively, in analogy with Kant's method in the "Principles of Judgment" in the first *Critique,* we may be intended to see not the proposition that rational being is the end in itself but rather the proposition that the only possible ends are empirical ends or rational being itself as a synthetic *a priori* proposition, with the elimination of the first disjunct then following from the earlier requirement that a moral law be universally valid.[18]

In any case, the assumption that there can be no direct and positive *argument* for the identification of reason as the objective end of rational willing is consistent with Kant's earliest and never retracted characterization of the methodology of moral philosophy in the essay *On the Distinctness of the Principles of Natural Theology and Morality.*[19] Here, where he already works with (though does not yet name) the distinction between hypothetical and categorical imperatives, Kant claims that a moral theory requires both a *formal* and a *material* first principle. This is because "it is impossible, by contemplating a thing or a concept of any kind whatever, to recognize or infer what one ought to do, if that which is presupposed is not an end."[20] So he holds that moral action may require a formal constraint, but also requires an end, because otherwise

---

[18] The analogy would be that in his proofs of the Analogies of Experience and Refutation of Idealism, Kant tacitly assumes that empirical judgments of temporal order could be made by either the perception of absolute time or inference from laws governing the behavior of objects in time, and then explicitly eliminates the first possibility. For further discussion of this as a method that is supposed to yield synthetic *a priori* principles of empirical knowledge, see my *Kant and the Claims of Knowledge,* especially pp. 418–21.

[19] Submitted in the fall of 1762 for the Berlin Academy of Sciences essay competition on the question of whether the principles of theology and ethics are as certain as those of mathematics, and published in 1764. I have discussed this essay and its implications for Kant's subsequent moral philosophy in Chapter 1.

[20] 2:299; translation by David Walford in Immanuel Kant, *Theoretical Philosophy, 1755–1770,* p. 273.

"no specifically determinate obligation flows from [the] rules of the good." But there cannot be a demonstration of what the fundamental end is, because such a demonstration could proceed only by showing that its candidate is a means to a further end, in which case of course it would not be the fundamental end after all. At this stage of his development, Kant concludes that the fundamental end must be recommended by feeling rather than reason, tacitly identifying the faculty of reason with the faculty of demonstration. The Kant of the *Groundwork* instead supposes that we can see that reason and only reason can be an end in itself, but still suggests no way of deducing that from any more evident premise. So we still seem to be left with the conclusion that there is no direct way to argue for FHE, although its assertion as a fundamental synthetic *a priori* proposition may be confirmed by the way it illuminates the examples of the four classes of duty that have already been derived from FUL.[21]

Even though the nature of Kant's argument for FHE remains obscure, the significance of his introduction of it into the sequence of formulas in *Groundwork* II can be further clarified by contrast to a complementary but distinct move in the introduction to the "Doctrine of Virtue" of the later *Metaphysics of Morals*. Here Kant claims that "[e]very action . . . has its end," or that "whatsoever is an act of *freedom* on the part of the acting subject, not an effect of *nature*," requires that the agent himself make "the object of his choice into an end" (*MM*, 6:385).[22] From this he infers that there must be ends that are also duties, and that can be universally commanded, for otherwise a CI would not be possible. "For were there no such ends, then all ends would hold for practical reason only as means to other ends; and since there can be no action without an end, a *categorical* imperative would be impossible" (*MM*, 6:385).[23] Kant then searches among the general classes of all our possible ends for some that could qualify as duties, excluding, for differ-

---

[21] Herman perhaps suggests a similar view when she writes, "The conception of value [in FHE] has no separate derivation" (*The Practice of Moral Judgment*, p. 240).

[22] Immanuel Kant, *Metaphysics of Morals*, trans. Mary Gregor (Cambridge: Cambridge University Press, 1991), pp. 189–90.

[23] Ibid., p. 190.

ent reasons, those that cannot, namely our own happiness and the perfection of others, and leaving those that can, our own perfection and the happiness of others. These then furnish the basis of the more specific duties of virtue.

This argument can be seen as based on the assumption that a rational being cannot perform any *particular* action without a particular end, and thus that there must be ends *compatible* with the adoption of CI if the latter is itself to be a possible rule of action for rational beings. But this assumes that the necessity and therefore the possibility of adopting CI has already been established: "one can begin with the maxim of actions in conformity with duty and seek out the end that is also a duty" (*MM*, 6:382).[24] In the *Groundwork*, however, Kant treats the adoption of CI as something that must itself be shown to be possible for a rational being, which it can be only if there is shown to be a necessary and universal end that any rational being would hold but that can be realized only through the adoption of CI. In other words, Kant conceives of a rational being as one for whom *every* level of action must have an end, not merely particular actions that need to be compatible with CI but also the higher-order action of making CI into its fundamental maxim.[25] The "Doctrine of Virtue" requires that there be ends that are *compatible* with the adoption of CI, but this presupposes the argument of the *Groundwork* that there be a universally valid end that offers a reason for the adoption of CI itself.[26]

---

[24] Ibid., p. 187.

[25] *Religion within the Boundaries of Mere Reason* provides clear textual evidence for conceiving of the adoption of CI as itself an action – and one of, as it were, a higher order than that of adopting particular maxims. There Kant writes that a good or evil disposition, "i.e., the ultimate subjective ground of the adoption of maxims, can be one only and applies universally to the whole use of freedom. Yet this disposition itself must have been adopted by free choice [*Willkür*], for otherwise it could not be imputed" (6:25; trans. Theodore M. Greene and Hoyt H. Hudson [New York: Harper, 1960], p. 20).

[26] Herman puts this point by describing rational agents as ones for "whom reasons go all the way down," who thus are never simply caused to act by a desire but who act for principles (whether of desire-satisfaction or of morality) that are themselves adopted for reasons. "It is for this reason," she says, "that the willings of rational agents are open to full justification" (*Practice of Moral*

Before leaving the discussion of FHE, I want to return briefly to the larger question of how the idea that rational nature is itself the universally necessary end of all rational willing is to be reconciled with Kant's earlier claim that moral action is "good in *itself*" (G, 4: 414) rather than in relation to any "other end" (G, 4:415). As is well known, in *Groundwork* I Kant argues that an action is morally praiseworthy because of the quality of its intention rather than actual outcome (G, 4:394); but the considerations he appeals to there imply only that, because of the ways in which forces beyond the foresight or control of an agent can intervene between the intended and actual outcome of an action, we should praise an agent in virtue of the *intended end* of his action rather than its *actual outcome*. Understood this way, Kant's claim would not imply that the moral value of an action is independent of any end altogether, but only that it is independent from the actual realization of its intended end. In *Groundwork* II, Kant seems to have a more controversial claim in mind. As we have seen, Kant never introduced any premise from which it would follow that a virtuous action can have no end at all; rather, his requirement that the adoption of CI depend upon no arbitrarily given end will be satisfied if the adoption of CI depends on the adoption of an end that is non-contingent. However, we can now go further and see that rational being as an end in itself is in a certain sense fulfilled in any action that is performed under its aegis, and is not merely an effect of it that could in principle be attained through some other means. That is, FHE can be interpreted as presenting rational being as both the means and the end of moral action, thus as introducing an end that is neither "another" end external to moral action nor an "arbitrary" end. The relation between action performed with the intention of satisfying CI and the end that makes the adoption of CI rational can be called constitutive rather than instrumental

Judgment, p. 228). Of course, this should not be taken to imply that the ultimate or most fundamental decision of rational agents (to act out of self-love or the principle of duty) is open to full *explanation*; there is nothing in the present view that is incompatible with Kant's thesis of the inscrutability of the most fundamental acts of choice.

in the sense that such an action is itself an *instance* of rational being (or of being rational), although there is also a way in which action on CI is instrumental to rational being as its end, since it is aimed at bringing about a state of affairs that goes beyond the *individual rational agent's* compliance with CI itself. That is, while there may be a kind of conceptual identity between moral action and its aim, insofar as the end of being rational is nothing other than rational being itself, and is therefore already reached in acting rationally, there is also an extensional difference between the rationality of any one action, and of any one agent, and rational nature in general, which allows rational nature to serve as an end of moral action the attainment of which goes beyond the individual agent's performance. For what is commanded by FHE is that "humanity in your own person as well as in the person of every other always be [your] end" (*G*, 4:429), that is, that each moral agent strive to preserve and promote rational nature in all persons or all rational agents affected by his actions, not just in himself. Thus, although every moral action is already an instance of the general idea and ideal of rationality, the outcome it is aimed to produce can be the preservation and promotion of rationality in a wide range of instances other than itself. In these two ways, then, any particular exercise of rational nature is itself an instance of that which is absolutely good and yet also has an aim that is outside of and larger than itself.[27]

Kant draws on this understanding of rational nature as an end

[27] Here I believe there is a significant difference between my interpretation and Herman's. She holds that it "misses the point" to ask for "some other good that" willing in conformity with the principle of CI "promotes or brings about" (*Practice of Moral Judgment*, p. 215), and thus concludes that the task of a Kantian conception of value is to show how action in accord with the CI manifests a conception of value "in action and judgment" (ibid., p. 216). This could suggest that this value must be fully realized within any instance of action on CI, or, in the language I have been using, that the relation between the CI and the objective end of rational being is entirely constitutive. But it is part of my view that since action on CI is rational because it is intended to preserve and promote rational being in general, not just in the agent's own case, there is also a sense in which any individual instance of rational action is indeed instrumentally related to rational being as an end in itself.

in itself in a final explanation of how FHE serves as the ground for the adoption of FUL, which without it would be fallacious:

> The ground of this principle is: *rational nature exists as an end in itself*. Man necessarily represents his own existence to himself in this way; insofar it is therefore a *subjective* principle of human actions. But every other rational being also represents its own existence to itself in this way in accordance with the same rational ground [*Vernunftgrundes*] that is also valid for me; thus it is likewise an *objective* principle, from which as a highest practical ground all laws of the will must be able to be derived. (G, 4:429)

If this were read to assert that just because I value *my* rational nature and every other human or rational being values *his* or *her* rational being, therefore *I* have a reason and an obligation to value the rational nature of *every other* human or rational being, it would be fallacious – that I love my wife and you love your husband obviously does not of itself give me a reason to love him. But I take it that what Kant means is rather that each of us values his or her own existence as a rational being because of the value of rational nature *in itself*, which however gives us the same reason to value rational nature in everyone else as in ourselves. There is no fallacious inference from love of self to love of others, but rather a valid inference from a general source of value to the value of each of its exemplifications. In this way my moral action is good in itself, because it is an instance of that which is fundamentally good, but at the same time has an end lying beyond itself, namely the preservation of rational agency in general and the promotion of it wherever that is possible and reasonable for me.[28]

FHE thus contributes an essential element to demonstrating the real possibility of CI by specifying an objective end that is realized in and through action on CI and that thereby makes it rational for a rational being to act in accord with CI. We now consider several further contributions to the demonstration of the real possibility of CI for rational beings in general that are made by Kant's discussion of FA and FKE.

---

[28] See also Chapter 4, section VI.

IV THE FORMULAS OF AUTONOMY
AND OF THE KINGDOM OF ENDS

At the outset of his discussion of "our third practical principle for the will" Kant states that the ideas of universal law and of rational nature as an end in itself can be combined into the complex *"idea of the will of every rational being as a universally legislating will"* (*G*, 4:431), which idea yields the command "to do everything from the maxims of one's will as one that can at the same time regard itself as universally legislating," that is, FA (*G*, 4:432). Then he says that "the concept of every rational being that must consider itself as universally legislating through all the maxims of its will" leads to the "fruitful concept" of a *"kingdom of ends"* (*G*, 4: 433), which in turn gives rise to FKE, the requirement "that all maxims from one's own legislating ought to harmonize into a possible kingdom of ends, as a kingdom of nature" (*G*, 4:437). This series of assertions seems to suggest that the idea of the kingdom of ends adds nothing new to the notions of universal law and rational nature as an end in itself.

At the same time, however, Kant also claims that the first two formulations of CI "were merely *assumed* to be categorical, because one had to assume them to be something like that if one would explain the concept of duty," and that something more needs to be done in *Groundwork* II, even though the final proof that there are practical propositions that command *us* categorically still awaits the argument of *Groundwork* III. This suggests that there is an essential contribution to the analysis of the conditions of the real possibility of action on CI for rational beings in general that must precede the final proof that we ourselves are rational beings bound by the moral law. What could this be?

I will suggest that in the course of his brief discussion Kant actually introduces two distinct ideas. First, FA, or the idea of the moral agent as not merely acting in compliance with universalizable maxims but also as conceiving of himself as a universal legislator and thus as the source of these maxims, characterizes the interest we have in acting on the categorical imperative, an interest necessary to compete with the empirical interests we have in acting on hypothetical imperatives. Kant's further characterization of rational beings as having a unique dignity as makers of their own laws continues this account of the necessary conditions of the CI by exhibiting rational nature as not only an objective end but also one that can motivate us. Second, conceiving of not only oneself but of all the others who may be affected by one's actions as universal legislators, that is, as agents who have not only particular empirical interests but also the same overriding interest in universal legislation that one has oneself – that is, postulating that those whom one's actions affect can be members of a kingdom of ends – is a necessary condition of acting on CI, for only the postulation that all who are affected by one's actions are capable of universal legislation can make it reasonable to suppose that a universal law can be accepted by a manifold of agents in spite of their diverse empirical interests. Thus FKE is necessary to prove that CI is not just, as it were, intensionally noncontradictory and coherent but also extensionally realizable – the final requirement for a demonstration of the real possibility of CI, analogous to the proof that a pure concept of understanding can actually be realized in a manifold of intuition given the form of such a manifold.

Kant begins his discussion of FA by claiming that the idea of the will of a rational being as one capable of universal legislation is necessary in order to explain the possibility of "the renunciation of all interest" required for action on a categorical rather than hypothetical imperative (*G*, 4:431). Kant's explanation of this claim is that prior efforts at moral theory have failed to see the human being "as subject *only to his own yet nevertheless universal legislating*," and thus have only been able to conceive of him "as subject to a law (whatever it might be) because it carries with it some interest as an attraction or compulsion [*Reiz oder Zwang*], since it does not arise as a law from *his* will, but the latter is necessitated in a lawlike way to a certain course of action by *something else*" (*G*, 4:432–33) – what Kant calls "heteronomy" rather than "autonomy" (*G*, 4:433). That is, on prior theories the moral agent would be capable of action in accordance with hypothetical imperatives, the adoption of which is always dependent on the presence of contingent aims or interests, but not capable of action on CI, which may require disregarding any contingent incentives. For if agents conceive of themselves as having merely empirical incentives, they may be able to conceive of themselves as using reason instrumentally in the pursuit of contingent goals, but only if they conceive of themselves as legislators or as having "a will that is itself supremely legislative" (*G*, 4:432) will they be able to see themselves as having an interest in using their reason for universal legislation rather than for the pursuit of contingent and private aims. In other words, the idea of oneself as a universal legislator rather than as a mere subject of universal laws imposed from without allows one to conceive of oneself as having an identity that is fulfilled by universal legislating. When we so conceive of ourselves, action in accord with CI seems like the realization of our own identity rather than submission to an external constraint, and is in this way well motivated. Thus, the idea of oneself as a universal legislator essential to FA introduces a self-conception that is a condition of the possibility of being motivated to act on a categorical rather than merely hypothetical imperative.

The depiction of a motive necessary for the intelligibility of the adoption of CI is continued in Kant's account of the dignity of autonomy. The real bedrock of Kant's moral thought is his vision of the value of autonomy, the idea that an incomparable dignity attaches to freeing oneself from nature and being one's own master in the most general possible sense. Law making has dignity, as opposed to mere "market" or "fancy" price (*G*, 4:434–35), because only through it can the will avoid being "imposed upon" or "wheedled" into doing something not of its own choice (*G*, 4:435), and law making can determine value for other things or even transmit it to them because it itself has the incomparable dignity that attaches to self-mastery. Rational nature can be seen as an end in itself when it is interpreted as not merely subjection to but the willing of universal law because then it can be seen as the means by which agents capable of being rational free themselves from natural law and attain the dignity of self-mastery.[29]

The thought that there is an incomparable value or dignity in

---

[29] In other words, the argument of the *Groundwork* reveals that the incentive of respect for the moral law, first mentioned at *G*, 4:435 and then so heavily emphasized in the *Critique of Practical Reason*, makes sense only because of the value we attach to that which is to be achieved through the adoption of that law, namely autonomy. For further discussion of this theme, see Chapter 4.

self-mastery over nature, which can be attained only through the willing of universal law, is what is ultimately necessary in order to explain why rational being is an end both in one's own person and in that of everyone else. The dignity of autonomy is what makes the preservation and promotion of one's own rational nature an absolute end; but it makes humanity an end in everyone else as well because one's own autonomy is not desired merely as a matter of personal preference but as something of incomparable dignity wherever it occurs. In Kant's words, autonomy is not an object of self-love but is rather "the ground of the dignity of human and of every rational nature" (*G*, 4:436).

It can here be noted only in passing that this conception of the goal of morality is the ground of the constraint on what one can do for others that Kant emphasizes in all his writings on ethics from his early lectures to the late "Doctrine of Virtue," namely that, since the end of morality is self-mastery, one cannot directly realize this end for others, but can at best help them in realizing it themselves. As Kant puts this point, "it is a contradiction for me to make another's *perfection* my end. . . . For the *perfection* of another human being, as a person, consists just in this: that he *himself* is able to set his end in accordance with his own concepts of duty" (*MM*, 6:386).[30] This overlooks the ways in which I may make it my goal to help others in realizing their own freedom, but just as clearly emphasizes that it is the rational exercise of freedom that is itself human perfection and thus the necessary and objective end of moral action.

Finally, Kant's introduction of FKE as well as FA constitutes the last step in his exhibition of the conditions of the real possibility of CI by demonstrating the assumption that is necessary in order to ensure that a universal law can be found for any manifold of agents. Kant defines a kingdom of ends thus:

> I understand, however, by a *kingdom* the systematic combination of different rational beings through common laws. Now since laws determine ends in accord with their universal validity, then, if one abstracts from personal differences of rational beings, as well as from all content of their private ends, a whole of all ends

---

[30] Translation by Gregor, *MM*, p. 191.

(both of rational beings as ends in themselves as well as of the individual ends which each may set for himself) in systematic connection, i.e., a kingdom of ends, can be thought, which is possible in accordance with the above principles. (*G*, 4:433)

This passage can be interpreted as making several claims. First, if one is to conceive of rational beings as abstracting from all personal ends but still as agents, that is, as still having some reason to act, then one must also conceive of them as universal legislators, that is, as agents who see their reason and capacity for universal legislation as itself a reason to will. This reiterates the point previously made, although it applies it to all members of a kingdom of ends and not just oneself. But, second, it is only if one sees both oneself and all others who may be affected by one's actions as having not only personal ends but also both the capacity for and interest in universal legislation that one can be sure that a systematic connection of ends is always possible, that is, that for any set of circumstances there is indeed some universalizable maxim that can be adopted by oneself and others. If agents have only individual ends and merely instrumental reason, there is no guarantee that in any given circumstances there will be any maxim of action that could be adopted by any single agent that will also be compatible with all those ends. But if all the agents involved have the capacity for and interest in universal legislation, they will all be able to abstract from the content of their personal ends and come up with a universally acceptable maxim, even if in some particular situations that will only be the maxim that in those circumstances everyone must refrain from seeking to fulfill any merely empirical interest. In other words, only in a community of universal legislators, where universal legislation itself is available as an end in addition to particular empirical interests, will it always be possible to formulate a universal law, and thus for any individual rational agent to comply with FUL; only in a community all of whose members see themselves as universal legislators and not just as pursuers of individual ends will there always be some maxim that is indeed not only acceptable to but well motivated for all. Thus, just as the absence of logical contradiction in the idea of a figure enclosed within two straight lines does not prove its possibility in the space permitted by our form of intuition,[31] and only figures actually constructible in that space are really possible, so too the practical concept of a universal law can be proved to be a real possibility only for a domain of agents all of whom are universal legislators capable of setting aside personal interests and acting out of their common interest in being such legislators.[32]

Thus, both FA and FKE bring out crucial features of Kant's analysis of the full conditions for the real possibility of action on CI that need to be in place before the demonstration that we are actually capable of satisfying all those conditions, to be offered in *Groundwork* III, can be contemplated. FHE took a first step toward the exhibition of these conditions in going beyond the formal requirement of the universalizability of one's maxims by introducing rational nature as an end of action; but the conceptions of the moral agent as a universal legislator and of the community of moral agents as a kingdom of ends are necessary in order to explain how an individual moral agent could possibly act apart from personal interest and how a community of moral agents could possibly arrive at a systematic union of maxims and ends. Thus, Kant was wrong when he said that the formulations of CI beyond FUL are necessary just in order to bring morality closer to intuition, and in a lesser way wrong when he suggested that three formulations of CI are necessary for a complete determination of the principle of morality: a complete account of the real possibility of action in accord with CI for any rational being requires reference to the four formulations FUL, FHE, FA, and FKE.

---

[31] *Critique of Pure Reason*, A 220–21/B 268.

[32] Herman's account of the function of FKE stresses that through this formula persons are seen as reasoners all the way down, but does not show how this yields a guarantee of the possibility of universalizability itself (see *Practice of Moral Judgment*, pp. 228–30).

Chapter 6

The Strategy of Kant's *Groundwork*

In this chapter I want to examine further the argumentative strategy of Kant's mature moral philosophy, as first laid out in the *Groundwork for the Metaphysics of Morals*, by exploring the relationship between "common" and "philosophical" "rational cognition of morals" (*sittlichen Vernunfterkenntnis*) that Kant has in mind in this much studied but still not well understood work.[1] One striking fact about the argument of the *Groundwork* is that philosophy appears in it in the guise of both "popular moral worldly wisdom" – here it may be best to translate *Weltweisheit* literally rather than as just an archaic word for "philosophy" – on the one hand and that of Kant's own "metaphysics of morals" and "critique of pure practical reason" on the other. More precisely, the *Groundwork* starts off by deriving its initial formulation of the categorical imperative from a "common rational cognition of morals" that every reasonable person is supposed to recognize as his or her own, and then relates both "popular worldly wisdom" and a genuine "metaphysics of morals" and "critique of pure practical reason" to this "common rational cognition of morals." What is the relation of these two

This chapter originally appeared under the title "Self-Understanding and Philosophy: The Strategy of Kant's *Groundwork*," in Marcelo Stamm, ed., *Philosophie in synthetischer Absicht* (Stuttgart: Klett-Cotta, 1998), pp. 271–97. That volume was a *Festschrift* for Dieter Henrich; here I omit an opening paragraph relating the paper to Henrich's philosophical concerns.

[1] I have touched upon this issue in a preliminary way in the final paragraphs of Chapter 4, section II.

forms of philosophy to each other and to the prephilosophical self-understanding from which Kant's argument seems to begin?

One interpretation might be this: Kant thinks that every normal human being innately possesses or early acquires an understanding of the demands of moral duty and of its worth, which, however, can be corrupted by bad but popular philosophy or "worldly wisdom." Such philosophy, a kind of empiricism in the sense that it bases its prescription of how moral agents ought to behave on observation of how humans are actually observed to behave, could corrupt our innate sense of duty and its merit in two ways: it would confuse us about the principle of morality by presenting our own happiness rather than duty as the object of morally worthy action; and it would give us an excuse for lapsing from the stern demands of duty by appealing to determinism as an excuse for our own moral frailty or evil. Kant's strategy, then, would be to counteract the deleterious effects of this "popular worldly wisdom" by showing, in his "metaphysics of morals" (i.e., Section II of the *Groundwork*), that happiness can never be the object prescribed by the categorical imperative, which we are all in some way disposed to acknowledge, and by showing, in his "critique of pure practical reason" (i.e., Section III of the *Groundwork*), that we really are always free to live up to the stern demands of morality no matter what our prior experience and history might seem to have determined us to do. In this way, a sound philosophy would save our innate self-understanding as moral agents from corruption by bad philosophy.

Such an interpretation of Kant's strategy in the *Groundwork* is almost right, but not quite. Dieter Henrich might seem to suggest such an interpretation when he writes:

> Man subtly refines the moral law until it fits his inclination and his convenience, whether to free himself from it or to use the good for the justification of his own self-importance. Kant considers his entire philosophy an attempt to refute the sophistry of reason that is in the service of pleasure. In this way he also attempts to give firm insight into the good against dialectical artifices.[2]

---

[2] "The Concept of Moral Insight into Kant's Doctrine of the Fact of Reason," in Dieter Henrich, *The Unity of Reason: Essays on Kant's Philosophy*, ed. Richard

But Henrich's references to the sophistry of *reason*, not to the sophistry of *popular philosophy* or "worldly wisdom," as well as to dialectical artifices, suggest a more subtle reading of Kant's argument. The risk to our moral self-understanding does not arise from without, from the wily artifices of corrupt philosophers who appear out of nowhere to darken our paths; the source of sophistry and corruption lies within us, in evil possibilities inherent to our own nature, which can in turn co-opt our own faculty of reason to produce a form of philosophy that would appear to justify our lapses from duty unless countered by a sounder philosophy that is itself another product of our own reason accessible to any of us by the reflective use of that reason. Just as our theoretical reason is inherently liable to irresolvable dialectical disputes or antinomies until we fully understand the proper conditions for its use – dialectical disputes that find expression in speculative philosophy but are by no means mere artifices of speculative philosophers[3] – so our practical reason is inherently liable to undermine our common rational cognition of morals by a dialectic that is entirely natural to it, which is thus not caused by but merely expressed in popular moral philosophy or worldly wisdom, and which can only be resolved by a sounder philosophical reflection on the nature of our practical reason and the conditions of its use, a reflection of which we are also capable. Kant's moral philosophy is not intended simply to rescue our moral self-understanding from bad philosophy contingently imposed upon us by bad philosophers. It is rather intended to give us the fuller self-understanding that we need in order to save our understanding of the moral law and

Velkley (Cambridge, Mass.: Harvard University Press, 1994), pp. 55–87, at p. 66; originally "Der Begriff der sittlichen Einsicht und Kants Lehre vom Faktum der Vernunft," in D. Henrich, W. Schulz, and K. H. Vollkmann-Schluck, eds., *Die Gegenwart der Griechen im neueren Denken: Festschrift für Hans-Georg Gadamer*, (Tübingen: J. C. B. Mohr, 1960), pp. 77–115.

[3] This is, after all, why Kant always treats the proponents of the dialectically opposed theses and antitheses of his antinomies, Leibniz and Wolff or Locke and Hume, with the utmost respect, rather than dismissing them as fools: they are only giving voice to natural illusions of human reason, which cannot fully be dispelled until the nature and conditions of the use of human reason are fully understood.

its demands from our own self-misunderstanding and the bad philosophy that we create for ourselves.

This subtle strategy might not be entirely obvious from Kant's first statement of the need for his moral philosophy in the preface to the *Groundwork*:

> A metaphysics of morals is therefore indispensably necessary, not merely because of a motive to speculation – for investigating the source of the practical basic principles that lie *a priori* in our reason – but also because morals themselves remain subject to all sorts of corruption as long as we are without that clue and supreme norm by which to appraise them correctly. For, in the case of what is to be morally good, it is not enough that it *conform* with the moral law, but it must also be done *for the sake of the law;* without this, that conformity is only very contingent and precarious, since a ground that is not moral will indeed now and then produce actions in conformity with the law, but it will also often produce actions contrary to the law. Now the moral law in its purity and genuineness (and in the practical this is what matters most) is to be sought nowhere else than in a pure philosophy. (G, 4:390)[4]

Initially, this passage simply leaves open the source of any tendencies to the corruption of morals. It then perhaps goes on to suggest that the problem is that while we may have a natural desire to conform to the requirements of morality, whatever they might be, without a clear recognition of the principle of morality and its requirements, particularly its requirement that we act for the sake of the moral law itself, we are open to all sorts of corruption. Thus we might suppose that Kant means to argue that our natural disposition to conform to the demands of morality has to be supplemented by a clearly formulated principle of morality, and that it is up to his moral philosophy to offer a sound one to

---

[4] Translations from the *Groundwork* in this chapter are based on those in Immanuel Kant, *Practical Philosophy*, ed. and trans. Mary J. Gregor (Cambridge: Cambridge University Press, 1996). In one major departure from Gregor's practice, however, I have not translated *Beurteilung* as "appraisal," but by means of the gerundive noun "judging." This makes clear the affinity of this term to the word *Urteil* ("judgment") and others of its derivatives.

compete with, and triumph over, the less sound ones offered by more popular worldly wisdom or philosophy.

The conclusion of Section I of the *Groundwork*, however, suggests the subtler strategy I have ascribed to Kant. Here Kant writes:

> Reason issues its precepts unremittingly, without thereby promising anything to the inclinations and so, as it were, with disregard and contempt for those claims. . . . But from this there arises a *natural dialectic*, that is, a propensity to rationalize against those strict laws of duty, and to cast doubt on their validity, or at least on their purity and strictness, and, where possible, to make them better suited to our wishes and inclinations, that is, to corrupt them at their basis and to destroy all their dignity – something that even common practical reason cannot, in the end, call good.
>
> In this way *common human reason* is impelled, not by some need of speculation (which never touches it as long as it is content to be mere sound reason), but on practical grounds themselves, to go out of its sphere and to take a step into the field of *practical philosophy*, in order to obtain there information and distinct instruction regarding the source of its principle and the correct determination of this principle in comparison with maxims based on need and inclination, so that it may escape from its predicament about claims from both sides and not run the risk of being deprived of all genuine moral principles through the ambiguity into which it easily falls. So there develops unnoticed in common practical reason as well, when it cultivates itself, a *dialectic* that constrains it to seek help in philosophy, just as happens in its theoretical use; and the former will, accordingly, find no more rest than the other except in a complete critique of our reason. (*G*, 4:405)

The dialectic of practical philosophy is not academic but natural: that is, the corruption of "common human reason" is threatened not from without, but from within, and "popular worldly wisdom" is not an external threat to "common human reason" but is itself an expression of something natural to human being that can be resolved only by the self-understanding afforded by a "complete critique of our reason." In particular, common human reason tends to confuse its natural recognition of the genuine principle of morality with "maxims based on need and inclination." Only a clear distinction between the fundamental principle of morality that we all intuitively recognize from any maxims based on need and inclination, but at the same time an equally clear understanding of the proper role of need and inclination in the conditions of human agency, will enable us to save ourselves from the dialectic of practical reason that is as natural to us as our recognition of the fundamental principle of morality itself.

This program of self-understanding is carried out in the *Groundwork*, I suggest, in the following three steps.

In Section I, Kant argues that a genuine even if less than entirely explicit understanding of the fundamental principle of morality is reflected in our common conceptions of good will and duty and in the moral judgments that we make about particular cases of human action, especially when those cases are presented to us in ways that do not immediately involve our own interests. From our common conception of good will and duty and from such particular cases, a clear formulation of the genuine principle of morality can be extracted (*G*, 4:402). This clear recognition of our duty, however, is threatened by two factors that are as natural to our condition as is the recognition of our duty itself. First, it is entirely natural for us each to seek our own happiness, and thus the risk of substituting an imperative to seek our own happiness for the imperative to perform our duty is equally natural to us. We also try to dignify this tendency by adopting a philosophy that seems to entail hedonism. Second, as far as we can see, human beings frequently succumb to this confusion; thus insofar as we try to base our moral principles on actual examples of human conduct, and moreover even try to dignify this procedure by thinking of it as dictated by what appears to be a respectably empiricist philosophy, we tend to substitute the principle of happiness for the genuine principle of duty.

In Section II of the *Groundwork*, Kant argues that this natural danger can be avoided only by making completely explicit the fundamental principle of morality that is merely implicit in our initial moral self-understanding. In the fuller development of his moral theory, however, he will also have to show how the interest in happiness, precisely since it is entirely natural to us and neither should not nor cannot be expected to be extirpated, is to be incorporated into the object of morality in the form of the highest good, the realization of happiness conditioned by the worthiness to be happy. If the principle of happiness were just a threat from bad moral philosophy, not an ineliminable feature of human nature, the theory of the highest good would not be a necessary part of Kant's moral philosophy. Although the *Groundwork*, unlike each of Kant's three critiques, does not itself mention the theory of the highest good, its dialectical strategy nevertheless shows why the theory of the highest good is essential to Kant's moral philosophy.

Section III of the *Groundwork* then takes up the second threat to our natural recognition of duty, a threat that is just as natural to us as the interest in happiness and just as much as that needs to find its proper place in a complete self-understanding of our moral agency. This is the threat of determinism, or as Kant himself calls it "predeterminism,"[5] the doctrine that our actions at any given moment are thoroughly necessitated by events at prior moments, from which it seems to follow that it is not always in our power to live up to the stringent demands of duty, which must therefore be weakened. Such a doctrine of determinism is clearly, in Henrich's term, a sophistry of our own reason by which we can excuse our failure to act always as we know we should, and needs to be answered by a critique of pure practical reason that will show that we do indeed always have the power to act as duty requires, no matter what our past might seem to predict. The doctrine of determinism, however, is not just a rationalization of our moral weakness offered to us by popular philosophy (although, of course, historically it was a prominent doctrine of the empiricist philosophies of Locke and Hume), but is itself a genuine aspect of our self-understanding, indeed the indispensable foundation of our theoretical understanding of the world of nature and our place in it. Thus, what is necessary is not a simple *refutation* of determinism but rather a proper *situation* of it in the fuller self-understanding that we can reach through a sound philosophy – which must also lie ready in ourselves. This is, of course, what Kant attempts to provide through the transcendental idealism that he

[5] See *Rel*, 6:49–50n.

invokes in Section III of the *Groundwork* and then again in the *Critique of Practical Reason*.[6] Just as Kant's theory of the highest good is his recognition that we cannot simply dismiss the principle of happiness but must incorporate it into a proper position in our full understanding of the object of morality, so he also recognizes that we cannot simply dismiss determinism as a groundless threat to our sense of duty but must rather show its proper place in relation to the indisputable fact of our freedom in the transcendental idealism that gives fullest expression to our self-understanding as moral agents.

Although I hardly have room here to explicate and argue for these three claims in the detail they require, I can present some of the key evidence for these claims and comment on some of the issues that they raise.

SECTION I

From the outset of the *Groundwork*, Kant insists that everything essential in moral philosophy is readily accessible to the ordinary human being. The Preface maintains that "in moral matters human reason can easily be brought to a high degree of correctness and accomplishment, even in the most common understanding"

---

[6] Dieter Henrich has discussed the vexed issue of the relation between Kant's treatment of freedom in the *Groundwork* and in the second *Critique* in his famous paper, "Die Deduktion des Sittengesetzes: Über die Gründe der Dunkelheit des letzten Abschnittes von Kant's *Grundlegung zur Metaphysik der Sitten*," in Alexander Schwann, ed., *Denken im Schatten des Nihilismus: Festschrift für Wilhelm Weischedel* (Darmstadt: Wissenschaftliche Buchgesellschaft, 1975), pp. 55–110. An English translation of all but the last three sections of this paper appears in Paul Guyer, ed., *Kant's Groundwork of the Metaphysics of Morals: Critical Essays* (Lanham: Rowman and Littlefield, 1998), pp. 303–41. In the present chapter, I assume that Kant's transcendental idealist conception of freedom is the same in both works, although the arguments by which he introduces it are different; and even then, as I suggest later, there is a crucial structural similarity between the two works' arguments for transcendental idealism, as Kant tries to argue that the transcendental idealist understanding of freedom is in fact just as natural to us as the natural theory of determinism which is the internal threat to morality that a fuller self-understanding must resolve.

(*G*, 4:391). The argument of Section I then takes the form of deriving the first formulation of the fundamental principle of morality from an analysis of the concept of a good will that is taken to be commonly acknowledged, where the common possession of this concept is itself confirmed by our common response to hypothetical examples of the performance of duty, such as the case of the man who has been created without sympathetic inclinations or lost them through his own misfortunes yet who can nevertheless act virtuously out of his respect for duty (*G*, 4:398). We can consider this style of argument to be continued in Section II of the *Groundwork* when Kant appeals to commonly accepted examples of duty – now ranged in four classes – to confirm now not the common concept of duty itself but rather the first and second formulations of the categorical imperative to which this concept of duty gives rise (*G*, 4:421–23 and 429–30). Throughout, Kant's strategy is to show that the moral principle that he proposes – which is hardly supposed to be a new invention, "as if, before him, the world had been ignorant of what duty is"[7] – is implied by the commonly shared conception of duty and expressed in commonly shared judgments about particular cases of dutiful action.

Kant does not make his assumption clear when he first introduces the analysis of the concept of a good will: here he just says, entirely without any methodological comment, that in order "to explicate the concept of a will that is to be esteemed in itself . . . we shall set before ourselves the concept of *duty*" (*G*, 4:397). Upon having derived his initial formulation of the only possible principle for the determination of the good will from this concept, however, he states that "Common human reason also agrees completely with this in its practical judging and always has this principle before its eyes" (*G*, 4:402). A page later, he reiterates that "we have arrived, within the moral cognition of common human reason, at its principle, which it admittedly does not think so abstractly in a universal form, but which it actually has before its eyes and uses as the standard for its judging" (*G*, 4:403). The fundamental principle of morality is implicit in our common conception of duty and in our common judgments about duties, and

---

[7] *CPracR*, 5:8; translation from Gregor, *Practical Philosophy*.

even if not already explicitly formulated by every normal human being it will still immediately be recognized and acknowledged when presented to any normal human being in its explicit form.

As I am here more concerned with the form of Kant's account than with its content, the details of his analysis and its confirmation can be recalled briefly. Kant analyzes the concept of a good will by means of three propositions that are obviously supposed to be acknowledged by anyone with common moral cognition: (i) good will consists in acting from duty rather than from inclination (*G*, 4:397); (ii) "action from duty has its moral worth *not in the purpose* to be attained by it but in the maxim in accordance with which it is decided upon, and therefore does not depend upon the realization of the object of the action but merely upon the *principle of volition*" (*G*, 4:399–400); and (iii) "*duty is the necessity of an action from respect for law*" (*G*, 4:400). The first proposition of the analysis in particular is confirmed by an appeal to an example: we all recognize that there is no manifestation of good will and thus no special moral worth in a grocer's maintaining a policy of honesty for the sake of his own long-term self-interest or in somebody preserving his life merely out of inclination (*G*, 4:397), but we do recognize good will and thus moral worth when somebody "preserves his life without loving it" or continues to act benevolently even though his mind has been "overclouded by his own grief" (*G*, 4:398). Our judgments of moral worth in such cases can only be explained by our assumption that moral worth lies in the performance of actions out of the motive of duty rather than out of inclination or self-interest. The first phase of Kant's analysis of the concept of a good will in terms of the concept of duty is thus confirmed by commonly accepted moral judgments.

After completing his analysis of duty, Kant then derives the formula "*I ought never to act except in such a way that I could also will that my maxim should become a universal law*," which he designates as the first formulation of the categorical imperative after he has introduced the concept of such an imperative in Section II, from the fact that since this analysis has "deprived the will of every impulse that could arise for it from obeying some law, nothing is left but the conformity of actions as such with universal law" (*G*, 4: 402). The validity of this formula is then again confirmed by an example: if we consider whether we may make a promise without the intention of keeping it in order to get out of a current difficulty, we all realize that the relevant question is not whether it is possible or prudent to do so, but rather simply "would I indeed be content that my maxim (to get myself out of difficulties by a false promise) should hold as a universal law (for myself as well as for others)?" (*G*, 4:403). Kant's previously cited claims that his formulation of the principle of morality is reflected in the practical judgments of common human reason immediately precede and succeed the exposition of this example (*G*, 4:402, 403). Kant's argument in *Groundwork* I thus has the following form: our common conception of good will as manifest in the performance of action from duty, which is supported by examples of virtuous action that we all recognize, combined with an analysis of the concept of duty that we all accept, gives rise to a formulation of the fundamental principle of morality, which, even if we do not explicitly recognize it in its most abstract form, is in fact the basis for the particular moral judgments that we make, as can again be confirmed by an appeal to any example of a duty that we all acknowledge.

Kant sums up this first stage of his argument by saying that "there is no need of science and philosophy to know what one has to do in order to be honest and good, and even wise and virtuous" (*G*, 4:404). If this is so, why does the argument of the *Groundwork* have to continue into its Sections II and III? Kant's answer to this question is not that we need philosophy simply in order "to present the system of morals all the more completely and comprehensibly and to present its rules in a form more convenient for use." His answer is rather that "innocence . . . is easily seduced," because the "human being feels within himself a powerful counterweight to all the commands of duty," namely, "the counterweight of his needs and inclinations, the entire satisfaction of which he sums up under the name happiness" (*G*, 4:404–5). The next stage of the argument of the *Groundwork*, which occupies Section II, must then be to distinguish clearly the principle of morality from the principle of happiness. In Kant's moral philosophy more generally considered, however, the next stage of the argument must be not merely to distinguish the principle of morality from the natural pursuit of happiness, but also to show how happiness, as the ineliminable natural end of human beings, does properly fit into the complete object of morality. Before turning to this next stage of Kant's argument, however, several comments on the character of its first stage are in order.

First, there is a question about what sort of moral principle could be derived by the appeal to common concepts and judgments that Kant presents in *Groundwork* I. Thus far, I have referred to both the fundamental principle of morality and the categorical imperative without distinction, but of course, these are not exactly the same: as Konrad Cramer has argued, the fundamental principle of morality can be considered a pure synthetic *a priori* principle, applicable to any and all rational beings, whereas the categorical imperative is an impure synthetic *a priori* principle, the form in which the fundamental principle of morality presents itself to beings like us, who empirically know ourselves to have inclinations and interests that may conflict with compliance with the fundamental principle of morality, and thus may experience the fundamental principle of morality as a constraining obligation – a categorical imperative – in a way that beings without such conflicting incentives would not.[8] Shouldn't a derivation of a moral principle that appeals to commonly shared concepts such as those of good will and duty and to commonly shared practical judgments or moral responses to particular examples of duties and dutiful sorts of persons yield at best an impure formulation of the fundamental principle of morality in the form of a categorical imperative applicable to beings like us only, rather than the fundamental principle of morality itself in its pure form? Indeed, shouldn't a derivation of a principle of morality in any form from common concepts and judgments yield only something empirical, not any sort of *a priori* principle at all, that is, a principle that is universally and necessarily valid for any species of rational agents, let alone all rational agents? To answer this question, we need to distinguish carefully between a derivation of the *formula-*

---

[8] Konrad Cramer, "Metaphysik und Erfahrung in Kants Grundlegung der Ethik," in Gerhard Schönrich and Yasushi Kato, eds., *Kant in der Diskussion der Moderne* (Frankfurt am Main: Suhrkamp, 1996), pp. 280–325; originally published in *Metaphysik und Erfahrung: Neue Hefte für Philosophie* 30–31 (1991): 15–68.

tion of the principle of morality (in any form) and a derivation of its *validity*. It clearly cannot be Kant's position that we derive the *validity* of the moral law by any sort of empirical method from commonly accepted concepts and judgments. Rather, it is clearly his view that by *reflection* on our common concepts of good will and duty and on common moral judgments about particular examples of duties and dutiful persons we can see that we already acknowledge the validity of the moral law even in its purest form, its form as the fundamental principle of morality, as well as in its form as the categorical imperative, and even if we have not previously explicitly formulated the principle in any abstract terms at all. We immediately see that our recognition of the principle is what explains our acceptance of the concepts and judgments that we all do accept; we do not only come to accept the principle because of our response to particular cases. As Kant says, "Nor could one give worse advice to morality than by wanting to derive it from examples. For every example of it represented to me must itself first be judged [*beurteilt*] in accordance with principles of morality, as to whether it is also worthy to serve as an original example" (*G*, 4:408).[9]

But at this point a second question about an argument involving appeal to examples arises. At the outset of Section II of the *Groundwork*, Kant inveighs against any attempt to derive the fundamental principle of morality in any form from *actual examples* of human conduct:

> If we have so far drawn our concept of duty from the common use of our practical reason, it is by no means to be inferred from this that we have treated it as a concept of experience. On the contrary, if we attend to experience of people's conduct we meet frequent and, as we ourselves admit, just complaints that no certain example can be cited of the disposition to act from pure duty; that, though much may be done *in conformity with* what *duty* commands, still it is always doubtful whether it is really done *from duty* and therefore has moral worth. . . . In fact, it is absolutely impossible by means of experience to make out with

---

[9] See also Kant's discussion of Christ as a model for our own morality in *Rel*, 6:62–64.

complete certainty a single case in which the maxim of an action otherwise in conformity with duty rested simply on moral grounds and on the representation of one's duty. (*G*, 4:406–7)

Doesn't this blunt statement completely undermine any attempt to derive anything about the moral law from examples of any kind?

To answer this question, we need to draw a firm distinction between the use of *actual* and of *hypothetical* examples of moral conduct. Kant's initial argument in Section II is that we cannot be sure that any *actual* conduct, that of others or even our own, has been performed out of the pure motive of duty, and thus we would be hard-pressed to derive a fundamental principle of morality from actual human behavior in the face of uncertainty; indeed, we might even take him to go on to argue that we can be reasonably sure that almost all actual deeds, whether our own or others', have been motivated by inclination and self-interest, thus that if we attempt to formulate a fundamental principle of morality by induction from actual conduct we shall almost certainly come up with the *wrong* principle. In particular, we know that in cases of actual actions in any way affecting our own interests, our judgments are likely to be distorted by self-love (*G*, 4:407). But the examples in *Groundwork* I are not actual examples of human conduct but hypothetical cases for moral judgment; and in the case of such examples what is at issue is only the question of how we judge that agents in such cases *ought* to be judged, not whether we ourselves or anyone else ever actually lives up to such judgments. Kant's claim is precisely that in the appraisal of hypothetical cases and situations of human action, where the threat of self-love can be certain to be set aside, we all immediately recognize how human agents ought to be motivated and to behave, even if we are not sure that any of us has ever actually been motivated in that way. And the basis of such acknowledgments of the principle of morality, Kant insists, is not experience but pure practical reason. Examples need to be adduced for the confirmation of our common concepts of good will and duty because pure practical reason commonly expresses itself in the judgment of particulars rather than in abstractions, but not because these concepts rest on experience rather than pure reason.

SECTION II

Kant's argument in *Groundwork* II is that the true principle of morality can never be discovered by examples from ordinary experience; rather it requires "pure rational concepts" and a "metaphysics of morals" (*G*, 4:410), although once "the doctrine of morals" has been "first *grounded* on metaphysics," it can be "provided with *access* by means of popularity" (*G*, 4:409). By a "popular philosophy" (here he does use the word *Philosophie* instead of *Weltweisheit*), he means simply a method "that goes no farther than it can by groping with the help of examples" (*G*, 4:412). Thus, he does not explicitly identify "popular philosophy" with a specific school of academic moral philosophy, such as the moral sense school as an applied form of academic empiricism. In fact, he clearly means to include the perfectionism of Wolff and his followers as well as the moral sense philosophy of Hutcheson and Hume under this rubric – what we get if we attempt to discover the principle of "morality in that popular taste" is a hodgepodge of principles identifiable with those of all the popular schools of moral philosophy: "One will find now the special determination of human nature (but occasionally the idea of a rational nature as such along with it), now perfection, now happiness, here moral feeling, there fear of God, a bit of this and a bit of that in a marvelous mixture" (*G*, 4:410). But the overall argument of Section II is certainly a polemic against the idea that Kant assumes would be inevitably suggested by basing our conception of the fundamental principle of morality on observation of actual examples of human motivation and behavior, namely, the idea that what morality prescribes is the pursuit of happiness as such – as Hume puts it in his *Enquiry concerning the Principles of Morals*, the cultivation of qualities useful and agreeable to ourselves and others.[10]

Kant carries on his polemic against any such principle in several stages. First, he derives the concept of a categorical imperative in general from what he clearly assumes to be the common

---

[10] David Hume, *An Enquiry concerning the Principles of Morals*, section IX, part I; in Hume's *Enquiries*, ed. L.A. Selby-Bigge, 2d ed. (Oxford: Clarendon Press, 1902), p. 268 (the pagination remains the same in the third edition of Selby-Bigge, rev. P. H. Nidditch, 1978).

understanding that the fundamental principle of morality must be an objectively necessitating principle, that is, a principle necessitating certain principles of action for all relevant agents (*G*, 4: 413–14), and then argues that a simple principle of pursuing happiness could never give rise to a categorical imperative but only a hypothetical one. Such a principle would be a hypothetical one not because whether anyone adopts happiness as an end is entirely contingent – on the contrary, Kant recognizes it as a fact of nature, a "natural necessity" (*G*, 4:415), that everyone does adopt happiness as an end – but rather because of the following sorts of considerations: what the *particular* ends are whose satisfaction would constitute anyone's happiness is contingent; whether the various particular ends the satisfaction of which would constitute a single person's happiness are conjointly realizable is contingent (*G*, 4:418); and, as Kant adds in the *Critique of Practical Reason*, whether two or more different persons' conceptions of happiness are conjointly realizable is also contingent (5:28). For these sorts of reasons, then, although it is not exactly contingent whether anyone has happiness as an end, it certainly would be contingent whether anyone has as his end a particular conception of happiness that could rationally be pursued in the actual circumstances of his life.

After his initial contrast between merely hypothetical imperatives and a categorical imperative, Kant argues that the very concept of a categorical imperative – again, presumably one that every normal human being has – gives rise to precisely the same formulation of the fundamental principle of morality that the previous analysis of the concepts of good will and duty yielded, the principle that one should only act on maxims that can at the same time be willed as universal law (*G*, 4:421). In the discussion of this and the following further formulations of the categorical imperative, especially the principle of humanity as an end in itself,[11] Kant continues to emphasize that the principle of morality is not "a

---

[11] For the classical exposition and discussion of the various formulations of the categorical imperative, see H. J. Paton, *The Categorical Imperative: A Study in Kant's Moral Philosophy* (London: Hutchinson, 1947). There has been much recent discussion of this subject; for my own approach, see Chapters 4 and 5 in this volume.

subjective principle on which we might act if we have the propensity and inclination," thus not a principle prescribing our happiness, but an "objective principle on which we would be *directed* to act even though every propensity, inclination, and natural tendency of ours were against it" (*G*, 4:425), thus a principle that apparently ignores all reference to our own happiness. Kant stresses that the categorical imperative abstracts from all "subjective ends" and is thus *formal* rather than *material* (*G*, 4:428); but since human beings cannot act without an end at all, he elevates humanity into "*an end in itself,*" "which is the supreme limiting condition of the freedom of action of every human being," "an objective end that, whatever ends we may have, ought as law to constitute the supreme limiting condition of all subjective ends" (*G*, 4:430–31). Thus, Kant insists – and he insists that we will all come to recognize this readily by reflection on concepts that we already acknowledge, such as those of the good will, duty, and the categorical imperative – the end of morality is not happiness, the satisfaction of our particular, subjective material needs and inclinations, but is rather something else, humanity as such, which is a limiting condition on the pursuit of happiness. This is not the result that we get by induction from actual examples of human motivation, even if we dignify such an induction with the name of philosophy, but is the result that we get from reflection on the pure concepts of a metaphysics of morals that is in fact accessible to each of us.

Now at the height of the polemic against founding a principle of morality on the object of happiness in *Groundwork* II, Kant goes so far as to say not merely that "all objects of the inclinations have only a conditional worth," but also that "the inclinations themselves, as sources of needs, are so far from having an absolute worth so as to make one wish to have them, that it must instead be the universal wish of every rational being to be altogether free from them" (*G*, 4:428). However, if this suggests that human beings either could or should eradicate all inclinations in themselves, thus eradicating everything the satisfaction of which could produce happiness, and that the goal of morality could or should be pursued by means of such a mass extinction of inclination, then it radically misrepresents what will become the considered position of Kant's moral philosophy. As Kant makes clear in *Religion within the Boundaries of Mere Reason*, we are not evil because we *have* sensuous inclinations but because of the attitude we adopt toward them as our fundamental maxim. We are not evil simply because we have such inclinations, first because we "cannot presume ourselves responsible for their existence" (6:35),[12] but even more because "predispositions in the human being" are "*original*," that is, "they belong to the possibility of human nature," and – certainly on the teleological view of nature, which Kant had long assumed should regulate our reflection on our natural endowments[13] – they must therefore be assumed to be "not only (negatively) good (they do not resist the moral law) but they are also predispositions *to the good* (they demand compliance with it)" (6:28). Further, Kant writes,

> *Considered in themselves* natural inclinations are *good*, i.e., not reprehensible, and to want to extirpate them would not only be futile but harmful and blameworthy as well; we must rather only curb them, so that they will not wear each other out but will instead be harmonized into a whole called happiness. (*Rel*, 6:58)

Other things being equal, the fulfillment of human inclinations can be assumed to be a part of what is good for human beings, which we represent to ourselves by conceiving of it as part of what nature intends for us. We realize our radical possibility for evil only if we "reverse the moral order of [our] incentives in incorporating them into [our] maxims," by placing the satisfaction of all of our own inclinations ahead of our obedience to the moral law. "Whether

---

[12] Translation by George di Giovanni, from Immanuel Kant, *Religion and Rational Theology*, trans. and ed. Allen W. Wood and George di Giovanni (Cambridge: Cambridge University Press, 1996).

[13] Of course, at the time of writing the *Religion* Kant had already defended the adoption of a *regulative* interpretation of a teleological view of nature as a single system directed to our own moral fulfillment in the *Critique of Judgment* (see especially §§83–84). But the view that we should conceive of every natural faculty and disposition of our own nature as having a proper and indeed properly moral use was hardly new to the third *Critique*; it is clearly expressed in the 1784 essay *Idea for a Universal History from a Cosmopolitan Point of View*, Proposition One (8:18), and in the *Groundwork* itself (4:395–96). See the conclusion of Chapters 4 and 11 in this volume.

the human being is good or evil must not lie in the difference between the incentives that he incorporates into his maxim (not in
the material of his maxim) but in their *subordination* (in the form of
the maxim): *which of the two he makes the condition of the other*" (6:36).
We are not evil simply because we satisfy natural inclinations, but
only if we make the satisfaction of our own inclinations the sole
condition under which we will comply with the moral law rather
than making the possibility of our complying with the moral law
the sole condition under which we will find it permissible to satisfy our natural inclinations (those of ourselves and of others whom
we can affect by our actions).

On Kant's view, then, there is one sense in which it is natural to
place our own happiness before all else and to try to dignify this
into a moral principle by purporting to philosophize from actual
examples of human conduct, but another sense in which the existence of inclinations the fulfillment of which would bring happiness is entirely natural and in itself a predisposition to the good
rather than to evil. If this is so, then inclinations and happiness as
their satisfaction cannot simply be banished from our conception
of ourselves as moral agents but must be given their proper place.
This is what Kant suggests in highly abstract form by arguing in
the *Religion* that being good lies not in eradicating but in subordinating natural incentives to the moral law, and what he expresses
more concretely in his doctrine of the highest good, the exposition
of which is found not only in the summation of each of Kant's
three critiques but also in the preface to the *Religion* itself[14] – a fact
that cannot but suggest the absolute centrality of this doctrine for
Kant. As Kant expounds this doctrine in the *Religion*, human beings cannot determine their wills to action except by the representation of some particular ends to be achieved by acting. That
is, in order to act we must have something specific we intend to
do, which can only be some particular action proposed as a way
to fulfill some human need or inclination. Even if it is conceived

---

[14] In the *Critique of Pure Reason*, in the "Canon of Pure Reason," A 804–19/B 832–
47; in the *Critique of Practical Reason*, in the "Dialectic of Pure Practical Reason,"
especially 5:110–13; in the *Critique of Judgment*, especially in "the moral proof
of the existence of God," §87, 5:447–53; and in the preface to *Rel*, 6:4–6.

of merely as "the supreme limiting condition of the freedom of action of every human being" (see *G*, 4:430–31), morality needs proposed particular courses of action to limit. But as Kant puts it better in the *Religion*, while the motivation to act (respect for duty) and a formal specification of the condition on all maxims of action (the fundamental principle of morality) can be acknowledged by us independently of "the representation of an end that would have to precede the determination of the will," morality itself must still have "a necessary reference to such an end" because without it we would be "instructed indeed as to *how* to operate but not as to the *whither*" (6:4) – that is, we wouldn't actually have anything particular to do. Particular things to do can only be suggested by nature, not by the pure rational idea of morality itself, and this means that such particular ends of action must be suggested by the various needs and inclinations that we all actually have. What morality imposes is not the eradication of such natural occasions for action, then, but "only the idea of such an object that unites within itself the formal condition of all such ends as we ought to have (duty) with everything that is conditional upon ends we have and which conforms to duty (happiness proportioned to its observance), that is, the idea of a highest good in the world" (6:5). Such a happiness proportioned to duty is not just one's own happiness pursued without regard to any constraints – that would be a goal liable to be incoherent both in itself and with the happiness of others – but is rather the conjoint satisfaction of the naturally good inclinations of oneself and others insofar as that is both licensed by and indeed also prescribed by the goal of adopting maxims that are also fit to be universal law.

Section II of the *Groundwork* thus initiates Kant's complex argument about happiness in his mature moral philosophy – an argument, however, that as we have seen already has its roots in his reflections on reason and morality in the 1770s.[15] The satisfaction of our inclinations, and thus the attainment of happiness, is a natural goal of human beings. Unfortunately, the disposition to place above all else the attainment of our own, individual happiness – or, even more precisely, the attainment of what seems to us

---

[15] See Chapters 2 and 3.

at a given moment the means to our own individual happiness – is also a natural tendency of human beings, and one that tries to dignify itself by co-opting an empiricist approach to philosophizing in order to dignify the actual conduct of human beings with an air of necessity. That tendency has to be resisted, but it cannot be resisted simply by extirpating all our natural inclinations. That would be both impossible and also incoherent, for it would leave us with no actions to undertake at all. Instead, we must combat our tendency to subordinate morality to our own happiness and to dignify this with the name of (popular) philosophy with a sounder philosophy and the proper subordination of happiness to duty that this philosophy prescribes – as we have always known. We misunderstand the conditions and requirements of our own agency both by subordinating morality to our inclinations but also by proposing to extirpate all our inclinations; we properly understand both our nature and our duty when we condition our pursuit of both our own happiness and that of others by the fundamental principle of morality, as is dictated by the concept of the highest good as the object of morality.

SECTION III

The other great mistake that we would make if we were to draw our moral principles solely from the observation of actual human conduct, and to rationalize such a restriction by elevating our actual conduct into a (popular) moral philosophy, would be to adopt the view that human actions are always entirely and solely determined by previous actions and events, leaving us no freedom of choice when faced with a particular moral issue. Such a view of the limits of human action would damage our original disposition to morality by transforming what we so often observe, namely human behavior falling short of the demands of morality because of frailty, impurity, or depravity (see *Rel*, 6:30), into a necessity of human nature, which would then lead us – quite reasonably, once the first step down this path has been taken – to cut and trim our original recognition of the stringent requirements of morality to whatever weaker principle might seem compatible with such a view of the limitations of human nature. If the actions commanded by morality seem to be "actions of which the world has perhaps so far given no example, and whose very practicability might be very much doubted by one who bases everything on experience," "then nothing can protect us against falling away completely from our ideas of duty and can preserve in our soul a well-grounded respect for its law" (*G*, 4:407–8). A revision of the principle of morality to reflect the limitations of what human beings can actually do would indeed be the only reasonable response to such limitations, on the principle of rationality that Kant always assumes we all share, that "duty commands nothing but what we can do" (*Rel*, 6:47).[16] On this principle, if we cannot do an action, then the principle of morality cannot command it, so the principle of morality must reflect what we can do.

Kant clearly must limit the damage that could be done to morality by the all too common examples of human frailty and the philosophy of determinism that dignifies such examples with the air of necessity. But, just as in the case of happiness, he cannot deal with the threat of frailty and its philosophical expression in the doctrine of determinism simply by "extirpating" or *refuting* this doctrine. For determinism is the keystone of Kant's own theoretical philosophy: the condition of the possibility of understanding nature, and of understanding ourselves as creatures in nature, is nothing less than the universal validity of the principle that every event in nature is determined to occur when it does in accordance with a law linking it to a prior occurrence that necessitates what follows. Determinism is not merely a natural attitude for us but the condition of the possibility of our understanding of nature itself. Thus, just as Kant's normative moral philosophy must deal with the natural interest in happiness not by eradicating it but by assigning it its proper place in the complete object of morality, so his account of the conditions of the practicability of the stringent principle of morality must still find a place for a doctrine of determinism. In Kant's own words, "Philosophy must therefore assume that no true contradiction will be found between freedom and natural necessity in the very same human actions, for it can-

---

[16] Kant repeatedly asserts the principle that we must be *able* to do what we *ought* to do in the *Rel*; e.g., 6:62, 63.

not give up the concept of nature any more than that of freedom" (*G*, 4:456).

It is hardly necessary here to go into the details of Kant's way of assuring that there is "no true contradiction" between "freedom and natural necessity": every reader knows that Kant argues that determinism is a necessary condition of assigning a determinate order to events as they occur *in time*, but that because time itself is a feature only of the *appearance* of things, not of those things as they are *in themselves*, it is entirely possible that the real agents of our actions are not – contrary to appearance – situated in time at all, and therefore are not subject to the condition of determinism, and so are instead free to act as morality requires regardless of what past experience might predict.[17] Nor do I here want to canvass the well-worn objections to this reconciliation of freedom and determinism. What I do want to emphasize is that it is part of Kant's view of our own self-understanding, thus of what must be reflected by a proper philosophy, that certainty of our freedom is just as readily and naturally *accessible* to every normal human being as confidence in determinism is: the "rightful claim to freedom of will" is "made even by common human reason" (*G*, 4:457). The assignment of determinism into its proper place in the more complex doctrine of transcendental idealism is not merely the speculative replacement of unsound philosophy by sound philosophy; it is, in Kant's view, itself the proper expression of ordinary human self-understanding.

It might not seem surprising to say this about Kant's defense of freedom in the *Critique of Practical Reason*, where he argues precisely that everyone immediately infers his freedom to act as the moral law requires directly from "the *moral law*, of which we become immediately conscious (as soon as we draw up maxims of the will for ourselves)" (5:29). On this account, "*practical reason*," starting from an indubitable consciousness of what the moral law demands of us, infers our freedom always to do what the law demands by the principle that "ought" implies "can," and then imposes the fact of freedom on "speculative reason," which has, as it were, no choice of its own but to secure (if not explain) at least

---

[17] Kant gives his fullest account of this analysis in the *CPracR*, 5:93–106.

the possibility of freedom (5:30). But, at least on one standard interpretation,[18] the *Groundwork* reconciles freedom and determinism by a more theoretical or speculative route than the *Critique of Practical Reason*: the *Groundwork* argues that the distinction between appearances and things in themselves is one that is introduced in theorizing about the nature of knowledge, and then carried over to reflection on practical reason, where it can directly establish the fact of our freedom from which in turn the validity of the moral law can be inferred (*G*, 4:451–53). But theorizing about the conditions of the possibility of knowledge can easily look like the furthest thing from an activity of "common human reason," and thus it might well seem surprising to claim that Kant's defense of freedom in the *Groundwork* is intended to be a proper expression of ordinary human self-understanding.

But even in the *Groundwork* Kant claims precisely that "no subtle reflection" is required to make the distinction between appearances and things in themselves; rather "one may assume that the commonest understanding can make it, though in its own way, by an obscure discrimination of judgment which it calls feeling." Even this commonest human understanding, Kant alleges, is aware of the difference "between representations given us from somewhere else and in which we are passive, and those that we produce simply from ourselves and in which we show our activity"; and this is enough to "yield a distinction, although a crude one, between a *world of sense* and the *world of understanding*," a distinction that will in turn allow anyone to conceive of the difference between the appearance of objects and their states that are fully governed by deterministic laws of nature and the spontaneous actions of things as they are in themselves that can only be governed by laws of reason rather than sensibility (*G*, 4:450–51). The *Critique of Practical Reason* may infer the fact of our freedom from our prior acknowledgment of our obligation under the moral law, whereas the *Groundwork* may infer our obligation under the moral law from the fact of our freedom, which is in turn inferred from the basic structure of human cognition, but the epistemological status of

[18] See Henrich, "The Deduction of the Moral Law," and Karl Ameriks, *Kant's Theory of Mind* (Oxford: Oxford University Press, 1982), ch. 6.

both arguments is intended to be precisely the same: each argument assumes that what it characterizes as the sufficient ground for knowledge of our freedom is just as available to every human being, just as much a part of our self-understanding as is the basis for the belief in determinism. In both arguments, Kant's philosophical reconciliation of freedom and determinism is supposed to be the expression of common human self-understanding.

This result leads to one last conclusion, which can tie together Kant's apparently optimistic moral writings of 1785 and 1788 with the apparently pessimistic *Religion* of 1793. If transcendental idealism with its reconciliation of freedom and determinism is really the proper expression of ordinary human self-understanding, then the belief in the philosophical doctrine of determinism could not possibly be due to an academic philosophical misunderstanding alone, any more than the elevation of one's own happiness into the unrestricted principle of morality could be the product of a merely speculative misunderstanding alone: the sounder philosophy that reconciles freedom and determinism, just like the sounder philosophy that subordinates but at the same time incorporates happiness into the complete object of morality, Kant has insisted, is just as available to common human reason as the one-sided philosophies are. Instead, the adoption of the one-sided "worldly wisdom" that would undercut our recognition that happiness is not the sole object of morality and human frailty not an excuse for trimming the demands of morality could only be the *product* or *expression* of the human possibility to be evil instead of good, not the *cause* of this evil. If the proper understanding of our own agency is always available to us, then misunderstanding the possibilities of our agency cannot simply be imposed upon us but must be self-imposed. We cannot blame philosophy for our own failings, Kant must hold, because the philosophy that can save us from these failings is always already available to us.

Part III
Duties

Chapter 7
Kantian Foundations for Liberalism

I IS LIBERALISM INCOHERENT?

Contemporary American liberals have been characterized as holding two distinct and potentially conflicting commitments rather
than "a single, articulate political creed." On the one hand, liberals "are heirs to the liberalism of the American Founding Fathers,
a liberalism that is expressed in the Bill of Rights, to the extent that
they believe in the importance of freedom of expression, association and religion, and in civic equality." On the other hand, "they
are heirs also to the liberalism of the New Deal in their conviction
that the state has a part to play in guaranteeing the basic welfare
of all citizens and in protecting employees from exploitation by
powerful corporations."[1] This conjunction may seem self-contradictory because it prescribes a high level of state intervention in
one aspect of the lives of citizens, their material well-being, while
proscribing a similar level of state intervention in another – the formation and expression of their intellectual, political, and spiritual
beliefs and attitudes. At the same time, contemporary conserva-
tives also seem to hold equally self-contradictory principles, since
they too both prescribe and proscribe a high level of state intervention in the lives of citizens, although they reverse the liberal

This chapter originally appeared in *Jahrbuch für Recht und Ethik/Annual Review of
Law and Ethics* 5 (1997): 121–40.

[1] K. Anthony Appiah, "The Marrying Kind," *New York Review of Books* 43 (20 June
1996): 48–54, at p. 52.

assignment of values – they recommend a high level of state intervention in the formation and expression of beliefs about matters that liberals would regard as essentially private and privileged, while advocating a low level of state intervention in matters of property and economy, those matters of welfare that liberals regard as preeminently suitable for public and political intervention and regulation in the name of the common weal. Is either contemporary liberalism or contemporary conservatism even a coherent, let alone plausible doctrine? And if so, which can be given a clear and coherent foundation?

I argue here that Kant showed how to construct a clear and coherent argument for the two basic principles of liberalism. He did this by showing that the fundamental premise of all his practical philosophy, the intrinsic value of human freedom, has very different implications with regard to claims to property rights on the one hand and the rights to freedom of belief and expression on the other. On Kant's analysis, property is by its very nature the subject of interpersonal agreement: a property right consists in the claim of one (natural or artificial) person to some form of control over some sort of object that is deferred to by others; but if property consists in mutual agreements about the control and use of objects, it can exist only in circumstances in which it is rational for all affected agents to uphold such agreements. Beliefs and their expression, however, are not inherently dependent on interpersonal agreement in the same way: although, of course, people are often passionately interested in having their beliefs accepted by others, it is nevertheless possible for one person to hold and express beliefs about all sorts of matters of both fact and value without the acceptance of those beliefs by anyone else. Thus, because property rights can exist only in circumstances in which it is rational for many who might make claims to the use of certain objects to defer to others, public regulation of such claims is both naturally inevitable and morally defensible; but the conditions of the possibility of the formation and expression of many sorts of belief do not include intersubjective agreement, and therefore do not automatically give rise to moral grounds for public regulation. On Kant's underlying assumptions that the essence of state regulation is coercion and that coercive law is appropriate only where it is necessary to preserve and promote the possibility of human freedom, the fundamental premises of contemporary liberalism, that the state must regulate claims to property rights in the interest of all but should regulate the formation and expression of belief as little as possible, turn out to be both coherent and necessary, while the inverted premises of conservatism turn out to be diametrically opposed to both the fundamental principle of morality and the ontology of property.

In Kant's own terms, this account of the twin foundations for liberalism goes like this. He begins with the premise that the only object of unconditional value for human beings is the freedom of human choice and action itself, and that the fundamental principle of morality is that we are all obliged to adopt maxims of action that preserve and promote the freedom of each to the maximal extent compatible with a like freedom for all. An innate right to the freedom of each compatible with a like freedom for all is the correlative to our fundamental obligation to preserve and promote such freedom. The moral worth or virtuousness of a human action, in contrast to its mere rectitude, is a reflection of its motivation – a virtuous action is one motivated solely by respect for the fundamental principle of morality itself – but the freedom that is to be preserved and promoted by right action, whether it is motivated by virtue or not, is in all cases freedom not only of choice but also of action in the world, the freedom of human beings to move their own bodies and to exercise them upon other objects in nature in accord with their own choices to the extent compatible with a like freedom for all other human beings. Political organization under public law is the collective use or threat of coercion to enforce outward compliance with some consequences of the fundamental principle of morality. Such coercion can be justified only when it is both logically possible and practically effective to use it to enforce the preservation and promotion of freedom within the limits of a like freedom for all. Coercive law cannot reasonably be used to force either virtuous motivation or the adoption of various virtuous policies as ends, because coercion cannot force more than the performance of particular outward actions.

These principles might seem to imply a minimalist conception of the state, on which the use of collective power is warranted only to prevent illegitimate intrusions on the innate right to freedom. Such a simple conclusion is precluded, however, by the fundamental difference between the conditions of the possibility of property rights and those of other kinds of rights, which Kant expounds by means of a distinction between innate and acquired rights. Holding a belief or opinion, for example, does not of itself impinge upon the freedom of anyone else, and the exercise of the right to freedom of thought is therefore simply an exercise of the innate right to freedom. Claiming a property right in an object, however, inherently impinges upon the freedom of others who might otherwise be able to control or use the object – as Kant says, "Possession is the connection of an object with myself so that on account of my freedom others restrain their will [*Willkür*] to use that object"[2] – and such a right must therefore be acquired through the deference of others. The restriction of the exercise of such a right to conditions upon which in principle all can agree, and the establishment of such political and therefore potentially coercive regulation as is necessary to make such claims determinate and to secure consent to them, are therefore not intrusions upon a pre-existent innate or natural right, but rather the very conditions of the possibility of the existence of such an acquired right. Now – and this is the key step in the argument, which Kant does not explicitly state but which he clearly presupposes – there are two ways in which we can reasonably be expected to agree with claims made against our freedom of action for the sake of the property rights of another: it will be rational for us to defer to another's claim to the control of an object in the face of a sheer threat of forceful coercion, given our natural and also moral interest in avoiding our own injury or death, or else it will be rational for us to agree to such deference in the absence of such a threat because doing so is still in our own interest as well as in the interest of the other making the property claim. It will be in our interest to agree freely to a property claim when the system of property rights within which such a claim is being made promises all of the participants in it

---

[2] *Vorarbeiten zur Rechtslehre*, 23:212. Translations from the *Vorarbeiten* are my own. In the case of other works by Kant, translations are my own unless otherwise indicated.

some reasonable level of access to its benefits. If we assume that gaining deference to property claims on the basis of sheer threat of force is excluded by the fundamental moral principle of respect for freedom, the only alternative for the foundation of morally acceptable property rights is that they be acquired within a system that is rational for all affected parties to adopt because it is in the interest of each. Thus, while political intrusion into matters of innate right such as freedom of belief is *prima facie* unwarranted and indeed immoral, the political regulation of property rights for the benefit of all is not an intrusion upon an innate right at all but the only condition under which an acquired right can be acquired in a morally acceptable way.

In this chapter, I do not give equal attention to each stage of this argument; after a brief exposition of the underlying principles of Kant's philosophy of right, I focus on Kant's analysis of the necessary conditions for rightful claims to property, his inference that, since there can be no rightful "unilateral acquisition" of property, there can be a rightful claim to property only within a system of "distributive justice" (*austheilende Gerechtigkeit*),[3] which is what grounds the "liberalism of the New Deal," and his contrast between the acquired right of property and the innate right of freedom that is directly expressed in such rights as the right of free expression, which is what grounds the "liberalism of the Founding Fathers."

II LIBERALISM AND THE DISTRIBUTION OF PROPERTY

1. The end or value which is served by adherence to the fundamental principle of morality is human freedom or autonomy; that is, adherence to the principle of morality, in whatever form it is expressed, preserves and promotes the exercise of freedom by all human beings. This is essentially the indemonstrable material first principle of Kant's moral philosophy, which cannot itself be derived from anything more fundamental.[4] Kant clearly implies

---

[3] Ibid. 23:281.

[4] The concept of an indemonstrable material first principle of morality is suggested in Kant's early comments on morality in *An Inquiry concerning the Distinctness*

it in the *Groundwork for the Metaphysics of Morals* when he states that the source of the priceless "dignity, i.e., unconditioned, incomparable worth," that makes any human being an end rather than a means is the freedom of a human being to obey only those laws "which he gives himself," or "autonomy" (*G*, 4:435–36). At the same time, he says it outright in his 1784 lectures on natural right, when he states that "The inner value of the human being rests on his freedom," and "If only rational beings can be ends in themselves, this cannot be because they have reason, but because they have freedom; reason is merely a means"[5] – that is, the moral law, which is formulated by reason, is binding only because it is the necessary means to the preservation and promotion of freedom. Or as Kant puts it a decade later in the *Metaphysics of Morals*, "On this concept of freedom . . . are based unconditional practical laws" (*MM*, 6:221).[6]

What Kant calls "right," the appropriate domain for the politically organized rule of law, concerns "the external and indeed practical relation of one person to another, insofar as their actions, as facts, can have (direct or indirect) influence on each other." Thus, when he says that right is "the sum of the conditions under which the choice of one can be united with the choice of another in accordance with a universal law of freedom," or that the Universal Principle of Right is that "Any action is *right* if it can co-exist with everyone's freedom in accordance with a universal law, or if on its maxim the freedom of choice of each can coexist with everyone's freedom in accordance with a universal law" (*MM*,

---

of the Principles of Natural Theology and Morality, written for the Berlin academy essay competition in 1762 and published by the academy in 1764; see 2:299 – 300. I suggest that the foundation of Kant's mature moral philosophy does not lie in surrendering the view of the *Inquiry* that a formal principle of morality must always be applied to a material one in favor of the view that morality can proceed with a purely formal principle alone, as is usually thought; rather, the fundamental change in the mature philosophy lies in the replacement of material first principles based on feelings detected by the moral sense with the indemonstrable principle of the dignity of autonomy. See Chapters 1, 4, and 5.

5 *Naturrecht Feyerabend,* 27:1319, 1321.

6 For translations in this chapter, I have generally followed the *The Metaphysics of Morals,* trans. Mary J. Gregor (Cambridge: Cambridge University Press, 1991); the present quote is from p. 48.

6:230),[7] what he means is that right is the condition in which the external *use* or the *expression* of any individual's freedom of choice in freedom of action can coexist with a like active expression of freedom on the part of all others. Thus the universal law of right is "to act externally so that the free use of your choice can coexist with the freedom of everyone in accordance with a universal law" (*MM*, 6:231).[8]

This emphasis on freedom of action or the external use of freedom of choice does not itself separate the principle of right from the fundamental principle of morality, as if that fundamental principle concerned only the freedom of choice and not external freedom of action. Throughout his moral philosophy, Kant assumes that the freedom that is fostered by the principle of morality is the freedom to choose to adopt maxims *of action* and to *act* in accordance with those autonomously chosen maxims. Although the moral worth of a particular action may be assessed in accordance with the maxim or intention its agent acts upon rather than the actual outcome of the action (see *G*, 4:394), the maxim or intention is by its very nature a maxim or intention *to act* in a certain way in order to bring about a certain outcome in the external world. Thus, to be free or autonomous is to be able to choose one's own maxims of action freely and to act freely in accord with those maxims. There would be many ways to argue this point; one way would be to appeal to Kant's doctrine of the highest good as the ultimate *object* of morality, because, as a conjunction of *happiness* with virtue or the worthiness to be happy, the highest good is clearly a condition that must obtain *in the world* as a result of *actions* performed with virtuous *intentions*. As Kant puts it in the *Critique of Judgment*, which includes the last major statement of his moral theory prior to the *Metaphysics of Morals*, the "final end" that is defined by the moral law is "the highest good *in the world* possible through freedom."[9] Kant's view is thus that the *external use*

---

[7] Ibid., p. 56.

[8] Ibid., p. 56.

[9] *CJ*, §87, 5:450; translation by J. C. Meredith, *Kant's Critique of Teleological Judgment* (Oxford: Clarendon Press, 1928), p. 118. For further discussion of Kant's theory of the highest good, see Chapter 6, section II, and Chapter 10 in this volume.

of freedom, or freedom of action, must be protected by a condition of right because human autonomy is the ultimate value, and freedom of action is the natural expression and concomitant of freedom of choice.

The claim that the condition of right consists in reciprocal freedom of external action, which is an indispensable premise for Kant's subsequent argument that there is a right to acquire property and that there must therefore be a rightful way to acquire property, is different from the claim that the condition of right is the legislation of external rather than internal *incentives*. Kant claims that "there is connected with right by the principle of contradiction an authorization to coerce someone who infringes upon it" (*MM*, 6:31);[10] that is, right is analytically equivalent to the regulation of the external use of freedom by the establishment of coercive external incentives (see *MM*, 6:219).[11] In Kant's opinion, only the performance of particular external actions, or external uses of freedom, can be coerced or compelled by the provision of aversive external incentives, that is, threats of punishment. The adoption of an internal incentive, or a particular motivation for performing an action, as well as the adoption of ends or policies, as contrasted to the performance of particular actions that might realize those policies, cannot be compelled by external incentives, because particular actions can always be performed in order to avoid a threatened sanction without the adoption of any motivation or policy other than that of avoiding the sanction. Thus, Kant argues that if the realm of right is defined by those violations of the laws of freedom for which coercive sanctions are both logically and morally possible, then it must be restricted to a proper subset of all the duties dictated by the moral law (and indeed even a subset of those actions that might be dictated by the universal principle of right): the realm of right or juridical legislation is limited to the regulation of external actions affecting the external use of the freedom of others, which it is morally legitimate and necessary to regulate and which can be effectively legislated. There is, in other words, both a theoretical and a practical restriction on the use of coercion:

---

[10] Gregor, *MM*, p. 57.
[11] Ibid., p. 46.

coercion can be rightfully legislated only where it is necessary to prevent a hindrance to a hindrance to freedom (*MM*, DR Introduction, §D, 6:31),[12] and only where it can be effective in preventing such a hindrance.

Yet this restriction of the realm of right to the coercive enforcement of duties regarding the external freedom of others should not be taken to mean that the realm of right has nothing to do with the fundamental principle of morality. The fundamental principle of morality dictates the protection of the external use of freedom or freedom of action, as a natural expression of freedom of choice and thus as part of autonomy as a whole; likewise the fundamental principle of morality dictates the restriction of the use of coercion to the regulation or prevention of those uses of freedom of action which would unlawfully restrict or destroy the freedom of action of others. At the same time, duties of virtue, those duties flowing from the fundamental principle of morality which for either theoretical or practical reasons cannot be coercively enforced, do not concern solely freedom of choice or the internal use of freedom. As Kant makes clear, while "the freedom to which [juridical or political] laws relate can be only freedom in the *external* use of choice, the freedom to which [laws of virtue] relate is freedom in both the external and the internal use of choice, insofar as it is determined by laws of reason" (*MM*, Introduction, 6:214).[13] Political regulation properly concerns only actions affecting the freedom of action of others, because the fundamental value of freedom protects the freedom of action as well as of choice but only licenses the use of coercion to prevent injuries to freedom of action; duties of virtue preserve and promote freedom of action as well as of choice even where juridical legislation cannot because freedom of action as well as of choice is part of the natural expression of autonomy.

2. The institution of property arises on the fundamental principle of morality because it is natural and necessary for us to exercise our external freedom of action not only in the motion of our own

---

[12] Ibid., p. 57.

[13] Ibid., p. 42. For more on the complex issue of distinguishing between duties of right and duties of virtue, see Chapter 9.

bodies but also in the use of other objects in nature, and the institution of property falls within the realm of right or juridical legislation because such an exercise of our right to freedom of action naturally affects the freedom of action of others who might use the same objects and who can also be influenced by coercive external incentives. Property rights are thus acquired rights, although the right to establish property rights is part of the innate right to freedom.

Kant presents his analysis of the concept of property and its consequences in a roundabout way. He begins by considering what conditions are necessary to make possible *injury* to the right of property rather than to the innate right to freedom and introduces his distinction between *sensible, physical* or *empirical* possession on the one hand and *intelligible, rational,* or *noumenal* possession on the other hand to explain what an injury to a property right is (*MM*, DR, §1, 2:245). Physical possession or detention is the bodily holding of an object or the bodily occupation of a place, and does not allow for a distinctive type of injury against property: to wrest an object from someone's hand or force him off of the spot on which he stands is an injury against his innate right to freedom conceived as including – or perhaps even consisting in – the right to maintain one's own body in particular states of rest or motion as one sees fit (*MM*, DR, §6, 6:250). For there to be a possibility of a distinct category of injury to property rights, there must be a relation between people and their property that does not consist in physical possession and that can be injured without violating the innate right to freedom by interfering with the bodily condition of persons. This form of control over objects and their use that can be violated by another's possession of an object or occupation of a position, even when that does not interfere with the current bodily condition of the rightful owner, is what Kant calls intelligible possession. In his exposition in the *Metaphysics of Morals*, Kant initially tells us more about what intelligible possession is not than what it is, but he eventually gives us a clue as to what it means when he states that "such a concept of possession (*possessio noumenon*) [is] a *giving of law* that holds for everyone . . . since by it an obligation is laid upon all others, which they would not otherwise have, to refrain from using the object" (*MM*, DR, §7,

6:253).[14] Intelligible possession, the basis for a right to property rather than the innate right to freedom of the person, consists in a relation among persons regarding objects, in which persons other than the owner agree that all but the owner are to refrain from using the object otherwise than as the owner chooses, or in which they defer to the will of the owner regarding the control and use of the object to which he claims a property right. Kant states this crucial point more clearly later in the text, when he writes that

> Now if these sensible conditions of possession, as a relation of persons to *objects* that have no obligation, are left out or disregarded (abstracted from), possession is nothing other than a relation of a person to persons, all of whom are *bound*, with regard to the use of the thing, by the *will* of the first person, insofar as his will conforms with the axiom of outer freedom, with the *postulate* of his capacity to use external objects of choice, and with the *lawgiving* of the will of all thought as united *a priori*. (MM, DR, §17, 6:268)[15]

Kant makes the initial point of this paragraph many times in the preparatory sketches for the "Doctrine of Right," sometimes more clearly than in the published text. Here is one citation that can stand for many:

> All right consists in the possibility (the capacity [*Vermögen*]) to necessitate the will of another through laws of freedom (although not solely through these). Thus it properly consists only in the relation of the will [*Willkür*] to the will of others and not immediately to objects of the will.[16]

In other words, property rights consist not in any immediate relation between a person and an object but in a relation among persons in which all who might claim control of an object consent to control of that object by one particular person. This relation is called intelligible, rational, or noumenal in a theoretical or ontological sense simply because it does not consist in any immediately perceivable physical relation between a person and an object, but in

---

[14] Ibid., p. 75.
[15] Ibid., p. 88.
[16] *Vorarbeiten zur Rechtslehre*, 23:227.

a relation among the minds and wills of persons (of which, of course, there may be physical marks or records, such as fences and deeds); it is also properly called by these terms in a *normative* sense, for, insofar as such a relationship is to be *freely* established or maintained, it must in fact be *rational* for all affected parties to agree to it. This crucial point emerges only gradually over the course of Kant's analysis, which is why I say that Kant suggests, rather than makes plain, an argument for the "New Deal" leg of liberalism.

The first point that Kant makes, under the rubric of the "postulate" of the capacity to use external objects of choice, is that, because physical objects themselves have no free wills to serve as the ground of an obligation on our part to them, it would be irrational or a contradiction in our own wills to deny ourselves the use of them in the absence of any reason stemming from other human wills not to do so. Kant expresses this irrationality by stating that if we were to deny the right to make mere objects into property "then freedom would be depriving itself of the use of its choice with regard to an object of choice, by putting *usable* objects beyond any possibility of being *used*" (*MM*, DR, §2, 6:246).[17] This would actually represent a *contradiction* in willing on the unstated assumption that objects are usable as means to all sorts of reasonable ends and on Kant's stated assumption that it is analytically true that to will the end is to will (permissible) means to it (*G*, 4:417): to put potentially usable objects beyond the sphere of our control when there can be no reason to do so coming from the object itself would be to deny ourselves possible means to our various ends, even though it is a fundamental canon of rationality that we should will the (availability of) means to our possible ends, and would thus be a contradiction in willing and therefore a violation of duty either to ourselves or to others (depending on who might otherwise get to use the object as a means to their legitimate ends).[18]

---

[17] Gregor, *MM*, p. 59. For a particularly clear statement of the "postulate" in the *Vorarbeiten*, see 23:213.

[18] Among currently standard accounts of Kant's theory of property, that by Leslie A. Mulholland comes closest to analyzing the contradiction underlying the postulate of pure practical reason with regard to property as a contradiction in willing; but he puts the point somewhat obscurely by appealing to formulations

This point, however, which is prominent in many of Kant's statements of the "postulate of practical reason with regard to rights,"[19] only expresses part of the conditions under which claims to property rights are permissible. It says that the denial of the right to property in objects would be an irrational contradiction in willing because there is no hindrance to such claims stemming from the objects themselves; but equally important, although less clearly stated, is the other part of Kant's argument, which says that the relation among wills in which the intelligible possession of property consists can be *rightfully* established only when there is no hindrance to a person's claim to an object arising from the *wills of the other affected persons*, or when the claim is consistent with the freedom of others and can therefore be established in accord not only with one's own unilateral will but with the will of all others who might also, as far as the object is concerned, raise a claim to control it. Thus Kant claims that "my *rightful* power to make use of" an object must "coexist with the freedom of everyone in accordance with a universal law" (*MM*, DR, §2, 6:246).[20] That is, the conditions for a *rightful* claim to property include not just the lack of any claim to rights on the basis of objects themselves but also the possibility of a universal will or agreement to an individual's use of such an object on the part of others who would otherwise be able to use it.

Kant expresses this point in one sketch by listing as two

in Kant's preparatory sketches, which suggest that "If a maxim of preventing use of external objects were to become a law, it would have the consequence of preventing some (otherwise possible) use of innate faculties"; see his *Kant's System of Rights* (New York: Columbia University Press, 1990), p. 250. He does not go back to the fundamental argument of the *Groundwork* that it is a contradiction in willing to deny ourselves the means to our possible legitimate ends, which is what requires that we be able to use our "innate faculties" for possible ends. It is important to recognize that this argument underlies the argument for the acquirability of property in the "Doctrine of Right," because it is also crucial for the doctrine of duties to oneself in the "Doctrine of Virtue" and thus constitutes a common bond between the two parts of the *Metaphysics of Morals* in spite of their other differences.

[19] Several particularly clear examples are at *Vorarbeiten zur Rechtslehre*, 23:288 and 23:291.

[20] Gregor, *MM*, p. 68.

separate conditions of the possibility of property defined as intelligible possession, first, the contradiction in willing that would arise if the will were made "dependent" on a mere object and then, second, the restriction of claims to property to conditions universally valid for rational beings: "All relation of right is a merely intelligible relation of rational beings to one another and thereby in relation to objects of the will, in regard to which their will is restricted by the law of universal validity of that will for everybody."[21] Or, in another passage, Kant again makes clear that there are at least two conditions for rightful claims to property, the second of which is the compatibility of any particular claim to property with a universal law allowing agreement about such claims among rational beings:

> Thus all synthetic propositions of right are possible only if
> (1) having external property [*Mein und Dein*] does not contradict freedom in accordance with universal laws, thus if it is possible to act without going against this law; (2) such a possession as merely rightful can be found only in a united will, hence the *a priori* condition of the unifiability of the will in regard to an object also constitutes the condition of possibility of a merely rightful possession of things and of external property.[22]

The possibility of rightful claims to property thus depends not only on the consistency of such claims with the nature of objects but also on the morally requisite consistency with the rational willing of the other rational beings affected by such claims, in whose deference the right to property ontologically consists, in accordance with a universal law of freedom or, in other words, in their free and rational consent to such claims.

The implications of this analysis should be obvious. Property rights extending in any way beyond the right to personal freedom in the current detention of an object or occupation of a position consist in the deference of others to one's control of that object or position. That is a purely theoretical or ontological point. In principle, such deference could be obtained in two distinct ways: by

---

[21] *Vorarbeiten zur Rechtslehre*, 23:213.
[22] Ibid., 23:227.

sheer threat or use of force or by freely and rationally given consent. (In practice, of course, consent might be obtained by a mixture of these two means.) But a *rightful* claim to property precludes its foundation in a sheer and unprovoked threat or use of force, which would violate the innate right to freedom (i.e., the obligation to respect the freedom) of anyone on whom it was exercised, and can therefore be grounded only in the freely and rationally given consent of those whose deference is needed. "For rightful possession consists solely in the capacity of the will to determine the will of others in regard to an object of the senses in accordance with laws of freedom."[23] But such consent can be given only if the claim to property is in accord with a universal law of freedom, which is presumably not just the moral law in general but a more particular law that makes the consent rational by making it in the interest of those who are to consent, which would in turn be achieved if the system of rules or conventions within which any individual property right is claimed extends to all those involved the possibility of making such claims of similar or equal value in their own reasonable judgment.[24]

---

[23] Ibid., 23:275.

[24] The currently standard accounts of Kant's theory of property all make clear that Kant's argument about property rests on the inference that since nonhuman things themselves do not have any rights, the only hindrances to the use of objects and the need to establish determinate particular rights to them arise from the fact that property rights consist in the deference of other people to someone's use of an object. But they do not, I believe, make sufficiently clear the normative character of the second step in Kant's argument, for they do not stress that ontology alone leaves it open *how* such agreement or deference is to be obtained and maintained, and thus that there is a moral choice to be made about whether property rights are to be established by force or by free consent, and that if they are to be established by the latter route then they are inherently limited to conditions under which it is rational for free parties to agree to them. Thus, Wolfgang Kersting presents Kant's argument as an immediate inference that since a thing has no rights, only the general will can establish such rights, and calls this an "eleutheronomic" theory of property, but he does not make explicit that there is a moral choice to be made whether to unite the wills of all into a general will freely or merely by force; see his *Wohlgeordnete Freiheit: Immanuel Kants Rechts- und Staatsphilosophie* (Berlin: Walter de Gruyter, 1984), pp. 138–99, 146–49. Bernd Ludwig follows Kant's own roundabout way of making the argument

3. Most of the time Kant seems content to state this implication in the most abstract terms possible, arguing simply that because property actually consists in the deference of others to the owner's control of an object, then if property is to be rightful, this deference must be freely granted, and thus cannot arise from an owner's unilateral act of will but can only arise from the consent of all, represented as given through a common or united will. Here is a particularly clear example of that argument:

> Empirical property [*Mein und Dein*] is grounded in the subsumption of the apprehension (of the object) under the idea of the united will with regard to outer objects in general.
>
> For through a unilateral *actus* of the will I would lay an obligation on others that does not rest on their own will, which would violate freedom in accordance with universal laws. Therefore with regard to property the will of others must agree *a priori*,

by invoking the common will of all, and thus the postulated agreement of others to anyone's property claims, to explain why one person does not injure another when he forcibly *defends* his property; but he does not make clear that freely obtaining the consent of all through a general will itself represents a decision to acquire property morally rather forcibly; see his *Kants Rechtslehre*, Kant Forschungen, vol. 2 (Hamburg: Felix Meiner, 1988), pp. 116–17. Mary Gregor argues that since property rights consist in the deference of others to one's use of objects, one can only rationally make property claims where one is prepared to defer to others' claims to what they *have* acquired; but this formulation, although not, I believe, so intended, makes it sound as if this is merely a matter of prudence, not a moral decision to claim property rights only when others would freely agree to them, whether they have already acquired anything or not; see her "Kant's Theory of Property," *Review of Metaphysics* 41 (June 1988): 757–87, at pp. 779, 785. Leslie Mulholland perhaps comes closest to making Kant's point clear when he writes that since intelligible possession cannot be understood "as a relation of a person to an object," it must instead be "a relation of a person to other persons through moral laws which determine obligations concerning the use of the object" (*Kant's System of Rights*, p. 241), but he still does not make clear that the decision to obtain the consent of others to one's property claims in accordance with moral laws is not dictated by ontology but is itself a moral decision. And none of these authors then analyzes the conditions under which intersubjective deference to property claims would be freely granted; thus, none discusses the liberal implications of Kant's theory of property.

which is only possible if the will of others is united with my own in one willing, i.e., through the idea of the united will.[25]

This sort of argument leaves unstated the natural assumption that rational beings with needs to use objects similar to those of the owner to whom they are deferring control of a particular object will only do so if by their deference they can enjoy similar rights, and thus leaves unstated the conclusion that a system of property rights can be freely agreed to by rational beings only if it is equitable to some suitable degree.

Sometimes, however, Kant comes closer to making this conclusion explicit. Here is one passage in which he does so:

> Through my acquisition there arises an obligation for others to do something or to refrain from something that they did not have before my action. – An obligation cannot arise for anybody, however, except what he himself incurs (*omnis obligatio est contracta*). Thus nobody can acquire through unilateral will . . . but only through the united will of those for whom an obligation is created in the acquisition and who reciprocally contract.[26]

The freely granted deference of wills that constitutes rightfully acquired or maintained property, in other words, is to be understood on the model of a multiparty contract: it is rational for a free agent to give up something of potential value, the claim to a particular object – only in exchange for something of similar value – presumably, a similar claim to another object. And not surprisingly, the right to enter into contracts is the first specific property right that Kant discusses after expounding his general theory of right. By comparing the conditions of the possibility of rightful acquisition to those necessary for making contracts, Kant clearly implies that a certain degree of reciprocity is inherent in the idea of such rightful acquisition. However, he does not attempt to define further what would be sufficient conditions of reciprocity in such a contract, that is, what would count as a sufficient level of fairness in a system of property rights to make it something that could be freely accepted as opposed to being imposed by force or its threat alone.

[25] *Vorarbeiten zur Rechtslehre*, 23:308–9.
[26] Ibid., 23:219.

Some further definition of such a minimal condition of fairness, however, might be gleaned from Kant's distinctive further argument that the rightful private possession of property must be conceived as a transfer to a particular possessor of a rightful original common possession of the basis of all property (land). Kant stresses that the idea of original common possession is not meant as a piece of history but instead furnishes the basis for a standard of justice in claims to property rights: "Original possession in common is, rather, a practical rational concept that contains *a priori* the principle in accordance with which alone men can use a place on the earth in accordance with principles of right" (*MM*, DR, §13, 6:262).[27] Understood normatively rather than historically, the argument about common possession that Kant constructs yields some further information about the minimal conditions of fairness for a rightful system of private property. The argument has both factual and moral premises.

The basic factual premise is that human beings occupy the undivided surface of a sphere, the physical features of which certainly make some parts harder to reach than others but do not absolutely preclude anyone from moving to any point on it from any other point. Thus, from a theoretical point of view the original possession of land can only be "possession *in common* because the spherical surface of the earth unites all the places on its surface" (*MM*, DR, §13, 6:262).[28] But precisely because the surface of the earth is undivided, mere geography (or any other empirical fact) cannot give any particular person a right to occupy any particular place.

There are then two basic moral premises to the argument. The first is that everyone has a right to exist unhindered in some place or other on the undivided surface of the earth. Kant does not spell this premise out in the text of the *Metaphysics of Morals*, but several passages in the *Vorarbeiten* make it clear that this premise is a consequence of the innate right to freedom: since to deprive someone of a place to stand on the earth requires the forcible removal of his person from that spot, the basic right to a place on the earth

---

[27] Gregor, *MM*, p. 84.
[28] Ibid., p. 83.

follows from the innate right to freedom of the person. In Kant's words, "The *Communio originaria* is not empirically grounded as *factum* or occurrence but is a right to the land without which no human being can exist and which itself follows from freedom in the use of things"; however, the right to a place on the land is "not a right to a thing but my innate right to freedom, which no one can take away from me."[29] The right to maintain one's own existence, which is also a perfect duty to oneself, entails a right to exist unhindered on some spot of land or other, even though no such spot is naturally divided from any other. But since the land of the earth is naturally undivided and every inhabitable point is ultimately accessible from every other, the innate right to freedom cannot by itself give anyone a right to any specific spot; rather it gives everyone an equal interest in the undivided or common possession of the surface of the earth.

The second moral premise of the argument is the assumption that any rightful claim to exclusive control of a specific portion of the undivided surface of the earth can only be conceived of as the product of a free transfer to an individual owner of the right of all to any place. Kant puts this point by saying that the right to individual possession presupposes an original common possession: "The schematism of external property rests on the agreement of all to universal *a priori* principles for the distribution of things in space within which property takes place: consequently it presupposes an original common possession."[30] The agreement of all to assign a particular place to a particular owner can create rightful possession only because it can be conceived of as if it were derived from a common possession of all land, a possession that can be freely divided and rightfully transmitted to particular owners.

But now, although Kant does not say so, these premises imply a certain constraint on any rightful system of private ownership. Because the original common possession of the land arises not just from geography but from the right of each to a place on the land, which flows from the innate right and indeed duty of each person freely to maintain his own existence, and because the transfer of

---

[29] *Vorarbeiten zur Rechtslehre*, 23:241, 281.
[30] Ibid., 23:273.

title from the commonality to any individual has to be imagined as occurring by the free consent of all, which consent has to be in accord with the universal laws of freedom, it follows that any system or "schematism" of individual property rights must allow each participant at least an opportunity to maintain his or her own existence equivalent to what he or she enjoyed under the original common possession: otherwise it would be irrational for anyone freely to consent to the transfer of rights, and it would indeed be a violation of the duty to strive to maintain one's own existence. This will certainly imply that in a fair system of property each individual must have a right to acquire property in land or other means of sustenance sufficient to maintain an opportunity for continued existence equal to anyone else's. The right has to be understood as one to an *opportunity*, of course, because the innate right to unhindered occupation of a place on the surface of the earth that is the basis for the acquired right of property itself does not guarantee continued existence but only the opportunity for continued existence; after the expulsion from Eden, the land has to be worked in order to provide sustenance, and nature as well as other humans have to cooperate for that end to be achieved. And the right has to be understood only as one to an equal chance to maintain one's own existence, not necessarily as a right to an equal share of any particular material goods. Nevertheless, the right to an opportunity to property sufficient to maintain existence or an equivalent that can produce the same result provides a minimum standard for the rational acceptability of any system of property rights, where the rational acceptability of such a system is in turn a necessary condition of its morality.

4. Kant's analysis of property, then, leads to the conclusion that an opportunity to maintain one's own existence at least equivalent to that which would have been enjoyed in an original common possession of the earth is a necessary condition of the rationality of free agreement to any system of property and thus a necessary condition of the rightfulness of property itself. It is the only condition under which a rational agent can freely agree to the existence of private property rather than the undivided possession of the entire surface of the earth.

This argument should not be understood in other ways, some of which Kant himself misleadingly suggests. First, it should be clear that it is neither a merely prudential argument that others will defer to one only if one gives them something of equal value in exchange for what they surrender, nor is it that the moral law of universalization is to be applied to a preexistent natural right to property, in the way in which a moral concern for the happiness of others can be superimposed on one's own natural desire for one's own happiness in order to make the pursuit of the latter morally acceptable. There is one passage in the published text of the "Doctrine of Right" that might be taken to suggest either of such arguments:

> When I declare (by word or deed) that I will that something external is to be mine, I thereby declare that everyone else is under obligation to refrain from using that object of my choice, an obligation that no one would have were it not for this act of mine to establish a right. This claim involves, however, acknowledging that I in turn am under obligation to refrain from using what is externally his; for the obligation here arises from a universal rule having to do with external rightful relations. I am therefore not under obligation to leave external objects belonging to others untouched unless everyone else provides me assurance that he will behave in accordance with the same principle with regard to what is mine. (*MM*, DR, §8, 6:255–56)[31]

Contrary to what the last sentence of this passage might suggest, Kant's argument is not that experience shows that anyone's claim to property will be insecure unless equal property rights are extended to others; unhappily, experience shows that if sufficient force is used or threatened, this is far from being true. Nor is the argument that morality requires that something that one *could* do on one's own, namely possess property going beyond what can be immediately physically possessed, is permissible only if that act can be universalized, as the second sentence might suggest. Such an interpretation brings morality onto the scene too late. Rather, Kant's argument is that since property is never a natural

---

[31] Gregor, *MM*, p. 77 (modified).

relationship between a person and an object, but literally consists in a relation among wills, namely, the deference of other wills to one's own regarding the use of a particular object, what morality requires is that such deference be obtained freely rather than forcibly; from that point on, the inference that a rightful system of property requires it to offer something of suitable value to all participants follows without any further appeal to moral law but from a theoretical analysis of the conditions under which free agents would consent to a transmission of their original undivided interest in common property. In other words, a direct appeal to the principle of morality – in the form of our fundamental obligation to respect the innate right of freedom – governs the initial decision to establish the relation among wills in which property consists freely rather than forcibly; it is not a later decision to extend a privilege that one enjoys oneself to others in the name of universalization.

This point is important, because, if the argument were understood in the latter way, it might seem as if the obligation to extend the right of property to others, like the obligation to make the happiness of others one's own end, would generate only an *imperfect* duty, requiring that one extend to others some sort of property right or other but leaving how much one extends exclusively up to one's judgment about an appropriate degree of benevolence, given one's other duties, interests, and so on. Rather, Kant's argument is that since free agreement to a system of property rights can be expected from rational beings only under a condition of minimum reciprocity or equability, satisfaction of the latter is a necessary condition of the possibility of a rightful system of property from the outset.

Another possibly misleading interpretation of the argument that any rightful system of property must satisfy a certain level of fairness is suggested when Kant argues that the state has the right of taxation for the support of the poor, such as foundling hospitals and charitable institutions, because

> The general will of the people has united itself into a society that is to maintain itself perpetually; and for this end it has submitted itself to the internal authority of the state in order to main-

tain those members of the society who are unable to maintain themselves. For reasons of state the government is therefore authorized to constrain the wealthy to provide the means of sustenance to those who are unable to provide for even their most necessary natural needs. (*MM*, DR General Remark (following §49) C, 6:326)[32]

This could make it sound as if wealth, like strength or talent, is a natural condition that is a means to the end of self-sustenance, which some may have while others do not, and that in recognition of the possible transitoriness of wealth, like that of health, those who have it enter into a state, like a health maintenance organization (HMO), to help them if they lose it by providing them with alternative means to their continued sustenance, which they can reasonably expect to enjoy only if they stand ready when they do enjoy wealth to help other members of the state who are already in the condition they hope to avoid. But such an argument is more purely prudential than what Kant's fundamental analysis of property implies. It would come close to an argument that the state ought to regulate property in the interest of the happiness of all its members, an argument the premise for which Kant strongly rejects in the essay *On the Common Saying: That Might Be Right in Theory but Not in Practice*, when he says that a "paternalistic" government, which makes its own judgments about what would best ensure the happiness of its subjects, "is the greatest conceivable despotism, i.e., a constitution which suspends the entire freedom of its subjects."[33] Kant's fundamental argument for the reciprocality of property rights is not drawn from the value of any particular ends to which people might use their freedom as a means, or the aggregation of such ends in the aim of happiness, but from the necessary conditions for preserving the rational exercise of freedom itself. Since property consists in the deference of the wills of others, nobody possesses wealth merely as a natural good, like health, strength, or talent, which might be lost as circumstances change; rather all wealth is a social creation, which, if it is to be

[32] Ibid., p. 136.
[33] 8:290–91; translation by H. B. Acton in Kant, *Political Writings*, ed. Hans Reiss, 2d ed. (Cambridge: Cambridge University Press, 1991), p. 74.

acquired or maintained freely rather than forcibly, can only be enjoyed under conditions in which it is rational for others to agree to it. And it will be rational for others to agree to a system that assigns wealth to anyone only if it provides all with a suitable level of property or access to it. In other words, the right of the state to control the distribution of property or wealth is a consequence of the fact that the possibility of the rational consent of all to the distribution of property is a necessary condition of the existence of property at all.

Thus, the fundamental premise of the "Liberalism of the New Deal," that the state, as the agency of the people as a whole, has the right and indeed the duty to provide a certain level of opportunity to acquire property or equivalent means of support for the existence of even its poorest members, is not an intrusion upon any natural right to property or the politicization of a moral principle of charity that ought to remain the province of private and voluntary institutions. It is a necessary condition of the rightful existence of any form of property other than undivided common possession of all the land and all that is upon it with all the inconveniences of this condition.

III LIBERALISM AND THE FREEDOM OF CONSCIENCE

We can now treat the other tenet of liberalism, what was referred to at the outset as the "liberalism of the Founding Fathers," much more briefly. In Kant's view, the principle that people must enjoy a wide latitude in forming, adopting, expressing, and publishing beliefs on almost any conceivable matter free of the fear of governmental intervention is a direct consequence of their innate right to freedom, itself the immediate consequence of our fundamental moral obligation to respect freedom above all else, combined with what we can call the ontological fact, parallel to but contrasting with the ontology of property, that one person's adoption or expression of a belief does not itself in any way directly impinge on the freedom of others or require any deference from their wills. Therefore one person's adoption or expression of virtually any belief whatever does not give anyone else a right to intervene in the former's exercise of his freedom in this form. This point is so obvious that Kant states it even before he describes the fundamental principles of property and the constitution of the state that is necessary primarily to make claims to property determinate and secure:

> *Freedom* (independence from being constrained by another's choice), insofar as it can coexist with the freedom of every other in accordance with a universal law, is the only original right belonging to every human being in virtue of his humanity. This principle of innate freedom already involves the following authorizations, which are not really distinct from it . . . : innate *equality*, that is, independence from being bound by others to more than one can in turn bind them; hence a human being's quality of being *his own master* (*sui juris*), as well as being a human being *beyond reproach* (*iusti*), because before he performs any act affecting rights he has done no wrong to anyone; and finally, his being authorized to do to others anything that does not in itself diminish what is theirs, so long as they do not want to accept it – such things as merely communicating his thoughts to them, telling or promising them something, whether what he says is true and sincere or untrue and insincere . . . ; for it is entirely up to them whether they want to believe him or not. (*MM*, DR, 6:237–38)[34]

Kant's assumption is that as long as a human being is a free agent, his knowledge that another person holds any particular belief cannot itself constrain his own opinions or actions, and that he therefore has no right to constrain the other in his formation or expression of beliefs. Of course, there may be circumstances in which this assumption does not hold: impressionable children may not yet have freedom over their own beliefs; people in a crowded theater who hear a convincing scream of "Fire!" may not be able to control their panic; and perhaps advocating the violent overthrow of the state would diminish what rightfully belongs to the law-abiding citizens of the state, namely the security of the rule of law. In such circumstances Kant's premises would allow for the regulation of speech, not however as the expression of

---

[34] Gregor, *MM*, p. 63, modified.

belief as such but rather as a form of action that has the predictable consequence of illegitimately constraining the freedom of others. But such special circumstances aside, Kant's argument is simply that in the ideal case, where all involved are mature and fully functioning free agents, no one person's adoption or expression of a belief consists in the deference of any other or intrinsically constrains the will of any other, and therefore there can be no right, whether exercised individually or transferred to the state, to regulate such matters.

Again, it is important to see what kind of argument this is. It is not the argument that Kant suggests in *The Conflict of the Faculties* that government has an interest in *truth* as such and therefore needs to preserve freedom of thought for at least one of the faculties in its state-supported universities, namely the faculty of philosophy (nowadays, arts and sciences), in order to increase the probability of the discovery of truth.[35] Nor is it an argument that the state (or any of its members) has an interest in the discovery of the truth about certain particular subjects in order to advance various of the material ends of itself or its subjects, such as well-being, and would therefore benefit by encouraging freedom of thought and its expression to increase the likelihood of the discovery of the truth about those matters – an argument of the sort that John Stuart Mill might be taken to suggest in chapter 2 of *On Liberty* when he argues that freedom of thought is the best condition for discovery of "Truth, in the great practical concerns of life," above all "human well-being."[36] Such an argument would sit ill with the antipaternalistic conception of the state to which, as we have seen, Kant was committed. Rather, Kant's argument is much more like the argument that Mill makes in chapter 1 of *On Liberty*, based on the blunt "principle . . . that the sole end for which mankind are warranted, individually or collectively, in interfering with the liberty of action of any of their number, is self-protection."[37] It is not an argument based on the value of any other end to which freedom

---

[35] *The Conflict of the Faculties*, 7:32.
[36] John Stuart Mill, *On Liberty*, in *Essays on Politics and Society*, *The Collected Works of John Stuart Mill*, vol. 18, ed. J. M. Robson (Toronto: University of Toronto Press, 1977), p. 254.
[37] Ibid., p. 223.

might be a means, but a direct expression, as Kant says, of the fundamental value of freedom itself. This can give rise to an argument that freedom of thought and conscience is the optimal condition for the realization of the ends of the state only if, as Kant intimates in the essay *What Is Enlightenment?* the end of the state itself is taken to be nothing more but nothing less than the maximal freedom of each of its subjects compatible with a like freedom for all, or where the ruler of the state is prepared to allow to develop "the germ on which nature has lavished most care, the inclination and vocation to free *thinking*," in order that his subjects may "gradually become more capable of the *freedom to act*."[38] But this is hardly to see freedom of thought or conscience as a *means* to any separate end at all, but as rather a *part* of the freedom that it is the fundamental aim of the state, as of any morally grounded human institution, to preserve and promote.

Thus Kant provides the foundations of a coherent liberalism, in which both the public regulation of property and the freedom of thought and conscience from public regulation are grounded in the innate right to freedom: the state needs to regulate the acquisition and accumulation of property in light of a conception of fairness because only under such a condition could its subjects freely agree to the institution of property, but it is barred from the regulation of thought and speech in any but special circumstances because any such regulation would be an unwarranted intrusion upon the freedom of its subjects which it is again the duty of a morally acceptable and necessary state to preserve and promote.

---

[38] 8:41; translation from Reiss, *Political Writings*, p. 59, modified.

Chapter 8

Life, Liberty, and Property: Rawls and Kant

I

Until recently, Kant's political philosophy has had little impact on American political thinking and political philosophy. Reasons for this are not hard to find. First, of course, the basic framework of American political thought was laid down in the 1770s and 1780s, a decade or two before Kant's "Doctrine of Right" was published – the U.S. Constitution, indeed, predates Kant's work by exactly ten years. But there also appears to be a fundamental philosophical difference between Kant's political theory and the basic tenets of American political thought.

The signers of the Declaration of Independence in 1776 and the framers of the Constitution in 1787 asserted a wide rather than narrow scope for their new government, including among its proper ends the advancement of its citizens' happiness or welfare as well as the preservation of their lives and liberty. The Declaration of Independence states that "Governments are instituted among men" in order to secure their "inalienable rights" to "Life, Liberty and the pursuit of Happiness." The Preamble to the Constitution states

This chapter, originally written for a conference on Kant's "Doctrine of Right" in Marburg in 1992, was previously published under the title "Life, Liberty and Property: Rawls and the Reconstruction of Kant's Political Philosophy," in Dieter Hüning and Burkhard Tuschling, eds., *Recht, Staat und Völkerrecht bei Immanuel Kant, Schriften zur Rechtstheorie*, vol. 186 (Berlin: Duncker & Humblot, 1998), pp. 273–91. It is reprinted here with several changes.

that its purpose is "to form a more perfect Union, establish Justice, insure domestic tranquillity, provide for the common defence, promote the general Welfare, and secure the Blessings of Liberty to ourselves and our Posterity." In neither case is there any explicit acknowledgment of the potential for conflict between the goal of securing life, justice, tranquillity, and the blessings of liberty, on the one hand, and the aim of advancing the happiness and welfare of the citizenry on the other. The underlying assumption is surely that a truly representative government of the people can just as wisely advance their happiness as defend their life and liberty. However, the Bill of Rights, which had to be appended to the Constitution in order to secure its ratification, might well be thought of as having made the defense of certain fundamental civil liberties an unconditional and inviolable constraint on all the activities of the government, to which even the legitimate end of advancing the happiness and welfare of the people must always be subordinated. The Bill of Rights could therefore be thought of as having introduced a lexical ordering of the two goals of preserving liberty and promoting happiness or welfare, yet without having excluded the latter from the proper sphere of the new government.

At least on its face, however, Kant's political philosophy confines the legitimate end of any government to the defense of the life and liberty of its subjects and strictly prohibits it from any effort to advance their welfare and happiness. Thus, in his most accessible work on political philosophy, the essay on *Theory and Practice* from 1793, Kant wrote that

> The concept of external right in general flows entirely from the concept of *freedom* in the external relations of men to one another and has nothing whatever to do with the end that all men naturally have (the goal of happiness), or with the prescription of means for the achievement of that end; so that the latter end simply must not be mingled with that law as its determining ground. *Right* is the limitation of the freedom of each to the condition of its harmony with the freedom of everyone, insofar as this is possible according to a universal law; and the *public right* is the sum of *external laws* which make such a thoroughgoing harmony possible.

263

A government confined to the defense of freedom safeguards the freedom of all of its citizens to pursue their happiness after their own conception of it, but does not itself take on the goal of more directly advancing their welfare or happiness in any particular way. Thus Kant characterizes the freedom that is the sole "principle of a commonwealth" in these terms:

> Nobody can coerce me to be happy in his way (as he conceives of the well-being of other men), but each may seek his happiness in the way that seems good to himself, if only he does not do injury to the freedom of others to strive after a similar end, which can consist with the freedom of everyone according to a possible universal law (i.e., this right of the other). – A government that was erected on the principle of benevolence toward the people, as a *father's* toward his children – i.e., a *paternalistic government* (*imperium paternale*) . . . [would be] the worst conceivable *despotism*. (*TP*, 8:289–91)[1]

Kant thus appears to draw a strict line between the establishment of justice in order to secure the inalienable rights of life and liberty on the one hand and the right to happiness and promotion of the general welfare on the other, which are conjoined as equally legitimate ends of government in the American constitutional tradition. It is thus initially difficult to see what connection there could be between the tacit political philosophy of the American constitution and the explicit political philosophy of Kant.

For nearly three decades, however, John Rawls has advocated a political philosophy that purports to provide a Kantian pedigree for the most basic principles of American political philosophy. Rawls's conception of "justice as fairness," as explicated by his two principles of justice with the second subordinated to or lexically ordered after the first, is supposed to be derived from an es-

---

[1] The translation from *Theory and Practice* in this essay is my own; for the "Doctrine of Virtue," however, I use *The Metaphysics of Morals*, trans. Mary Gregor (Cambridge: Cambridge University Press, 1991). I follow Gregor here in giving the section (§) numbers of the "Doctrine of Right" (DR) from Kant's *Metaphysics of Morals* as they appear in the *Akademie* edition, and not as they appear in Bernd Ludwig's revised edition of Kant's text (Hamburg: Felix Meiner, 1986); this is for the sake of convenience, and not a rejection of Ludwig's revisions.

sentially Kantian conception of free and equal moral agents yet to provide a version of the American conception of the ends of government as originally stated by the Declaration of Independence and then modified by the amendment of the Constitution with the Bill of Rights. The latter is to be accomplished by the two principles that assign to a just government the dual ends of protecting the liberties of all and intervening in the arrangement of inequalities in the distribution of primary goods so as to maximize the welfare of the worst-off members of society, where, however, pursuit of the second goal is always to be limited by the first. In the terms of Rawls's final formulation of the fundamental principles of justice for institutions in his *A Theory of Justice*:

> *First Principle*: Each person is to have an equal right to the most extensive total system of equal basic liberties compatible with a similar system of liberty for all.
>
> *Second Principle*: Social and economic inequalities are to be arranged so that they are both:
> (a) to the greatest benefit of the least advantaged . . . and
> (b) attached to offices and positions open to all under conditions of fair equality of opportunity.
>
> *First Priority Rule* (The Priority of Liberty): The principles of justice are to be ranked in lexical order and therefore liberty can be restricted only for the sake of liberty. (*TJ*, 302)[2]

That is, the first goal of a just government is the preservation of equal liberty for all; its next goal is that of allowing or establishing social and economic inequality only to maximize the condition of the worst-off; but liberty itself is never to be restricted solely for the sake of improving the condition of those who are socially and economically least well off. This set of principles can be thought of as reflecting the idea that both the protection of liberty and the promotion of the general welfare constitute the legitimate ends of

---

[2] TJ stands for *A Theory of Justice* (Cambridge, Mass.: Harvard University Press, 1971). This essay was written before the appearance of Rawls's *Political Liberalism* (New York: Columbia University Press, 1993), and does not take account of that work, which in any case modifies Rawls's theory of the justification of the basic principles of justice but not his account of their content.

government but that the former end gives rise to a bill of inviolable civil rights that can never be overridden, even in the interest of advancing the latter end.

How can such a conception of social justice be considered Kantian? Doesn't Rawls at best only introduce a Kant-like principle of the priority of liberty into a fundamentally non-Kantian conception of the ends of government? That is, isn't Rawls's principle permitting governmental intervention in social and economic inequalities in order to improve the condition of the worst-off fundamentally non-Kantian, his alleged Kantianism thus being confined solely to his principle that the preservation of an equally and maximally extensive system of liberties for all must always take priority over considerations of welfare – a principle already tacitly acknowledged by the U.S. Bill of Rights?

In what follows I argue that Rawls's conception of the principles of justice is not incompatible with Kant's conception of the limited sphere of government but is actually required by it. What appears to be the strict separation between the preservation of equal liberty and any concern for welfare, *a fortiori* for equality in the means of welfare, advocated by Kant's essay on *Theory and Practice* turns out to be more subtle than it first appears when we examine Kant's analysis of the very conditions of the possibility of the existence of property that is central to his mature political theory in the "Doctrine of Right" of the *Metaphysics of Morals*. As we saw in Chapter 7, this analysis of property makes the preservation of the liberty to acquire property the fundamental reason for the creation and maintenance of government, yet entails that a system of property can be rationally and morally accepted by the citizens of a state only when it is in the interest of all who are or will be affected by it. A plausible interpretation of the latter requirement would certainly be that inequalities in the distribution of property are rationally acceptable only when they are in the interest of everyone affected by them, including those who are least well off. Rawls's second principle of justice is thus compatible with Kant's conception of the connection between property and the state. Indeed, Rawls's conception of social justice by means of his two principles plus the accompanying principle of priority can be conceived of as a plausible reconstruction of Kant's political philosophy, although Rawls himself has never appealed directly to the texts of Kant's own political philosophy in support of the view that he has presented as inspired only in a general way by basic features of Kant's general approach to moral philosophy.

If Rawls's principles of justice are in fact a plausible reconstruction of Kant's conception of external right, yet also provide a philosophical model for the basic principles of American constitutionalism, does that mean that Kantian and American political philosophy are basically identical, even though Kant could not have influenced American political thought and does not seem to have been influenced by it? Such a conclusion would be a little too hasty. For there still remains a certain latitude in the Declaration of Independence's conception of the pursuit of *happiness* with which Kant would be unhappy, and which indeed I believe has often clouded American political debate. Any idea that the government might directly assist in the pursuit of happiness as long as it does not thereby violate any of the inviolable civil rights would still run afoul of Kant's concern that a paternalistic imposition of the government's conception of happiness upon the governed might thereby be licensed. It might therefore be better to suggest that Rawls's reconstruction shows there to be a deep connection between the Kantian conception of the legitimate concerns of the state and the *Lockean* conception of the ends of government that inspired the Declaration of Independence but was broadened by it. Locke, of course, assigned to government not the protection of life, liberty, and the pursuit of *happiness* but rather the "mutual *Preservation* of [the citizen's] Lives, Liberties and Estates, which I call by the general Name, *Property*": "though Men when they enter into Society, give up the Equality, Liberty, and Executive Power they had in the State of Nature, into the hands of the Society . . . yet it [is] only with an intention in every one the better to preserve himself his Liberty and Property."[3] Here there is no suggestion that a government should attempt to advance the

---

[3] *The Second Treatise of Civil Government*, ch. IX, §§123, 132; in the edition by Peter Laslett, *John Locke: Two Treatises of Government*, 2d ed. (Cambridge: Cambridge University Press, 1967), pp. 368, 371. See also ch. I, §3 (p. 286), and ch. VIII, §95 (p. 349).

happiness of its subjects directly, but only the requirement that government should secure their property so that they may use it as the means for their own advancement of their happiness after their own conception of it. Thus, the threat of paternalism does not arise on the Lockean conception of the goals of government, although it can on the American transformation of Locke's formulation. My argument might then be put by saying that while Kant might properly have had qualms about assigning to government the protection of life, liberty, and the pursuit of happiness, his own theory of property does require him to assign to government a concern for distributive justice in the system of property as the means to happiness as well as the protection of life and liberty.[4]

II

Rawls conceives of his two principles of justice, the principle of equal liberty and the so-called difference principle that inequalities must always be arranged so as to improve the condition of the least well off, plus the priority rule that lexically orders them so that in any case of conflict the difference principle must always give way to the principle of equal liberty, as "the principles that free and rational persons concerned to further their own interests would accept in an initial position of equality as defining the fundamental terms of their association" (*TJ*, 11). That is, these principles are conceived of as the fundamental rules of social association that would be chosen by prudential agents with no special interest in the welfare of others who have to choose their political principles in an "original position" in which they are barred by a "veil of ignorance" from knowledge of their own goals and desires as well as their own socioeconomic position. This characterization has left Rawls open to the natural objections that we should

---

[4] As I argued in the previous chapter, however, Kant's theory of property itself should not be understood as Lockean. Locke believed that property could be created by a natural relation between an individual and an object, and that an individual who has property should enter into a state for prudential reasons, that is, to protect his property; Kant believes that property is created only by interpersonal agreement, and that the creation of the state is necessary and obligatory in order to make such agreement conclusive rather than merely provisional.

not look to the choices of merely prudential, self-interested agents to discover principles of justice, and that in any case we do not choose our political or moral principles in a situation of ignorance like that postulated as the "original position." Such objections, however, miss the point of Rawls's approach. Rawls conceives of the original position as a device of reasoning by means of which persons who are morally committed to a conception of themselves and all those others with whom they have to interact as free and equal persons can determine what principles would best express their conception of themselves as such free and equal persons and allow that self-conception to govern the basic principles of their society. The requirement of ignorance that is built into the conception of the original position excludes precisely that information which morality deems to be irrelevant to the choice of social principles, thus providing an epistemologically clear method of arriving at morally desirable principles. As Rawls puts it in *A Theory of Justice,*

> The principles of justice are chosen behind a veil of ignorance. This ensures that no one is advantaged or disadvantaged in the choice of principles by the outcome of natural chance or the contingency of social circumstances. Since all are similarly situated and no one is able to design principles to favor his particular condition, the principles of justice are the result of a fair agreement. . . .[5] For given the circumstances of the original position, the symmetry of everyone's relations to each other, this initial situation is fair between individuals as moral persons, that is, rational beings with their own ends and capable, I shall assume, of a sense of justice. (*TJ*, 12)

The *motivation* to discover and abide by the principles that would be chosen in the original position is moral from the outset, and the exclusion of information that characterizes it is morally determined. In addition, the denial of any direct interest in others to the agents in the original position is only meant to ensure that it is solely the

---

[5] The words omitted are "or bargain." But since Rawls subsequently argues that the principles of justice are not arrived at by any actual process of bargaining between different parties making trade-offs between themselves, this ellipsis seems appropriate. See TJ, 139–40.

underlying conception of ourselves as free and equal persons, which is assumed to be the essential conception of morality, that determines the choice of principles. The original position is thus only a heuristic device for discovering what principles such a moral conception of ourselves actually requires. As Rawls puts it in the 1980 Dewey Lectures:

> The essential thing is that, when we formulate the . . . conception of the original position, we must view the parties as selecting principles of justice . . . for social cooperation among persons who conceive of themselves as free and equal moral persons. . . . the conception of moral persons as free and equal . . . must be appropriately reflected in its description. Otherwise the original position cannot fulfill its mediating role to connect a certain conception of the person with definite first principles by means of a procedure in which the parties, as rationally autonomous agents of construction, adopt principles of justice.[6]

In other words, we see what principles of social justice free and equal persons ought to agree to by seeing what principles rational but self-interested agents in the original position would agree to; but we agree to be bound by the principles that would be chosen in the original position precisely because of our underlying moral commitment to see ourselves and to treat others as free and equal moral persons.

Rawls has a complex argument by means of which alternatives to his own principles of justice are eliminated as irrational for persons in the original position, but his positive argument for it is straightforward. The underlying assumption is that free and equal persons will want maximally equal shares of certain primary goods, resources that "normally have a use whatever the person's rational plan of life." These goods, which for simplicity are designated as "rights and liberties, powers and opportunities, income and wealth" (*TJ*, 62), are resources of which any rational individual would prefer more rather than less, because "with more of these goods men can generally be assured of greater success in

---

[6] "Kantian Constructivism in Moral Theory: The Dewey Lectures 1980," *Journal of Philosophy* 77 (September 1980): 522; see also p. 552.

carrying out their intentions and advancing their ends, whatever their ends may be" (*TJ*, 92). There are in fact two reasons why rational persons should define their fundamental needs in terms of such primary goods: within the original position, of course, no one knows what their specific needs and desires are, so everyone must instead focus on securing resources that can serve as means for all possible ends; but, even in real life, rational persons will understand that their needs and desires can both become known only over the course of their lives and also change during their lives, and so there too they should be concerned that their social system secures them the basic means for attaining possible ends rather than directly satisfying any particular ends that they take themselves to have at a given time. This conception of the rationality of seeking primary goods is, of course, profoundly Kantian, as the *Groundwork*'s example of the duty to cultivate one's talents as means "for all sorts of possible purposes" (4:423) reveals.[7]

But rational agents will not treat all of these primary goods the same way. Rather, Rawls argues, they will not ordinarily agree to anything less than maximally equal rights, liberties, and opportunities, but will agree to inequalities in powers, income, and wealth

---

[7] Many commentators have misunderstood Rawls's theory of primary goods. Thus, Andrew Levine's argument that Rawls's conception of the rational agent is anthropological and Hobbesian rather than pure and Kantian depends upon his interpretation of the primary goods as universal objects of natural desire that all but only natural human beings want, whatever other desires they may also happen to have, rather than as universally valid means that any rational agent would recognize as necessary for the satisfaction of the kinds of needs any rational beings in the situation of human beings could possibly have, thus as means that are recommended by pure reason itself. See "Rawls' Kantianism," *Social Theory and Practice* 3 (1974): 47–63, especially pp. 50–51, 54–55. Arnold I. Davidson's defense of Rawls's Kantianism is also weakened by a similar misunderstanding of Rawls's conception of primary goods; see "Is Rawls a Kantian?" *Pacific Philosophical Quarterly* 66 (1985): 48–77, especially pp. 59–60. This leads to the attribution of a more dualistic conception of human motivation to Rawls than is necessary, a conception on which a purely naturalistic instrumental rationality is seen as being externally constrained by an independent moral self-conception, rather than the recognition of the need for primary goods and the moral conception of the self being seen as aspects of an integrated conception of rationality As we have seen in Chapter 6, precisely the same difficulty often infects the understanding of Kant's conception of the relation between morality and happiness.

when such inequalities have the effect of bettering the lot of everyone including the worst-off members of the society. The reasons for this difference are these. First, rational persons who do not know what particular socioeconomic position they will occupy will only consent to a society in which each individual enjoys the maximal set of basic liberties consistent with a like liberty for everyone else (*TJ*, 62–63, 150). "Indeed, this principle is so obvious that we would expect it to occur to anyone immediately." Second, however, rational persons will also agree to permit economic and social "inequalities in the basic structure that work to make everyone better off in comparison with the benchmark of initial equality" (*TJ*, 151). That is, if certain inequalities in the distribution of resources would improve the circumstances of everyone, even those who are worst-off, over what they would be if strict equality were maintained, then anyone who for all he knows may end up in the worst-off position in the society (and who is not moved by the irrational sentiment of envy) would have reason to prefer that unequal distribution of resources even to a more equal distribution. (This is what Rawls calls the maximin principle, the principle of maximizing your outcome in the worst case [*TJ*, 152–53].) Thus "inequalities are permissible when they maximize . . . the long-term expectations of the least fortunate group in society" (*TJ*, 151). Further, if the second clause of Rawls's second principle is adopted, and thus all positions are equally open, then rational agents will know not only that the inequalities that are permitted in a just society will benefit them even if they occupy the worst-off position in it, but also that there is no institutional bar to them or their offspring occupying a better position in it by dint of their own efforts. However, Rawls assumes, no rational person who conceives of himself as a moral agent free and equal to all others would be willing to trade off a basic liberty for a mere improvement in economic well-being: "if the parties assume that their basic liberties can be effectively exercised, they will not exchange a lesser liberty for an improvement in economic well-being" (*TJ*, 151–52). Rational persons will be willing to tolerate an unequal distribution of basic liberties only when they see that as a necessary condition for the realization of a higher level of moral rather than material civilization, which will eventually yield a higher level of liberty for everyone. Thus reasoners in the original position will adopt the principle of equal liberty and the difference principle, but will subordinate the second to the first. They will never tolerate the limitation of equal liberty for the sake of economic gain, although they will tolerate unequal distributions of liberty now for the sake of greater liberty for everyone later.

Rawls argues that the same principles of justice can be reached by arguing from an explicitly Kantian conception of morality. As he puts it, "the principles of justice manifest in the basic structure of society men's desire to treat one another not as means only but as ends in themselves" (*TJ*, 179). This is because "treating men as ends in themselves implies at the very least treating them in accordance with principles to which they would consent in an original position of equality" (*TJ*, 180). And, Rawls argues, what people in such a situation would agree to are the principles of justice he has defined. The basic argument is simple. Treating everyone, oneself and others, as ends and not merely as means requires treating them all in accord with principles each would freely adopt under conditions in which each has an equal freedom of choice. In such a situation, it can be assumed, no one would consent to sacrifice any of her liberty for the liberty of another, unless doing so promised subsequently greater freedom for all; and no one would agree to suffer economic inequality solely for the sake of the higher expectation of another, that is, to be used merely as a means for the ends of another. Instead, to regard all "persons as ends in themselves in the basic design of society is to agree to forego those gains which do not contribute to their representative expectations" and to permit only those unequal gains which improve the expectations of all better than any other alternative (*TJ*, 180). To gain the free consent of everyone who may be affected by the basic principles of a society, in other words, requires the preservation of the equal liberty of each person and the acceptance of only those inequalities to which everyone, even the worst-off, would consent as being in their own interest – in other words, the two principles of justice. Thus, Rawls concludes,

> Kant held . . . that a person is acting autonomously when the principles of his action are chosen by him as the most adequate

possible expression of his nature as a free and equal rational being. . . . Assuming, then, that the reasoning in favor of the principles of justice is correct, we can say that when persons act on
these principles they are acting in accordance with principles that
they would choose as rational and independent persons in an
original position of equality. (*TJ*, 252)

There can be no doubt that the idea that justice requires that all
those affected by the actions of others be able to give rational consent to those actions because they see them as being in their own
interest as well expresses the fundamental conception of Kantian
morality. What it is to treat others as ends Kant defines as to regard them "as such who must also be able to contain the end of
[another's] action in themselves" (*G*, 4:430). At the very least, obviously, Kant's principle of morality precludes actions that unnecessarily injure the freedom of others; but this formulation seems
to suggest the stronger requirement that those who are affected by
another's action must be able to find an end of their own in that
action, which it is natural to interpret as requiring that they must
be able to find a way in which that action actually serves their own
interest as well as the other's. Perhaps this will be too stringent as
a general standard for moral permissibility; but, as we will see, it
is a good expression of the requirement of reciprocity that is built
into Kant's theory of justice by the analysis of property.

There is also a further step to Rawls's "Kantian interpretation"
of his principles of justice. These principles, he argues, are those by
which persons can best "express their nature as rational and equal
members of the intelligible realm with [the] liberty to choose,"
those principles which "will best manifest this freedom in their
community, most fully reveal their independence from natural contingencies and social accident" (*TJ*, 255). If we naturally aspire to
behave rationally and freely, failure to live up to these principles
will give rise to shame but compliance with them will lead not to
mere obedience to universal law but "to an ethic of mutual respect
and self-esteem" for ourselves as free beings who can rise above
enslavement to contingency (*TJ*, 256). In particular, Rawls argues,
the absolute priority of liberty over other primary goods serves to
express and secure the fundamental human desire for self-respect

and self-esteem in society: given the "central place of the primary good of self-respect and the desire of human beings to express their nature in a free social union with others," it is only natural that "the desire for liberty is the chief regulative interest that the parties must suppose that they will have in common" (*TJ*, 543). "In a well-ordered society then self-respect is secured by the public affirmation of equal citizenship for all" (*TJ*, 545). Thus the two principles of justice can be traced to our moral self-conception as free and equal beings, and the priority of the first over the second principle in particular can be traced to the primacy of the value of self-respect.

I have no doubt that this argument, and especially the argument for the priority of liberty as the fundamental condition of self-esteem, is true to Kant's own deepest thought about the ultimate function of the principle of morality. Kant's revisionary argument in the *Lectures on Ethics* that "duties toward ourselves constitute the supreme condition and the principle of all morality" because above all else "we must reverence humanity in our own person, because apart from this man becomes an object of contempt, worthless in the eyes of his fellows and worthless in himself,"[8] places the basis of morality precisely in the contrast between the shame that accompanies treating ourselves merely as natural instruments for obtaining sensuous pleasure and the self-esteem that attaches to living up to the ideal of free and rational agency in which we are ends and never merely means for ourselves. Kantian morality is based on nothing less than the supposition that we can respect ourselves only by attempting to live up to the ideal of free rationality, the guidelines for the realization of which are expressed by the moral law.[9]

Let us grant, then, Rawls's argument that his principles of justice are precisely those that would be arrived at by persons seeking to give expression to their *moral* ideal of themselves and others as equally rational and independent persons. From the Kantian point of view, there would still be a question as to whether these

---

[8] *Lectures on Ethics,* trans. Louis Infield (from the edition by Paul Menzer) (London: Methuen, 1930), p. 121; cf. *Moral Mrongovius,* 27:1482.

[9] See Chapters 4 and 5.

undeniably valid *moral* principles of *social justice* can be made into *external laws* of *public right*, that is, fundamental principles of political organization. In Kant's framework, this question would be whether free and rational persons would be willing to countenance *coercive enforcement* of both of the Rawlsian principles of justice. Coercion is not an issue that Rawls raises while searching for the social expression of our moral conception of ourselves, but for Kant it is the essence of external law. An external law is precisely one to which it is morally permissible and pragmatically effective to attach a coercive sanction as a nonmoral motive for its fulfillment; so where it is neither morally nor pragmatically possible to constrain a person to fulfill a law by the threat of coercion, there one has a duty of virtue but not of right (*MM*, 6:219). Now, on Kant's view that coercion is permissible and indeed necessary as a hindrance to the hindrance of freedom (*MM*, DR Introduction, 6:231), it is easy to see how Rawls's first principle of justice can become the subject of coercive enforcement: any attempt to introduce an unequal abridgment of basic liberty in a society could without injustice be forcibly resisted as a hindrance to the preservation of equal and maximal liberty. Further, any rational person who conceived of himself as both free and equal to all others in his right to freedom would consent to the forcible defense of equal maximal liberty, since he might fear that someone else would attempt to abridge his liberty but would have no reason to want to abridge the liberty of anyone else. But it is less clear that rational and moral persons would consent to the coercive enforcement of the difference principle. For if the difference principle could be enforced only by coercion, that might appear to be precisely the case in which the difference principle could be realized only at the cost of an abridgment of someone's liberty, and in which the priority of the principle of equal liberty over the difference principle would therefore be violated. Rational persons might thus prefer to see the difference principle realized but not be prepared to permit the coercive enforcement of it. The second principle of justice would then describe a desirable ideal of social morality without giving rise to a genuine coercively enforceable public law. In other words, Rawls's conception of justice might appear to be a genuinely Kantian ideal of social *morality* but to go beyond the bounds of genuinely Kantian *duties of right*.

I propose here at least a restricted solution to this problem by arguing that Kant's own conception of property commits him to something very much like Rawls's difference principle for the distribution of the primary goods of income and wealth, and then that if he is prepared to countenance the coercive establishment and maintenance of the institution of property itself through the instrument of the state, as he surely is, he must also be prepared to countenance the coercive enforcement of something like the difference principle. Although Kant may well have good grounds to resist the incorporation of the pursuit of *happiness* in general into the ends of just government, he is himself committed to the enforcement of a just principle for the distribution of *property* as part of the proper ends of government.

III

Kant defines the principle of right or justice solely in terms of the preservation of freedom: "Any action is *right* if it can coexist with everyone's freedom in accordance with a universal law, or if on its maxim the freedom of choice of each can coexist with everyone's freedom in accordance with a universal law" (*MM*, DR Introduction, 6:230). This is virtually identical to Rawls's first principle of justice, that "Each person is to have an equal right to the most extensive total system of equal basic liberties compatible with a similar system of liberty for all," for if the only ground for the restriction of the freedom of anyone is compatibility with the freedom of others, then what results can only be the maximally compossible preservation of freedom for all. Precisely because of this identity, however, Kant's conception of external right appears to be confined to the first rather than to include both of Rawls's principles of justice.

Kant also expresses this restriction of the concept of justice by maintaining that freedom so constrained by the possibility of equal freedom for others is the only "innate" or "original right belonging to every man by virtue of his humanity" (*MM*, DR Introduction,

6:237). Kant spells out several consequences of this innate right, but does not explain why or in what sense it is innate or original. Presumably what he has in mind is simply that the foundation of all of our *perfect duties to others*, the sole form of *duty* to which the constraint of external legislation can be attached, is the duty to preserve and protect from injury the freedom of others and their physical and moral being, insofar as it is a condition of their freedom (cf. *MM*, 6:214, 220). For such a perfect duty can give rise to a determinate claim or right on the part of others that their freedom not be destroyed or abridged, a claim that, it will turn out, is physically possible and morally permissible to enforce. In contrast, our *imperfect duty* to advance or improve the conditions under which others can exercise their freedom does not give rise to any determinate obligations to perform particular actions in their behalf in any particular circumstances, and so cannot give rise to any determinate let alone morally enforceable claims or rights on their part.[10]

The next step in Kant's theory of justice is the claim that "Right Is Connected with an Authorization to Use Coercion" (*MM*, DR Introduction, 6:231). His argument for this claim is simply that "Resistance that counteracts the hindering of an effect promotes this effect and is consistent with it"; "whatever is wrong is a hindrance to freedom," and thus in general coercion would be wrong as a hindrance to freedom; but coercion in opposition to such coercion, as the hindrance of a hindrance to freedom, is consistent with freedom, and therefore authorized and even, one could presumably add, required for the preservation of freedom. Now, as it stands, this argument seems too simple, and open to the obvious objection that two wrongs do not make a right.[11] What has to be shown is that coercion in opposition to a hindrance to freedom is indeed consistent with freedom and would not itself have the same effect of abridging or destroying freedom as the hindrance it is trying to hinder. But here there are two things that could be said to

---

[10] The distinction between perfect and imperfect duty is touched upon again in Chapter 9.

[11] See Leslie A. Mulholland, *Kant's System of Rights* (New York: Columbia University Press, 1990), pp. 186–87. His solution to the problem, however, suggests only the first of the two points I make (p. 187).

flesh out Kant's argument. First, an initial act that would hinder the freedom of another by abridging or destroying it is not itself a use of freedom that is compatible with the equal freedom of the other, and so is not itself protected by the Universal Principle of Right. Second, perhaps less obviously, it could also be argued that at least the threat of coercion against a hindrance to freedom does not itself automatically deprive the would-be perpetrator of the initial hindrance to freedom of his own freedom and is thus itself consistent with freedom. For while the perpetrator who would simply abridge the freedom of another gives the other no choice in the matter, the threat of coercion against such a perpetrator leaves *him* with the free choice to desist or suffer the consequences of his act; thus the perpetrator is not in fact deprived of his freedom in the way that his victim would be. If this is so, then a hindrance to the hindrance of freedom is indeed consistent with the preservation of freedom and can be authorized and even required in the name of the perfect duty and innate right to freedom.

The next step in Kant's argument is the introduction of the right to property. This takes place by means of the "Postulate of Practical Reason with Regard to Rights" (*MM*, DR, §2, 6:246), the argument for which is as brief as the argument for the legitimacy of coercion and the interpretation of which is even more vexed.[12] Basically, Kant's argument is just that it would be irrational or self-contradictory for freedom to deprive "itself of the use of its choice with regard to an object of choice" where that object does not itself have any rights "by putting *usable* objects beyond any possibility of being used" (6:246); so reason mandates that we create conditions under which objects can in fact be used by particular agents in the rational pursuit of their various ends. This is presupposed without much argument to require not just that agents be permitted to dispose freely of objects currently in their physical

[12] For interpretations of Kant's argument for the practical postulate of property, see Mulholland, *Kant's System of Rights*, pp. 245–57; Mary Gregor, "Kant's Theory of Property," *Review of Metaphysics* 41 (1988): 757–87, especially pp. 775–76; Wolfgang Kersting, *Wohlgeordnete Freiheit: Immanuel Kants Rechts- und Staatsphilosophie* (Berlin: Walter de Gruyter, 1984), pp. 127–34; and Bernd Ludwig, *Kants Rechtslehre, Kant Forschungen*, vol. 2 (Hamburg: Felix Meiner, 1988), pp. 110–15.

possession – any interference with that would be a direct violation of the agent's freedom of person anyway and would not require any special right to property (*MM*, DR, §6, 6:250) – but that agents must have the power to plan on the use or disposition of objects that are not currently in their physical possession. Thus the possibility of the existence of property requires what Kant calls "intelligible" rather than merely "physical possession" (*MM*, DR, §1, 6:245). And – this is the key to Kant's argument – the conditions of the possibility of intelligible possession require the consent of others to any individual's claims of property for both ontological and moral reasons.

Kant claims that the "question, How is it possible for *something external to be mine or yours?* resolves itself into the question, How is *merely rightful* (intelligible) *possession* possible?" (*MM*, DR, §5, 6:249). His reason for this claim is not initially stated and is subsequently spelled out only in an argument that is still too compressed:

> When I declare (by word or deed) that I will something external to be mine, I thereby declare that everyone else is under an obligation to refrain from using that object of my choice, an obligation no one would have were it not for this act of mine to establish a right. This claim involves, however, acknowledging that I in turn am under an obligation to every other to refrain from using what is externally his: for the obligation here arises from a universal rule having to do with external rightful relations. (*MM*, DR, §7, 6:255)

This needs to be understood as an argument in two steps. The first step is the assumption that since the possession of property must involve more than merely momentary physical control, it must instead consist in a recognition of one's right to dictate the use of an object that one does not currently physically possess, which is nothing other than the agreement of others that one has such a right. In other words, the consent of others to one's control of property is an ontologically necessary condition of the possibility of the existence of property – it is only the acknowledgment of others that extends one's possession beyond one's mere physical control. But this in turn has a moral as well as a pragmatic implication: one has no moral right to *claim* the consent of others to one's control of property unless one is willing to extend a similar right to control (other, perhaps comparable) property to them, and one also has no pragmatic reason to *expect* others actually to agree to one's control over any property if that agreement is not part of a system of property rights that is sufficiently advantageous to them as well – unless one is prepared to obtain their agreement by sheer coercion, which could not, however, be justified in the only way that coercion can be justified, as a hindrance to a hindrance to freedom. Thus, one has a right to the establishment of property because it would be irrational to deny oneself the kind of long-term planned use of objects that property allows, but one can have such a right only if one is willing to extend a like right to others, because otherwise one has no right to claim their consent to one's claim of property and they have no reason to give it. The ontology of property thus demands its morality.

As we saw in Chapter 7, beyond a general appeal to the reciprocity of property rights (*MM*, DR, §8, 6:256), Kant does not do very much to spell out precise conditions under which it is reasonable for persons to consent to a system of such rights. But one could surely argue that Rawls's difference principle is a plausible interpretation of the conditions under which it would be morally permissible to demand the agreement of others to a system of property and rational for them to consent to it. From a purely pragmatic point of view, if all the members of a society know that even if they occupy (or could come to occupy) the worst-off position in their society they will still be better off under a proposed system of property than under any other distribution of property, and if they know moreover that there is no societally institutionalized impediment to changing their positions and thus enjoying the even greater opportunities the system has to offer, they would have no reason not to consent to it. However, weaker constraints on the distribution of property than the stringent constraint of Rawls's difference principle might also make it rational to consent to a system of property rights (especially if the possible costs of resistance to such a system are also calculated). But Kant's analysis of property does not just require us to calculate pragmatically under what conditions it is reasonable to *expect* others to consent to our property claims; it also requires us to consider what it is moral to *demand* of others. And here it might be argued that the morality of demanding consent from others requires a higher level of equality than the more purely pragmatic consideration of what level of equality is necessary to obtain their actual consent. In particular, it might be argued that morality's requirement that the system equally serve the interest of all begins by requiring that it be in the best interest of the worst-off. Thus even if the difference principle does not follow from pragmatic considerations alone, it could be argued to follow from the moral constraints on demanding the consent of others to one's property claims. I do not attempt to pursue this issue further. Let us just stipulate that Kant has established in a general way that one can neither reasonably expect nor reasonably demand to establish a property right of one's own without the consent of others, and that they will give that consent only if they see the system of property rights thereby implied as in their own best interest as well. In other words, one has a right to property as an exercise of one's own freedom, but only under the condition that one is willing to concede an analogous right to property to others.

This brings us to the conclusion that Kant cannot subsume the right to property under a principle of liberty akin to Rawls's first principle of justice without also acknowledging something very much like Rawls's second principle. But it does not yet take us all the way to the recognition that both of Rawls's principles are principles of external law or public justice in the Kantian sense of being coercibly enforceable. But this conclusion follows from Kant's suppositions that property rights can be established only within a state and that anyone has the right to coerce any others who might interfere with his use of objects into membership in a state for the purpose of establishing property rights. Here again there would be a two-stage argument moving from ontological to moral considerations.

The first step would consist of Kant's argument that because property can exist only by the consent or will of all rather than by any individual's unilateral act of will, which "cannot put others under an obligation they would not otherwise have," and further because "the condition in which the will of all is actually united for giving law is the civil condition," property therefore cannot actually exist except in a civil condition or under a rule of law (*MM*, DR, §15, 6:264). Presumably Kant has in mind the traditional assumptions that actual law and not just general consent is needed both to make property claims determinate, for example, by recording deeds, and also to enforce them, by police power. But Kant does not take this to mean that property rights are logically prior to the establishment of the state and only improved or reinforced by the latter.[13] Rather, he argues that without the state property rights are only provisional, being made in anticipation of and with a willingness to subscribe to the laws of a state that would recognize one's right to property while extending the same privilege to others. Only with the establishment of a system of law establishing such a mutual system of rights does anyone's claim to property become what Kant calls conclusive (6:264).

The trickier part of the argument concerns coercion, for here is where the moral grounds for consent to a system of property must be considered. Kant asserts that one who provisionally claims property rights with a willingness to join in a state that would conclusively establish such rights both for himself and others has the right not only to resist others who would injure his property but even to coerce them to join in such a state with him. For the right of resistance to attacks on provisional claims to property he argues thus:

> Prior to entering [an *actual* civil] condition, a subject who is ready for it resists with right those who are not willing to submit to it and who want to interfere with his present possession; for the will of all others except for himself, which proposes to put him under obligation to give up a certain possession, is merely *unilateral*, whereas his at least has the advantage of being compatible with the introduction and establishment of a civil condition. (*MM*, DR, §9, 6:257)

The argument is that if another would take property for himself without being willing to recognize my claim to my own property,

---

[13] In this regard Kant's theory of property is certainly not Lockean. This point has been particularly stressed by Wolfgang Kersting in "Eigentum, Vertrag und Staat bei Kant und Locke," in Martyn P. Thompson ed., *John Locke und/and Immanuel Kant: Historische Rezeption und gegenwärtige Relevanz/Historical Reception and Contemporary Relevance* (Berlin: Duncker and Humblot, 1991), pp. 109–34.

then he would simply be abridging my freedom rather than recognizing it, and may thus be coercively resisted; but because I am claiming property for myself only while also recognizing the other's right to property, then I am not abridging his freedom and do not fall under the same restraint. Thus my coercive resistance to him is justified in the name of freedom while his coercive attack upon me is not.

Kant's further claim is then that one not only has the right to resist attacks upon one's provisional claims to property but can actually rightfully coerce others with whom one unavoidably comes into contact to join one in a civil condition: "Hence each may impel the other by force to leave [the state of nature] and enter into a rightful condition" (*MM*, DR, §44, 6:312). Here Kant's argument must be that no one is free from fear for their property in the state of nature, even when it falls short of an actual state of war; that one has a right to property as long as one is willing to concede a similar right to others, and thus a right to freedom of fear for one's property, which can only be secured by the establishment of the state or civil condition, thus that the creation of such a condition is a rightful extension of one's freedom; and, moreover, that one can do no injury to others by enforcing the creation of such a condition because, since one is willing to extend to them a right to property equal to one's own, one would be doing no injury to their rightful exercise of their own freedom. One would be forcibly depriving them of a freedom that is incompatible with an equal freedom for everyone else, but that sort of freedom has no claim to protection; one would be extending to them a freedom equal to that enjoyed by oneself and everyone else. Thus departure from the state of nature and entry into the civil condition is right and indeed obligatory in order to avoid the threat of injury, and no one has any reason to resist it because in it each is extended the same right as every other.[14] Coercive resistance to the establishment of

---

[14] As Leslie Mulholland has stressed, this argument departs from traditional social contract theory by making the empirical fact of the actual consent of others irrelevant to the justness of the state, grounding its justness instead on the ideal rationality of the consent they ought to give (*Kant's System of Rights*, pp. 278–81). One might argue that Locke had already tacitly recognized the point by his theory of tacit consent.

a state that would make provisional property claims conclusive is wrong, therefore, because it would be a unilateral violation of freedom; but coercive establishment of the civil condition is not wrong because it actually extends the offer of omnilateral freedom for the acquisition and use of property. One therefore has the right to enforce the creation of a state recognizing property rights as a rational extension of individual freedom, but only insofar as the right to property is extended to all upon terms to which all can rationally consent.

Thus Kant is committed to the conclusion that there can be external or public legislation enforcing the right to property, but only under conditions of equality like those defined by Rawls's second principle of justice. Thus something like Rawls's second principle as well as his first is a necessary principle of justice in the Kantian sense of a coercibly enforceable principle of external freedom.[15]

This completes my argument that Rawls's principles of justice are the necessary reconstruction of Kant's own conception of right, and thus that, although there was no influence between Kant's political philosophy and the political philosophy of American constitutionalism, there is also no conflict between them, at least as reconstructed by Rawls. Before I conclude, however, I add one further comment on Kant and liberalism. I would like to suggest that the juxtaposition between the antipaternalism of *Theory and Practice* and the commitment to something like the Rawlsian difference principle that we have found in the Doctrine of Right's theory of property is not in fact a conflict, but rather a model for resolving the apparently paradoxical nature of political liberalism. For what Kant has actually argued is that it is despotic for government to interfere with its citizens' *conceptions of happiness*, thus with their beliefs, convictions, and personal goals, but that it is only right for government to intervene in the distribution of the resources which are the *means to happiness*. For while no one needs the consent of

---

[15] I have here omitted a paragraph concerning Kant's defense of taxing the wealthy for the preservation of the poor (see *MM, DR*, 6:325–26) found at pp. 290–91 of the original version of this essay; I now prefer the treatment of this paragraph given in Chapter 7.

anyone else to her beliefs and convictions and thus her conception of happiness, everyone needs the consent of everyone else to their property claims, and can both expect and demand that consent only if they are willing to consent to a system of property that is in some sense fair to all, a condition that can in turn be realized only through the instrumentality of a system of public civil law.[16] So while in practice it may seem paradoxical for liberalism to insist upon maximal freedom of belief on the one hand but intervention in the distribution of income and wealth on the other, in theory it is not, for the freedom of belief and the freedom to claim property have fundamentally different ontological and moral conditions of possibility.

[16] This distinction is made more extensively in Chapter 7.

Chapter 9
Moral Worth, Virtue, and Merit

This chapter presents Kant's account of the relation between moral worth and motivation by respect for duty alone as well as his conceptions of virtue and merit as aspects of his underlying theory of free human agency. In the first section, I try to undercut recent debates about whether Kant's account of moral worth as motivation by respect for duty alone allows for the presence of "cooperating" inclinations by arguing that on Kant's account of free human agency there is no room for any conception of merely cooperating inclinations; instead, inclinations can only be granted motivational force by a person's freely chosen fundamental maxim and are, to some extent, even to be seen as products of that choice. In the second section, I argue that Kant's conception of virtue and his ultimate catalog of duties of virtue in the *Metaphysics of Morals* can also be explained only by reference to his conception of free human agency: what all forms of virtue and duties of virtue share is that they are all forms of conduct to which we can be constrained only by our own free choice of fundamental moral maxim. In the final section, I show how Kant's conception of merit fits into his image of human conduct as ruled by such a freely chosen fundamental moral maxim.

I MORAL WORTH

In the first section of the *Groundwork for the Metaphysics of Morals*, Kant notoriously claims that an action has "moral worth" (*sittlicher* or *moralischer Wert*) only when it is performed out of the motive of respect for duty alone rather than from any inclination, including any feeling favorable to the person who is the object of the action, whether that person be oneself or another. He writes, for example,

> To be beneficent where one can is a duty, and besides there are many souls so sympathetically attuned that, without any other motive of vanity or self-interest they find an inner satisfaction in spreading joy around them . . . But I assert that in such a case an action of this kind, however it may conform with duty and however amiable it may be, has nevertheless no true moral [*sittlichen*] worth but is on the same footing with other inclinations, for example, the inclination to honor, which, if it fortunately lights upon what is in fact of general utility and in conformity with duty, and hence worthy of honor, deserves praise and encouragement but not esteem; for the maxim lacks moral content, namely to do such actions not from inclination but *from duty.* Suppose, then, that the mind [of a] philanthropist were clouded over by his own misery, which extinguished all sympathy with the fate of others, and that while he still had the resources to do good for others suffering from need their need did not touch him because he was fully occupied with his own, and now, when no longer incited to it by any inclination, he nevertheless tears himself out of this deadly insensibility and does the action without any inclination, strictly from duty, only then does it first have its genuine moral [*moralischen*] worth.[1]

Here Kant appears to claim that a performance of an action has genuine moral worth and is worthy of genuine esteem (whatever

---

[1] *G*, 4:398. My translations of Kant's published works in moral philosophy in this chapter are based upon but do not always adhere to those in Immanuel Kant, *Practical Philosophy*, trans. and ed. Mary J. Gregor, introd. Allen W. Wood (Cambridge: Cambridge University Press, 1996); my citations from Kant's lectures on ethics follow the translations in Immanuel Kant, *Lectures on Ethics*, ed. Peter Heath and J. B. Schneewind (Cambridge: Cambridge University Press, 1997). In the present quotation, I have noted that Gregor treats *"sittlich"* and *"moralisch"* interchangeably; *sittlich* could also be translated as "ethical" and could sometimes even be linked to terms like "ethos" or "mores" without a strictly moral connotation; but in this passage it does seem equivalent to *moralisch*.

exactly that is) only if a person does it out of respect for duty alone, without the cooperation and indeed in the absence of any naturally occurring feelings, such as love, sympathy or benevolence, which might otherwise have inclined the agent to perform the same action. Kant's apparent commitment to such a position has engendered scorn and ridicule from the outset, even from his friends and supporters. Friedrich Schiller's famous lampoon exemplifies the reaction of many:

> Gladly I serve my friends, but alas I do it with pleasure.
> Hence I am plagued with doubt that I am not a virtuous person.
> Sure, your only resource is to try to despise them entirely,
> And then with aversion to do what your duty enjoins you.[2]

Surely, Schiller and many others since have felt, Kant's position is a grotesque distortion of anything that we would recognize as a morally praiseworthy disposition and motivation for performing a morally desirable or requisite action, such as helping another in need.

Defenders of Kant have naturally sought to find ways to save him from the sting of this criticism. The most obvious move has been to suggest that Kant is simply characterizing an extreme and perhaps abnormal case of praiseworthy motivation for its heuristic value in identifying the fundamental principle of morality, which is the real focus of the first two sections of the *Groundwork*, and by no means attempting to give his full account of morally praiseworthy motivation and character at this early stage of the *Groundwork* or indeed anywhere in this preliminary work at all.[3]

---

[2] From Friedrich Schiller and Johann Wolfgang von Goethe, *Xenien*. This translation, by A. B. Bullock, is found in H. J. Paton, *The Categorical Imperative: A Study in Kant's Moral Philosophy* (London: Hutchinson, 1947). Paton in turn borrowed it from Hastings Rashdall, *The Theory of Good and Evil* (London, 1907), 1: 120.

[3] This approach goes back at least to Paton's "method of isolation," in *The Categorical Imperative,* pp. 47–48. For more recent versions of this approach, see Christine M. Korsgaard, "Kant's Analysis of Obligation: The Argument of *Groundwork* I," originally published in the *Monist* 72 (1989): 311–40, reprinted in her *Creating the Kingdom of Ends* (Cambridge: Cambridge University Press, 1996), pp. 43–76, and, slightly abbreviated, in Paul Guyer, ed., *Kant's Groundwork of the*

On this account, Kant's point is simply that since it is still possible for a person in the unfortunate position of the miserable philanthropist to act in a morally estimable way, undesirable as it would be for anyone actually to be in this situation, the fundamental principle of morality must be one upon which a person in such a situation could act, and thus must be a principle the motivational force of which does not depend on any inclinations but on something else altogether, something that Kant will shortly identify as the pure form of an agent's maxim.

There can be no doubt that Kant does intend his examples of agents who act out of respect from duty in the absence of inclination to "bring out" the nature of the good will "by contrast and make it shine forth all the more brightly" (*G*, 4:397), and that he then goes on to identify the fundamental principle of morality precisely by asking what kind of law could be acted upon by an agent moved by respect for duty in the absence of any inclination. This happens when he asks and then answers the question:

> But what kind of law can that be, the representation of which must determine the will, even without regard for the effect expected from it, in order for the will to be called good absolutely and without limitation? Since I have deprived the will of every impulse that could arise for it from obeying some law, nothing is left but the conformity of actions as such with universal law, which alone is to serve the will as its principle. (*G*, 4:402)

Metaphysics of Morals: Critical Essays (Lanham: Rowman and Littlefield, 1998), pp. 41–79; see p. 61, and Marcia Baron, "Kant on Acting from Duty," ch. 5 of her *Kantian Ethics Almost without Apology* (Ithaca: Cornell University Press, 1995), pp. 146–87, at pp. 147–48. Most recently, see Nelson Potter, "Kant and the Moral Worth of Actions," *Southern Journal of Philosophy* 34 (1996): 225–41. In his article, Potter goes on to argue, against, for example, Keith Simmons in "Kant on Moral Worth," *History of Philosophy Quarterly* 6 (1989): 85–100, that Kant does not really have a concept of the moral worth of actions that has distinct conditions from a concept of the moral worth of persons, but is rather interested in morally worthy actions only as expressions of the good will of morally worthy agents, which can be used to identify the chacter of the fundamental maxim of the morally worthy agent. In what follows, I accept Potter's conclusion and offer an interpretation of Kant's account of the motivational structure of a morally worthy agent.

However, it is too quick to say that Kant's elimination of any inclination from the motivation of the morally worthy agents in the examples of *Groundwork* I is meant merely to lead the reader to a recognition of the purely formal character of the moral law and not to provide a complete characterization of the motivation of a morally worthy agent. If Kant had intended these examples to play such a merely heuristic role, he might have said it must be possible for an agent's motivation to be morally worthy or estimable, *even if* he is moved only by duty in the absence of inclination. But Kant does not put his point that way. Rather, he says quite pointedly and at least twice that the performance of an action *first* (*allererst*) *has* genuine or proper moral worth if it is done out of (respect for) duty rather than out of inclination: in the passage already quoted, where the depressed philanthropist tears himself out of his deadly insensibility and acts "without any inclination, simply from duty; then the action first has its genuine moral worth" (*G*, 4:398), and then, in the next example, when a sufferer from gout forgoes momentary pleasures of the table not because of "the perhaps groundless expectation of a happiness that is supposed to lie in health . . . but from duty; and it is then that his conduct first has proper moral worth" (*G*, 4:399). In other words, Kant does not say that the absence of inclination merely helps to *reveal* the true nature of moral worth and the character of the moral principle that implies; like it or not, he seems to insist that the performance of an action has moral worth only if it is performed from duty in the absence of any inclination.

Alternative approaches to this issue were tried out in the well-known debate between Richard Henson and Barbara Herman.[4] Both parties to this debate assume that inclinations do have motivating force for human agents, that the presence of inclinations

[4] Richard Henson, "What Kant Might Have Said: Moral Worth and the Overdetermination of Dutiful Action," *Philosophical Review* 88 (1979): 39–54, and Barbara Herman, "On the Value of Acting from the Motive of Duty," *Philosophical Review* 90 (1981): 359–82, revised as chapter 1 of her *The Practice of Moral Judgment* (Cambridge, Mass.: Harvard University Press, 1993), pp. 1–22. Both articles are discussed in Tom Sorrell, "Kant's Good Will and Our Good Nature," *Kant-Studien* 78 (1987): 87–101, reprinted in Guyer, *Kant's Groundwork of the Metaphysics of Morals*, pp. 81–100.

cannot really be thought to be incompatible with an agent's moral worth in the performance of an action that is in conformity with duty, and that some way must therefore be found to reconcile the presence of inclination in the full motivational state of a morally worthy agent with Kant's insistence that only action from duty has genuine moral worth. Henson's approach is to argue for the over-determination of actions; ultimately, he claims, Kant settled on a subjunctive or counterfactual approach: an agent's performance of an action could be motivated by both inclination and respect for duty as long as the motive of respect for duty *would have been* strong enough to move the agent to the action in question, even if the inclination had been absent. Herman's approach, also adopted by Marcia Baron,[5] is to interpret respect for duty as a "limiting condition" on a morally worthy agent's performance of an action. The presence of an inclination, Herman holds, can be what actually moves even a morally worthy agent as long as that inclination is subject to respect for duty as a limiting condition; that is, the morally worthy agent is one who allows herself to be moved to act on and by an inclination as long as doing so is consistent with the requirements of duty, but would reject acting on the inclination if so doing would violate those requirements. On neither of these accounts do we have to think that only the dyspeptic philanthropist is the paragon of moral worth; we can think that a cheerful philanthropist acting on his sympathetic inclinations to others can be a paragon of moral worth as long as he has a respect for duty that would be strong enough to move him to his philanthropic actions, even if his cheerful inclinations should fail him (Henson), or as long as he would be prepared to refrain from acting on those inclinations if so doing would violate the limiting condition of respect for duty (Herman).

Herman's idea of respect for duty as a limiting condition on other motives assigns the fundamental principle of morality a central place in her interpretation of Kant's conception of morally worthy motivation, whereas Henson's account threatens to remove respect for duty entirely from the causal loop of at least some apparently estimable performances of action by relegating it to the

---

[5] *Kantian Ethics Almost without Apology*, ch. 4.

status of an alternative cause that *could* and *would have* kicked in if there had not been an adequate inclination to do the action required by duty. But both of these accounts seem to differ from Kant's own position by treating inclinations as potentially independently motivating factors in the first place, that is, factors that are themselves ever *sufficient* to bring about an action, which can be *allowed* to move the morally worthy agent as long as they are consistent with the requirements of duty or can cooperate with the motive of respect for duty itself in producing the morally requisite action.

This assumption is faulty in two ways, one rather abstract and one more concrete. First, it does not seem to do justice to what Henry Allison has called Kant's "Incorporation Thesis," the position that feelings, inclinations, or any other naturally occurring psychological states never move the free human agent to action on their own, but do so only insofar as they have been incorporated by an act of choice into an agent's *maxim*, the subjectively effective principle by means of which an agent decides upon a certain action in order to realize a certain end.[6] On this account, an agent might decide to act upon a certain inclination because he has made it his maxim to act for the sake of gratifying his inclinations, or he might decide in certain circumstances to act on a particular inclination because his respect for duty tells him that in those circumstances it is permissible or even mandatory to gratify that inclination; but an agent never acts without some maxim or other, and thus the presence of an inclination is never by itself the complete explanation of an action, even in the case in which gratifying the inclination would be compatible with respect for duty as a limiting condition. Second, the assumption of the potentially independently motivating efficacy of inclinations does not seem to capture fully what Kant has in mind when he says that morally worthy action must arise *from* duty, for Kant does not suggest that

---

[6] In *Kant's Theory of Freedom* (Cambridge: Cambridge University Press, 1990), Allison writes that according to Kant's model of "the spontaneity of an agent as rational deliberator . . . the intentional actions of a rational agent are never '*merely*' the causal consequences of the agent's antecedent psychological state (or any other antecedent conditions for that matter) but require, as necessary condition, an act of spontaneity" (p. 5).

the presence of inclination is merely compatible with the morally worthy agent's respect for duty, but rather assumes that morally beneficial feelings or inclinations are in some ways and to some extent themselves the *products* of that respect for duty, which must therefore be seen as the ultimate cause of the particular actions of morally worthy agents even when such feelings or inclinations might appear to be all or part of the proximate cause of such action. I address these two points in the remainder of this section.

First, Kant's "Incorporation Thesis" implies that a naturally occurring inclination is never the cause of a human action by itself, but can be a cause of action only if it is granted efficacy by an agent's underlying decision either always to do what morality requires or to act out of self-love even when that conflicts with duty. As Allison observes,[7] Kant makes the "Incorporation Thesis" explicit in *Religion within the Boundaries of Mere Reason* when he states that

> Freedom of the power of choice has the characteristic, entirely peculiar to it, that it cannot be determined to action through any incentive *except so far as the human being has incorporated it into his maxim* (made it into a universal rule for himself, according to which he wills to conduct himself); only in this way can an incentive, whatever it may be, coexist with the absolute spontaneity of the power of choice (freedom). (*Rel*, 6:23–24)

Two points about the theory of motivation that Kant presents in the *Religion* are crucial. First, as this passage makes clear, an "incentive" – a psychological state such as an inclination – is not by itself a cause of action in a free agent, but can lead to action only insofar as the agent's maxim makes that incentive a reason for his action. Thus, an incentive cannot coexist or cooperate with any other motive as one sufficient or independent cause might coexist or cooperate with another, but can become a cause of action only by a maxim that makes it into a reason for that action. Second, as Kant makes clear as he continues, a free agent's actions are not the product of some number of maxims that are adopted and function

---

[7] *Kant's Theory of Freedom*, pp. 39–40.

independently of each other, one of which might perhaps recommend acting on one sort of psychological incentive or inclination while another recommends against acting on some other sort of inclination. Rather, it is Kant's view that the particular maxims a person adopts are always adopted as a consequence of his commitment to one or the other of two alternative fundamental and overarching maxims: the maxim always to do, out of respect for duty, all and only what duty requires or permits, and thus to act as an inclination would suggest only if so doing is compatible with or conducive to doing what duty requires; or the maxim always to do, out of self-love, what inclination suggests, even when so doing is incompatible with doing what duty requires.[8]

Kant argues that an agent's fundamental maxim and the disposition or attitude of which it is the expression is unitary: "This disposition, i.e., the first subjective ground of the adoption of the maxims" – that is, the various particular maxims adopted by a particular agent – "can only be a single one, and it applies to the entire use of freedom universally" (*Rel*, 6:25). His argument for this claim is that it would be a contradiction to suppose that an agent could at one and the same time[9] be committed to the universal principle of morality, which prescribes a course of action wherever it applies, and yet to another fundamental maxim that might prescribe or permit an action incompatible with that prescribed by the maxim of morality. In his words:

---

[8] Nelson Potter introduces a useful distinction between "action-maxims" and an agent's "fundamental maxim"; in this terminology, an agent's more particular action-maxims, such as "I will always make every effort to repay my debts by any lawful means available to me" or "I will make every reasonable effort to develop what seem to be my potentially best talents within the limits that my other duties allow," would be applications of his fundamental maxim, either always to do what duty requires or always to do what self-love requires, even when that conflicts with duty. See "Kant and the Moral Worth of Actions," p. 232.

[9] Kant does not mean, of course, that a person cannot have a change of heart and thus a change of fundamental maxim at some point in her life; on the contrary, one of the fundamental objectives of the *Religion* is surely to defend the inscrutable reality of radical freedom (with the concomitant possibility of radical evil) from the predeterminism of orthodox Lutheranism and Calvinism.

Nor can a human being be morally good in some parts and, at the same time, evil in others. For if he is good in one part, he has incorporated the moral law into his maxim. And were he, therefore, to be evil in some other part, since the moral law of compliance with duty in general is a single one and universal, the maxim relating to it would be universal yet particular at the same time: which is contradictory. (*Rel*, 6:24–25)

As a matter of logic, one's fundamental maxim must either be to make no exceptions for any reason to the universally valid and binding requirements of duty, or to make exceptions to those requirements when, for whatever reason, one is so inclined. The latter policy is what Kant calls the maxim of self-love, although of course this does not mean that actions undertaken in its name must be what we ordinarily call selfish or purely self-regarding: one can have an inclination to act for the pleasure of any particular person as well as for one's own pleasure, but as long as one chooses to gratify such an inclination simply for the pleasure of gratifying it and regardless of what duty requires, then one's action falls under the maxim of self-love. Thus Kant concludes that our most fundamental choice is simply whether to act for the sake of duty, regardless of what self-love might dictate, or to act for the sake of self-love, regardless of what duty might dictate; he expresses this as a choice of *priorities*, that is, a choice to give duty the priority over self-love or self-love over duty, because he believes, for obvious reasons, that no one is free of inclinations that could be acted upon out of self-love, but at the same time, perhaps for less obvious reasons,[10] that no one is simply ignorant of the moral law and the requirements of duty. So no one can act out of self-love because of actual ignorance of duty; instead, anyone who acts out of self-love when that is contrary to duty must prefer self-love to duty. In Kant's words,

Hence the difference, whether the human being is good or evil, must not lie in the difference between the incentives that he incorporates into his maxim (not in the material of the maxim), but in their *subordination* (in the form of the maxim): *which of the*

[10] See Chapter 6.

two he makes the condition of the other. It follows that the human being (even the best) is evil only because he reverses the moral order of his incentives in incorporating them into his maxims ... he makes the incentives of self-love and their inclinations the condition of compliance with the moral law – whereas it is this latter that, as the *supreme condition* of the satisfaction of the former, should have been incorporated into the universal maxim of the power of choice as the sole incentive. (*Rel*, 6:36)

So such incentives as inclinations can never either cooperate or conflict with the demands of duty on their own: when we act against an inclination in order to perform our duty, that action must of course reflect our fundamental choice to do our duty whether we are inclined to or not; but even when we act in a way that both conforms to duty and is also how we are inclined to act, that must still either reflect our fundamental commitment to do our duty, in a case in which our inclination contingently coincides with our duty, or else our commitment to acting out of self-love, in a case in which acting out of self-love contingently coincides with acting as duty would demand.[11]

Thus Kant's basic conception of free agency commits him to the claim that a person always acts either out of the motive of respect for duty, which is of course morally worthy and estimable, or out of the motive of self-love, which is not.[12] From this it is not much of a leap to the following judgments: that it is morally worthy for

[11] Tom Sorrell argues against both Henson and Herman that there can be no co-operating inclinations in morally worthy action because purity of motivation really does require the absence of such inclinations; see "Kant's Good Will and Our Good Nature," Guyer, *Kant's Groundwork of the Metaphysics of Morals*, p. 86. I agree with Sorrell that there can be no such thing as a cooperating motive on Kant's account, not because purity of will requires the absence of inclination, however, but because the cooperation of inclination must itself be seen as a product of purity of will.

[12] In saying this, I ride roughshod over the distinction that Kant makes in the *Religion* between mere human frailty and actual evil or malice (*Rel*, 6:29–30), where the former involves a failure to act on the moral maxim which the agent does recognize, while only the latter involves prioritizing the maxim of self-love over the maxim of morality. For a useful discussion of some of the issues raised by this distinction, see Robert N. Johnson, "Weakness Incorporated," *History of Philosophy Quarterly* 15 (1998): 349–67.

a person to act as duty requires even when he has no inclination to do so; that when a person who acts as duty requires because of his respect for duty also has an inclination to do so, what is morally worthy and estimable is still the fact that he acts out of respect for duty, or even acts upon his inclination out of duty, but not the mere fact that he is naturally inclined to act as he does; and that when a person who has no respect for duty happens to do what duty requires simply because that is what he is inclined to do and out of self-love he does what he is inclined to do, there is nothing morally worthy about his action even though for various reasons the rest of us might do well to praise and encourage it (see *G*, 4:398) – after all, we do want duty to be done, whether or not anyone is to be esteemed for doing it.

So Kant's view of the connection between an agent's moral worth or estimability and his fundamental maxim precludes any idea that there are inclinations or incentives that can of themselves *cooperate* with duty any more than they can of themselves *conflict* with duty. It might be objected that this conclusion differs from Herman's conception of respect for duty as a limiting condition merely in emphasis: while on her account inclinations might be seen as potential causes of action that may have to be restrained by the agent's principle of respect for duty as a limiting condition, on the present account the agent's principle of respect for duty can be seen as empowering inclinations that could lead to the actions that duty requires, as it were, elevating them to the rank of causes. But there is a substantive difference between the two approaches, which brings us to the second main point of this section. Emphasizing the primacy of the principle of respect for duty in the morally worthy agent's motivational structure treats it as the first cause of the agent's actions, and thus suggests in turn that the agent is at least to some extent causally responsible for the kinds of feelings and inclinations that he has, and is not, as the model of respect for duty as merely a limiting condition might suggest, a passive subject in whom feelings and inclinations simply occur although an active agent insofar as he can restrain the causal efficacy of those causes by virtue of the limiting condition of respect for duty. This assumption may not be evident in Kant's brief and abstract treatment of moral worth in the *Groundwork*, which indeed often treats all inclinations as if they were nothing but naturally occurring nuisances from which any rational agent would wish to be liberated (see *G*, 4:428). But it is central to Kant's mature account of human virtue in the "Doctrine of Virtue" of the *Metaphysics of Morals* that the virtuous agent has a duty to *cultivate* feelings and inclinations that are useful in the performance of duty and can even, although Kant seems initially hesitant to admit this, *cause* morally beneficial feelings to develop as a result of his commitment to the fundamental maxim of respect for duty. Such an account makes sense only if inclinations are not seen as natural occurrences in the passive sensibility of human subjects, who can at best limit such inclinations or allow them to cooperate with the moral determination of the will, but are instead seen as themselves products of the human will.

To be sure, Kant begins the "Doctrine of Virtue" with an account of moral feelings that does seem to presuppose that such feelings lie largely outside of the reach of the will and its principles, and are therefore independent causes that might be allowed to cooperate with the principle of respect for duty but are not actually products of it. Thus, in a section of the Introduction to "Doctrine of Virtue" that is to deal with "Concepts of what is presupposed on the part of feeling by the mind's receptivity to duty as such," Kant discusses "moral feeling," "conscience," "love of human beings," and "respect." By "moral feeling," Kant means the general "susceptibility to feel pleasure or displeasure merely from being aware that our actions are consistent with or contrary to the law of duty," a feeling that accompanies our consciousness of duty whether that is a duty to self or others. Kant argues that this feeling is not a product of will, thus "there can be no duty to have moral feeling or to acquire it; instead every human being (as a moral being) has it in him originally" (*MM*, DV Introduction, §XII, 6:399); however, he does allow that we do have an "obligation with regard to moral feeling," namely, the obligation "to *cultivate* it and to strengthen it through wonder at its inscrutable cause" (6:399–400). To be sure, the action that is hereby enjoined upon us appears to be rather restricted: an act of cognition or contemplation which would then have the effect of strengthening a feeling to which we are innately disposed; still, it is more than just a duty to allow a natural feeling to cooperate with the maxim of duty. Second, Kant argues that a more specifically directed feeling of "love of human beings . . . is a matter of *feeling*, not of willing, and I cannot love because I *will* to, still less because I *ought* to (I cannot be constrained to love); so a *duty to love* is an absurdity" (6:401); the duty of benevolence, he holds, is a duty "to *do good* to other human beings . . . whether one loves them or not" (6:402), that is, regardless of what feelings one may have toward them. Yet no sooner does Kant insist upon the difference between our active duty to do good for others and the apparently entirely passive feeling of love toward them then he goes on to say "*do good* to your fellow human beings, and your benevolence will produce love of them in you (as an aptitude of the inclination to beneficence in general)" (6:402). So even here it seems clear that he does not think of feelings as causal agents that are entirely independent of our will but which can be allowed to act as long as they cooperate with duty; rather, he supposes that morally appropriate feelings can be products of the morally disposed will, though they may not be direct products that are immediately willed to exist, but rather indirect products that can be expected to result over time from the performance of the kind of actions that are dictated by the will whose fundamental maxim is respect for duty.

As Kant proceeds to expound our particular duties of virtue to ourselves and others, an even more nuanced picture of the connection between duty and feelings emerges. Kant recurs to the subject of morally beneficent feelings at two important places in the "Doctrine of Virtue." The first is an "Episodic Section" at the end of his discussion of perfect duties to ourselves, in which Kant argues, by way of sorting out a potential confusion between certain duties to ourselves and duties to other, nonhuman beings, that we in fact do have a duty to ourselves (but "regarding" other beings), which turns out to be a duty *not to destroy or damage* certain morally beneficial inclinations. What he has in mind are naturally occurring feelings of pleasure at the beauty of inanimate nature, of humaneness toward animals, and of awareness of moral laws represented as divine commands; and what he argues is that we have a duty not to damage such feelings, at least in the first two cases, by unnecessarily destructive behavior toward their objects. Thus he claims that

> A propensity to wanton destruction of what is *beautiful* in inanimate nature (*spiritus destructionis*) is opposed to a human being's duty to himself; for it weakens or uproots that feeling in him which, although not of itself moral, is still a disposition [*Stimmung*] of sensibility that greatly promotes morality or at least prepares the way for it. (*MM*, DV, §17, 6:443)[13]

Here Kant could be taken to assume that there are naturally occurring feelings, that is, feelings that occur independently of an act of our will, that can be conducive to our behaving as morality requires us to do, and which could thus be allowed to cooperate with our maxim of respect for duty as long as they fall within it as a limiting condition; but even if the existence of such feelings is not itself a product of our will, Kant argues that we have a positive duty, requiring an act of our will, not to undertake actions, such as needlessly damaging the environment or treating animals cruelly, that would weaken or destroy such feelings. This is already more than simply a duty to confine the motivational efficacy of our feelings by respect for a limiting condition.

Further, Kant argues that we have a positive duty both to *use* morally beneficent feelings and to *cultivate* or *strengthen* them by undertaking actions that can be expected to have such an effect. He makes these claims in his discussion of "sympathetic feeling," or "*sympathetic joy* and *sadness* (*sympathia moralis*)," which are "sensible feelings of pleasure or displeasure . . . at another's state of joy or pain" (*MM*, DV, §34, 6:456). First, Kant claims that we have a duty to employ these feelings, which themselves occur naturally, in the fulfillment of our general duty to be beneficent to others: "Nature has already implanted in human beings receptivity to these feelings. But to use this as a means to promoting active and rational benevolence is still a particular, though only a

---

[13] See also the parallel passage in the Vigilantius transcription of *Kant on the Metaphysics of Morals*, 27:709–10, in Kant, *Lectures on Ethics*, ed. and trans. Heath and Schneewind, pp. 434–35.

conditional, duty" (6:456). It is an indirect duty insofar as our respect for duty as an end gives rise to a requirement to use everything that is available as a means to the realization of that end, but also a conditional duty since we must of course use such means only insofar as their use is consistent with the ultimate end of duty. This latter can of course be seen as a limiting condition, but it is still important to see that we here have an active and positive duty to *use* naturally occurring feelings and not merely a passive and negative duty to *allow* them to work as long as they are not inconsistent with duty. Second, Kant goes on to argue that we have an affirmative duty to strengthen and cultivate these feelings:

> But while it is not in itself a duty to share the sufferings (as well as the joys) of others, it is a duty to sympathize actively in their fate; and to this end it is therefore an indirect duty to cultivate the compassionate natural (aesthetic) feelings in us, and to make use of them as so many means to sympathy based on moral principles and the feelings appropriate to them. – It is therefore a duty not to avoid the places where the poor who lack the most basic necessities are to be found but rather to seek them out, and not to shun sickrooms or debtors' prisons and so forth in order to avoid sharing painful feelings one may not be able to resist. (*MM*, DV, §35, 6:457)

Here Kant reiterates the previous point that we have a positive duty to make use of naturally occurring feelings that incline us to do what duty requires of us and adds that we have a positive duty to take steps to cultivate and strengthen such feelings. (The example, of course, makes the empirical assumption that visits to hospitals and the like will strengthen and not weaken feelings of sympathy.) Thus we have not only the duty to use feelings as a means to the ends imposed by duty, and not only the duty not to destroy or damage such means, but also the duty to do what we can to improve the availability and efficacy of such means. All of this seems to go well beyond any model of simply allowing naturally occurring inclinations to move us to action as long as the actions to which they would move us are consistent with duty as a limiting condition. Instead, making morality rather than self-love our fundamental maxim enjoins upon us the duty to preserve, strengthen and employ all the means naturally available to us for the performance of our duty as our ultimate end, including the preservation, cultivation, and use of naturally occurring inclinations.

There seems good reason, then, to conclude that Kant does not think of the morally good agent as one whose actions are either overdetermined by both moral principle and inclination or one whose actions are prompted by inclinations that pass the test of moral principle as limiting condition. Instead, Kant thinks of the morally worthy agent as one who, to put it abstractly, makes his inclinations into causes by freely incorporating them into his maxim, and who, to put it more concretely, develops and/or preserves and strengthens naturally occurring inclinations as means to the ends he imposes upon himself by his commitment to the fundamental principle of morality as his fundamental maxim, operating under the completely general canon of rationality to make use of all available means suitable for and compatible with one's ends (*G*, 4:417).

II VIRTUE

In this section, I want to show how Kant's apparently diverse conceptions of virtue and the duties of virtue are all grounded in his basic theory of the moral worth of an agent as his commitment to act out of the fundamental maxim of respect for duty; in everything that Kant calls a virtue, the self-constraint possible by means of such a commitment is the only form of constraint that is possible.

Kant uses the term "virtue" (*Tugend*) or expressions including it in at least three apparently different senses. First, by "virtue" or "virtuous disposition" (*tugendliche Gesinnung*) he often means to refer simply to the morally worthy motivation of an agent, that is, adherence to the maxim of respect for duty, as a disposition expressed in the particular actions and omissions of the agent. Kant also calls the obligation to make nothing but respect for duty itself our motivation in any action or omission required by duty the "obligation of virtue" (*Tugendverpflichtung*) or "*obligatio ethica*" (*MM*, DV Introduction, §XVII, 6:410). Second, he uses the word "virtue" to designate a standing disposition or a constant effort to perform what duty requires in the face of resistance arising from within human nature itself: "the capacity and considered resolve to withstand a strong but unjust opponent is *fortitude* (*fortitudo*) and, with respect to what opposes the moral disposition *within us, virtue* (*virtus, fortitudo moralis*)" (*MM*, DV Introduction, §I, 6:380); "*Virtue* is the strength of a human being's maxims in fulfilling his duty" (*MM*, DV Introduction, §IX, 6:394); and "Virtue signifies a moral strength of the will" (*MM*, DV Introduction, §XIII, 6:405). Finally, Kant uses the term "duty of virtue" (*Tugendpflicht, officium ethica sive virtutis*) to refer to any of the subset of our duties that is not a duty of right, that is, a duty that is legitimately enforced by coercive sanctions in a polity. This term, unlike the term "obligation of virtue," naturally admits of a plural usage, "duties of virtue" (*Tugendpflichten*), since there can be only one obligation to make respect for duty our fundamental maxim but many specific duties that we are obliged but cannot properly be coerced to fulfill; perhaps the distinction between Kant's terms *Tugendverpflichtung* and *Tugendpflicht* would be clearer if the former were translated as "obligation *to* virtue" and the latter as "duty *from* virtue."

This triplex of senses of "virtue" naturally raises the question of whether there is a single thread that ties them together. My claim is that it is perfectly natural for Kant to use the term "virtue" and its compounds to designate strength and perseverance in the performance of duty generally as well as the class of noncoercively enforceable duties because both of these have a causal relation to "virtue" in his initial sense of the morally worthy motivation by respect for duty alone. That is, only the motive of respect for duty alone is adequate to give rise to constant effort and perseverance in the cause of duty, and only the motive of respect for duty alone is available as a source of self-constraint in the fulfillment of particular duties when the agent cannot properly be constrained to their fulfillment by external, coercive threats or sanctions.

1. Kant does not always use the term "virtue" to refer to the basic fact of an agent's being moved to action by respect for duty alone. Notably, in his analysis of the good will in Section I of the *Groundwork* where (as we saw) he argues that only such a motive first

gives "moral worth" to actions (*G*, 4:398, 401) and to the character that they express (*G*, 4:398), he does not use the noun "virtue" (*Tugend*) as a straightforward synonym for good will. Even there, however, he does argue that his conception of the good will is precisely what "common human reason" uses, without any need of "science and philosophy," as its "compass" to determine "what one has to do in order to be honest and good, and even wise and virtuous [*tugendhaft*]" (*G*, 4:403–4). Moreover, there are many other passages in which Kant does define "virtue" in precisely the same terms he uses to define "genuine moral worth" or uses the former term as if it were interchangeable with the latter. In the lectures known as *Naturrecht Feyerabend*, delivered in the fall of 1784 just while he was writing the *Groundwork*, Kant is recorded as stating that "The disposition to act from duty, from respect for the law, is virtue" (27:1327). In the *Critique of Practical Reason*, he equates virtue simply with "a disposition conformed with law *from respect for law*" (5:128). Half a dozen years after the second *Critique*, in the lectures on the metaphysics of morals transcribed by Johann Friedrich Vigilantius in the winter semester of 1793–94, in its culminating contrast between religion and morality, Kant states that:

> In the latter, the dutifulness of our moral actions appears as *virtue*, i.e., under the disposition to perform all the duties we have, to ourselves or any other world-beings, on account of the obligatory character of the action, disclosed through reason; and this is *virtus*.[14]

Finally, in the Introduction to the "Doctrine of Virtue" in the *Metaphysics of Morals* Kant also defines virtue as simply the capacity to determine oneself by respect for duty, and a virtuous action as one that results from such a motivation: "Because the moral capacity for [self-coercion] can be called virtue, . . . the action arising from such a disposition (respect for the law) can be called an action of virtue [*Tugendhandlung*] (ethical)." For this reason, Kant argues here, even respect for the coercively enforceable rights of others can be called virtuous when it is motivated not by the fear

---

[14] "Kant on the Metaphysics of Morals," *Vigilantius*, 27:715; in Kant, *Lectures on Ethics*, ed. and trans. Heath and Schneewind, p. 438.

of coercion but by respect for duty itself, "for it is the *doctrine of virtue* that commands us to hold the right of human beings sacred" (*MM*, DV Introduction, §IX, 6:394). So although Kant does not use the word "virtue" as a synonym for the morally worthy motivation of a good will in the *Groundwork* itself, there is ample evidence that in both his lectures and his publications from the time of the *Groundwork* until that of the *Metaphysics of Morals* he was prepared to do so. Virtue in this sense then functions as the natural basis for the other kinds of virtues.

2. Sometimes Kant seems to define virtue as if it were simply the constant disposition and strength to do what duty requires in the face of obstacles, arising mostly from within, but without reference to the particular motivation by which a person manages to do so. The first definition of virtue in the Introduction to the "Doctrine of Virtue" is that it is "the capacity and considered resolve to withstand a strong but unjust opponent . . . with respect to what opposes the moral disposition *within us*" (*MM*, DV Introduction, §I, 6:380). A striking passage in the Vigilantius lectures also characterizes virtue as simply an agent's "persistent, steadfast endeavor, by overcoming of his inclination, to bring about agreement, in his action, with the law of humanity."[15] The last clause, of course, means that virtuous actions are ones in accord with the moral law, and the second clause makes clear what is also obvious, that regularly complying with the law of humanity will often require overcoming inclination; but a characterization like this does not make explicit in virtue of what motivation an agent who does steadfastly and persistently endeavor to overcome inclination in order to comply with the law of humanity can or will do so. In another passage in the same lectures, Kant also characterizes virtue as, "precisely, the strength of the resolve to perform our duties, and to strive against the constant enticements to do otherwise, which sensory feelings inspire."[16] Such definitions of virtue at least appear to leave open what the motivation for such a steadfast and persistent endeavor is, and thus to raise a question about the con-

---

[15] *Vigilantius*, 27:609; *Lectures on Ethics*, p. 354.
[16] *Vigilantius*, 27:570; *Lectures on Ethics*, p. 323.

nection of this sense of "virtue" with the sense in which virtue is simply the morally worthy motivation of respect for duty itself.

Others among Kant's characterizations of virtue, however, make it explicit that virtue as the persistent and steadfast endeavor to overcome inclination in order to comply with the moral law can only be expected to arise from the motivation of respect for duty itself. Thus, later in the Introduction to the "Doctrine of Virtue" Kant first characterizes "*Virtue* [as] the strength of a human being's maxim in fulfilling his duty," but then immediately goes on to say that "virtue is not merely a self-constraint (for then one natural inclination could strive to overcome another), but also a self-constraint in accordance with a principle of inner freedom, and so through the mere representation of one's duty in accordance with its formal law" (*MM*, DV Introduction, §IX, 6:394). Ten pages later Kant says that "Virtue is thus the moral strength of the will of a *human being* in the prosecution of his *duty*: which is a moral *necessitation* through his own law-giving reason, insofar as this constitutes itself into a power *executing* the law" (*MM*, DV Introduction, §XIII, 6:405; here I have modified Gregor's translation). These passages suggest that the motivation to maintain a steadfast and persistent endeavor to comply with the law of humanity can only come from an act of inner freedom, which can be nothing other than an agent's adoption of respect for the moral law as his fundamental maxim.[17]

Perhaps this inference should be obvious, because on Kant's account of inclination any motive for complying with the demands of duty other than sheer respect for duty – for example, a prudential concern for one's public reputation – is just as much a matter of inclination as a passing desire for some particular pleasure, and thus to suppose that a persistent and steadfast endeavor to

---

[17] Nelson Potter suggests that virtue can be understood as the exemplification of the moral worth of an agent under the concrete and typically adverse circumstances of human existence ("Kant and the Moral Worth of Actions," p. 232). I am going beyond that account in stressing that the relation between good will or the moral worth of an agent and virtue should be seen as a causal relation, with the morally worthy motivation of respect for duty functioning as the only possible cause of a steadfast endeavor to do what duty requires under the sometimes adverse conditions of human existence.

comply with duty could be based on any such motivation would be to suppose that virtue could be based on the constraint of one inclination by another, which would in fact be utterly unreliable. But Kant at least suggests three more specific reasons why a persistent endeavor to do what duty requires can only be grounded in the motive of respect for the moral law.

Two of these reasons are suggested quite early in the Introduction to the "Doctrine of Virtue," when Kant states that

> Virtue is not to be explained and valued merely as an *aptitude* [*Fertigkeit*] and . . . a long-standing *habit* [*Gewohnheit*] of morally good actions acquired by practice. For unless this aptitude results from considered, firm, and continually purified principles, then, like any other mechanism of technically practical reason, it is neither equipped for all cases nor adequately secured against the alteration that new temptations can produce. (*MM*, DV Introduction, §II, 6:383–84)

The statement that nothing except "purified principles" equips one to do what is right in all cases implies that inclination, that is, everything other than the motivation of respect for the moral law itself, only contingently coincides with what the moral law requires, and thus may sometimes but will not always tell one what would be right to do. The statement that nothing except "purified principles" adequately secures the agent against changing temptations suggests that even if the agent knows what it is right to do, inclination is an unreliable motivation for doing what is right: sometimes it might move one to do what one knows to be right, but other times, when one is presented with new temptations, it might not. Thus, only respect for the moral law itself can serve as a basis for virtue as the steadfast and persistent endeavor to conform with the law of humanity because only it provides both a reliable criterion of what is right and a reliable motivation for doing what is right.

Kant more frequently stresses the second rather than the first of these functions of respect for duty in the production of virtue; thus, some pages later in the Introduction to the "Doctrine of Virtue" he writes that only through virtue understood as constraint through law-giving reason is the agent ensured that he "can suffer no loss by chance or fate" (§XIII, 6:405), and then this:

> Since virtue is based on inner freedom, it contains a positive command to a human being, namely to bring all his capacities and inclinations under his (reason's) control and so to rule over himself, which goes beyond forbidding him to let himself be governed by his feelings and inclinations . . . ; for unless reason holds the reins of government in its own hands, his feelings and inclinations play the master over him. (§XV, 6:408)

Similarly, in the Vigilantius lectures Kant states that it is only by means of the "active power" that lies in "the existing freedom of the human being, or his independence of necessitation *per stimulos*," that the human agent "is at all times in a position to gain the upper hand, or act virtuously."[18] But at least some other passages do suggest that Kant has in mind both the criterial as well as motivational necessity of respect for the moral law in maintaining virtue; in one place he characterizes *"lack of virtue"* as consisting in "weakness in the use of one's understanding coupled with the strength of one's emotions" (*MM*, DV Introduction, §XV, 6:408), implying that both of these problems could be corrected by respect for the moral law as such. His position is thus that it is only adherence to the fundamental maxim of respect for duty that will both always tell what it is right to do and always afford the motivation to do it even in the face of resistance.

Finally, Kant suggests one more reason why virtue understood

---

[18] *Vigilantius*, 27:570; *Lectures on Ethics*, p. 323.

Robert N. Johnson has argued that Kant should be seen as holding that respect for duty is always a reliable criterion of what is right, but not that it is always accessible as a reliable motive for doing what is right; see his "Expressing a Good Will: Kant on the Motive of Duty," *Southern Journal of Philosophy 34* (1996): 147–68. This conclusion might be required by Kant's insistence on the inscrutable fact of human wrongdoing, which implies that the motive of respect for duty is not always available to everyone; but passages like those just cited suggest that it is Kant's view that, at least to the extent to which anyone does reliably act rightly in the face of temptations to do otherwise, it can only be the agent's adherence to the fundamental maxim of respect for duty which explains that constancy.

as a persistent and steadfast endeavor to comply with the requirements of duty can only be grounded in virtue as the morally worthy motive of respect for duty as such. This is that although virtue must be *like* a habit in producing a consistent pattern of behavior, it cannot merely *be* a habit, a pattern of behavior that has become unthinking and automatic, because then it would no longer be an expression of the inner freedom of the agent:[19]

> An *aptitude* (*habitus*) is a facility in acting and a subjective perfection of *choice.* – But not every such *facility* is a *free* aptitude (*habitus liberatis*): for if it is a *habit* (*assuetudo*), that is, a uniformity in action that has become a *necessity* through frequent repetition, it is not one that proceeds from freedom, and therefore not a moral aptitude. . . . [Only an] aptitude [that] is not a property of choice but of the *will*, which is a faculty of desire that, in adopting a rule, also gives it as a universal law . . . can be counted as virtue. (*MM*, DV Introduction, §XIV, 6:407)

Of course, Kant does maintain that virtue must be acquired, as a habit is, simply because human beings naturally have inclinations and thus are not naturally disposed to be steadfastly virtuous – this is simply an expression of his basic assumption that the adoption of a fundamental maxim is an act of free choice:

> For while the capacity (*facultas*) to overcome all opposing sensible impulses can and must be simply *presupposed* in man on account of his freedom, yet this capacity as *strength* (*robur*) is something he must acquire; and the way to acquire it is to enhance the moral *incentive* (the thought of the law), both by contemplating the dignity of the pure rational law in us (*contemplatione*) and by *practicing* virtue (*exercitio*). (*MM*, DV Introduction, §X, 6:397)

Yet the habit of virtue is not acquired once and for all, by an act or period of practice after which it is automatic. No matter how long one contemplates or practices acts of virtue in order to make virtue a disposition, even the best-entrenched practice of virtue

---

[19] This point is also suggested by Mary Gregor; see *The Laws of Freedom* (Oxford: Basil Blackwell, 1963), pp. 71–72.

must still represent a continuing free choice of the law over inclination. Thus Kant writes:

> Virtue is always *in progress* and yet always starts *from the begin-*
> *ning.* . . . For moral maxims cannot, like technical ones, be based
> on habit (since this belongs to the natural constitution of the
> will's determination), because even if their practice were to be-
> come a habit, the subject would thereby sacrifice *freedom* in the
> adoption of his maxims, which is, however, what characterizes
> an action out of duty. (*MM*, DV Introduction, §XVI, 6:409)

In sum, then, virtue in the sense of a strong and persistent endeavor
to do what duty requires in the face of resistance and temptation
can only be conceived as the product of virtue in the sense of motivation by respect for duty alone, because only the latter, unlike
any mere inclination, can always tell the agent what it is right to
do, only it is always available to the agent as a motive to do what
is right, and only it can always be available to the agent while remaining an expression of the freedom of the agent.

3. I now turn from virtue to duties of virtue. Kant's definition of
what he specifically calls duties of virtue is clearly narrower than
either of the two senses of virtue thus far considered. Yet Kant
subsumes *more* under the rubric of duties of virtue than fits this
definition, and indeed holds that *any* requirement of duty can be
fulfilled in a virtuous way. Is Kant's catalog of the duties of virtue
a tissue of confusion, or is there a perspicuous way to relate the
duties of virtue properly so called to virtue in its more general
forms?

Kant starts the "Doctrine of Virtue" with the claim that ethics
goes beyond right "and provides a *matter* (an object of free choice),
an *end* of pure reason which it represents as an end that is also objectively necessary, that is, an end that, as far as human beings are
concerned, it is a duty to have" (*MM*, DV Introduction, §I, 6:380).
A duty of virtue, as the subject of ethics as the doctrine of virtue,
is *"an end that is also a duty,"* or a duty to adopt an end. To adopt
an end is to adopt a general policy of attempting to bring about a
certain kind of result, such as the cultivation of one's own talents
or the improvement of the lot of others who are in need, but to

adopt such a general policy does not always and automatically commit one to performing actions of a certain determinate type: to adopt the policy of cultivating talent does not of itself commit one to developing a particular talent, say that for doing philosophy, and even making it one's end to cultivate that particular talent would only commit one to the most general sorts of further actions, such as reading and talking enough, and would not commit one to any fully determinate pattern of action, such as taking four specific classes a semester and reading a thousand specific pages a month for some determinate number of semesters. Since having an end does not entail the necessity of performing actions that are specific in this sense, Kant infers that it is not possible for anyone to be *compelled* to have an end in the same way that one can be both logically and, under appropriate circumstances, morally compelled to perform a determinate action or omission. In Kant's word, "I can indeed be constrained by others to perform actions that are directed as a means to an end, but I can never be constrained by others *to have an end:* only I myself can *make* something my end" (6:381).

From this Kant infers that if any constraint at all is available for the adoption of ends, it can only be self-constraint: since only I can make something my end, *a fortiori* only I can force myself to make something my end. For this reason, Kant says, *all* duties consisting in the requirement to have or adopt an end can only be ethical duties or duties of virtue, "since *self-constraint* in accordance with (moral) laws belongs to the concept of ethics alone" (6:381); they cannot be duties of right, which are duties where external constraint is both logically and morally possible. However, Kant also maintains that duties to have or adopt an end are the *only* duties that are ethical duties or duties of virtue, for they are the only duties that cannot be the subject of external constraint: "determination to an *end* is the only determination of choice the very concept of which excludes the possibility of constraint *through natural means* by the *choice* of another" (6:381). Finally, we can now see why duties to have an end are called duties of *virtue*: if fulfilling them requires constraint at all – if, for example, making it one's end to cultivate talent or to cultivate some particular talent is the kind of thing one may have to force oneself to do – then the only constraint available for this purpose would be that which one's own reason could exercise over one's inclinations by means of a motive available to that reason. Since the motive of respect for the moral law is the only motive available to reason that is not a matter of mere inclination, and that motive constitutes a virtuous disposition in the initial sense of that which has genuine moral worth, duties to adopt ends can then be called duties of virtue because virtue in its primary sense is the only motive by means of which we can constrain ourselves to adopt ends when we have to constrain ourselves to do so.[20]

In spite of this neat analysis, however, Kant's list of duties of virtue clearly includes duties that are not duties to adopt an end, and thus casts doubt on his claim that it is *only* duties to adopt an end that are duties of virtue. The duties to cultivate our talents and to be benevolent to others are clearly duties to have general ends rather than to perform any very determinate types of actions. But other duties that Kant includes in the "Doctrine of Virtue" in the published *Metaphysics of Morals* as well as in his lectures on ethics from the mid-1770s to the mid-1790s, such as the duties to refrain from suicide, self-abuse, drunkenness and gluttony, lying, avarice, and servility, which are duties to ourselves, as well as the duties of respect to others, the duties to avoid arrogance, calumny, and mockery, all seem to be duties to refrain from determinate types of actions, duties that we would appear to be obliged to fulfill no matter by means of what motives we manage to do so or what ends we have. They are in fact all duties of omission, all of which seem to be narrow duties, whereas duties to have or adopt an end are duties of commission, and at least in these cases broad duties. So why are these duties of omission with regard to both self and others listed by Kant as duties of virtue rather than of right?

One answer to this question might seem to be that, contrary to initial appearance, even these duties of omission are duties to have

[20] This general approach is suggested by Gregor in *The Laws of Freedom*, p. 69. She does not, however, pursue at any length the question of whether everything Kant labels a duty of virtue is actually a duty to adopt an end. Neither the German transcription of the *Vigilantius* lectures on the metaphysics of morals nor its English translation, which as we will see reveals the difficulty of Kant's thought on this issue, were available to her at the time that she wrote.

an end. For these duties, duties such as refraining from suicide or avoiding the mockery of others, also derive from our general obligation to "use humanity, whether in your own person or in the person of any other, always at the same time as an end, never merely as a means" (*G*, 4:429): while being benevolent to others is surely treating the humanity in them as an end, gratuitously vilifying them is just as surely treating the humanity in them merely as a means to our own perverse pleasure. Kant might seem to suggest such an answer when he writes:

> The supreme principle of the doctrine of virtue is: act in accordance with a maxim of *ends* that it can be a universal law for everyone to have. – In accordance with this principle a human being is an end for himself as well as for others, and it is not enough that he is not authorized to use either himself or others merely as means (since he could then still be indifferent to them); it is in itself his duty to make the human being as such his end. (*MM*, DV Introduction, §IX, 6:395)

The problem with such an answer is that it would seem to make *all* of our duties into duties of virtue, even paradigmatic duties of right such as the duties not to injure others' innate right to freedom of the person or their acquired right to freedom in the acquisition and use of property and contract; for *all* of our duties are clearly supposed to be derivable from the fundamental injunction always to use humanity as an end and never merely as a means. In other words, if it were the completely general duty to make humanity our end that Kant had in mind in defining duties of virtue, the definition would be far too general. Does Kant avoid this problem?

Kant's actual list of duties of virtue seems to reflect the assumption that our duties of omission with regard to ourselves and even some of our duties of omission with regard to others, those he calls "duties of respect," should be classified along with duties such as those to cultivate talents or to practice benevolence as duties of virtue solely because in their case too, if constraint is needed, it can only be self-constraint deriving from the virtuous motivation of respect for duty as such. In the case of these duties, which are not duties to adopt an end but still permit only of self-constraint, however, the reason for this is not that it would be logically or theoretically impossible for one person to be compelled to fulfill such duties by another, as it is logically or theoretically impossible for one person to compel another to have a particular end. Rather, the reason why only self-constraint is possible in these cases is that it would be morally impossible to enforce them by means of coercion: no one else has the requisite standing to compel another to fulfill these duties to the self or duties of respect to others. Kant assumes this when he states that "What essentially distinguishes a duty of virtue from a duty of right is that external constraint to the latter kind of duty is morally possible, whereas the former is based only on free self-constraint" (*MM*, DV Introduction, §II, 6:383), though he does not offer an explanation of why external constraint is not morally possible in the case of, for example, the negative duties to oneself. Nor does he offer an adequate explanation of his assumption in the Vigilantius lectures when he says that there are "*officia stricta*, to which I may be compelled without anyone else being able to compel me. For example, it is a strict duty to humanity in my own person that I be unable to dispose over my body as the owner of it; nor can another person compel me directly in that respect."[21] What Kant needs here is an explanation of why others do not have moral standing to compel us to comply with our duties of omission to ourselves or even with our duties of respect regarding others. Such an explanation would presumably have to have the form of showing that, while coercion can only be justified when it is a hindrance to a hindrance of freedom (*MM*, DR Introduction, §D, 6:231), that account only works when what is at issue is one agent's would-be hindrance to the freedom of *another*, so that there can be no justification for another's hindrance to one who would in some way hinder his own freedom. Perhaps such an argument would ultimately have to turn on the fact that one person cannot hinder the freedom of another who would hinder his own freedom without depriving the other of precisely that which the first person's intervention is supposed to preserve, namely, the latter's own freedom; but Kant certainly never spells such an argument out.

[21] *Vigilantius*, 27:581; *Lectures on Ethics*, p. 332.

Along with Kant's silence about the ultimate basis for his supposition that our perfect duties or duties of omission to ourselves as well as certain of our perfect duties to others are only fit for self-constraint or internal legislation, not coercive enforcement or external legislation, there goes a lingering uncertainty about the best way to classify the duties of self-constraint that is evident even in the brief period between the delivery of the Vigilantius lectures of 1793–94 and the publication of the "Doctrine of Virtue" in 1797. In the Vigilantius lectures, Kant starts by firmly equating the distinction between duties of right and duties of virtue with the distinction between *officia stricta* or *perfecta*, that is, duties to avoid the commission of certain relatively specific types of action, and *officia lata* or *imperfecta*, that is, the broad duties to adopt a relatively general sort of end, which cannot be mechanically translated into duties to perform specific types of actions in specific circumstances: all *officia stricta* or perfect duties are duties of right, and all *officia lata* or imperfect duties are duties of virtue.[22] The criterion of whether a duty permits of external, coercive enforcement is clearly subsidiary, and thus can be used to mark a distinction within the duties of right without transforming the latter into duties of virtue. The duties of right thus include "strict or internal duties of right, i.e., the right of humanity in our own person," and "strict or external coercive duties, i.e., the rights of men in regard to one another," whereas the duties of virtue include "broad or internal duties of virtue, the end of humanity in our own person, or that end which humanity imposes on us," and "broad or external duties of virtue, i.e., ends toward other men."[23] So "not every *officium strictum*, or duty of right, is a coercive duty" in the usual sense "whereby the *obligatus* can . . . be coerced by another into the act of duty"; "on the contrary, coercion is conceivable, without it presupposing a duty toward others; there are duties of right, or *officia stricta*, to which I may be compelled without anyone else being able to compel me."[24] On this account, then, no duties of right are duties to adopt an end, but only some duties of right permit of

[22] *Vigilantius*, 27:581 (c); *Lectures on Ethics*, p. 332.
[23] *Vigilantius*, 27:583; *Lectures on Ethics*, p. 333.
[24] *Vigilantius*, 27:581 (c); *Lectures on Ethics*, p. 332.

external coercion, and others allow only self-constraint, whereas all duties of virtue remain duties to adopt an end (and for that reason none of them permit of external coercion). Kant tries to mark the distinction between the two types of duty of right with a subtle verbal distinction: Vigilantius says that

> Professor Kant therefore sets forth this distinction as follows: Duties of right, both to oneself and to others, are *officia juris*, the former *interna* and the latter *externa*. The *externa* are of that type which he calls coercive duties, or genuine *officia juridica*, legal duties, and in regard to them the coercion from without is an authentic feature.[25]

Thus, all perfect duties, whether to self or others, are duties of right, but within this class only some are juridical or legal duties, that is, duties for which publicly managed constraint or coercion is both possible and appropriate. The remainder permit only of self-constraint, but this does not make them into duties of virtue, which are always imperfect duties or duties that are broad because they are duties to adopt an end rather than omit or commit some determinate action. This classification is possible only because in these lectures the adoption of an end rather than the necessity of self-constraint is unequivocally the criterion of a duty of virtue.

In the "Doctrine of Virtue," however, published just three years later, although Kant begins with the same set of equations – all duties of right are *officia stricta* and all duties of virtue are *officia lata* – he subsequently proceeds as if the necessity of adopting an end were just a particularly salient feature of many duties of virtue that leads us to the more fundamental recognition that duties of virtue require inner rather than external coercion, that is, self-constraint rather than constraint by others; this then becomes the most fundamental criterion of duties of virtue, so that all duties for which only self-constraint is possible are now classified as duties of virtue. Here Kant argues that there must be ends that are also duties, because some duties of virtue are clearly duties to adopt ends, which would not make any sense unless there are ends that

---

[25] *Vigilantius*, 27:582; *Lectures on Ethics*, p. 332; see also 27:587, p. 337.

it can be a duty to adopt; but he also holds, as we have already noted, that "What essentially distinguishes a duty of virtue from a duty of right is that external constraint to the latter kind of duty is morally possible, whereas the former is based only on free self-constraint" (*MM*, DV Introduction, §II, 6:383). He then goes on to include all of the perfect duties to oneself and even some perfect duties to others, namely the duties of respect, as duties of virtue. He is now inclined to treat the distinction between allowing external constraint and allowing only self-constraint as the primary criterion for distinguishing between duties of right and duties of virtue, even if it may be a reflection on the impossibility of anything other than self-constraint in the setting of ends that leads us to this distinction in the first place.

A decision to make self-constraint into the sole criterion for all duties of virtue, moreover, would have the merit of explaining why duties of virtue are so called: while there may not be an obvious or analytical connection between the idea of setting an end and the concept of virtue as motivation by respect for duty as such, there is a crucial connection between the idea of self-constraint and this basic notion of virtue, because on Kant's view the only motive available for self-constraint is the virtuous motivation of respect for duty – any other motivation could only be a form of inclination, and therefore not a form of self-constraint. So compliance with the duties of virtue defined simply as duties for which only self-constraint is possible can only be a product of virtue.

Yet in spite of this advantage of using self-constraint as the primary criterion for duties of virtue, and thus revising the definition of duties of virtue in a way that would capture all of the duties he actually listed as duties of virtue, Kant was obviously loath to reject outright the approach to the distinction between duties of right and virtue that he had been using in his lectures. Toward the end of the Introduction to the "Doctrine of Virtue" he therefore tries to maintain the equal importance of both criteria. He does this by distinguishing between "formal" and "material" aspects of the distinction between duties of right and of virtue.[26] In formal

[26] This manuever was anticipated in the Vigilantius lectures; see *Vigilantius*, 27: 542; *Lectures on Ethics*, p. 300.

terms, Kant holds that duties of virtue may be distinguished from duties of right "by laying it down (1) that duties of virtue are duties for which there is no external lawgiving; (2) that since a law must yet lie at the basis of every duty, this law in ethics can be a law of duty given, not for actions, but only for the maxims of actions; (3) that (as follows in turn from this) ethical duty must be thought as *wide*, not as narrow, duty." Then he goes on to say that "the principle of division must *secondly*, in terms of what is *material*, present the doctrine of virtue not merely as a doctrine of duties generally but also as a *doctrine of ends*, so that a human being is under obligation to regard himself, as well as every other human being, as his end" (*MM*, DV Introduction, §XVII, 6:410). While the formal criterion of the impossibility of external lawgiving would leave room for those duties of omission that are not coercively enforceable duties of right to count as duties of virtue, the material criterion for the distinction would require that every duty of virtue be a requirement to adopt an end. Here Kant even suggests that the impossibility of external lawgiving itself implies this, because since the law in ethics cannot be a law for actions, it must be a law for maxims of actions (step (2) of the "formal" characterization). This inference is problematic, however, because external lawgiving for a duty might be impossible, not because the duty does not involve or prohibit a determinate action but because no one other than the agent has standing to enforce such a duty. The impossibility of external constraint to the performance of a particular duty does not by itself imply that the duty is a duty to adopt an end, so it seems as if Kant should choose whether the impossibility of external constraint or the adoption of an end is the primary criterion for a duty of virtue, and not just assume that the former implies the latter.

There is a similar uncertainty in Kant's classification of the fundamental obligation to make respect for the moral law itself our motive, or what Kant calls the obligation *of* or *to* virtue itself (*Tugendverpflichtung*). On the one hand, in the same section of the Introduction to the "Doctrine of Virtue" that we have just been considering, Kant explicitly denies that "every *obligation of virtue* (*obligatio ethica*) is a duty of virtue (*officiam ethicum s. virtutis*)," because "respect for law as such does not yet establish an end as a duty, and only such an end is a duty of virtue" (*MM*, DV Introduction,

§XVII, 6:610). Precisely because the general obligation to make respect for law our fundamental motive does not by itself enjoin any determinate end, Kant maintains, it is not itself a duty of virtue, and can indeed be "our subjective determining ground to fulfill ... duties of right" as well as specific duties of virtue. On the other hand, in the catalog of duties of virtue that constitutes the body of the "Doctrine of Virtue," Kant includes the duty to increase one's moral perfection, that is, the "perfection consist[ing] subjectively in the *purity (puritas moralis)* of one's disposition to duty, namely, in the law being by itself alone the incentive, even without the admixture of aims derived from sensibility, and in actions being done not only in conformity with duty but also *from* duty," as one of our two chief duties of virtue to ourselves (*MM*, DV, §21, 6:446): our duty to increase our natural perfection is our duty to develop our talents of spirit, mind, and body, and our duty to increase our moral perfection is our duty to increase the purity of our moral disposition. This duty to increase our moral perfection seems identical to the general obligation to virtue of which Kant earlier spoke, so it seems as if Kant both asserts and denies that the obligation to virtue is a duty of virtue. He can't have it both ways, so which way should he have gone?

If we should watch what Kant does and not what he says, then his actual enumeration of the duties of virtue clearly shows that he ultimately regarded the general obligation to virtue as a duty of virtue. If Kant had stuck to the idea that the possibility of self-constraint alone is a sufficient criterion for a duty of virtue, he could readily have argued for this position on the ground that no one but the agent himself can compel him to make respect for the moral law his fundamental motive. Without using the term *Tugend-verpflichtung* ("obligation to virtue"), Kant suggests precisely such an argument in yet another passage in the Vigilantius lectures. Here he equates the distinction between duties of right and of virtue with that between *officia justi et honesti* (duties of justice and of honor), and then says that it is precisely when an "action is performed solely for the sake of the law, i.e., [when] the law alone is the action's determining ground or moving cause, motive and norm," that the action is *"aliquid honestum"* or a duty of virtue. He then goes on to explain that this is true because "a coercive law can be confined only to the legality of the action, but is not think-able in regard to its morality"; the reason for this is that "neither man nor a God is in a position to compel the agent to adopt the *animus legis,* since he has been granted the power to follow the law with free choice, and not with a mechanism."[27] The decision to make respect for the moral law one's fundamental motive is an es-sential expression of inner freedom or freedom of choice; because it is such an expression, it can never be compelled by anyone other than the agent himself, even someone else with superhuman powers; because it cannot be compelled by anything other than self-constraint, it is an *aliquid honestum,* apparently, that is, a duty of virtue. This argument would have been completely consistent with Kant's statement in the "Doctrine of Virtue" that the impos-sibility of anything other than self-constraint is what is essential to any duty of virtue (*MM,* DV Introduction, §II, 6:383).

Again, however, Kant tries to evade this straightforward solu-tion in the Introduction to the "Doctrine of Virtue." Instead of ei-ther standing by his statement that the obligation to virtue is not a duty of virtue or else granting that it is one because it can only be a matter of self- rather than external constraint, Kant ultimately tries to argue that the obligation to make respect for moral law as such one's fundamental maxim does involve adopting an end and is an imperfect duty for that reason after all:

> Although there is nothing meritorious in the conformity of one's actions with right . . . , the conformity with right of one's max-ims of such actions, that is, *respect* for right, is *meritorious.* For one thereby makes the *right* of humanity . . . one's *end* and in so doing widens one's concept of duty beyond the concept of what is *due* (*officim debitis*), since another can indeed by his right re-quire of me actions in accordance with the law, but not that the law be also my incentive to such actions. The same holds true of the universal ethical command, "act in conformity with duty *from duty.*" (*MM,* DV Introduction, §VII, 6:390–91)

However, Kant does not worry that interpreting the fundamental moral maxim of respect for the moral law as positing an end will

---

[27] *Vigilantius,* 27:582; *Lectures on Ethics,* pp. 332–33.

transform duties of right into duties of virtue, and thus end up making all duties into duties of right, because duties of right can still be coercively enforced without concern for the agent's maxim at all.

Further, explicitly under the rubric of an "Exposition of Duties of Virtue as Wide Duties," Kant next argues that "the cultivation of morality" in ourselves is an imperfect rather than a perfect duty because, unlike a duty of right, it commands the adoption of a maxim and not by itself the performance of any specific actions:

> The greatest perfection of a human being is to do his duty *from duty* (for the law to be not only the rule but also the incentive of his actions). – At first sight this looks like a *narrow* obligation, and the principle of duty seems to prescribe with the precision and strictness of a law not only the *legality* but also the *morality* of every action, that is, the disposition. But in fact the law, here again, prescribes only the *maxim of the action*, that of seeking the basis of obligation solely in the law and not in sensible impulse (advantage or disadvantage), and hence not the *action itself*. (*MM*, DV Introduction, §VIII, 6:392)

Moreover, Kant adds further reasons why the fundamental obligation to make duty one's maxim is like an imperfect duty. He continues here to argue that this obligation can only be broad and imperfect because we can never be certain that we have succeeded in making it our motive, and later he argues that it is imperfect because on account of human frailty we can in fact know that we make at best imperfect progress to truly making respect for the law our fundamental motive (*MM*, DV, §22, 6:446–47). If we consider these further claims by themselves, Kant could seem just to want to argue that the general obligation to virtue is a duty of virtue because like other duties of virtue it is imperfect, although the reasons for its imperfection are not the same as in other cases of duties of virtue: other duties of virtue constitute only imperfect and broad duties because the ends they set are general rather than specific, whereas in the case of respect for law as one's fundamental maxim there is nothing nonspecific, but just uncertainty as to whether that is really our maxim or even certainty that because of our frailty it may never be entirely our maxim. But Kant's whole shift from denying that the general obligation to virtue is a duty of virtue to affirming that it does appear to involve a subtle shift from a definition of a duty of virtue as one that necessarily involves the adoption of an *end* to a definition of such a duty as one that involves the adoption of a *maxim*. Since the general obligation to virtue is precisely to make respect for the law our fundamental maxim, this can now count as a duty of virtue even if it is also sometimes taken (when it is a motive for compliance with duties of right) to require us merely to treat others as ends without making the humanity in them our end.

In the end, perhaps we can conclude that Kant could have avoided a lot of obscurity if not actual confusion simply by treating the impossibility of anything other than self-constraint as the sufficient condition for a duty of virtue, as he was sometimes clearly tempted to do. Then he could just have argued that both duties to adopt various ends such as benevolence or the cultivation of talents as well as the duty to make respect for the moral law as such our fundamental motive are duties of virtue because they all admit only of self-constraint, not external coercion. This would have preserved the connection between the concept of duty and the primary sense of virtue as morally worthy motivation, while other similarities or differences among the various kinds of duties of virtue could then have been explored for what they are without being denied or distorted for the sake of the classification. For instance, Kant could have observed that we must always be uncertain to what extent we have really made respect for duty our fundamental motive, indeed even while being certain that we can never wholly succeed in so doing, without misleadingly suggesting that this sort of imperfection is the same sort of imperfectness, that is, simple nonspecificity, which is characteristic of those duties of virtue that involve the adoption of some particular end such as benevolence.

III MERIT

I conclude with a few words about Kant's conception of merit (*Verdienst*). Kant treats merit as what we esteem in an agent who does more than what is owed. In the Vigilantius lectures, he says that *"Meritum* or service [*Verdienst*] is the quality of an action in which more good occurs than the one who was acting was liable for under laws of right, or a lawful action in which, however, the action could not have been compelled in the measure in which it took place, e.g., when beneficence and philanthropy are combined with it."[28] It therefore seems most natural to assign merit to the performance of duties of virtue, for the reason that the degree – or "measure" (*Maaße*) – to which we fulfill them is always optional and thus more than what is owed. Thus, some pages later in the Vigilantius lectures Kant says the following about "Duties of love (*officia meriti*), meritorious duties": "They always go beyond what is merely due from us, i.e., precisely because they are supposed to be merits they always contain in themselves more moral goodness than is determined as necessary by the law."[29] However, the suggestion that the performance of duties of love, that is, imperfect duties to others, or even duties of virtue more generally, is meritorious because the fulfillment of such duties is always more than what is owed creates two problems. First, it suggests that the fulfillment of such duties is always optional and thus supererogatory, which is clearly not Kant's considered position.[30] Second, it might make it difficult to explain a connection between the concept of merit and Kant's fundamental conception of moral worth, that is, the general obligation to virtue or the motivation to act out of respect for duty itself; for while Kant clearly supposes that "the conformity with right of one's maxims of . . . actions, as duties, that is, *respect* for right, is *meritorious*" (*MM*, DV Introduction,

---

[28] *Vigilantius*, 27:558; *Lectures on Ethics*, p. 313 (modified).

[29] *Vigilantius*, 27:600; *Lectures on Ethics*, p. 347.

[30] In one of the first important modern publications on the "Doctrine of Virtue," Paul Eisenberg criticized Kant for not having room for the concept of the supererogatory; see his "From the Forbidden to the Supererogatory: The Basic Ethical Categories in Kant's *Tugendlehre*," *American Philosophical Quarterly* 3 (1966): 255–69. Others have gone to interpretative extremes to find room for the supererogatory within Kant's ethics, for example, by trying to associate it with the aesthetic category of the sublime; see Richard McCarty, "The Limits of Kantian Duty, and Beyond," *American Philosophical Quarterly* 26 (1989): 43–52. Most recently, Marcia Baron has offered an extensive defense of Kant's elimination of the category of the supererogatory from his ethics; see *Kantian Ethics Almost without Apology*, especially chs. 1 and 2.

§VII, 6:390), it hardly seems optional that we should strive to make respect for duty our fundamental motivation. We must clear up these two issues before we can understand the relation of merit to particular duties of virtue (*Tugendpflichten*) and the general obligation to virtue (*Tugendverpflichtung*).

Kant does sometimes make it sound as if duties of virtue are optional and thus any particular fulfillment of them supererogatory and meritorious because it is more than what is owed. Thus at one point in the Vigilantius lectures he says that "duties of broader obligation" or imperfect duties "may also be called neglectable [*nachläßliche*] or better optional duties [*Wahlpflichten*], since they leave it to the person how far the end proposed to him by humanity, whether in his own person or for the happiness of others, can be fulfilled."[31] But even this statement itself suggests that the fulfillment of such duties is not so much optional as adjustable in degree. More fully, Kant's account of the fulfillment of such duties suggests that one does have a general obligation to fulfill them, but that this cannot be mechanically translated into an obligation to perform any specific action for several reasons: first, because the *kind* of action one can undertake in fulfillment of a general objective such as benevolence depends on one's particular circumstances and talents; second, because the *degree* of action one can undertake also depends on such factors; and, perhaps most importantly, because whether one can undertake to fulfill an imperfect duty in any particular circumstances is always conditional upon what *other* imperfect as well as perfect duties one might have and whether compliance especially with the latter would preclude performance of the former. Thus, in the "Doctrine of Virtue" Kant stresses not that imperfect duties are simply optional, that it is simply a matter of indifference whether we act to fulfill them on any particular occasion, but that they are *limited, constrained,* or *conditioned* by our other duties: "a wide duty is not to be taken as permission to make exceptions to the maxim of actions but only as permission to limit one maxim of duty by another (e.g., love of one's neighbor in general by love of one's parents), by which in fact the field for the practice of virtue is widened" (*MM*, DV

---

[31] *Vigilantius*, 27:578; *Lectures on Ethics*, p. 330.

Introduction, §VII, 6:390). On Kant's considered account it is certainly not optional that we make benevolence our end, for example, but in any actual circumstances we will have to use our judgment to determine whether our own needs, resources, and other obligations will permit a particular benevolent action and if so how much of one. For this reason, in turn, no other person, no matter what her circumstances, no matter how needy of benevolence she may be, automatically has a claim on my benevolence, and thus I cannot be said to owe a determinate act of benevolence to any other particular person. This is the sense, then, in which any particular act in fulfillment of a duty of love or duty of virtue goes beyond what is owed: such an act is never automatically owed to another particular person, although in the particular circumstances it may not in fact simply be optional for us to perform the act in question.[32] Thus Kant writes:

> The love of humanity in particular, as that to which we are bound by obligation to the universal rule, and which constitutes practical love, seems, when considered as a *debitum*, to be in contradiction to the law that enjoins us, since the latter is fulfilled only out of respect for it, and not out of love. Moreover, it seems to be a meritorious thing, when we love people, and we only enlarge such a disposition by that which relates to the good as such. In itself, too, the duty that refers to love toward other people is merely an *officium meriti*, never a *debitum*; for it rests on the fact that we have a demand and a will to contribute to their happiness; now nobody has a claimant's right to demand that I promote his well-being.[33]

In other words, a duty like benevolence both is and isn't owed, and thus is and isn't meritorious: in general, it is incumbent upon us to be benevolent, and thus it would seem that we earn no special merit by making benevolence our general maxim or policy; yet no specific act of benevolence is owed to any specific person apart from detailed consideration of particular circumstances, so the

---

[32] This point is well made by Eisenberg; see "From the Forbidden to the Supererogatory," pp. 266–67.

[33] *Vigilantius*, 27:669; *Lectures on Ethics*, p. 402.

performance of any particular act of benevolence is always more than is strictly owed and is therefore meritorious.

We can say something similar about the general obligation to virtue, or our obligation to make respect for duty itself our fundamental maxim. On the one hand, this is something that Kant clearly assumes is expected of us all. On the other hand, while everyone has a claim that others should act toward them as this maxim demands, no one has a claim that any other person act toward him out of this maxim as his actual motive. Two cases should be distinguished here. As we have just seen, at least apart from very special circumstances, no other particular person can demand that I make him the object of my policy of, for example, benevolence; *a fortiori*, he cannot demand that I make him the object of my benevolence out of my respect for duty itself. But even where another does have a particular claim upon me, for example, that I repay a debt that I have freely contracted and thus have a duty of right to pay, he still cannot demand that I repay this debt out of any particular motive, *a fortiori* out of the virtuous motive of respect for duty as such. As Kant puts it,

> Another can indeed by his right demand of me actions in accordance with the law, but not that the law be also my incentive to such actions. The same holds true of the universal ethical command, act in conformity with duty *from* duty. To establish and quicken this disposition in oneself is, as in the previous case, *meritorious*, since it goes beyond the law of duty for actions and makes the law itself also the incentive. (*MM*, DV Introduction, §VII, 6:391)

In other words, even if there is some general sense in which we are obliged to make respect for the law itself our maxim, we do not owe this to any other particular person, so in fact making it our maxim is more than what is owed, at least to any other person, and is therefore meritorious.

Finally, Kant also suggests not merely an analogy but also a causal link between the merit in the fulfillment of an imperfect duty and the merit in making duty our fundamental maxim, a link that confirms our earlier argument that duties of virtue are so called because virtue in its primary sense of morally worthy motivation is the only motivation available for fulfilling them when so doing requires any self-constraint. This suggestion comes in a remark in the Vigilantius lectures where Kant maintains that purity of motivation is meritorious not only in itself but also because it in fact leads to a fuller realization of specific duties of virtue than could otherwise be expected:

> [To] make myself *worthy of honor* . . . the dutifulness of the action must be supplemented by moral goodness, viz., that the idea of duty should have been the motive to the action, and that we should thus have acted from duty and no other motive. To attune our moral disposition to this, and order our conduct thereby, is a duty, and one whose fulfillment lies in the *honeste vive*; it is that which does us honor. Toward men we realize more morality than is incumbent on us, and in this, therefore, lies at the same time the merit of our actions. This *honestas* can be attained by practice, no less in conduct toward our own humanity than in serving the ends of other men – for example, when the manual worker cultivates his talent beyond the call of duty, so as thereby to become more useful to others, and is guided by the dutiful conviction that he is bound to cultivate his talents to the best of his ability.[34]

Perhaps the arguments that making duty one's maxim and even performing particular deeds of benevolence are meritorious simply because these are not owed to particular claimants will seem strained. But here Kant suggests that truly making respect for duty as such one's fundamental maxim will lead one to take steps, such as cultivating talents, that will actually put one in a better position to fulfill one's duties, particularly duties of virtue, than one would otherwise be in, and surely this seems genuinely meritorious. Kant's suggestion is thus that to make duty one's fundamental maxim is not merely in itself more than what is owed to any other claimant but will also put one in a position actually to do more than what would otherwise be owed to any particular claimant. This does not seem like an implausible account of merit.

---

[34] *Vigilantius*, 27:668; *Lectures on Ethics*, pp. 401–2.

I conclude with a summary of this long argument. Kant's fundamental conception of the moral worth of an agent as consisting in
making respect for duty itself one's fundamental maxim gives rise
to a distinctive position on the moral significance of inclinations:
on Kant's account, no inclinations, no matter how sympathetic,
are ever in themselves independent but cooperating motives in
morally worthy action; only if inclinations, however cooperative
they might seem to be on their own, have been freely chosen as
means to an end dictated by the fundamental maxim of respect for
duty can they be a sign of the moral worth of an agent. Further,
virtue in Kant's primary sense, which is equivalent to this notion
of the moral worth of an agent, is causally connected to the further sense of virtue as the steadfast and persistent effort to do what
is right in the face of resistance and to the duties of virtue, because
only the fundamental maxim of respect for duty as such can be
counted on to produce a constant yet free effort to do what is right
and, further, an effort to fulfill those duties for which no external
constraint is theoretically possible or morally permissible. Finally,
merit attaches to both the fulfillment of imperfect duties and to
the very fact of making respect for duty one's fundamental maxim
because both of these are more than what is owed to any particular
person, but also because the latter, respect for duty as such, is an
indispensable condition for maximizing the former, one's ability
to fulfill one's imperfect duties to the fullest extent possible.

Part IV
Hopes

Chapter 10

From a Practical Point of View: Kant's Conception of a Postulate of Pure Practical Reason

From the first edition of the *Critique of Pure Reason* in 1781 (see A 634/B 652, A 828/B 856) to the 1793 draft of an answer to the Berlin Academy's question "What Real Progress Has Metaphysics Made since the Time of Leibniz and Wolff?" Kant argued that the necessity of conceiving of the highest good as the object of morality leads to a "practical-dogmatic" proof of the existence of God, immortality, and (sometimes) freedom that is valid "only in a certain regard." In such a proof, the existence of God or the other objects of belief is postulated "not in order to ground the laws and even the final end of morality . . . but in order to secure reality . . . in a practical point of view [*in praktischer Absicht*] for its idea of a highest good possible in a world, which considered objectively and theoretically lies beyond our capacity [*Vermögen*]" (*RP*, 20:305). Or as Kant put his position in the *Critique of Judgment*:

> The *highest good* that can be effected in the world through freedom, [is a] concept [which] cannot be demonstrated in any experience possible for us, whose objective reality hence cannot be adequately demonstrated for the theoretical use of reason, but whose use for the best possible effectuation of that end is yet commanded through practical reason and hence must be assumed to be possible. This commanded effect *together with the*

A German translation of an abbreviated version of this chapter appeared previously as "In praktischer Absicht: Kants Begriff eines Postulats der reinen praktischen Vernunft," *Philosophisches Jahrbuch* 104 (1997): 1–18.

only conditions of its possibility conceivable for us, namely the existence of God and the immortality of the soul, are *matters of
belief.* . . . Only objects of pure reason can be matters of belief in
any case, but not as objects of mere pure speculative reason; for
then they cannot even be counted with certainty among the
matters, i.e., objects of cognition possible for us. On the contrary, the highest final end to be effected by us, that through
which alone we can become worthy of ourselves being the final
end of a creation, is an idea that has objective reality for us in a
practical relation. . . . If the highest principle of all moral laws is
a postulate, then at the same time the possibility of its highest
object and hence also the condition under which we can think
this possibility is also postulated. Now the cognition of the latter becomes thereby neither knowledge nor opinion of the existence and the constitution of these conditions, as a theoretical
sort of cognition, but merely an assumption in a practical and
commanded relation to the moral use of our reason. (*CJ*, §91, 5:
469–70).

In such passages Kant commits himself to two controversial claims.
First, our obligation under the moral law is an obligation to realize
the condition of the highest good, a condition that Kant elsewhere
describes as the conjoint maximization of virtue and happiness,
and indeed, in spite of the reference to immortality, an obligation
to realize this condition so far as possible "in the world," that is,
in the course of our sensible existence. Second, while the command
of morality entails the possibility of the highest good, the possibility of this good in turn requires the assumption, although only
from a practical point of view, of the actual existence of God and
other matters as the necessary conditions of this possibility. These
two assumptions immediately raise three questions: First, how
can the moral law, which apparently obligates all rational beings
without reference to ends at all (e.g., *G*, 4:415), at the same time
command pursuit of a single "final end," the highest good? Second, even if we can understand how the rationality of acting in accord with the moral law requires the possibility of the highest good,
why does the latter possibility entail, even if only "from a practical point of view," the actual existence of God or the other postulates? Third, what does it mean to consider an inference to an idea

or proposition to be valid "from a practical point of view" when we know that there is no adequate theoretical justification for it, and how is it even possible for us to believe something "from a practical point of view" that we know to be theoretically indemonstrable?

The final question about the coherence of practical belief in a theoretically indemonstrable proposition arises particularly because of the inference that the very possibility of a practically obligatory end presupposes the actual existence of its necessary conditions. This inference rests on a strong conception of the possibility of an object as involving more than just the absence of any contradiction in its concept. Occasionally Kant seems willing to employ a weaker conception of the conditions of rationality. Thus, writing in the *Metaphysics of Morals* about the duty to seek perpetual peace, Kant says:

> Now it is evident that what would be made our duty in this case is not the *assumption* (*suppositio*) that this end can be realized, which would be a judgment that is merely theoretical and, moreover, problematic; for there can be no obligation to do this (to believe something). What is incumbent on us as a duty is rather to act in conformity with the idea of that end, even if there is not the slightest theoretical likelihood that it can be realized, as long as its impossibility cannot be demonstrated either. (*MM*, 6:354)[1]

Kant's position here seems to require simply that if an end is sufficiently important to us, then all that is required to make the pursuit of it rational is the conviction that its realization is not impossible, which in turn seems to require only that the concept be free of contradiction. No further theoretical belief seems to be necessary, and here Kant adds that it would not even make sense to bring any further theoretical belief into an account of our duties, since in any case theoretical belief cannot be commanded in the way that action can be. Such a model of rationality would then suggest that the rationality of action aimed at bringing about the

---

[1] Translation from Immanuel Kant, *The Metaphysics of Morals*, trans. Mary J. Gregor (Cambridge: Cambridge University Press, 1991), p. 160; orthography modified.

highest good – for which perpetual peace is in fact just the complete political condition – requires only that there be no contradiction in the concept of the conjunction of virtue and happiness. In the case of perpetual peace, at least, there is no hint of any further inference from the possibility of perpetual peace to the actual existence of any ground for its existence other than our own actions in its behalf. So the question naturally arises, Why should the possibility of the highest good lead to the postulation of the actual existence of any necessary conditions beyond the noncontradictoriness of the concept of this end of practical reason?

The answer to this question is connected to the answer to my third question. Both the necessity but also the possibility of believing in the actual existence of theoretically indemonstrable conditions for the realization of the ultimate end defined by the moral law lie at the deepest level of the dualistic conception of human nature that underlies Kant's moral psychology: to act effectively to bring it about, we need to believe not just in the possibility of the highest good but in the actuality of its conditions just because we are not purely rational creatures, but creatures with both reason and sensibility who must exploit the natural means afforded by the latter to bring it into conformity with the former. The postulates of pure practical reason, like the aesthetic experience of beauty as a symbol of the morally good, are products of human psychology that can be used by the moral will as naturally occurring means to the realization of its morally necessary end; indeed, the will that has made the fundamental principle of morality its supreme maxim and is also governed by the fundamental maxim of technical reason, to use all appropriate means for its ends, must use such naturally occurring means to its morally necessary ends.

My argument for this claim has two parts. In the first, I examine Kant's argument for the necessity of adopting the highest good as the ultimate end of morality itself as well as his argument from this concept to the postulates of practical reason. In the second part, I explain how Kant can respond to the objection that his doctrine is a paradox absurdly requiring us to believe in that for which we can readily recognize ourselves to have inadequate theoretical grounds. This explanation of the possibility of the practical postulates shows it to be a part of the moral psychology that

Kant was developing in all the major works of his final decade of philosophical activity, the view of us as complex creatures with both reason and sensibility who can never simply ignore or extirpate our sensibility but must learn to direct and cultivate it in accordance with the demands of reason. Of course, this moral psychology may not prove the necessity of the religiously inspired postulates to which Kant himself was committed but may still provide a general model for the efficacy of moral ideals.

I FROM THE HIGHEST GOOD TO THE POSTULATES OF PRACTICAL REASON

1. Kant's argument for the postulates consists of two parts: first, the contention that the fundamental principle of morality calls for the production of a certain state of affairs as the intended outcome of our action in accordance with that principle, leading to the claim that it is rational for us to act as the principle requires only if we can also assume that it is possible for us to realize that intended outcome; and, second, the inference from the possibility of that intended outcome to the existence of the necessary conditions of this possibility. Thus Kant first argues that the rationality of adhering to the moral law requires the possibility of the state of affairs that he calls the "highest good," and then that the possibility of the highest good in turn presupposes the existence of the freedom of the human will, the immortality of the human soul, and of God as the intelligent Author of nature – or better, as he puts it in *Real Progress*, of God as the intelligent Author of the disposition to morality within us and of the receptivity to our moral disposition of nature outside us (*RP*, 20:300).

To start, we have to put together several of Kant's remarks to get a complete characterization of what he means by a postulate of pure practical reason. In the *Critique of Practical Reason*, Kant's first explicit account of such a postulate is that it is "a *theoretical* but as such indemonstrable proposition . . . insofar as it is inseparably connected to an *a priori* unconditionally valid *practical* law" (*CPracR*, 5:122). This tells us little about the content of a postulate – only that it is a "theoretical proposition" and so is not itself an imperative but an indicative, presumably existential statement – but more about its status; namely, it is not demonstrable by any theoretical means but is some sort of corollary of a "practical law," which presumably is an imperative rather than indicative statement. Kant tells us more about the content of the postulates several pages later, when he tells us that "by their means concepts which are otherwise problematic (merely conceivable) . . . are now assertorically declared to be ones to which actual objects pertain, because practical reason unavoidably requires their existence for the possibility of its practically absolutely necessary object, the highest good" (*CPracR*, 5:134).[2] Kant's repeated use of the word "object" (*Objekt*) in its two different senses of aim or intended outcome on the one hand and entity on the other makes this statement confusing, but what he means is that the pursuit of the highest good is mandated by the moral law, that the realization of this object or aim of our moral action must be at least possible for our action in accordance with the moral law to be rational, and that this possibility of the highest good in turn requires the assertion of the actual existence of objects or states of affairs – God, freedom, and immortality – that are theoretically indemonstrable, although they must also be at least theoretically possible, but which can be asserted to exist, in ordinary existential propositions, solely on the basis of their status as necessary conditions of the possibility of morality.

These claims raise two questions. First, why does adherence to the moral law require the possibility of the highest good? Second, why does the possibility of the highest good require the presupposition of the actual existence of such objects and states of affairs as God, freedom, and immortality, and how is it even possible for us to believe in these existential propositions when we know that they are theoretically indemonstrable?

---

[2] Here Kant adds what would seem to be the counterintuitive claim that this practical necessity makes *theoretical* reason "justified in presupposing" the existence of these objects; but he immediately adds that this "extension of theoretical reason" is no "extension of speculation, i.e., from a *theoretical point of view*," but that it is only practical reason whose concepts are hereby allowed to be "real and actual" (*CPracR*, 5:134). So the unexpected concession he grants with one hand is immediately taken back with the other.

2. Kant introduces the concept of the highest good in the *Critique of Practical Reason* with his famous statement that, although virtue is the "*supreme condition* of everything that may seem desirable to us," it is not the "entire and complete good as the object of the faculty of desire of a rational finite being; in order to be that, *happiness* is also required" (5:110). This may make it sound as if the highest good is the composite of two independent aims or ends – virtue as our end as rational creatures, and happiness as our end as finite and therefore sensible creatures – and that these two separate ends have to be reconciled by pursuing our natural end of happiness within the limits set by virtue, which intrinsically has nothing to do with happiness. This reading, however, which from the beginning has occasioned no end of misinterpretation,[3] is not what is implied by Kant's central statements about the content of the moral law, especially in the *Critique of Pure Reason* and the *Groundwork for the Metaphysics of Morals*. What the moral law requires is universal respect for rational being or humanity in all human beings as ends in themselves, which is to say above all else as beings capable of freely and rationally setting their own ends, for "The capacity to set oneself an end – any end whatsoever – is what characterizes humanity (as distinguished from animality)" (*MM*, 6: 392). This in turn entails that it must be the purpose of each of us in acting in accordance with the moral law to establish the kingdom of ends, namely a "whole of all ends (both of rational beings as ends in themselves as well as of the individual ends that each may set for himself) in systematic connection" (*G*, 4:433). That is to say, it must be our end in acting in accordance with the moral law to treat all persons – therefore including ourselves – as agents capable of freely setting and pursuing their own ends within the general constraint of allowing each agent the same freedom to set and pursue ends. But Kant also defines happiness as nothing other than the collective satisfaction of an individual's jointly satisfiable

---

[3] Within five years of the publication of the *Critique of Practical Reason*, Kant was already responding to Christian Garve's misplaced criticisms of the doctrine of the highest good in the first section of the 1793 essay *On the Common Saying: That Might Be Right in Theory but Not in Practice* (see 8:278–89).

ends or purposes (see *G*, 4:417–18), and so the realm of ends that we are each mandated to make our end is nothing other than the condition within which all rational finite agents can and do pursue their own happiness within the constraint that each not only recognizes the rational agency of all others as a limit on his own pursuits but also makes the happiness of all his own end; it is thus the framework within which the maximally lawful happiness of all can and must be sought. This lawfully regulated pursuit of the ends and therefore the happiness of all is not in fact a natural goal of human beings merely constrained by virtue – for the natural goal of human beings is just their own individual happiness or that of some others connected to them by contingent bonds of affinity – but is an objective goal that virtue mandates. Therefore, the highest good, conceived as the condition that would obtain if the kingdom of ends were established, is not a composite of two separate ends, one constraining the other, but is rather the object defined by virtue itself as respect for all free rational agents and for the reasonable pursuit of particular ends in which the exercise of their free rational agency consists.

This conception of the object commanded by the moral law itself will be controversial, because the moral law is ordinarily interpreted as establishing the framework of constraints within which individual happiness can be pursued by the negative limiting condition of respect for rational beings as ends rather than means (*G*, 4:437), not as itself mandating the satisfaction of ends and therefore happiness.[4] I would defend my interpretation in two ways. First, note that in his characterization of the kingdom of ends Kant says that we are to establish a whole of rational beings *as* ends and *of* their individual ends; this commands respect both for the existence of rational beings as ends in themselves and for their pursuit of particular ends (*G*, 4:433). Second, the four examples of duty in the *Groundwork* (see especially *G*, 4:429–30) and their amplification and refinement in the "Doctrine of Virtue" show that the general requirement of respect for humanity gives rise to a com-

---

[4] This is implied by the conception of duty as a limiting condition favored even by such sophisticated interpreters as Barbara Herman and Marcia Baron; see Chapter 9, notes 4 and 5.

plex set of duties including the moral duty to work toward the fulfillment of particular ends, and therefore happiness, within the general framework of this respect. From the first example, the prohibition of suicide, we see that we have a duty to preserve human life in ourselves and others as the underlying condition of the *existence* of humanity. Second, from the prohibition of deceitful promises, we see that we have a duty to preserve the *free* exercise of humanity in both others and ourselves in the form of the actual setting of and consenting to ends. Third, from the duty to develop our talents, we see that we have a duty to promote the conditions for the *successful* exercise of agency in both ourselves and others by developing capacities for the successful pursuit of all sorts of possible ends. Finally, from the duty of beneficence, we see that we have a duty to promote the actual *fulfillment* of the particular ends of ourselves and others by creating a condition in which, if the permissible ends of one person cannot be fulfilled by that person's own capacities and efforts, they will be fulfilled by the efforts of others.[5] The latter two duties, but especially the last, are the basis for my claim that the moral law itself requires not just that we recognize lawful constraints on the individual pursuit of happiness but also that we actually pursue the happiness of all within these constraints.

This implication is particularly clear in the "Doctrine of Virtue," where after his initial and unsatisfactory suggestion that we have a duty only to the happiness of others (e.g., *MM*, DV Introduction, §IV, 6:386), Kant argues that the duty of benevolence, the requirement to take "satisfaction in the happiness (well-being) of others," gives rise to the duty of beneficence, "the maxim of making others' happiness one's end" (*MM*, DV, §30, 6:453), but then also argues that this gives rise to a truly universal duty to produce happiness, "since all *others* with the exception of myself would not be *all*" and therefore "lawgiving reason, which includes the whole species (and so myself as well) in its idea of humanity as such, includes me as giving universal law along with all others in the duty of

---

[5] There are a variety of reasons why in practice some of these duties yield particular duties to self and others particular duties to others, but for our purposes here we do not need to go into these issues.

mutual benevolence, in accordance with the principle of equality" (*MM*, DV, §27, 6:451). On this account, the practice of universal beneficence is the final duty commanded by the moral law, and the moral law includes a direct command to establish permissible happiness as part of virtue itself.

The highest good is therefore the object to which our efforts are directed by morality itself, not by the mere conjunction of morality and natural inclination. This was already apparent in the "Canon of Pure Reason" in the first *Critique*. Kant here defined a "moral world" as "the world as it would be if it were in conformity with all moral laws" (A 808/B 836), and then introduced the idea of the highest good in the form of the claim that it is necessary to assume that "everyone has cause to hope for happiness in the same measure as he has made himself worthy of it, and that the system of morality is therefore inseparably combined with the system of happiness, although only in the idea of reason" (A 809/B 837). This claim is not grounded on a conception of human or divine justice as requiring an apportionment of a degree of happiness to a corresponding degree of virtue, as is often thought, but is introduced as the inevitable consequence of compliance with the demands of morality under ideal circumstances. In Kant's words:

> Now in an intelligible world, i.e., in the moral world, in the concept of which we have abstracted from all hindrances to morality (inclinations), such a system of happiness proportionately combined with morality can also be thought as necessary, since freedom, partly moved and partly restricted by moral laws, would itself be the cause of the general happiness, and rational beings, under the guidance of such principles, would themselves be the authors of their own enduring welfare and at the same time that of others. (A 809/B 837)

Kant even called this a "system of self-rewarding morality," thereby implying that morality is not an extrinsic constraint on happiness, nor happiness an extrinsic reward for morality, but rather that morality is a law for the exercise of the free will of rational agents, which itself commands the lawful pursuit of individual ends and which would therefore, at least under ideal circumstances, have as its outcome a lawfully maximal distribution of happiness as the satisfaction of those ends.

Before we can proceed further, we must consider a traditional objection to this conception of the highest good. Kant obviously did not want morality to be confused with any form of hedonism, but also thought that he could avoid such a risk even while maintaining his conception of the highest good by distinguishing between the *motive* and the *object* of morality, that is, between our reason for acting morally and the state of affairs we are trying to bring about in and through acting morally. His claim is that we can act out of the virtuous and praiseworthy motive of respect for the moral law itself rather than out of the, at best, morally indifferent and, at worst, reprehensible motives of self-love or sympathetic inclination to particular others,[6] whereas the moral law itself, out of respect for which the virtuous agent acts, is such that complete compliance with it would ipso facto establish a systematic union of ends, and a law that under the ideal circumstances in which all systematically consistent purposes were actually attained, would produce the maximum of lawful happiness as well as virtue.

This position is already at work in the *Critique of Practical Reason*, where Kant's whole argument for the postulates is based on the premise that "the maxims of virtue must be the efficient cause of happiness" (5:113), and the existence of God as the Author of nature is postulated only to complete the conditions for this efficient causation, which experience shows are not supplied by the power of human virtue alone. But Kant's clearest statement of his position may be in the 1793 essay *On the Common Saying: That Might Be Right in Theory but Not in Practice*, the first section of which is his reply to Christian Garve on precisely this point. In Kant's words,

---

[6] Whether these motives are indifferent or blameworthy would, of course, depend on whether the actions they would lead agents to do in particular circumstances (if given the opportunity to do so by the principle of self-love; see Chapter 9, section I) are in outward conformity with the requirements of duty or not: being led to do actions in outward accordance with duty out of what Kant calls "pathological love" will be morally indifferent, but violating an outward requirement of duty because of self-love or sympathy for others will be blameworthy.

Garve had interpreted his position that the moral law dictates a maximum of both virtue and systematic happiness, the possibility of which in turn requires the presupposition of God, freedom, and immortality, to mean that "The virtuous person cannot and may not ever lose sight of this point of view (of his own happiness) – because otherwise he entirely loses access to the invisible world, to conviction of the existence of God and immortality" (*TP*, 8: 280).[7]

In Kant's view, however, this is a double misinterpretation of his own position: it confuses aiming at one's *own* happiness alone with aiming at the happiness of *all* including oneself; and it confuses making happiness in the latter sense the *object* or goal of one's action with having the natural inclination to happiness (whether of oneself or others) as the *motive* for one's action. Thus Kant argues that the virtuous person "must indeed strive to become conscious, as far as is possible, that no *motive* [*Triebfeder*] derived from [happiness] steals unnoticed into the determination of his duty," which is part of the reason, Kant adds, why duty is best represented as connected with sacrifices; but to say this, Kant continues, is not incompatible with holding that "the concept of duty, [although] it need not be grounded in any particular purpose, nevertheless *introduces* another end for the human will, namely to work with all of one's capacities towards the *highest* good possible in the world (the universal happiness which is connected in the world-whole with the purest morality and is appropriate to it)" (*TP*, 8:279). Kant expands on this by arguing that while all willing must have an end and thus an object as well as a motive, for the possibility of virtue this end as well as the motive must be unselfish; but the apparent paradox that any rational action must be directed at an end and therefore potentially at happiness yet must also be unselfish can readily be dissolved by distinguishing between the selfish end "of one's own happiness" and the unselfish

---

[7] Kant refers to Garve's essay "Über die Geduld," in Christian Garve, *Versuche über die verschiedene Gegenstände aus der Moral, der Litteratur und den gesellschaftlichen Leben*, Erster Theil (Breslau, 1792), pp. 3–116, at pp. 111–14. (Citation from Immanuel Kant, *Über den Gemeinspruch: Das mag in der Theorie richtig sein, taugt aber nicht für die Praxis/Zum ewigen Frieden*, ed. Heiner F. Klemme [Hamburg: Felix Meiner, 1992], p. 106.)

end of the "whole of all ends under a principle of a comprehensive final end" – an end that, Kant explicitly states, goes beyond the mere "observation of formal laws to bring about the production of an object (the highest good) of the *ampliative* unselfish will" (*TP*, 8:279–80n).[8] Kant thus argues that while the virtuous motive must be respect for the moral law, this law, as a universal law for rational wills that necessarily have ends, itself defines an object, the systematic union of ends. Adherence to the moral law as motive satisfies the virtue component of the concept of the highest good, whereas the realization of the end defined by this law constitutes the happiness component of the highest good. Of course, as Kant points out in this same passage, the attainment of this good "is in our power in one of its sides but not in both taken together" (*TP*, 8:279) – that is, it is entirely in our own power to determine our motivation but not equally in our own power to create ideal circumstances for the realization of the systematic union of ends. That is why the concept of the highest good leads to the practical postulates, which do bear on those conditions; but as should now be clear, contrary to what Garve supposed, these postulates bear on the conditions of the possibility of the end of universal and unselfish happiness defined by the moral law itself and not on any merely selfish inclination toward happiness.

3. With this understanding of the concept of the highest good in hand, we can now turn to Kant's argument from the highest good to the postulates of God, freedom, and immortality. The argument for the postulates rests on two fundamental assumptions: first, a canon of rational willing according to which it is only rational to adopt a maxim that defines a certain end or goal and to act in accord with such a maxim if we have reason to believe that the

---

[8] The distinction between the selfish end of one's own happiness and the unselfish end of happiness in general is not clearly stated in the *Critique of Practical Reason*, but is necessary to complete the argument that Kant begins with the statement that "Now it is clear from the Analytic that the maxims of virtue and those of one's own happiness are entirely heterogeneous in regard to their supreme practical principle" (5:112); this heterogeneity can be removed only by connecting general rather than individual happiness with the principle of virtue.

realization of that end is possible; second, an assumption about possibility itself, namely that the real possibility of any object requires not just that the concept of it be free of internal contradiction but also that the possible object have some sort of ground in something that actually exists – an assertion of possibility must be more than an internally coherent fantasy. The first of these premises is explicitly stated in the course of Kant's exposition of the postulates; the latter is not explicitly stated but is clearly used in the course of the argument. It also has a long and complex history in Kant's theoretical philosophy.[9]

The canon of rationality that all rational willing presupposes the possibility of its object is clearly stated in the conclusion of the argument for the postulates: "the subjective effect of the [moral] law, namely the *disposition* to advance the practically possible highest good which is appropriate to it and also necessary through it, presupposes at the least that the latter is *possible,* because otherwise it would be practically impossible to strive after the object of a concept that is fundamentally empty and without a concept" (*CPracR,* 5:143). Here Kant argues that it cannot be rational to adopt the moral law even as our motive or give it "subjective effect" on our disposition unless we believe that our action on this motive can at least under ideal circumstances have its intended "objective" or external effect and produce its object.

Kant gives another clear statement of his canon of rationality in a long reflection from the 1790s that was also included as a footnote in Jäsche's edition of Kant's lectures on logic. Here Kant expresses the contrast between the motive and the end of an action as a contrast between considering actions in themselves and extending our consideration of them to take in their ends, and says that belief in the postulates

> Is the necessity of accepting the objective reality of a concept (of the highest good), i.e., the possibility of its object, as *a priori* necessity of the object of choice. If we look merely to actions, we do not need this belief. But if we wish to extend ourselves through

---

[9] We have already seen one application of Kant's distinction between logical and real possibility in Chapter 5.

actions to possession of the end that is thereby possible, then we must accept that this end is completely possible. (*JäL*, 9:69n)[10]

What he means here is presumably that in order to see an action as our duty, we need only to look at it and its relation to the maxims of duty. But when we consider more fully the conditions of rationally willing an action, then we recognize that the action must have an end and that it must be at least possible for us to realize this end if it is to be rational for us to will to take any actions to achieve it.[11]

The second premise of Kant's argument for the postulates is not as explicitly stated as the first in the *Critique of Practical Reason*, although Kant does state it plainly elsewhere. Thus, the *Jäsche Logic* also says: "The disposition in accordance with moral laws leads to an object of choice that is determinable through pure reason.

---

[10] Translation from Immanuel Kant, *Lectures on Logic*, trans. and ed. J. Michael Young (Cambridge: Cambridge University Press, 1992), p. 573. The original of the passage is to be found at *R* 2793 (16:515).

[11] Kant's canon of rationality is also expressed in a different context, namely the *Critique of Judgment*'s classification of a representation of the faculty of desire as a mere "wish" in the case in which "one works toward the production of one's object through one's representation alone, yet can expect no success, because he is conscious that his mechanical forces . . . through which that representation must be determined in order to effect the object . . . are either inadequate or even aim at something impossible, e.g., undoing what is done" (*CJ*, 5:177–78n). If aiming at something which we know to be impossible is the definition of a mere *wish*, then by contrast we can take it as a definition of *willing* that we aim our efforts at something that we know to be at least possible, and then what I have called the canon of rational willing could even be considered an analytic proposition. Kant does not offer any argument from a more fundamental premise for this canon of rationality; perhaps characterizing it as analytic would explain why no further argument can be offered for it, just as in the case of that other canon of rationality which Kant does explicitly classify as analytic, namely the proposition that "he who wills the end also (so far as reason has the decisive influence on his actions) wills the indispensably necessary means thereto" (*G*, 4:417). Both of these canons of rationality would then be fundamental premises on the basis of which argumentation in moral philosophy is conducted. See Onora O'Neill's account of requirements of rationality in "Consistency in Action," in her *Constructions of Reason: Explorations of Kant's Practical Philosophy* (Cambridge: Cambridge University Press, 1989), pp. 81–104, especially pp. 89–94.

The acceptance of the feasibility [*Thunlichkeit*] of this object, and hence of the reality of its cause, is a moral belief" (*JäL*, 9:69n).[12] But even without such an explicit statement, Kant's commitment to this premise becomes fully apparent in the course of the exposition of the argument itself.

Having defined the highest good as the complete object of morality, Kant starts the argument for the postulates by setting up an antinomy. He rejects the view that the connection between virtue and happiness is analytic, as was held by the Stoics who simply identified being happy with being virtuous or by the Epicureans who simply identified being virtuous with being happy (*CPracR*, 5:111–12).[13] Instead, he claims, the connection must be synthetic, which he takes to mean that it must be causal. But here an antinomy arises because both of the obvious candidates for a causal relation between virtue and happiness seem impossible: that action motivated by the search for happiness (whether one's own or others') should lead to virtue is excluded by the nature of morally praiseworthy motivation itself; but that action motivated by respect for duty alone should necessarily lead to happiness (whether one's own or others') seems to be belied by everything that we know about "all practical connection of causes and effects in the

---

[12] Translation modified from Young, *Lectures on Logic*, p. 572. The original for this passage is in *R* 2794 (16:515).

[13] See also Kant's lectures on ethics, e.g., *Moral Mrongovius*, 27:1400–4, or in the English translation, Immanuel Kant, *Lectures on Ethics*, trans. Louis Infield (London: Methuen, 1930), pp. 6–11. One point should be noted here. Both the Stoics and Epicureans were presumably seeking for an "analytic" connection between one's own virtue and one's own happiness, not universal happiness. Kant's introduction of the discussion of the Stoics and Epicureans also starts off by stating that "virtue and happiness together constitute the highest good for one person" (*CPracR*, 5:110). But the happiness of oneself alone cannot be a moral goal, and therefore the conjunction of one's own virtue and happiness cannot be a completely moral goal. The happiness of all within the framework of universal respect for humanity as such is a moral goal, and one's own happiness as part of this is part of a moral goal. The argument for the postulates as conditions of *pure* practical reason, or a *moral* argument for the postulates, therefore cannot turn on a link between individual virtue and happiness, as this initial discussion might suggest, but only on a link between the universal realization of virtue and the universal realization of lawful happiness.

world," where outcomes depend not just on "moral dispositions of the will, but on the knowledge of natural laws and on physical capacities" (*CPracR*, 5:113), both of which are often imperfect. Virtue does not always have its intended effect, we might say, for reasons both inside and outside the skin of the virtuous agent: sometimes our best intentions fail to produce appropriate actions, and sometimes even our appropriate actions fail to produce their intended effects.

However, Kant's next move is to argue that the falsehood of this second alternative, that virtue can be the cause of happiness, is only apparent, arising from an empirical restriction of our conception of causality to our own causality in the sensible world of appearance. When we introduce the distinction between the appearance of the world and how it really is or may be, we realize that we can adopt a view on which this conclusion is not necessarily false. Here Kant introduces the specific postulate of the existence of God, arguing that while our own efforts at virtue may seem an obviously inadequate or at best contingent cause of happiness as long as we only consider "a nature that is merely object of the senses," we can think otherwise if we posit that "the morality of disposition has if not an immediate yet a mediate and indeed necessary connection as cause with happiness as effect in the sensible world (by means of an intelligent Author of nature)" (*CPracR*, 5:115). In other words, if we consider only our own empirically discernible powers as grounds for the causal connection between our virtuous motives and the achievement of happiness, they obviously fall short, but if we consider that there may be intelligently directed forces in nature greater than our own then we realize that our efforts at virtue may have the effect of happiness *within* sensible nature because of the character of the *supersensible* ground *of* nature.

Kant's subsequent more detailed account of the postulation of the existence of God makes the general form of his argument for the postulates even clearer. He begins by restating the assumption made at the outset that "in the moral law there is not the least ground for a necessary connection between virtue and the happiness proportionate to it in the case of a being that belongs to the world as a part of it and that is dependent upon it, which is thereby not the cause of this nature by its will" (*CPracR*, 5:124). In other words, the powers of human beings considered merely naturally are not great enough to ensure that the complete happiness that would flow from their morally perfect intentions under ideal circumstances does flow from them. But since "we *should* seek to advance the highest good (which must therefore also be possible)," we must *"postulate* a ground of this connection" in the form of "the existence of a cause of the whole of nature which is distinct from this nature," and whose powers are therefore not limited in the way that ours as creatures within and dependent upon nature are (*CPracR*, 5:125). Now we come to the clearest use of what I earlier called Kant's second premise for the argument for the postulates: having explicitly stated that our obligation to pursue the highest good presupposes its possibility, Kant also argues that this possibility of the highest good requires a ground in the existence of an object with power sufficient to produce this possibility itself. As Kant puts it, "the highest good in the world is only possible insofar as a supreme cause of nature is assumed, which has a causality appropriate to a moral disposition," which can only be God; "Consequently the postulate of the possibility of the *highest derived good* (the best world) is at the same time the postulate of the actuality of a *highest original good,* namely the existence of God. . . . the possibility of this highest good . . . occurs only under the condition of the existence of God" (ibid.).

4. The arguments for the other two postulates also have the form of inferences from the possibility of a power or condition to the actual existence of its ground as well: the possibility of any virtuous disposition of the will entails the existence of transcendental freedom, although the existence of freedom entails only the possibility of virtue, because we can also use our virtue for evil; and the possibility of the perfection of our virtuous disposition requires our actual immortality, although again even our actual immortality would entail only the possibility of moral perfection, because we could also use our extra time to perfect an evil disposition. And although Kant initially uses his distinction between the sensible and the supersensible to introduce only the postulate of the existence of God, he subsequently argues that all three postulates of

God, freedom, and immortality depend on this distinction. Later in the second *Critique*, for example, Kant describes the three postulates as those of *"immortality, freedom* positively considered (as the causality of a being, so far as it belongs to the intelligible world), and the *existence of God."* The postulate of immortality requires this distinction because the duration of human life-spans in the sensible world is too short a "duration for the completeness of the fulfillment of the moral law." The postulate of freedom requires this distinction because of the "necessary presupposition of independence from the sensible world and of the faculty of the determination of one's will in accordance with the law of an intelligible world." And the postulate of the existence of God requires the distinction because only through it can the connection between virtue and happiness, which would be contingent in a merely sensible world, acquire the necessity it would have if the sensible world were in fact authored in accordance with the design of an intelligible world (*CPracR*, 5:132). However, there is a fundamental difference between the grounds for the postulation of freedom on the one hand and of God and immortality on the other: freedom is a condition of the very possibility of virtuous action, for it is the necessary condition of ever making the moral law the fundamental maxim of any of our actions, whereas God and immortality are conditions specifically of the possibility of the ultimate *object* of virtue, the highest good – immortality is the condition for the *perfection* of virtue and God that for the realization of happiness. Kant recognizes this distinction at least tacitly in the *Critique of Practical Reason* by lumping all three postulates together but in fact providing detailed discussion only of the postulates of God and immortality. In the *Critique of Judgment*, he explicitly acknowledges this problem, and in the draft of the essay on the "Real Progress" of metaphysics he suggests a solution to it. Yet there is also a problem with the postulate of immortality, which Kant does not recognize at all but which may ultimately leave the existence of God as the intelligible Author of nature as the only real postulate of pure practical reason. I briefly discuss these issues before continuing.

Kant's argument for the postulate of immortality is based on the premises that *"complete fitness* of the dispositions to the moral law" is "the supreme condition of the highest good" but is also *"holiness,* a perfection of which no rational being in the sensible world is capable at any point in time of his existence" (*CPracR*, 5:122). His argument then is that since the perfection of virtue that is required by the moral law as such and is in turn the first component of the highest good cannot be achieved in the finite empirical life-span of a human being, we must at least postulate that humans have a nonempirical and therefore at least possibly infinite life-span in which to perfect their virtue. This argument is clearly problematic. The problem is not with the claim that moral perfection cannot be reached within a normal human life-span; while empirical, this claim is not seriously debatable. Rather, the problem is with the conception of moral perfection itself, that is, with the argument's assumption that moral perfection requires not merely acting in the right way with the right motives on every relevant opportunity in one's life, regardless of whatever other inclinations one might feel, but also achieving a state of holiness in which one not merely never wills maxims and actions except in accordance with the moral law but never even has any inclination to do otherwise. To achieve such a will might well take an infinite life-span, but ordinarily Kant denies that such holiness is an intelligible goal for us and indeed argues that the imperatival character of the moral law – its presentation to us as the categorical imperative – cannot even be understood if we fancy ourselves as potentially holy wills (*G*, 4:414). In the argument for immortality Kant's ordinarily realistic although already sufficiently demanding conception of virtue, the demand that we always act out of the motive of duty regardless of any contrary inclinations we may (and usually do) have has given way to an unrealistic demand for holiness of will solely to justify a dogma to which Kant is obviously predisposed. Without the assumption that virtue requires holiness, the argument for immortality collapses; if virtue requires only commitment to the moral law as one's fundamental maxim regardless of contrary inclinations, and this commitment itself would under ideal circumstances produce universal lawful happiness, then the highest good can be realized without immortality.[14]

---

[14] This argument is probably a bit too strong. One could argue that the presence of inclinations contrary to the moral law would itself be a source of unhappiness,

The second problem is with the postulate of freedom. Although Kant typically lists freedom as one of the three postulates derived from the highest good (e.g., *CPracR*, 5:132; *RP*, 20:298–99), he does not in fact give a separate argument for the postulate of freedom. This is obviously because freedom has already been introduced (e.g., *CPracR*, 5:29–33) as the presupposition of our obligation under the moral law in general long before the introduction of the concept of the highest good as the object of freedom: we do not need to postulate freedom to explain the possibility of the realization of the *object* or intended outcome of action in compliance with the moral law, but to explain the possibility of making the moral law our fundamental maxim and acting in accordance with it in the first place. The postulate of freedom thus does not have a specific connection to the highest good as the supreme end of morality. In fact, Kant makes precisely this point in the *Critique of Judgment*. Concluding his important exposition of the doctrine of the postulates there, Kant asserts two premises: first, that "the freedom of man under moral laws" is the necessary condition of the validity of the moral law that "prescribes" the highest good as our "final end"; and second – here he is obviously alluding to the "fact of reason" argument of the second *Critique* – that it is "the only concept of the supersensible that proves its objective reality (by means of the causality that is conceived in it) in nature through the effect possible in it." Because the assumption of freedom is the foundation of the objective validity of the moral law itself, it is our primary justification for "the idea of the supersensible in us"; and because the moral law defines the object of the highest good for

therefore that perfect (individual?) happiness cannot be achieved until the will is not only fully lawful but also holy, and thus that if the achievement of a holy will would require immortality so would the achievement of complete happiness. Perhaps such an argument could be inferred from Kant's famous comment (in reply to Schiller) about the "aesthetic character" or "temperament of virtue" in the *Religion* (6:23–24n); but Kant does not make any such argument in the *Critique of Practical Reason*, so the official argument for the postulate of immortality would seem to fall to the present objection. And in any case, if immortality were admitted, there might be further problems about happiness, for it is far from obvious in what sense immortals could have desires and therefore enjoy happiness. In fact, when we think about immortality, we cannot but fall into incoherent because incompletely conceived possibilities.

which the postulation of God and immortality are further necessary conditions, the cognition of the reality of freedom – "although only in a practical regard" – is in turn the foundation for any idea of the supersensible "outside us." Thus "the concept of freedom (as the fundamental concept of all unconditionally practical laws) can extend reason beyond those boundaries within which every (theoretical) concept of nature must otherwise remain hopelessly restricted" (*CJ*, 5:474). So the assumption of freedom precedes and grounds those of God and immortality: the fact of freedom is the necessary condition of the validity of the moral law itself, and our most fundamental basis for any claims about how any things – in the first place, we ourselves – really are, and it is only because of it that morality can also define an object for us from the possibility of which any further postulates can be drawn. The reality of freedom is thus not a ground of the possibility of the highest good in particular but of morality in general.

The problems with the postulates of immortality and freedom are thus quite different. The concept of the highest good is not sufficient to ground the postulate of immortality unless a particular and implausible conception of moral perfection is added; the concept of the highest good is not necessary to ground the postulate of freedom, which is already implicit in the validity of the moral law. Thus only the postulate of God as the author of the laws of a nature in which it is possible for virtue to result in happiness is a necessary and sufficient condition of the possibility of the highest good. Kant seems to recognize this point in at least one passage in his final restatement of the doctrine of the postulates in *Real Progress*. Here, although he first characterizes the doctrine in religious language as "the *credo* of the three articles of the confession of pure practical reason" and identifies these three articles in his usual fashion as God, freedom, and immortality (*RP*, 20:298), he subsequently switches from the language of traditional religion to the language of his teleology and states that the three propositions that are proved practically rather than theoretically are "There is a God, there is in the nature of the world an original although incomprehensible disposition for agreement with moral purposiveness, and there is finally in the human soul a disposition that makes it capable of a never ending progress to this moral purposiveness"

(*RP*, 20:300). This could be taken to say that what the possibility of the highest good as the complete end of morality requires is "confidence in the success of the intention [*Absicht*]" to morality (ibid.), which in turn requires the possibility of freely forming completely virtuous disposition within human souls on the one hand and of finding successful execution of human intentions in the external world on the other hand, both of which in turn are conceived to depend on the existence of God as the author of the legislation of both freedom and nature. This formulation of the doctrine would not specifically commit Kant to the postulation of immortality but just to the general condition for the perfection of virtue, whatever that happens to be. Nor need it be read as first introducing the reality of freedom; rather its reference to the disposition of the human soul could be taken to refer to the possibility of harmonizing the intelligible freedom of the human soul as it really is with the natural disposition of the human psyche as it appears. On such a reading, the overall structure of the argument for the postulates could be simplified into the form that I have already given: the possibility of the successful formation of moral intentions on the one hand and of their fulfillment with its ensuing happiness on the other would both be possibilities supposed to be grounded in the actual although theoretically indemonstrable existence of God as the author of the legislation of nature.

The argument of the postulates thus reduces to the claim that the possibility of the realization of the highest good, which is a condition of the rationality of conduct in accordance with the moral law although not its motivation, in turn requires the postulation of the actual existence of God as its ground, although of course this is valid only from a practical and not a theoretical point of view. But now we can return to our underlying questions: why does Kant suppose such an inference from possibility to actuality is necessary, and how is such an inference even possible?

5. The basis of this inference lies in one of the oldest parts of Kant's philosophy, the distinction between real and merely logical possibility, a distinction that Kant had worked out by the early 1760s and used as the foundation for an argument for the existence of God as early as 1763. Kant's fundamental idea is that the internal

coherence or noncontradictoriness of the predicates comprising a concept, or logical possibility, is only a necessary condition of the real possibility of an object, a sufficient condition which always requires a ground in some other object that actually exists.

In the *Critique of Pure Reason* Kant first introduces this claim as a restraint on *empirical* knowledge, in the section entitled "The Postulates of Empirical Thinking in General"; this title, however, already suggests that there may well be a parallel between Kant's assumptions here and in the doctrine of the postulates of pure practical reason, and thus that we should conceive of the postulates of pure practical reason as well as of empirical thought as depending on the distinction between merely logical and real possibility. The general premise of "The Postulates of Empirical Thinking" is that the modal concepts of possibility, actuality, and necessity must be associated with forms of experience in order to have any empirical use.[15] In the case of possibility, Kant holds that to establish the objective reality of a concept, which is equivalent to the possibility of the existence of an object for that concept, the requirement "That in such a concept no contradiction must be contained is, to be sure, a necessary logical condition; but it is far from sufficient for the objective reality of the concept, i.e., of the possibility of such an object as is thought through the concept" (A 220/B 267–68). What must be added, depending on whether the concept at issue is an *a priori* concept or an empirical one, is connection with the form or content of experience: in the case of a concept of a geometrical figure, for instance, what must be shown is that the concept is not only logically non-contradictory but also constructible in pure intuition (A 221/B 268); in the case of empirical concepts – for instance, "new concepts of substances, of forces, and of interactions" – if these are to be more than mere "figments of the brain, for the possibility of which there would be no indications at all," then there must be not only logical noncontradictoriness but also a plausible causal connection to something actually experienced in perception (A 222–23/B 269–79). (Of course,

---

[15] See my article "The Postulates of Empirical Thinking and the Refutation of Idealism," in Georg Mohr and Marcus Willaschek, eds., *Immanuel Kant: Kritik der reinen Vernunft* (Berlin: Akademie Verlag, 1998), pp. 297–324.

the concept of a possible empirical object cannot be *directly* exemplified in perception, because then the object would be actual and not merely possible.)

In the "Doctrine of Method" of the first *Critique*, Kant introduces a conception of theoretical hypotheses that is a straightforward application of this conception – indeed, much of the same language and many of the same examples recur in Kant's exposition. Here Kant claims that we cannot simply open up a limitless field for hypotheses, because the "*possibility* of the object itself" "must be fully certain and not invented"; again, hypotheses are not to be "empty figments of the brain rather than concepts of things." For this to be avoided, hypotheses must not be merely logically noncontradictory but "must be connected as a ground of explanation with that which is actually given and consequently certain" (A 770/B 798). Again Kant says that, for instance, "we are not allowed to think up any sort of new original forces . . . or a new kind of substance"; these two examples suggest that hypotheses must employ causal laws of a kind for which we already have some evidence ("forces") or which can at least be subsumed under more general causal laws that are already established, and must by means of those laws connect hypothesized objects with actual objects of which we already have some experience ("substances"). Otherwise the concepts of hypotheses, "although free of contradiction, would nevertheless also be without any object" (A 771/ B 799). What we do when we introduce theoretical hypotheses, then, can be no more than introducing variations and refinements into a conceptual framework for which we already have confirmation in the forms of experience and actual empirical experience, and then looking for further pure or empirical confirmation of these refinements.

Now obviously this model cannot be directly applied to the postulates of pure practical reason, for they posit the existence of supersensible objects and conditions, for which confirmation by reference to the forms or contents of experience is excluded from the outset. Nevertheless, Kant does not restrict the requirement that concepts of possible objects must have some ground in actual existence to empirical objects but takes it as a general canon of rationality. Indeed, he insisted on this general rule long before he arrived at his specific treatment of the empirical possibility of theoretical concepts. In his 1763 book on the *Only Possible Basis for a Proof of the Existence of God*, after rejecting the ontological argument for the existence of God, Kant bases his own replacement for this proof on the premise that "possibility disappears not only when an internal contradiction, as the logical element of impossibility, is present, but also when there exists no material element, no *datum*, to be thought." Kant's basis for this claim is in fact the same as for his rejection of the ontological argument: "there is no internal contradiction in the negation of all existence," yet with the negation of all existence even determinate possibilities would vanish. Thus he concludes that "to say there is a possibility and yet nothing real at all is self-contradictory" (*OPP*, 2:78).[16] So he argues that for there to be any well-defined possibilities there must be something that actually exists to create some possibilities, and because this existence is necessary even for possibility, it is necessary in itself – that is, there is a necessary being, and that is God.

This argument is clearly problematic, especially in its inference from the necessity of some actuality to ground possibility to the intrinsically necessary existence of God, a move that depends on the trick premise that it is necessary that there be determinate possibilities because no possibilities would be the same as impossibility, that is, impossible (*OPP*, 2:79). But in spite of the flaws in the argument, Kant continued to see the idea that all possibility must have a ground in actuality, indeed in a single existence, as a natural assumption of human reason. Thus, prior to the demolition of the three traditional arguments of rational theology in the *Critique* – that is, the ontological, cosmological, and physico-theological arguments, the first of which succumbs precisely to the failure to distinguish between merely logical and real possibility – he first gives a much more sympathetic analysis of reason's tendency to construct an "Ideal of Pure Reason" as the single source of all the possibilities reflected in the complete determination of particular objects. This construction is based not only on the idea that in principle a complete determination of the predicates of any

---

[16] Translation from Immanuel Kant, *Theoretical Philosophy, 1755–1770*, ed. David Walford (Cambridge: Cambridge University Press, 1992), p. 123.

particular object requires reference to all possibilities for objects (A 571–72/B 599–600), but also on the further ideas that (i) negations can only be thought by reference to the opposed affirmations, thus that all possibilities must ultimately have positive grounds (A 575/B 603), and (ii) there must be a single entity that grounds all possibilities by itself containing all affirmative realities, "the entire storehouse of material from which all possible predicates of things can be taken . . . an All of reality (*omnitudo realitatis*)" (A 575–76/B 603–4). The hypostatization of this idea, Kant claims, is what leads to the idea of God (A 580/B 608).

The assumption that the real possibility of the highest good must have a ground in the actual existence of God thus seems to be grounded in Kant's underlying assumption that all real possibilities must have a ground in actual existence and indeed, ultimately in the actual existence of God. Since the possibility of the highest good is just the possibility of the conjunction of two particular positive predicates among others – virtue and happiness – it would seem to follow directly from this reasoning that it must have its ground in the existence of God just as any other object does.

But if this is so, then we must also consider that Kant is ultimately critical of any theoretical use of reason to infer from sensible conditions to supersensible causes. Theoretical hypotheses that remain within the limits of the sensible are permissible because they are just loans on future experience: to explain an experienced phenomenon, one posits an as yet unexperienced cause or type of causality but one that could be sensed in the forward march of experience, and ultimately the hypothesis is only confirmed when sensible evidence for its truth is forthcoming. But hypotheses about the supersensible can never be confirmed, even if it is natural for our reason to make them and even if we can conceive no satisfactory alternative to them, and therefore they can never be asserted to be more than logically possible. This is the gist of Kant's critique of rational theology in both the fourth Antinomy and in his treatment of the three traditional arguments for the existence of God, and although Kant may initially be kinder to the child of his own theological imagination in the first part of the "Ideal of Pure Reason" than he is to the arguments of earlier rational theologians, he ultimately criticizes his own use of the assumption that all possibility must have a ground in actuality for any metaphysical inference:

> This use of the transcendental idea would already be overstepping the boundaries of its vocation and its permissibility. . . . This latter is a mere fiction, through which we encompass and realize the manifold of our idea in an ideal, as a particular being; for this we have no warrant, not even for directly assuming the possibility of such a hypothesis. (A 580/B 608)

Thus Kant concludes that, although the tendency to think that there must be a real ground for any possibility is a natural tendency of human thought, any use of it beyond the limits of theoretical hypothesis, where there is at least the possibility of eventual empirical confirmation, is unwarranted and leads to "a natural illusion" (A 582/B 610).

Indeed, Kant concludes his critique of rational theology with the assertion "that all attempts of a merely speculative use of reason in regard to theology are entirely fruitless and by their internal constitution null and nugatory, . . . and consequently, if one did not ground it on moral laws or use them as guides, there could be no theology of reason at all" (A 636/B 664). It is plain that by a theology grounded on moral laws he is referring to the theory of practical postulates, which was indeed first explicitly referred to two pages before (A 634/B 662). But now Kant seems to be trapped in a vicious circle: for practical purposes, we must be able to conceive of the possibility of the highest good, because that is an end that must be possible if it is to be rational for us to act in accord with the moral law that defines that end for us, and it seems to be only a need of theoretical reason that leads us to add a ground in actual existence to that possibility; but now we have been told that theoretical reason is not in fact licensed to make this inference from the possible to the actual, and thrown back onto the resources of practical reasoning, which did not seem to need this inference for its own purposes in the first place. Hasn't the doctrine of the practical postulates – although not the moral necessity of aiming at the highest good – thereby been undermined?

From one point of view, this is entirely correct, and Kant himself says as much. In spite of everything that has led up to it, he actually concludes his discussion of the postulates in the second *Critique* by himself insisting that "the expansion of theoretical reason," which we seem to gain through the postulates, is "no expansion of speculation" at all, and that we cannot make any theoretical use of it, for instance to determine the predicates of God (5:134).[17] From a theoretical point of view, in fact, all that can be established is that the concepts of the conjunction of virtue and happiness as well as of its alleged grounds are noncontradictory and therefore that the highest good and its grounds are logically possible; as Kant puts it, "The three ideas of speculative reason are not in themselves cognitions; they are (transcendent) *thoughts,* in which there is nothing impossible" (5:135). Thus, we seem to come back to the point Kant himself reached in his treatment of perpetual peace, the thought that, given the moral necessity of pursuing the highest good, all that we need for pursuing it to be rational is that we know it is not impossible to achieve it, a condition that in the end seems to be satisfied as long as its concept is not self-contradictory. In this case, why are the postulates of the actual existence of the conditions of morally requisite goals anything more than natural illusions?

II THE PARADOX OF MORAL BELIEF AND THE DUALITY OF HUMAN NATURE

1. The present question can be put even more pointedly by reference to the distinction between "opinion" and "belief" that Kant makes in the "Canon of Pure Reason" in the first *Critique,* in the *Critique of Judgment,* in the *Real Progress* draft, and in the *Jäsche Logic.* Kant argues that the appropriate propositional attitude to theoretical hypotheses or, in his language, the appropriate way of "taking them to be true" (*Fürwahrhalten*) is *opinion,* whereas the

[17] Here Kant introduces an argument, already made in the *Critique of Pure Reason* (A 814–15/B 842–43) and subsequently amplified in the *Critique of Judgment* (§86, 5:444), that the only determinate predicates that can be attributed to the idea of God are those required by its role as the ground of the possibility of the highest good – omniscience, omnipotence, and benevolence, necessary for God to know what virtue has been achieved, to want to add happiness to it, and to be able to do so.

appropriate attitude toward the practical postulates is *belief*. In the case of an opinion we are conscious that our evidence for it "is subjectively *as well as* objectively insufficient," whereas in the case of a belief we recognize that our evidence of its truth "is only subjectively sufficient and is at the same time held to be objectively insufficient" (A 822/B 850; *JäL*, 9:66). We have opinions about theoretical hypotheses because we do not have adequate empirical evidence to exclude alternatives and confirm them, and we recognize that we do not, and therefore recognize that the evidence for our hypotheses is both subjectively and objectively inadequate. But in this case we may gradually add more evidence to what we have, and thus our evidence may become both psychologically and logically compelling, that is, subjectively and objectively sufficient. Thus opinion is at one end of a scale on which knowledge is the other end, and opinion about the empirical and sensible can be transformed into knowledge by the addition of further evidence. For example, "the ether of modern physicists . . . is a mere matter of opinion, but still of the sort that, were our external senses sharpened to the highest degree, it could be perceived" (*CJ*, §91, 5: 467). It makes sense to assign a degree to opinion, and to treat the difference between empirical knowledge and opinion as one of degree, because empirical evidence can be augmented. For the same reason, one can also speak of the probability of an opinion, because probability is "a mathematical determination of the modality of holding something to be true, where its moments must be assumed to be homogeneous, and where an approximation to certainty is therefore possible" (*RP*, 20:299).

In a postulate of pure reason, however, the object is by definition supersensible, so there is no empirical evidence for it in the first place and therefore no possibility of adding homogeneous moments to that evidence to transform a belief into a certainty. For this reason, no matter how subjectively compelling the belief in the reality of the postulate may be, there is nothing that can be conceived that would remedy the objective insufficiency of the evidence for it. For this reason, Kant maintains, "Objects of mere ideas of reason, which cannot be exhibited in any possible experience for theoretical cognition, are thus altogether *unknowable* things, and hence one can never have an *opinion* about them" (*CJ*, §91, 5:

467). Thus the postulates must remain *beliefs* – which seems to mean they are propositions recognized to be subjectively sufficient but also objectively insufficient, that is, to have a psychologically compelling effect on us but no possible confirmation of their truth.

2. But then the question becomes *how* can propositions that are *recognized* to be incapable of objective confirmation still have a subjectively compelling effect on us? Kant might seem to proceed as if he could sidestep this question by emphasizing that the ultimate point of the postulates is to increase our effectiveness in the performance of our duty rather than to augment our stock of theoretical knowledge – indeed, that we cannot have a duty to believe anything in particular but we do have a duty to act, and that the significance of the postulates is exhausted in their contribution to the fulfillment of that duty. He puts this point in a variety of ways. In the *Critique of Practical Reason* he claims that although it is absurd to command a theoretical belief (and thus we cannot actually have a duty to assert the postulates), it is not absurd to conceive of a free choice to affirm them as part of our morally requisite but free choice to do everything in our power to promote the highest good: "the principle that here determines our judgment is to be sure *subjectively* a need, but at the same time, as a means for the advancement of that which is *objectively* (practically) necessary, it is the ground of a *maxim* of holding-to-be-true from a moral point of view. . . . This is therefore not commanded, but itself arises from the moral disposition as freely willed compatibly with the morally (commanded) intention." (5:146). Once beyond the logical requirement of noncontradiction, in other words, all that we do with the postulates of practical reason is form practically effective moral intentions.

In the *Critique of Judgment*, Kant also stresses the strictly practical effect of the postulates: "Now through the moral law, which enjoins [the final end] upon us, we have reason to assume, from a practical point of view, namely to apply our powers to the realization of this end, the possibility or achievability of that end" (*CJ*, §88, 5:455). Here it seems explicitly asserted that to adopt something "from a practical point of view" is simply to make it effective in the concentration of one's powers in a way demanded by practical reason, and does not imply any cognitive attitude toward the proposition at all.

Finally, the *Real Progress* draft also seems to stress that to adopt something "from a practical point of view" is to make it effective in one's production of action rather than to take any cognitive attitude toward it. Here Kant combines the recognition that from a theoretical point of view all that can be established is the noncontradictoriness of the postulates with an exposition of the efficacy of belief that sounds thoroughly psychological. Kant begins with a point not made in the second *Critique*, that "belief in a moral-practical regard also has a moral worth in itself, because it is a free undertaking," and then goes on to combine the two points just mentioned: the "credo" consisting of the postulates

> is no proof of the truth of these propositions theoretically considered, thus no instruction in the reality of their objects, for that is impossible in regard to the supersensible; rather it is only a subjective and indeed practically valid and, from this point of view, sufficient instruction to act as if we knew that these objects were real, which kind of representation . . . is only necessary from a moral point of view in order to add through mere ideas of reason a final touch to the theory of the possibility of that to which we are already of itself obligated, namely striving after the advancement of the highest good in the world, while we ourselves make these objects, God, freedom in a practical quality, and immortality, only as a result of the advancement of moral laws and freely give them objective reality, because we are assured that no contradiction can be found in these ideas. (*RP*, 20:298–99)

We are freely to act *as if* these ideas had objective reality because that will make us more effective in striving after that which we are obligated to strive after, the highest good in this world. Thus Kant's position seems to be that while assurance that the noncontradictoriness of an end would be all that is needed from a theoretical point of view to make a course of action aimed at that end rational, human psychology is such that in fact it needs a greater incentive, a positive reason to believe its end is realizable, but that to accommodate that feature of human psychology we can ourselves introduce and then act under the ideas of positive grounds for the reality of the highest good as well as under theoretical proof of its noncontradictoriness.

But merely to say that the *point* of the postulates is to give us psychological assistance in the performance of morally requisite action rather than to augment our body of knowledge does not itself solve any of our outstanding issues. First, it does not resolve the paradox of belief. While we might ordinarily be able to explain the difference between the theoretical and the practical point of view by saying that practical propositions are not indicative or *descriptive* propositions at all but only *prescriptive* propositions – in Kantian terms, they do not say what *is* but what *ought* to be – we cannot use that account of the distinction here, because the postulates of practical reason are not prescriptive, but have the same form as any theoretical proposition, namely, that of asserting that a certain object or property with certain predicates exists. Belief in these propositions is supposed to assist us in carrying out a prescriptive rather than descriptive proposition, namely the categorical imperative, but that does not transform the postulates themselves from descriptive to prescriptive propositions. So we still have to ask how a theoretical proposition for which we recognize ourselves to have necessarily insufficient evidence *can* be psychologically effective. Second, there are questions about just how the psychological effectiveness of the postulates is supposed to come about. Kant has insisted that the doctrine of the highest good concerns not the motivation but the object of morality, but how can this talk of making our use of our powers more effective be understood except in terms of increasing our motivation? And what is the practical status of these propositions or ideas about God and the like supposed to be, anyway: are we supposed to be able to induce these beliefs or ideas in ourselves, and if so can we know that we do that and yet still have these self-induced cognitive contents be psychologically effective on our course of conduct?

3. The answer to these questions lies in precisely what leads Kant to the doctrine of the postulates in the first place. This is nothing less than his profoundly dualistic conception of human nature – by which I mean to refer not to a dualism of mind and body as

separate substances, a metaphysical position on which Kant is of-
ficialy agnostic (A 379–80), but the dualism of reason and sensibility as distinct human capacities with their own laws and characteristics, which runs throughout Kant's theoretical and practical
philosophy. Kant conceives of us as creatures who must and can
act in accordance with the laws valid for all rational creatures, but
he never conceives of us as creatures who can act in accordance
with these laws by means of our reason alone, without also recognizing our sensibility and inducing this sensibility to act in
accordance with the demands of reason by means appropriate to
sensibility. This is evident throughout the *Critique of Judgment* and
the *Metaphysics of Morals*, where Kant's position is never that reason must ignore sensibility but rather that it must, out of respect
for the duty imposed by reason, nurture every means to the performance of our duty that sensibility affords, such as the natural
feelings of beauty and the sublime, sympathetic emotions, natural feelings of gratitude and friendship, and so on. Inclination and
reason do not necessarily follow the same laws, so inclination does
not always automatically point in the same direction as duty, but
it must be cultivated when it does as well as made to conform with
duty when it does not. The same potential for both independence
but also cooperation between reason and sensibility underlies the
doctrine of the postulates.[18]

Indeed, Kant explicitly recognizes that the need for the doctrine
of the postulates arises in the first place because of the difference
in the conditions of human sensibility and human reason: it is a
fact about the limits of human sensibility, not about reason itself,
that the world does not seem to us to be a place in which virtue is
accompanied with happiness:

> I had said above that in accordance with the natural course of
> the world happiness exactly proportionate to moral worth is not
> to be expected and is to be held impossible, and that therefore
> the possibility of the highest good from this side can be conceded

---

[18] In addition to Chapter 9, section I of this volume, see also my *Kant and the Ex-
perience of Freedom* (Cambridge: Cambridge University Press, 1993), ch. 10, and
Nancy Sherman, *Making a Necessity Out of Virtue: Aristotle and Kant on Virtue*
(Cambridge: Cambridge University Press, 1997), ch. 4, especially pp. 135–41.

only under the presupposition of a moral author of the world. I carefully held back the restriction of this judgment to the *subjective* conditions of our reason, in order to make use of it only when the way in which it is held to be true had been more closely determined. In fact, the impossibility in question is *merely subjective*, i.e., it is *impossible for* our reason to make comprehensible in accord with a merely natural course such an exactly proportionate and thoroughly purposive connection between two events in the world which take place in accordance with such different laws, even though its impossibility cannot be proved in accordance with general laws of nature. (*CPracR*, 5:145)

In other words, the entire doctrine of the postulates of pure practical reason is stated within the limits of human psychology. It is a subjective limit of human psychology that we cannot see the possibility of the highest good to be compatible with the laws of nature, and it is a subjective necessity for us to compensate for this limitation by introducing ideas of grounds for this good that are theoretically noncontradictory but otherwise have no recommendation except that they are effective in motivating creatures like us to act in the way and toward the end that reason demands.

Now how does the general distinction between the way in which human sensibility and psychology work and the way in which pure reason works solve the specific questions about the efficacy of the postulates that have been raised? First, the dualism of reason and sensibility solves the paradox of belief, the question about the possible efficacy or subjective sufficiency of a proposition recognized to have theoretically and objectively insufficient grounds, simply by insulating sensibility from reason to some extent. Because sensibility does not automatically accord with reason, the recognition that there are no theoretically adequate grounds for the assertion of the postulates does not automatically render the sensible representation of their objects either impossible or psychologically ineffective. Humans are imperfectly rational creatures, and even if the possibility of morality demands that humans must always be able to force their sensible incentives to action (*Triebfedern*) to accept the intentions of pure reason (*Bewegungsgründe*), that does not mean that the whole subjective state of even a virtuous human being is dictated by pure reason alone. Cognitive limits recognized by pure reason, whether in the person of the professional philosopher or in the person of each one of us, can remain without effect on our sensibility, and representations can have an effect on sensibility that is not mandated by pure reason although it is harmonious with the demands of the latter. Thus, aesthetic experiences and symbols can be useful in making our sensibility harmonize with the demands of practical reason even though we know that they are no more than analogies for practical propositions (see *CJ*, §59, 351–54); and there is no reason why the religious ideas and symbols cannot have the same subjective power to affect human emotions and impel human actions – from the theoretical point of view they are illusions, but from the psychological point of view they remain natural. It might seem to be a crucial difference between the theory of the beautiful as the symbol of the morally good, for instance, and the doctrine of the postulates that the latter clearly posits the psychological efficacy of representations with the form of theoretical propositions while the former does not, but there is no reason why this should be a crucial distinction – there is no obvious reason why the *representation* of a proposition cannot itself be subjectively efficacious even when the *truth* of the proposition cannot be confirmed by the criteria of a purely rational agent.

This statement still leaves open questions about how precisely the psychological effect of the postulates is supposed to take place. The first question here was how can the postulates be construed as merely subjectively efficacious representations without collapsing the distinction Kant was so careful to draw between the pure motives and the object of morality? The answer to this question is that we must recognize the complexity of human psychology as understood by Kant, and not collapse all subjective states into inclinations that are candidates for motives competing with the pure motive of duty. Even subjectively, there will be representations of circumstances as well as desires – in fact, the latter cannot exist without the former – and the postulates can be construed as subjective representations of possible outcomes and their grounds that can prevent the subjective effect of the motive of duty on our psychological state from being undermined by beliefs in an inhospitable world in which the intended outcome of duty is impossible. In spite of the examples of *Groundwork* I (4:397–98), Kant does not seem to believe that the motive of duty typically works in spite of and in the absence of all subjective conditions, but that it works *on* our actually occurrent subjective incentives, strengthening some and weakening others.[19] The postulates could then be subjectively effective by preventing a subjective disposition of the will (*Willkür*) that is in accord with the motive of morality from being weakened by a subjective representation of an inhospitable rather than hospitable arena for moral conduct.

This still leaves the question of how a belief or an idea that we produce for ourselves (see *RP*, 20:299) can be psychologically effective. How can we consciously induce a belief in an allegedly external object and then have it be effective on our action? How can we recognize that we ourselves have produced the idea of this object and still be moved by it? To answer this question we can appeal to the model of the moral effect of aesthetic experience that underlies Kant's theory of both the beautiful and the sublime and that becomes explicit in the "Doctrine of Virtue." Here Kant argues that "a disposition to love something (e.g., beautiful crystal formations, the indescribable beauty of plants) even apart from any intention to use it" is "a natural predisposition that is very serviceable to morality in one's relations with other men," and that because this natural predisposition *regarding* nonhuman nature is "serviceable to morality" – by assisting in the subjective efficacy of moral motivation – we have a duty *to* ourselves not to "weaken or uproot" that feeling but on the contrary to preserve and promote it by cultivating our sensibility (*MM*, DV, §17, 6:443).[20] Kant does not argue that someone lacking this propensity could inculcate it *ab novo*, but rather that it is a naturally occurring disposition that we do not have to induce but which we do have to protect and cultivate. The same reasoning could then apply to the postulates: these could be construed as naturally occurring subjective representations – again, "natural illusions," as Kant called them in his critique of rational theology – that we do not have to produce literally for ourselves but which we do have to preserve

---

[19] Again, see Chapter 9, section I.
[20] Gregor, *MM*, p. 237.

and cultivate because of their subjective efficacy in promoting moral action. Once again, the fact that the subjective representation of the postulates is in propositional form rather than mere feeling, although it does call for a theoretical critique not necessary in the case of, say, aesthetic experience, would not be an essential difference when it comes to the beneficial psychological force of these ideas.

Kant comes very close to making this approach explicit by dealing with a duty regarding God but to ourselves immediately after his treatment of the duty regarding nature but to ourselves in the "Doctrine of Virtue." Here he discusses not the idea of God as the intelligent Author of nature, which is postulated for the sake of the highest good, but the idea of God as lawgiver, through which we recognize our duties as divine commands,[21] and he says that this idea unavoidably presents itself to reason rather than to sensibility; but the key point is his argument that although we in fact have no direct duties to God, once this idea occurs to us "it is a duty of man to himself to apply this idea, which presents itself unavoidably to reason, to the moral law in him, where it is of greatest moral fruitfulness. In this (*practical*) sense it can therefore be said that to have religion is a duty of man to himself" (*MM*, DV, §18, 6:443–44).[22] If we take the claim that the idea of God is a product of reason phenomenologically, that is, if we ascribe it to reason understood as part of our empirical psychology rather than to reason understood in some transcendental sense, then the difference between the sensible dispositions of aesthetics and this idea of reason is not important; the key point remains that human psychology affords us a variety of natural representations that are morally efficacious in spite of their lack of theoretical confirmation or justification, and that because making virtue our end requires among other things that we cultivate all naturally occurring

---

[21] This version of the idea of God and its explicitly subjective origins was to become increasingly prominent in the final stages of the *Opus postumum*; for further discussion, see my essay "The Unity of Nature and Freedom: Kant's Conception of the System of Philosophy," in Sally S. Sedgwick, ed., *Systematicity in Kant and German Idealism* (Cambridge: Cambridge University Press, forthcoming).

[22] Gregor, *MM*, p. 238.

means to morality, we have a duty to preserve and promote all such naturally occurring dispositions and representations, the postulates of practical reason as much as the forms of aesthetic experience.

In the end, then, Kant's moral theology stands alongside his aesthetics as an essential part of the moral anthropology that was the heart of his enterprise throughout his last decade of philo-sophical activity, and it is no accident that his most detailed state-ment of his moral theology is the culmination of the "Critique of Teleological Judgment," just as his most extensive statement of his moral aesthetics is the culmination of the "Critique of Aesthetic Judgment." Just as aesthetic experiences of the beautiful and the sublime, of the ideal of beauty, and aesthetic ideas as the contents of works of artistic genius are natural dispositions of human sen-sibility, which nevertheless can and must be put to work in the in-terest of reason to support our disposition to morality, so the pos-tulates of pure practical reason must ultimately be understood as natural products of teleological judgment that can and must be put to work in the interest of reason to allow sensibility to coop-erate with the interests of reason.

Chapter 11

Nature, Freedom, and Happiness: The Third Proposition of Kant's *Idea for a Universal History*

I

It is difficult to interpret Kant's aim in the *Idea for a Universal History from a Cosmopolitan Point of View*[1] (1784) – the page and a half of generalities that precedes the nine "propositions" that constitute the body of the essay do not contain a clear statement of why he is enumerating and expounding these propositions. It might be thought that in these propositions Kant is stating the metaphysical presuppositions necessary to write a scientific history of human activities on a global scale, just as in the *Metaphysical Foundations of Natural Science* of two years later (1786) he lays out what he takes to be the metaphysical presuppositions of a unified terrestrial and celestial physical science.[2] But Kant hardly suggests that he assumes that there is anything like a going practice of scientific

---

A French translation of this chapter is to appear in Jean-Christophe Merle, ed., *L' "Idee d'une histoire universelle du point de vue cosmopolitique" de Kant* (Paris: Ophrys, forthcoming).

[1] Translations from the *Idea for a Universal History* and the *Critique of Judgment* are my own; translations from the *Groundwork of the Metaphysics of Morals* and the *Critique of Practical Reason* will be based on those by Mary Gregor in Immanuel Kant, *Practical Philosophy*, trans. by Mary J. Gregor (Cambridge: Cambridge University Pess, 1996).

[2] That Kant's essay is concerned with theoretical foundations for a science of history is at least part of what is suggested by Pauline Kleingeld in *Fortschritt und Vernunft: Zur Geschichtsphilosophie Kants* (Würzburg: Königshausen and Neumann, 1995), e.g., p. 18.

history,[3] and there is no hint that he intends his procedure in this essay to be understood as anything like that in the *Prolegomena to Any Future Metaphysics* of the year before (1783) or the subsequent *Metaphysical Foundations of Natural Science*, where the application of an "analytical" method to an established body of science unexpectedly reveals synthetic *a priori* propositions at its foundation. Indeed, Kant says nothing about the logical and epistemological status of his nine propositions, and thus raises no expectation that he will try to show them to be synthetic *a priori* presuppositions of any established scientific discipline. But even if Kant were attempting to ground a science of history, it seems as if his interest in such a history would itself be moral and political – that is, that he is aiming to explain what assumptions about human nature would have to be made in a historiography that would support our deepest moral and political ends by describing human history as compatible with the realization of those ends. But then the premises of a possible universal history would be the conditions of the possibility of human moral and political development itself, thus premises that we would have to be able to adopt from a practical point of view, for the sake of morality, even if there were no theoretical necessity for assuming these premises in order to ground any scientific discipline of historical inquiry. I take this to be the implication of Kant's concluding statement in his discussion of the Second Proposition of the essay, where he writes that, if we cannot foresee a point in time at which the human species would have perfected its collective capacity for rationality,

> then the natural dispositions [of mankind] would have to be regarded as in large part vain and purposeless; which would suspend all practical principles and through which nature, whose wisdom must otherwise serve as the principle in the estimation of all other arrangements, would be suspect of childish play in the case of mankind alone. (8:19)

[3] Kleingeld cites a number of titles, including some owned by Kant, to show that there was a genre of "universal history" (ibid., p. 14), but Kant does not say enough in the first page and a half of his essay to prove that he is seriously concerned with the possibility of history as a scientific discipline in this essay. Concern with that possibility was typical of some neo-Kantians (e.g., Dilthey), but it seems to me anachronistic to ascribe it to Kant.

The assumptions that we would have to make in order to write a universal history of mankind from a cosmopolitan point of view are just the assumptions that we have to make about nature in order to see our own commitment to our practical principles as rational rather than vain and purposeless. This in turn suggests that the propositions enunciated in the *Idea for a Universal History* should be conceived of as more like postulates of pure practical reason than like necessary conditions of the possibility of experience or science.

If this is so, then the propositions of the *Idea for a Universal History* should obviously be consistent with the fundamental principles of Kant's moral philosophy as those would be expounded beginning with the *Groundwork for the Metaphysics of Morals*, which Kant was composing at the very moment when the essay on history was published (November 1784) and which would itself be published the following spring. But the Third Proposition of the history essay seems strikingly inconsistent with several of the apparently most fundamental tenets of Kant's moral philosophy, and indeed in at least one point inconsistent with commonsense assumptions about morality as well. Here is Kant's statement of the Third Proposition and some key extracts from the page of exposition that follows it. First, the proposition itself:

> Nature has willed that mankind should bring forth entirely out of itself everything that goes beyond the mechanical organization of its animal existence and should partake of no other happiness or perfection than that which it has created itself, free from instinct, through its own reason. (8:19)

Next, several key passages from the following text, first this:

> Since nature gave mankind reason and the freedom of the will grounded thereupon, that was already a clear indication of its intention with regard to its endowment. Mankind is not to be led by instinct, or cared for and instructed by inborn knowledge; it should rather bring forth everything from itself. . . . Nature seems here to have pleased itself in its greatest economy and to have measured out mankind's animal equipage so tightly, so precisely in accord with the greatest need of a rudimentary existence, that it seems as if nature wanted mankind, if it would

work its way up from the greatest crudeness to the greatest skill, to inner perfection of its manner of thought and thereby (so far as this is possible on earth) to happiness, to have the merit of this entirely on its own and to have only itself to thank; just as if nature were concerned more with mankind's rational *self-esteem* than with its well-being. . . . Nature seems not to have been concerned that mankind live well, but that it labor so as to make itself through its conduct worthy of life and of well-being. (8: 19–20)

Finally, Kant adds this:

It always remains disconcerting that the older generations seem to undertake their laborious business only for the sake of the later ones, in order to prepare for these a platform on which they can build higher the structure that nature has as its aim, and that only the latest generations will have the good fortune to dwell in the edifice on which a long series of their ancestors have labored (without, to be sure, so intending) without themselves being able to take part in the good fortune they have prepared. (8:20)

In these passages Kant seems to state three presuppositions of a history of mankind, which should in turn express the conditions of the possibility of human morality, yet which instead appear to contradict what we would otherwise assume to be the fundamental tenets of his moral philosophy.

First, particularly in our second passage, while describing the object of morality as "self-esteem" or being "worthy" of happiness, as we would expect, Kant suggests that this object is something that nature intends for us and that (as the Fourth and Fifth Propositions suggest) it can even bring about in spite of our own intentions, rather than something that can only be intended by an act of our own free will, indeed by nothing less than the free choice to liberate the determination of our will from all natural forces such as inclination and instead to determine it by pure reason alone. In other words, there seems to be a contradiction in the very idea that nature can intend us to be free: what is merely natural is precisely what would seem to be unfree rather than free.

Second, in the initial statement of the proposition itself, Kant suggests that what nature intends for us is that by our own rational action, explicitly "free of all instinct," we should produce both "happiness" and "perfection," presumably meaning by the latter moral perfection, or what the ensuing discussion refers to as "self-esteem" or "worthiness" to be happy. This not only repeats the apparent contradiction that we must conceive of our own freedom as an intended product of nature, but now also seems to undermine Kant's understanding of virtue alone as the distinctive object of morality by *including* happiness as well as worthiness to be happy in the object of morality that nature paradoxically intends for us.

Finally, the last portion of the exposition seems to undercut an expectation that has been part of commonsense morality at least since Plato's *Republic*, the expectation, namely, that the effort at being moral must have some kind of benefit, if not happiness then at least some form of contentment, for the agent who makes that effort; instead Kant suggests that, in a monumental case of deferred gratification, the payoff of morality may only accrue to the descendants of those who make the effort to be moral. And this is not merely a commonsense assumption but also an assumption to which Kant himself seems to subscribe when he introduces the concept of the highest good in the *Critique of Practical Reason*. Here Kant initially describes "virtue and happiness together [as] constitut[ing] possession of the highest good in a person," and states that any rational agent, even an omnipotent one, expects happiness to be combined with virtue as the worthiness to be happy in the person of any agent who does cultivate virtue: "For to need happiness, to be also worthy of it, and yet not to participate in it cannot be consistent with the perfect volition of a rational being that would at the same time have all power" (*CPracR*, 5:110). But Kant's account of the propositions that are apparently supposed to express the presuppositions of a view of history that would in turn be the condition of the possibility of morality seems to say that early generations, perhaps most generations, can only expect the happiness that should attend their own efforts to be virtuous to be enjoyed by later generations of human beings.

Thus what would seem to be intended as part of Kant's statement of the conditions of the possibility of morality instead seem to contradict his conception of morality on three crucial points: instead of being separated as they should be, the intentions of nature and the exercise of human freedom are conflated; instead of being separated as they should be, the goals of virtue and happiness seem to be conjoined in what nature intends for us; but instead of being conjoined as they apparently should be, in the highest good of each individual person or at least each generation, virtue on the one hand and happiness on the other seem to be separated by many generations. How are these claims about the role of nature in history to be reconciled with Kant's conception of morality?

One form of solution to what may be, at least from a metaphysical point of view, the most fundamental of these problems, the apparently paradoxical idea that our freedom itself is actually a product of nature, clearly won't do. Some commentators, such as Yirmiahu Yovel, have attempted to deal with this paradox by appealing to Kant's later distinction between right (*Recht*) and virtue (*Tugend*), and the associated distinction between *external* and *internal* legislation, arguing that there is no contradiction in thinking of a just *political* constitution emerging from entirely natural processes, since such a constitution is only the *external condition* for the exercise of a nonnatural freedom of the will. Neither the creation of nor compliance with such a constitution requires an especially moral motivation – although the moral motivation of respect for duty does require the creation of and compliance with such a constitution – and therefore such a constitution does not itself have to be produced by any nonnatural forces.[4] Such a simple solution of the apparent paradox at the heart of the Third Proposition cannot be right, however, because even though the Fifth through Seventh Propositions do concern the natural genesis of a political rather than moral constitution, in the Third Proposition Kant clearly ascribes to nature the aim of realizing our moral perfection itself, not merely an external framework within which

---

[4] Yirmiahu Yovel, *Kant and the Philosophy of History* (Princeton: Princeton University Press, 1981), p. 141. Yovel thinks that there is no solution at all to the second problem I have mentioned, which he thinks is "just another facet of human finitude" (p. 145).

virtue might be realized: as we have already seen, Kant's discussion of the Third Proposition explicitly states that nature is concerned with mankind's "*self-esteem*" rather than with its "well-being" (8:20). Here Kant says that nature has aimed at mankind's moral worth or virtue itself, thus excluding the proposal that nature brings forth merely the external and political conditions for virtuous human action as a sufficient interpretation of his claims.

Instead, a solution to the puzzles of the Third Proposition requires a reexamination of the presuppositions about the relations between nature and freedom as well as between virtue and happiness in Kant's moral philosophy that underlie the aparent paradoxes I have described. This in turn requires some reflection on Kant's teleology, as the locus where the apparently "boundless gulf between the territory of the concept of nature, as the sensible, and the territory of the concept of freedom, as the supersensible," is to be bridged (*CJ*, II, 5:175–6). Once we see that even within Kant's moral philosophy neither freedom and nature nor virtue and happiness are simplistically opposed, but rather that each of these apparent polar opposites is instead intimately connected with the other, then we will be able to see that the claims suggested by the Third Proposition do not undermine this moral philosophy but are indeed apt expressions of the conditions of its possibility.

I argue for this conclusion on two fronts. First, focusing on the normative implications of Kant's moral philosophy, I argue that the traditional assumptions that Kant's moral philosophy concerns solely the purity of intentions without regard to their realization in nature, and that it prescribes as the object of moral willing solely virtue and not happiness, are misleading. Kant's conception of moral assessment, to be sure, focuses on agents' maxims rather than on the outcomes of their actions in nature, but their maxims are expressions of intentions to act *in nature;* so as to bring about certain outcomes *in nature;* thus in order for any attempt to be moral to be rational, nature must be seen as, if not itself *intending* morality, at least *compatible* with morality. Further, in spite of Kant's emphasis that a desire for one's own happiness is not a virtuous or morally praiseworthy *motivation*, virtue and happiness are far from being entirely separated; on the contrary, although respect for duty is the only virtuous motivation for human beings, in Kant's view the *object* of morality – the highest good – can only be the preservation of human beings as ends in themselves together with the promotion and fulfillment of their permissible ends. Since the latter is in turn what constitutes the maximally permissible happiness of all, virtue and happiness are not separated but at least ideally joined at the hip. Moreover, Kant generally conceives of the highest good as a condition to be realized *in nature*, thus nature, even if it does not *intend* the conjoint realization of human virtue and happiness, must be at least compatible with it.[5]

Second, turning to the metaphysics of Kantian morality, I argue that Kant's talk of nature as intending human freedom should not be seen as incoherent, but rather as a colorful expression of his view that we must be able to see human action as subsumable under laws of both nature and freedom,[6] a view for which he argues not merely in his specific treatments of the problem of free will, as in the *Critique of Practical Reason*, but also in the teleology of the *Critique of Judgment* and even in his final attempts at a statement of his transcendental philosophy in the *Opus postumum*. Ultimately, Kant's transcendental philosophy implies that it is not incoherent to see nature as intending human freedom because nature itself must be seen as the product of an intelligible authorship. Of course, Kant's writings from the *Critique of Judgment* to the end of his life make it clear that any such conception of nature must be conceived of as a regulative ideal or principle, valid from the standpoint of reflective rather than determinant judgment; indeed, even the postulates of pure practical reason themselves become regulative principles when they are incorporated into the framework of a critique of teleological judgment. In the essay on the *Idea for a Universal History*, Kant does not explicitly say that the claims about nature that must ground a universal history of mankind because they must ground the practice of morality itself are regulative

---

[5] This interpretation of the highest good has been developed in Chapter 10 as well.

[6] See Chapter 6, section III.

principles or postulates, but perhaps that is what he means to convey simply by the mere use of the word "Idea" in his title.[7]

Another way of dividing the issues to be discussed in what follows is this: in section II, we see how freedom and nature must be compatible, and virtue and happiness not merely compatible but intimately connected; in section III, we see what sense can be given to the claim that nature actually intends either our virtue alone or our virtue in conjunction with happiness.

II

In this section, I argue for three claims grounded in the content of Kant's moral philosophy. (1) Although moral worth may be strictly a matter of what intentions human agents have, morally worthy intentions are themselves intentions to act *in nature*, so the laws of nature must in fact be compatible with the morality of human action. (2) Although morally worthy action is not *motivated* by a desire for personal happiness, the conjunction of virtue and the lawfully permissible happiness of all in the form of the highest good is in fact the inevitable *object* of morally worthy intention, and so the realization of both "happiness and perfection" *in nature*, and in the language of the Third Proposition intended by nature, is a condition of the possibility of morality itself. Thus, the laws of nature must in fact be compatible with the possibility of both action in accordance with the dictates of virtue and the realization of both virtue and happiness in the form of the highest good. (3) The idea that our efforts at morality might bring more happiness to future generations than to ourselves is not a violation of common sense, and certainly not incompatible with Kant's moral philosophy, but is a natural consequence of a synchronic interpretation of his ideas of a kingdom of ends and its realization in the form of the highest good.

---

[7] See Reinhard Brandt, "Zum 'Streit der Facultäten,'" in Reinhard Brandt and Werner Stark, eds., *Neue Autographen und Dokumenten zu Kants Leben, Schriften und Vorlesungen, Kant-Forschungen*, vol. 1 (Hamburg: Felix Meiner, 1987), pp. 31–78, at pp. 42–43.

1. In the complex of rhetorical stratagems that compose Chapter I of the *Groundwork for the Metaphysics of Morals*, a chapter that is only supposed to contain the introductory transition from commonsense assumptions about morality to an initial formulation of the fundamental principle of morality in a work that is itself supposed to be only an introduction to a systematic metaphysics of morals, Kant offers several arguments that have long been taken to entail that in his ethical theory the sole object of concern must be the formal structure of virtuous intentions in the mind of the moral agent rather than the actual outcome of the agent's actions in the natural world. In his initial analysis of what he takes to be the common understanding of the value of a good will, he argues that "A good will is not good because of what it effects or accomplishes, because of its fitness to attain some proposed end, but only because of its volition," thus that good will is "a jewel" that "would still shine by itself" regardless of its "usefulness or fruitlessness" (*G*, 4:394). In his subsequent discussion of what he takes to be an equally common understanding of the character of virtuous motivation, he argues that the fundamental principle of morality must be such that a virtuous agent can be motivated to act upon it even in the complete absence of any inclination that would move him in that direction – the principle must be such that even someone whose "own grief" has "extinguished all sympathy with the fate of others" could still both know what has to be done and motivated to do it in order, for example, "to benefit others in distress" (4:398).

The first claim might be taken to mean that the fundamental principle of morality, action on which constitutes having a good will, can have nothing to do with the consequences of our actions, but it doesn't entail that: the commonsensical assumption that evaluation of an agent's moral worth should concern the intention with which the agent acted rather than the actual outcome of her action can certainly be taken to mean just that in such an evaluation we should focus on the *intended outcome* of the action rather than its actual outcome, and is thus compatible with any conception of the content of the fundamental principle of morality, consequentialist as well as otherwise. The lesson of Kant's subsequent examples such as the unsympathetic but nevertheless virtuous benefactor is certainly that the fundamental principle of morality must be able to bind and move us without inclination, and from this perhaps there is a route to the conclusion that this principle must require above all a certain kind of formal consistency or universalizability in our maxims.[8] But even if that is true, it hardly follows that the principle requires anything other than the application of the appropriate formal constraint to our *intentions or maxims to act so as to produce certain outcomes in the world* – that is, in the physical realm of objects and events lying beyond our own thoughts, including our intentions. Indeed, Kant's requirement that even the agent rendered insensible to sympathy by his own grief must still be able to be moved by the fundamental principle of morality *to benefit others in distress* implies precisely this: benefiting others in distress is an action that must take place in the natural world beyond one's mere thoughts, although, to revert to Kant's first point, we may evaluate an agent's moral worth on the basis of her *having intended* to benefit others in distress rather than her actual success in so doing. Thus, Kant's appeals to common sense in *Groundwork* I may suffice to establish that an agent's moral worth must depend upon her commitment to a fundamental principle of morality, rather than on either the actual outcome of her actions or the presence of any, even sympathetic inclination to perform those actions, but cannot by themselves establish that the fundamental principle of morality itself does not direct us to choose to perform actions in the world outside our mere thoughts, actions that must therefore be at least possible effects of our free choices *in nature* if moral conduct itself is to be rational.

Kant's more "philosophical" derivation of the fundamental principle of morality from the concept of a categorical imperative in *Groundwork* II also fails to block the natural assumption that morality requires us to pursue certain courses of conduct rather than

---

[8] See Nelson Potter, "The Argument of Kant's *Grundlegung*, Chapter 1," *Canadian Journal of Philosophy*, suppl. 1 (1974): 73–91, and Christine M. Korsgaard, *Creating the Kingdom of Ends* (Cambridge: Cambridge University Press, 1996), ch. 2 ("Kant's Analysis of Obligation: The Argument of *Groundwork* I"). Both of these essays are reprinted in my *Kant's Groundwork of the Metaphysics of Morals: Critical Essays* (Lanham, Md.: Rowman and Littlefield, 1998). See also Chapter 6, section I, and Chapter 9, section I, in this volume.

others in the natural world, with the possibility of which that world must be at least compatible; indeed, everything that Kant says about the fundamental principle of morality implies that it must be applied to maxims to act in certain ways in the world, ways of acting with which the world itself must be compatible if so acting is to make any sense. Kant starts his argument off with the assumption that a fundamental principle of morality must present itself to us as a categorical rather than a hypothetical imperative, thus as a principle that must be able to bind and move us independently of any *particular* end we may have for acting. He infers from this that the fundamental principle of morality must impose a formal constraint rather than material end or objective on our particular maxims of action. But the maxims of action to which such a formal principle is to be applied, whether or not they turn out to satisfy this formal constraint, are themselves maxims to act in particular ways, for particular ends, in the world – maxims, for example, to make false promises of repayment in order to obtain money to pay off debts or to cultivate one's talents in order to be prepared for the pursuit of particular ends in the future. The actions prescribed or licensed by such maxims, actions such as making promises or cultivating talents, are actions intended to take place in the world beyond one's own thoughts and intentions, and ends such as paying off debts or satisfying future ends are likewise states of affairs that are to be brought about in the real world. Thus, although the fundamental principle of morality is supposed to hold independently of our particular inclinations and ends, it is to be applied to maxims or intentions to act in various ways in the world. The very idea of adopting and applying this principle thus makes no sense unless the maxims in accordance with which it ultimately directs us to act can be conceived of as maxims that can be effective in nature or the world beyond our mere thoughts. At the very least, even if nature need not be conceived of as *intending* us to act, free from inclination, in accordance with a formal conception of moral perfection, it must be compatible with our so acting.

The same result follows from consideration of the system of duties that Kant finally elaborates in the *Metaphysics of Morals* (1797) to which the *Groundwork* was all along supposed to be the introduction. This work is as complex as it is compact and divides its contents on the basis of several assumptions, the discussion of which would go well beyond the bounds of the present chapter.[9] Even restricting ourselves to the system of noncoercively enforceable duties to ourselves and others that Kant expounds in its "Doctrine of Virtue," we see a complex division of our duties into duties to ourselves as "moral" beings and as "animal" beings (*MM*, 6: 420) and duties of "respect" and of "love" to others (6:448). Duties to ourselves as moral beings are, for example, the duties to cultivate self-knowledge (6:441) and conscience (6:438–40), whereas duties to ourselves as animal beings are such duties as, on the one hand, those to avoid drunkenness and gluttony that would interfere with the exercise of our reason (6:427) and, on the other, duties to cultivate our natural powers of both mind and body "as means to all sorts of possible ends" that we might form during our lives (6:444–46). Duties of respect to others are duties not to diminish their dignity by showing contempt in the forms of arrogance, defamation, and ridicule (6:465) or even to tempt them into violation of their own self-esteem by such forms of contempt (6:642), whereas duties of love to others are such duties as those to be beneficent, grateful, and sympathetic (6:452) to others with regard to their own animal needs and also their duties to themselves as animal beings.

Now, it should be obvious that our duties to ourselves as animal beings and our duties of love to others are duties that can only be carried out in the natural world, and in that world only if it is compatible with our fulfillment of such duties; the *moral worth* of our performance of such duties may be a matter of our intention in performing them, or the character of the principle that moves us to fulfill them, but the duties themselves are clearly duties to act upon the natural world – ourselves and others as natural beings – and can only be rationally undertaken insofar as nature itself is at least compatible with the successful performance of such duties. It may be less obvious that our duties to ourselves as moral beings and our duties of respect to others also concern our actions in the

---

[9] In addition to Chapter 9 in this volume, see also Alan Donagan, "The Structure of Kant's *Metaphysics of Morals*," *Topoi* 4 (1985): 61–72.

natural world, and thus presuppose the possible efficacy of our freedom in the realm of nature, but a case could be made that this is so: moral self-knowledge is a *task* for us, for example, precisely because our inclinations *naturally* tend to lead us to self-deception; and the very possibility of showing either respect or contempt not only *for* but also *to* one another depends on the fact that we are embodied beings capable of communicating with each other, expressly or not, not merely by vocalization but by look and bearing as well, all of which are physical as well as mental. To make a long story short, all of our actual duties of virtue both to ourselves and to others are duties to act in a variety of ways as beings who are part of the physical reality of nature, and it can be rational for us to choose to fulfill these duties and to act so as to attempt to fulfill them only if nature is compatible with the freedom of both our choice and our action.

These arguments should suffice to establish the minimal first step in reconciling Kant's premises for a universal history with the fundamental tenets of his moral philosophy: even confining ourselves to Kant's conception of virtue, we can readily see that he conceives of virtue as something that must be practiced in nature, and we must therefore assume not merely for writing history but for the rationality of morality itself that nature is at least compatible with the freedom of our choice and action, that we can as natural beings choose to act as our free and rational will requires and that it is at least possible that our freely chosen actions can have their intended effects in ourselves and others as part of nature. We now turn to the next step of our argument, which is to show that the conjunction of virtue and happiness described in the Third Proposition as intended by nature is also an essential part of Kant's moral philosophy.

2. The Third Proposition states that nature intends us to use our freedom to achieve both "happiness and perfection," the latter presumably meaning moral perfection or virtue. This seems contrary to Kant's moral philosophy, at least as often understood, according to which it is virtue alone, regardless of happiness or any other consequences of our virtuous actions, that should be the motive of virtuous action and the concern of the fundamental principle of

morality. But Kant made it clear beginning with the "Canon of Pure Reason" of the *Critique of Pure Reason* – published four years before the *Groundwork* – that the complete *object* of virtuous action, although not its *motive*, is the highest good, or a conjunction of maximal virtue with maximal permissible happiness; and the doctrine of the postulates of pure practical reason, also already adumbrated in the first *Critique*, requires that we have an adequate ground for holding the realization of this object as a whole – both virtue and happiness – to be possible if it is to be rational for us to act on the fundamental principle of morality, even if our motivation in so acting is a concern for virtue alone. The claim that nature intends us to use our freedom to achieve both virtue and happiness, interpreted to mean at the very least that nature must be compatible with our realization of the highest good, can thus be taken as an expression of the assumption that we have to be able to make about nature, as the sphere of our action and the arena in which alone happiness can be achieved, in order for moral conduct to be intelligible.

For this thesis to be accepted, it must be recognized that the highest good is not, as its introduction in the *Critique of Practical Reason* might make it seem, a conjunction of two separate aims, the aim to be virtuous, which we have as purely rational beings, and the aim to be happy, which we have as merely animal or natural beings, both of which must be satisfied in order to please our dual nature, perhaps with the additional rider that our happiness must be proportional to (especially no greater than) our virtue being added as an expression of the priority of our moral over our animal nature. As the "Canon of Pure Reason" and many other texts make clear, the connection between virtue and happiness is more intimate than that: because virtue requires treating all human beings as ends in themselves, because treating all human beings as ends in themselves requires doing what one can both to preserve the freedom of all to set their own ends and to promote the fulfillment of the morally permissible ends of all (which are just those ends the pursuit and fulfillment of which are compatible with the freedom of all others to pursue and fulfill their ends), and because happiness just consists in the fulfillment of ends, it follows that virtue itself prescribes the fulfillment of the maximally com-

possible set of all human ends, thus that at least under ideal circumstances maximal compliance with the fundamental principle of
morality would itself result in maximally permissible human happiness. On this account what the Third Proposition suggests is that
the end of nature would indeed also be the object of morality itself.

The *Critique of Practical Reason* may suggest that our interest in
virtue on the one hand and our desire for happiness on the other
have two separate sources, and that the basic form of the relationship between them is that virtue, as the worthiness to be happy,
is the precondition of our right to enjoy happiness but not itself
the source of our desire for it. Thus Kant concludes the paragraph
which first introduces the highest good into the argument of the
second *Critique* with these words: "happiness is something that,
though always pleasant to the possessor of it, is not of itself absolutely and in all respects good but always presupposes morally
lawful conduct as its condition" (5:111). But Kant had already implied a more intimate connection between virtue and happiness,
one that can be interpreted as based on the argument outlined in
the previous paragraph, when he stated the following in the first
Critique:

> Now in an intelligible world, i.e., in the moral world, in the con-
> cept of which we have abstracted from all hindrances to moral-
> ity (of the inclinations), such a system of happiness proportion-
> ately combined with morality can also be thought as necessary,
> since freedom, partly moved and partly restricted by moral
> laws, would itself be the cause of the general happiness, and ra-
> tional beings, under the guidance of such principles, would
> themselves be the authors of their own enduring welfare and at
> the same time that of others. (A 809–10/B 837–38)

This statement can be explained precisely on the basis of the assumption that morality prescribes universal respect for human
beings as ends in themselves, which in turn requires both the
preservation of their free agency, the conditions of which Kant ultimately spells out in his list of perfect duties to both self and others, and the promotion of the ends of all lawfully set by their free
agency, the requirements for which Kant spells out in his system
of broad or imperfect duties to both self and others. Under ideal

circumstances, compliance with the latter set of duties in particular would result in the maximal permissible happiness.

Of course, as Kant immediately observes, ideal circumstances do not always obtain, or in any case certainly do not appear to obtain, and our actions, no matter how virtuously motivated, do not always have their intended outcome; thus in the sensible and natural world happiness does not always seem to be the inevitable outcome of virtue, and the happiness of all would not seem to be the inevitable outcome even of universal virtue. It is for this reason that the rationality of acting with the highest good as our object requires us to postulate the existence of an all-powerful as well as benevolent author of nature, who can supply the happiness that in the ordinary course of affairs does not in fact seem to follow inevitably from virtue:

> Thus happiness in exact proportion with the morality of rational beings, through which they are worthy of it, alone constitutes the highest good of a world into which we must without exception place ourselves in accordance with the precepts of pure but practical reason, and which, of course, is only an intelligible world, because the sensible world does not promise us that sort of systematic unity of ends, the reality of which can be grounded on nothing other than the presupposition of a highest original end, because self-sufficient reason, armed with all the sufficiency of a supreme cause, in accordance with the most perfect purposiveness, conserves and completes the order of things which is universal, although well hidden from us in the sensible world. (A 814/B 842)

Now this kind of statement is typically taken to mean that the happiness included in the highest good cannot be expected to be achieved in the natural lifetime of a human being, or in the lifetimes of human beings, but is rather something that could only be expected to be achieved in nonnatural circumstances, just as the perfection of virtue in the form of the achievement of holiness of will – the obliteration of all desire contrary to the virtuous will – could only be expected to be achieved in an immortal afterlife rather than in a natural life-span. In fact, however, whatever he might think about the necessary condition for the achievement of moral perfection, Kant does not actually say that the happiness of the highest good can only be expected in an afterlife, but he instead characterizes it as something that must be achieved "in the world," and must therefore be facilitated by God postulated as the author of *laws of nature* that are, contrary to what might appear to us to be the case in our initial view of the sensible world, in complete harmony with the law of morality. Kant makes the premise of this conclusion plain in the *Critique of Judgment*:

> The moral law as the formal rational condition of the use of our freedom binds us for itself alone, without depending on any end as material condition: but it determines for us, and indeed *a priori*, a final end, to strive after which it makes obligatory for us: and this is the *highest good* possible through freedom *in the world*. (§87, 5:450)

He makes what follows from this premise clear in the *Critique of Practical Reason* itself:

> The existence of a cause of all nature, distinct from nature, which contains the ground of this connection, namely of the exact correspondence of happiness with morality, is also *postulated*. However, this supreme cause is to contain the ground of the correspondence of nature not merely with a law of the will of rational beings but with the representation of this *law*, so far as they make it the *supreme determining ground of the will*. . . . Therefore the highest good in the world is possible only insofar as a supreme cause of nature having a causality in keeping with the moral disposition is assumed. (5:125)

And it is entirely correct for Kant to infer that the rationality of our compliance with the demands of morality requires us to think that the happiness of the highest good is at least possible in nature. For however it may be with the perfection of virtue – and one could argue that Kant's assumption that the perfection of virtue must be a holiness of will that could not be achieved in an ordinary human life-span is simply mistaken,[10] that perfect virtue instead consists simply in having the strength of will that is necessary to resist whatever temptations to violate the moral law that might present

[10] See Chapter 10, section I.

themselves within a normal human life[11] – it should be clear that happiness can *only* be a natural condition, for the simple reason that the needs and desires, the fulfillment of which, when permissible, constitutes permissible happiness, only occur within nature or within our lives as natural beings. At least as far as we can tell, all our needs to act arise solely from the fact that we are mortal, embodied creatures, although morality requires us to impose constraints of a reason that itself may be supranatural on these needs and desires.

Thus, it is quite proper for Kant to suggest that nature can intend for us to use our freedom to achieve both our own happiness as well as our perfection, interpreting this claim now to mean not only that the laws of nature must be able to be regarded by us as compatible with both our virtue and our happiness but also that our happiness certainly and perhaps our moral perfection as well can only be achieved in nature, that is, within our existence as natural, embodied creatures. The happiness included in the highest good must therefore be at least possible within human history, not somewhere else. Taken in this sense, then, the Third Proposition is not at odds with Kant's moral philosophy but instead expresses an assumption that we must make about nature in order for our attempt to be moral even to be intelligible.

3. Further reflection on Kant's conception of the highest good can also alleviate the discomfort that might be experienced at Kant's final claim in the discussion of the Third Proposition, his claim that only later generations of mankind may get to enjoy the happiness earned by the virtuous efforts of earlier generations. The key point to keep in mind here is that the happiness that is included in the conception of the highest good and promised by the postulation of an intelligent author of nature as at least a historical possibility is not the happiness of any individual agent, construed as a reward for personal merit, but rather some sort of collective happiness of mankind, construed as the ideal outcome of the virtuous action of all. Only happiness in this sense can be included in the concept of the highest good, because happiness only gets included

---

[11] See Chapter 9, section II.

in this happiness as the ideal outcome of the respect for the ends of all free agents that is prescribed by the moral law, compliance with which is of course the first object of morality.

Kant makes this point most clearly in his polemic with Christian Garve in the first section of his 1793 essay *On the Common Saying: That Might Be Right in Theory, but Not in Practice*.[12] Garve took Kant to be arguing in his doctrine of the highest good that "the virtuous person can never lose sight" of the perspective of "his own happiness" (8:281), an interpretation that Kant dismissed as a complete misunderstanding. Kant argues that *one's own* happiness is merely a natural end, not an end of reason (8:278) – actually, as he had already made clear in the *Groundwork*, even one's own happiness is not always one's natural end, because one is often tempted by an immediate promise of pleasure to actions that are incompatible with one's long-term happiness, as in the case of the gouty man who is tempted by the pleasure of a present indulgence to undermine his future health (4:399) – but that the happiness that morality makes our object is not our own "selfish" happiness but the "unselfish" end of the satisfaction of the ends of all:

> Without some end there can be no *will*, although, if it is a question only of lawful necessitation of actions, one must abstract from any end and the law alone constitutes its determining ground. But not every end is moral (e.g., that of one's own happiness is not), but this must rather be an unselfish one; and the need for a final end assigned by pure reason and comprehending the whole of all ends under one principle (a world as the highest good and possible through our cooperation) is a need

---

[12] This essay, like the *Idea for a Universal History*, was published in the *Berlinische Monatsschrift* (November 1793) and was thus intended for the same audience as the history essay: not an audience of academic philosophy professors but an audience of the enlightened classes of German society. After the death of Frederick the Great, the intellectually oppressive regime of his successor, and the recent spectacle of the French Revolution's collapse into terror, these people composed a far more embattled group than they were when Kant addressed them in the optimistic tones of the history essay nine years earlier. But the essay on theory and practice is a plea for continued optimism about the moral destiny of mankind in spite of these recent events.

of an unselfish will *extending* itself beyond observance of the
formal law to production of an object (the highest good).
(8:279–80n)

This makes clear that it is never merely one's own happiness that
is aimed at in the highest good, and that the highest good itself is
not a condition that may be attained by an individual – although
it must be aimed at by every individual – but a condition that may
be realized only by mankind as a whole. In fact, it would still take
Kant several years to recognize that one's own happiness, which
he here denies to be a moral end, is even properly aimed at as *part*
of the highest good: not until his discussion of the duty of benevolence late in the *Metaphysics of Morals* does he recognize that
"since all *others* with the exception of myself would not be *all*, so
that the maxim would not have within it the universality of a law,
which is still necessary for imposing obligation, the law making
benevolence a duty will include myself, as an object of benevolence, in the command of practical reason" (*MM*, DV, §27, 6:451).
Likewise, striving to promote the permissible ends and thus the
happiness of all except myself would not be aiming at the happiness of all, and thus the happiness that is part of the highest good
must include my own. But in no case can the happiness of the highest good be limited to my own, no matter how richly I might deserve it (of course, I couldn't deserve my own happiness unless I
aimed at the happiness of all). The happiness of the highest good
can only be the unselfish end of the happiness of all.

Now it still might not seem to follow from this that members
of earlier generations can rationally strive to be virtuous when the
benefit of their efforts in the form of happiness might accrue only
to later generations. But here one must remember that the highest
good is an ideal, a goal to which we must seek to make the sensible world conform, to which it must therefore be possible for the
sensible world to conform, but to which the sensible world would
actually conform only under ideal circumstances. Of course, ideal
circumstances don't always obtain, especially in the historical circumstances of human action. Even God's intelligible authorship
of the laws of nature only suffices to make those laws compatible
with the laws of morality; human beings retain the radical free-

dom to live up to the latter or not, and if they use that freedom to violate the laws of morality they cannot expect the laws of nature to produce maximally permissible universal happiness anyway. So at the very least, the efforts of virtuous human agents to bring about the highest good, including but not limited to their own happiness, can be frustrated by the vice of others. In this case, the virtuous agent might have to be satisfied with the self-content-ment that follows from the knowledge that she has done her duty, a form of satisfaction that Kant takes pains to distinguish from happiness as the actual satisfaction of one's ends (*CPracR*, 5:117–18). So in the actual rather than ideal circumstances of human his-tory, mere contentment rather than actual happiness may often be all that the individual can hope for. Still, that does not free one from the obligation of striving for universal happiness, including one's own, as the outcome of virtue; and the realization of the highest good must at least be possible in order for this effort to be intelligible. As far as it implies this, Kant's explanation of the Third Proposition of the history essay is certainly compatible with the basic tenets of his moral philosophy.

III

We must now turn from the normative to the metaphysical, from the compatibility of the Third Proposition's image of the ends for which nature intends us to use our freedom to the question about how nature can intend us to be free at all. Connecting nature and freedom, let alone attributing to nature an intention regarding our freedom, looks like mixing oil and water. Kant's standard con-ception of nature treats it as a realm of events completely subject to deterministic causal laws: "the combination of appearances as regards their existence, in accordance with necessary rules, i.e., in accordance with laws" (A 216/B 263). There seems to be room for neither freedom nor intentionality in nature so conceived, and thus it seems that room for freedom can be created only by reduc-ing nature to a realm of *mere* appearances and positing an under-lying reality where intentions can be freely formed independently of the causal determinism of nature. This certainly seems to be Kant's position in the "Antinomy of Pure Reason" in the first

Critique when he proposes to solve the conflict of determinism and freedom by transcendental idealism, which makes room for the position that "the dynamic series of sensible conditions . . . allows of a further condition different in kind, one that is not a part of the series but, as merely *intelligible*, lies outside the series" (A 530/B 559). This position in turn allows for a dualistic conception of human agency, according to which "In its empirical character," the human "subject, as appearance, would be subject to the causal connection, in accordance with all the laws of determination. . . . But in its intelligible character (even though we can have nothing more than merely the general concept of it), this subject would nevertheless have to be declared free of all influence of sensibility and determination by appearances" (A 540–41/B 568–69). But if by his own already published account Kant is committed to the view that room for freedom can be found only by looking outside of nature altogether, what can he possibly mean by ascribing an intention regarding our freedom to nature itself?

To answer this question fully would require a detailed study of Kant's claims and arguments about nature and freedom from the first *Critique* to the *Opus postumum*. That would obviously go well beyond the bounds of a single essay, and in any case we could only speculate about how much of this picture was already clear to Kant at the time that he wrote the *Idea for a Universal History*. All that I can do here is to offer a schematic reconstruction based on his subsequent works of what Kant might have meant by his ascription of an intention regarding the use of our freedom to nature in the popular essay of 1784. The main points of such a reconstruction would be the following.

1. The freedom of human *choice*, although it may be grounded in the noumenal realm, has to be at least compatible with the appearance of human character in the natural realm of phenomena. This point was first made clear in 1788, in the *Critique of Practical Reason*, but was probably already intended in 1781, in the first *Critique*'s distinction between empirical and intelligible character.

2. Second, as is posited in the doctrine of the highest good that is a part of each of Kant's three critiques, nature has to be compatible not only with the freedom of human *choice* but also with the efficacy of human *action*, for morality calls upon us to try to

bring about a certain state of affairs *in the world* and it would be irrational for us to strive to do so if we could not posit that the laws of nature at least allow for the possibility of realizing this end. But, Kant argues, we can make intelligible to ourselves the compatibility of the laws of nature and the moral laws of freedom only by positing an intelligent and purposive author of both sets of laws, whose intention it is that the laws of nature permit the realization of the happiness mandated in the highest good, if we indeed use our freedom virtuously. Thus we can at least conceive of an intention *for* nature and *for* ourselves as well as an intention for *us in nature*. Of course, as Kant stresses throughout his culminating exposition of this argument in the "Critique of Teleological Judgment," this conception of an intelligent intentionality behind nature is only a regulative principle of reflective judgment, which plays a heuristic role in our scientific inquiry and our moral conduct; it cannot be the subject of a theoretically valid deduction from either *a priori* argumentation (the traditional arguments for the existence of God) or empirical observation (physicotheology or the argument from design of eighteenth-century natural religion).

3. In his final writings, the last strata of the *Opus postumum*, Kant makes even clearer the merely regulative status of the conception of an intelligent intentional author of the laws of both nature and freedom by characterizing the images of both a law-governed nature and a giver of the moral law as projections of ourselves; we are the source of both natural laws and moral laws, and we can therefore speak of the intention behind the laws of nature as well as the moral law because we, the source of both, are fully capable of intentionality.

4. But, finally, this leaves the question, What is the value of speaking of nature's intention for us, as Kant does in the Third Proposition, rather than saying from the outset that all intentionality is a projection of our own? Here we can only speculate on an answer. This answer will have two parts. First, Kant may use this imagery to acknowledge that even though we ourselves are the fundamental source of the basic laws of both nature and morality, in both cases we have to accommodate our use of those laws to constraints that come from beyond ourselves, thus from nature in a common sense of the term – to empirical observations in the case

of laws of nature and to the raw material of needs and desires that has to be regulated by moral law. In both scientific inquiry and moral conduct, we must bring the formal laws that we project onto nature in both theoretical and practical reasoning into balance with the raw materials that emanate from empirical intuition and desire. But second, he may also use the image of nature's intention for us rather than our own intention to emphasize the authority this intention itself must have over other, more immediate needs and desires we might feel. Perhaps it is this complex of perspectives that Kant means to suggest through the otherwise paradoxical image of nature's intention for our use of our own freedom.

In what follows, I will amplify each of these points at least a little.

1. The laws of nature must be compatible with the freedom of human choice. If it was not already clear in the *Critique of Pure Reason*, Kant makes it more than clear in the *Critique of Practical Reason* that the freedom of human choice cannot be rendered intelligible simply by declaring what goes on in accordance with causal laws in the natural realm of appearances irrelevant to the freedom of choice posited to hold in the noumenal sphere; rather, the phenomenal appearances of human choices, their antecedents in and consequences for human characters, must be able to be seen as an expression of free human choice in spite of their subsumption under causal laws. Kant's device for sustaining this claim is transcendental idealism, namely his view that the temporal structure of appearances and nature, which can only be rendered determinate by subsumption to causal laws, does not apply to things as they are in themselves; thus our free choices are not subject to the temporal structure of our empirical character, and we can instead view our whole empirical character, even though it seems to unfold in time in accordance with the same sort of causal laws that govern everything else in nature, as an expression of our own free choices rather than as a deterministic constraint upon them. In Kant's words,

> The very same subject, . . . conscious of himself as a thing in itself, also views his existence *insofar as it does not stand under con-*

ditions of time and himself as determinable only through laws that he gives himself by reason; and in this existence of his, nothing is, for him, antecedent to the determination of his will, but every action – and in general every determination of his existence changing conformably with inner sense, even the whole sequence of his existence as a sensible being – is to be regarded in the consciousness of his intelligible existence as nothing but the consequence and never as the determining ground of his causality as a *noumenon*. (5:97–98)

Because the real act of choice does not have to be assigned a determinate place in the temporal history of a human character, it does not have to be considered as the causally determined consequence of antecedent states of that character, but can be considered as the free source of that whole character and everything that appears to follow in it and from it in accordance with causal laws of nature.

Resting as it does on Kant's transcendental idealism, this reconciliation of freedom and determinism has not found much favor. I certainly do not intend to defend it, but cite it only as a reminder that for Kant freedom and nature must be compatible, at least in the sense that nature can intelligibly be seen as an expression of human freedom. Of course, it still remains to be seen what sense can be given to the idea that human freedom is itself an expression of the intentionality of nature, as the Third Proposition suggests.

2. Again, Kant moves closer to an idea of the intentionality of nature – at least to an idea of the expression of an intention for us *in* nature – in the doctrine of the highest good. This doctrine is nothing less than the claim that the laws of nature must be able to be seen as compatible not only with the freedom of human *choice* but also with the efficacy of human *action*, at least with human action as the expression of the virtuous exercise of freedom of choice in accordance with the fundamental principle of morality. It is Kant's view that we can render this compatibility intelligible to ourselves only by conceiving of the laws of nature – presumably not just the laws of human character, but all the laws of nature, because humans can act on anything in nature and thus the outcomes of

human action can be impinged upon by any of the laws of nature –
and the moral law as the products of a single intelligent and purposive authorship of both mankind and the rest of nature. Kant
stresses that this conception is inevitable for us yet also merely
subjectively and regulatively valid. Thus it is inevitable for us to
conceive of nature as expressing the intention that we realize the
highest good – the production of happiness through virtue alluded
to in the Third Proposition – although this thought is only meant to
guide our action rather than add to our knowledge of reality.[13]

As we have already seen, although Kant is bent on giving a practical justification to the idea of immortality, and thus supposes
that virtue cannot be perfected in a finite life-span, he does not
usually make a parallel assumption that the happiness included
in the concept of the highest good is to be achieved in an afterlife;[14] rather, he typically supposes that the happiness that should
be the consequence of universally virtuous action must be *possible*
in nature, thus that we can render this possibility intelligible to
ourselves only by postulating a purposive ground or author *of nature*. He should argue this way because if happiness is conceived
of as the systematic and thus permissible fulfillment of our natural needs and desires, then it can only occur in nature, for that is
where our needs and desires arise. And he does argue in this way,
even in the *Critique of Practical Reason* immediately following his
exposition of the postulate of immortality (5:122–23): he does so
when he states that "*Happiness* is the state of a rational being in the
world in the whole of whose existence *everything goes according to
his wish and will*, and rests, therefore, on the harmony of nature with
his whole end as well as with the essential determining ground of
his will" (5:124); when he adds the premise that if it is "the practical task of pure reason" that "we *ought* to strive to promote the
highest good" and this "must therefore be possible"; and when he
concludes that

> Accordingly, the existence of a cause of all nature, distinct from
> nature, which contains the ground of this connection, namely of
> the exact correspondence of happiness with morality, is also *pos-*

[13] See Chapter 10, section II.
[14] For a possible exception to this generalization, see A 811/B 839.

tulated. . . . Therefore the highest good in the world is possible
only insofar as a supreme cause of nature having a causality in
keeping with the moral disposition is assumed. (5:125)

Kant's claim is that for it to be rational for us to strive to realize
the object of morality, we must believe that the appropriate form
of happiness is at least a possible outcome of our virtuously motivated action; that because happiness is a condition that can only
obtain in nature, this requires us to believe that the causality of
nature is in keeping with our moral disposition; and that we can
in turn believe this only if we ascribe the laws of nature as well as
the law of morality to a common supreme cause. We must conceive of this cause as both intelligent and purposive:

> A being capable of actions in accordance with the representa-
> tion of laws is *an intelligence* (a rational being) and the causality
> of such a being in accordance with this representation of laws is
> his *will*. Therefore, the supreme cause of nature, insofar as it must
> be presupposed for the highest good, is a being that is the cause
> of nature by *understanding* and *will* (hence its author), that is,
> God. (5:125)

Thus the rationality of our efforts at realizing the task imposed
upon us by morality requires that we see nature as an expression
of the same purposive and intentional authorship that is the source
of our "moral disposition," which presumably includes both our
obligation under the moral law and our capacity for living up to
this obligation.

In the *Critique of Judgment*, Kant not only reiterates that the highest good is an object of morality that is to be realized in nature (see,
again, §87, 5:450), but also stresses that the "postulate" of an intelligent and purposive author of both nature and our moral disposition is in fact a regulative idea, valid only for the guidance of
our conduct and not otherwise. The *Critique of Judgment* reaches
this conclusion by a convoluted argument that cannot be fully explicated here. But the key steps in the argument are these. First,
Kant argues that a characteristic difficulty that we have in comprehending certain processes in *organisms* requires us to introduce
the idea of an intelligent and purposive author of *them*, which it is
then inevitable for us to extend to the idea of an intelligent and

purposive author of nature *as a whole*. He then argues that we cannot determinately conceive of nature as a whole as a single system except by conceiving of the moral vocation of mankind as its ultimate goal, thus that we must conceive of the author of this system by means of the properties necessary to conceive of it as the author of a causality of nature in keeping with our moral disposition. At the same time, he argues, the moral imperative to realize the highest good independently drives us to the same conception of the author of both nature and our own moral disposition. Thus, both science and morality independently drive us to a conception of an intelligent and purposive ground of both natural and moral law, thus to a conception of nature as the expression of our moral vocation.[15]

From the outset of the scientific argument, however, Kant emphasizes that the difficulty in comprehending organic processes that drives us to the postulation of an intelligent ground for them, a conception that can be fleshed out only by the turn to morality, is a *subjective* restriction, a feature of the human cognitive condition that may not be universally valid. We have to conceive of an organic whole not merely as a product of its parts but also as the cause of them, something that we, with our unilinear conception of causation (*CJ*, §65, 5:372), can only do by representing the cause of the parts of an organism as a purposive agent with an antecedent representation of the whole organism (5:373), a conception that we form in analogy with our own capacity for artistic production (5:374). But because we have no ground for believing that the incapacity for understanding organic processes except by this analogy is anything but a peculiarity of our own cognitive capacity, we likewise have no ground for believing that the idea of an intelligent and purposive author of both organisms and then nature as a whole, which this incapacity drives us to introduce, is anything

---

[15] See my essays, "The Unity of Nature and Freedom: Kant's Conception of the System of Philosophy," in Sally S. Sedgwick, ed., *Systematicity in Kant and German Idealism* (Cambridge: Cambridge University Press, forthcoming), and "From Nature to Morality: Kant's New Argument in the 'Critique of Teleological Judgment,'" to be published in the proceedings of a conference on "The System of Reason in Kant and German Idealism," Vienna, October 1997 (Hamburg: Felix Meiner, forthcoming).

but a subjective peculiarity of human cognition, a thought of heuristic value for us in our scientific inquiry but of no other theoretical validity. Precisely because it is only *"the peculiar constitution of my cognitive faculties"* that determines "that I cannot judge otherwise of [organisms] and their generation except by thinking for them a cause that acts in accordance with intentions," I cannot ascribe any "objective reality" to this concept, but can only use it as a "principle" or "maxim" for reflective judgment (*CJ*, §75, 5:398).

Thus Kant argues that science and morality point us to the same concept, the concept of an intelligent author of the laws of both nature and morality and of their compatibility, and that it is thus not merely intelligible but inevitable for us to conceive of nature as expressing an intention in regard to our moral end if not as itself the source of that intention. At the same time, Kant stresses that the same restriction on the validity of this idea arises on both theoretical and practical grounds: the validity of the idea of such an author introduced as a precondition of understanding organisms is limited to us because the problem in understanding organisms arises from what may only be our own limit in the first place; and the necessity of introducing such an idea as a precondition of the rationality of moral conduct can never give rise to a theoretical argument at all, but only to a postulate valid from a practical point of view. Thus, the idea of the intentionality expressed in nature is inevitable for us, but valid only as a heuristic principle and practical postulate.

In summing up the "Analytic of Teleological Judgment," Kant gives an extraordinary argument in confirmation of the merely regulative and heuristic status of teleological judgment:

> In order to avoid all suspicion of presuming to mix up among our cognitive grounds something that does not belong to physics at all, namely a supernatural cause, one speaks about nature in teleology as if the purposiveness in it were intentional, but in such a way that one ascribes this intention to nature, i.e., to matter; by which means (since here there can be no misunderstanding, since nobody would ascribe intention in its proper sense to a lifeless stuff) one will indicate that this word here signifies only a principle of the reflective, not of the determinant power of judgment. . . . Hence in teleology, so far as it is applied to

physics, one speaks quite rightly of the wisdom, the economy, the foresight, the beneficence of nature, without thereby making an intelligent being out of it (for that would be absurd); but also without daring to set above it as its master craftsman another, intelligent being, since this would be extravagant. (*CJ*, §68, 5:383)

Here Kant claims, at least insofar as nature is identified with physical matter, that it is self-evident that it cannot harbor any intentions at all, and therefore that it is self-evident that any talk of the intentions of nature must be regulative and heuristic rather than constitutive. He takes this to apply to the idea of a supersensible cause of nature as well. This almost suggests that his lengthy argument in both the preceding and succeeding sections of the "Critique of Teleological Judgment" should be unnecessary: it should be self-evident that any talk of intentions either in or for nature, other than our own, is figurative, of heuristic value for either scientific or moral purposes, but of no theoretical force. Thus he seems to argue that for both scientific and moral reasons it is inevitable that we conceive of nature as manifesting intentionality but at the same time equally self-evident that this conception is figurative rather than literal, reflective rather than constitutive.

3. In the final stages of the *Opus postumum*, his last preserved writing, Kant goes even further in presenting whatever intentionality we might find in either nature or its supersensible ground as a reflection of our own intentionality. In the Seventh and First Fascicles (folders) of the *Opus postumum*, apparently the last two sets of these notes to be written, Kant left behind the attempt to discover the full extent of synthetic *a priori* principles in a science of both inorganic and organic nature that had occupied him in the earlier fascicles, and instead focused on the relation of the ideas of both nature and God to human reason. In the Seventh Fascicle, he devoted much of his effort to describing the idea of God as an idea that we create for ourselves in order to express the authority over all of our natural inclinations and desires that we ourselves give to the categorical imperative. A statement like this is typical:

The categorical imperative represents all human duties as divine commands: not historically, as if [God] had ever issued certain orders to man, but as reason [presents] them through the supreme power of the categorical imperative, in the same manner as a divine person can rigorously command submission to himself.[16]

Kant's idea seems to be that we assign the origin of the moral law to a figure other than ourselves in order to express the distinction between mere inclination and reason within ourselves, and we characterize this other figure as divine in order to represent the authority of the fundamental law of reason over our inclinations; but on reflection, we are well aware that the source of moral law is actually our own reason and that the authority of reason over mere inclination is self-created. Thus he also writes that "The categorical imperative does not presuppose a highest commanding substance outside me, but lies within my own reason,"[17] and that the idea of God is only an "ideal, which we create for ourselves, of a substance," just in order to represent "the imperative . . . as governing and absolutely commanding."[18] Thus "There is a God in moral-practical reason, that is, in the idea of the relation of man to right and duty. But not as a being outside man."[19] The idea of God is only a projection of our own capacity for giving ourselves an authoritative moral law.

In the final folder of the *Opus postumum* (confusingly labeled the First Fascicle because, as the last to be written, it was apparently left on top of the pile of his manuscript), Kant appropriates the traditional Wolffian division of the subjects of special metaphysics into God, the world, and the soul of man for the numerous drafts of a title page for his proposed work.[20] But unlike Wolff, who saw both the world and man as depending on God, or Spinoza, who saw material and thinking substance as just two different modes of the appearance of God, Kant sees both the world and

---

16 *Opus postumum*, VIIth Fascicle, sheet V, p. 2, 22:51–52; translation from Eckart Förster, ed., *Immanuel Kant: Opus postumum* (Cambridge: Cambridge University Press, 1993), pp. 211–12.

17 *Opus postumum*, VIIth Fascicle, sheet V, p. 3, 22:56; Förster, p. 214.

18 *Opus postumum*, VIIth Fascicle, sheet X, p. 4, 22:130; Förster, p. 209.

19 *Opus postumum*, VIIth Fascicle, sheet V, p. 4, 22:60; Förster, p. 217.

20 E.g., *Opus postumum*, Ist Fascicle, sheet II, p. 4, 21:14; Förster, p. 229; sheet III, p. 3, 21:32; Förster, p. 235; and sheet III, p. 4, 21:34; Förster, p. 237.

God as products of "the spirit of man which thinks both."[21] We
have already seen what he means by saying this about God. By
saying this about the world, he seems to have two things in mind.
First, he stresses throughout the *Opus postumum* that the unity of
experience from a theoretical point of view – the unity of space,
time, and the entire system of forces within them – is the product
of human thought in the sense of depending upon *a priori* principles furnished by us.[22] But second, in the First Fascicle he also
means that the idea of the world as an arena hospitable to our own
action is also, ultimately, a product of our own thought, because
"the categorical imperative . . . commands for nature freedom under laws."[23] Kant explicates this thought in a passage like this:

> God and the world are ideas of moral-practical and technical-
> practical reason, founded on sensible representation . . . both to-
> gether in one system, however, and related to each other under
> one principle, not substances outside my thought, but rather the
> thought through which we ourselves make these objects (through
> synthetic *a priori* cognitions from concepts) and, subjectively, are
> self-creators of the objects thought.[24]

Now, it might seem natural to read this to say that God and the
world are ideas of moral-practical and technical-practical reason
respectively, that is, to interpret the idea of God as the personifica-
tion of our own categorical imperative and the idea of the world
as the domain of causal laws, knowledge of which permits us to
formulate technical hypothetical imperatives. But Kant says that
the two are to be taken "together in one system," implying that
the idea of the world is an idea of both moral-practical and technical-practical reason, that is, that we must impose upon it both
the idea of natural laws necessary for the use of technical imperatives and also the idea that it is a domain hospitable to the realization of the ultimate object of our self-imposed morality, a realm
compatible with the realization of the highest good. In this way,

---

[21] *Opus postumum*, Ist Fascicle, sheet III, p. 1, 21:29; Förster, p. 233.
[22] Relevant texts are too numerous to cite, but just to pick one virtually at ran-
dom, see Xth Fascicle, sheet IV, p. 1, 22:329–30; Förster, p. 106.
[23] *Opus postumum*, Ist Fascicle, sheet II, p. 3, 21:21; Förster, p. 227.
[24] *Opus postumum*, Ist Fascicle, sheet II, p. 3, 21:21; Förster, p. 228, modified.

we would gain just as much right to talk of the intentions of the world with regard to our realization of moral perfection and happiness through our own freedom as we would to talk of God's intentions for us, because in fact both the world and God are projections of ourself and our own intentions.

4. The *Opus postumum* clearly manifests Kant's loss of organizational powers but is not a lapse into senility or second childhood and a surrender of his lifelong beliefs. In spite of what some of the passages cited may suggest, the final stages of the *Opus postumum* are actually, among other things, an extended polemic against the nascent absolute idealism represented for Kant by the young Friedrich Schelling.[25] So Kant does not mean that we literally produce the world out of our own heads, thus literally imbuing it with our own intentions. Even in the passage last quoted, he implies that we do not literally produce the world out of our own minds by parenthetically stating that "we ourselves make these objects (through synthetic *a priori* cognitions from concepts)"; he does not say that we make the *intuitions* necessary to have knowledge of the world ourself, so his view presumably remains his lifelong view that we make a unified *representation* of the world by using self-given concepts and principles to impose a coherent order on intuitions that are not entirely self-produced. This naturally raises the question, What if anything could Kant have meant (to be sure, nearly two decades earlier), beyond the postulate that we must at least believe that nature is compatible with the realization of our obligatory end, by ascribing what must be our own intentions for moral perfection and happiness to nature?

We saw from our last citation from the *Critique of Judgment* (§68, 5:283) that Kant takes the ascription of any actual intentions to nature to be self-evidently paradoxical and for that very reason a way of manifesting that such an ascription must be regulative rather than constitutive. Why then should he even have bothered to say, in the Third Proposition, that nature intends us to use our freedom to achieve our moral perfection and happiness rather than merely saying that nature must be compatible with the realization of these

[25] See "The Unity of Nature and Freedom," final section.

goals? Perhaps an answer is suggested by Kant's approach to the idea of God in the *Opus postumum*. As we have seen, Kant's final view of God is that we personify our own capacity to give ourselves moral law through reason in order to express the distinctness of reason from other aspects of ourselves and its authority over other possible motives to action in ourselves: it is *as if* the commands of reason were divine in comparison to our other impulses to act, which are not. Perhaps Kant simply meant to convey the authority of the objective of our moral perfection and happiness over our other inclinations by ascribing the intention that we use our freedom to achieve this dual goal to nature – or maybe "Nature" – rather than ourselves, to remind us that this conjoint goal is not in fact the one that always immediately occurs to us but is at least sometimes one that we must represent as if it were set over us.

This might seem conceivable in the case of virtue but paradoxical when it comes to happiness: while it may seem coherent to say that we can represent the authority of the categorical imperative over our merely natural inclinations by conceiving of the moral law as a divine command, it might appear self-contradictory to say that we can represent the authority of the objective of the highest good by saying it is nature's intention for us. Isn't that just to say that we represent nature as having authority over our natural inclination to happiness? But here one must recall that the happiness mandated as our object by the concept of the highest good is not in fact the immediate object of our inclinations. As we saw from Kant's reply to Garve, the happiness included in the highest good is the unselfish happiness constituted by the fulfillment of the permissible ends of all, not merely oneself, and this is an objective that must be conceived of as distinct from and authoritative over one's own inclinations. Indeed, as the *Groundwork for the Metaphysics of Morals* had already made clear with its example of the gouty man who might prefer the immediate pleasure of a drink or some rich food to his own long-range comfort (4:399), even one's own true happiness is not necessarily the immediate object of one's inclinations but is instead a rational goal that must be represented as distinct from and authoritative over one's momentary inclinations. Writing the essay on history at almost the same time as the *Groundwork*, but in a more figurative style fit for a wider expected audience, Kant may have meant the image of nature's intentions for us precisely to convey the authority enjoyed by the goals of moral perfection, permissible happiness for self and for all, and permissible happiness as achieved through virtue over mere inclinations – the mere inclinations that might previously have been taken by less philosophical historians to be the moving forces of human history.

Chapter 12

Nature, Morality, and the Possibility of Peace

This chapter will address two questions: (1) Does Kant's tract *Toward Perpetual Peace* (1795) present the view, which could also seem to be suggested by his earlier essay *Idea for a Universal History from a Cosmopolitan Point of View* (1784), that the cosmopolitan state of international peace, although required by morality, can be expected to be brought about entirely by natural processes, specifically through the exercise of human prudence as a natural phenomenon and a natural response to the lessons of human history? Or does *Perpetual Peace* argue that world peace can be achieved only by a free and morally motivated exercise of human will, which must be seen as being compatible with the natural course of history but which cannot itself be considered a merely natural phenomenon? (2) Whether Kant's position in *Perpetual Peace* is that the natural history of humankind might itself bring about perpetual peace, or is rather the more cautious view that the history of human nature is merely compatible with the achievement of perpetual peace but that this achievement can only be accomplished through a moral exercise of free human will, what is the epistemological status of Kant's claim about the natural history of mankind? Is it (i) a constitutive principle of history as a natural science,

An earlier version of this essay was presented at the Eighth International Kant Congress in Memphis in 1995, and published in the *Proceedings* of that Congress, edited by Hoke Robinson, vol. 1, part 1 (Milwaukee: Marquette University Press, 1995), pp. 51–69.

on an epistemological par with other laws of natural science; (ii) a postulate of pure practical reason; or (iii) a regulative ideal that does not fall neatly into either of those two categories but which would nevertheless dovetail with much else in Kant's philosophy as clarified by the *Critique of Judgment*?[1]

I argue that in spite of what might seem to be evidence to the contrary in both *Universal History* and *Perpetual Peace* itself, Kant's argument in the latter work represents a definitive rejection of any claim that natural processes alone can bring about moral progress, a rejection that is entirely consistent with and indeed necessitated by the understanding of the character of freedom of the will that Kant reached in the 1790s; and at least a clarification of the epistemological status of any claim about the moral destination of history that is required by the clarification of Kant's thought about teleology in the same period. First, although, the *Universal History* and much in *Perpetual Peace* might seem to suggest that the morally requisite goal of perpetual peace can be brought about entirely by natural means, namely the famous "unsocial sociability" of human nature (*IUH*, Fourth Proposition, 8:20), not only would such a position contradict the view of human freedom in Kant's mature moral philosophy, but the first appendix to *Perpetual Peace* explicitly argues that the moral goal of peace cannot be expected to come about by merely natural means but only through the affirmation of morality by moral politicians. Thus the historiographical thesis of *Perpetual Peace* can be only the proposition that the natural history of mankind is compatible with the achievement of peace, not a claim that the history of mankind renders this achievement

---

[1] In the previously published version of this chapter, I presented *Perpetual Peace*'s regulative principle of nature's progress toward world peace as a fundamental revision of a constitutive view of nature's contribution to moral progress that I then found in *Universal History*. The work that I did for the previous chapter (which was written after this one) persuaded me that the earlier essay was already intended in the spirit of a regulative ideal, and I have revised the references to the 1784 essay in this chapter accordingly. That view of the 1784 essay was pressed upon me in Memphis by Reinhard Brandt, and had earlier been argued for in his essay "Zum 'Streit der Facultäten,'" in Reinhard Brandt and Werner Stark, eds., *Neue Autographen und Dokumente zu Kants Leben, Schriften und Vorlesungen, Kant Forschungen*, vol. 1 (Hamburg: Felix Meiner, 1987), pp. 31–78. I am happy to acknowledge Brandt's contribution here.

inevitable. This is my primary point. Second, even though *Universal History* no doubt already intended its historical tale as a regulative ideal – a concept already introduced in the *Critique of Pure Reason*, after all – Kant's later treatment of progress toward peace is both more explicit that this is the case and clearer about what this means. *Perpetual Peace* explicitly treats nature's compatibility with moral progress as neither a constitutive law of theoretical reason nor a postulate of practical reason, but as a regulative principle that is necessary to make our morally motivated efforts in behalf of cosmopolitan peace rational. Further, although *Perpetual Peace* itself may not adequately explain what such a regulative ideal actually means, Kant's other discussions of progress toward peace in the 1790s – those in *Theory and Practice* (1793), the "Doctrine of Right" in the *Metaphysics of Morals* (1797), and *An Old Question Raised Again: Is the Human Race Constantly Progressing?* (1798) – do offer a clearer view of what such an ideal actually maintains than anything Kant wrote in the 1780s. *Perpetual Peace* thus develops a view about the conditions of the possibility of human progress that Kant had long held but also refines it in precisely the ways required by the maturation of his thought in both moral philosophy and teleology in the 1790s.

I CAN PERPETUAL PEACE BE ACHIEVED BY MERELY NATURAL MECHANISMS?

Before we can answer this question a brief review of Kant's conception of the moral status of perpetual peace and of his conception of the institutions that are necessary to attain it is necessary.

It should not take much argument to establish that the duty to achieve perpetual peace is the ultimate consequence of our duty to establish and preserve the necessary conditions of right or justice. For Kant, the source of all duties is the dignity of humanity as an end in itself, which grounds the fundamental principle of morality that each human being must do what he can to preserve and promote free rational agency in both himself and others.[2] The

---

[2] I have argued for this view in Chapters 4 and 5. See also Thomas E. Hill Jr., "Humanity as an End in Itself," in his *Dignity and Practical Reason in Kant's Moral Theory* (Ithaca: Cornell University Press, 1992), pp. 38–57.

fundamental principle of duties of right or justice is the obligation to maintain the external conditions necessary in order to preserve the maximally possible free exercise of rational agency: "Right is therefore the sum of the conditions under which the choice of one can be united with the choice of another in accordance with a universal law of freedom" (*MM*, DR Introduction, §C, 6:230);[3] this principle of right is to be contrasted to the principle of specific duties of virtue, which is the requirement to adopt the end of enhancing free agency itself in both oneself and others, as well as to the general obligation of virtue, which is the duty to satisfy all of one's specific duties, whether of justice or of virtue, out of respect for the idea of duty itself.[4] Securing the maximally compossible spheres for the external exercise of free choice as required by the principle of right, or "a condition of distributive justice" (*MM*, DR, §42, 6:307),[5] requires the creation of laws to make determinate the boundaries of these spheres of free agency, or private right, and laws to enforce the preservation of these boundaries, or public right. These laws cannot be created and preserved by human beings in the state of nature, where claims to freedom in person or property are merely provisional, but only in a civil condition, or a political state with a constitution committed to the principle of right, where such claims can be made conclusive (*MM*, DR, §43, 6:311).

Now it might seem as if such a constitutional condition could be established and maintained by any group of human beings in a limited region of the globe independently of the behavior of human populations elsewhere, and in historical fact some groups of humans have obviously approximated just constitutions before others. But it is Kant's view that since all human beings live on the surface of a single globe, no part of which is entirely inaccessible from any other, the establishment of the condition of right in any one region of the globe cannot be secure until conditions of right obtain everywhere on the globe and are established and maintained in the relations among different states as well as in the relations among the individuals within a single state. "Nature has enclosed

---

[3] Translation by Mary J. Gregor, in Immanuel Kant, *The Metaphysics of Morals* (Cambridge: Cambridge University Press, 1991), p. 56.

[4] For a discussion of these distinctions, see Chapter 9.

[5] Gregor, *MM*, p. 122.

[all the nations on the earth] together within determinate limits (by the spherical shape of the place which they live in, a *globus terraqueus*). And since possession of the land, on which an inhabitant of the earth can live, can be thought only as possession of a part of a determinate whole, and so possession of that to which each of them has a right, it follows that all nations stand *originally* in a community of land," which must be transformed into a *"rightful* community of possession" (*MM*, DR, §62, 6:352)[6] by securing the necessary conditions for perpetual peace among nations as well as for civil constitutions within nations. Thus, Kant's principle of right requires that each individual act in a way compossible with the free agency of all others who might be affected by his actions; in principle, the exercise of free agency by any individual on earth may be affected by the actions of any other; so the principle of right requires the establishment of nothing less than perpetual peace among all the inhabitants of the globe.

Because the principle of right requires the preservation and maximization of conditions for the external exercise of free agency rather than the enhancement of free agency itself, Kant also holds that the duties of right admit of *external legislation* or *coercive enforcement*, through which behavior in conformity with law, thus both the establishment and maintenance of a civil condition, can be achieved through external constraints rather than internal moral motivation (*MM*, DR Introduction, 6:214, 218–19).[7] This might appear to imply that the global condition of perpetual peace could also be established and maintained through external legislation or

[6] Gregor, *MM*, p. 158.

[7] Gregor, *MM*, pp. 42, 46. I have touched upon Kant's argument for the compatibility of freedom and coercion in Chapters 7, 8, and 9. As I have suggested, the argument that Kant presents for this thesis in the Introduction to the "Doctrine of Right" is incomplete. What he says is simply that because a hindrance to freedom is wrong, a hindrance to a hindrance to freedom is right. He needs, however, to show that a hindrance to a hindrance to freedom does not itself undermine freedom, so that he does not end up with two wrongs that do not make a right. The way to show this is to show that coercive enforcement of a law does not deprive a would-be lawbreaker of his freedom in the way that the latter's breach of law would deprive his victim of freedom, because, even in committing a crime and thus bringing punishment down upon himself, a criminal exercises a freedom of choice which he does not allow his victim.

coercion independently of any explicitly moral motivation. If this is so, then it would further seem possible that this condition of peace, although required of us by the fundamental principle of morality, could in fact be brought about through natural mechanisms of merely prudential reasoning generating external legislation, which could be coercively enforced even in the absence of moral motivation in those establishing and maintaining this condition. Kant might seem to suggest such a position both in *Universal History* (see 8:18) and in his famous suggestion in *Perpetual Peace* that "the problem of setting up a state can be solved even by a nation of devils (as long as they possess understanding)" (8:366).

As many commentators have observed, the achievement of perpetual peace through the mechanism of a merely prudential response to the threats of history would legally satisfy the requirement of morality but would not suffice to earn moral merit for any of the agents of such a peace, because moral merit can be achieved only through action motivated by respect for duty itself.[8] However, consideration of both Kant's prescription of the means for achieving perpetual peace and his mature theory of the nature of human freedom will reveal less obvious problems in the assumption that perpetual peace can be achieved by merely natural mechanisms leading to external legislation. First, the institutions of cosmopolitan peace to which mankind may be led by prudential reasoning may be necessary but are not sufficient to ensure perpetual peace. Second, no matter what institutions we may be led to by prudential reasoning, we retain the freedom to pervert their naturally beneficial effects unless we make a radical commitment to the principle of morality itself.

1. Let us consider first the limits that will be inherent in the institutions of peace that Kant prescribes even if these institutions themselves can be established by the entirely natural means of merely prudential reasoning.

---

[8] See, for example, William Galston, *Kant and the Problem of History* (Chicago: University of Chicago Press, 1975), p. 240; Yirmiahu Yovel, *Kant and the Philosophy of History* (Princeton: Princeton University Press, 1980), pp. 188–89; and Harry van der Linden, *Kantian Ethics and Socialism* (Indianapolis: Hackett, 1988), p. 143.

Kant begins *Universal History* with the claim that "Whatever concept of the *freedom of the will* one may form in a metaphysical regard, its *appearances*, human actions, are like every other natural occurrence determined in accord with universal natural laws" (8:17). Considered in isolation, this statement might be taken to mean[9] that even free human decisions intentionally made from the motive of respect for duty will always appear consistent with natural laws of human behavior because even natural laws are in the last analysis creations of the human mind. But it could also mean that the motive of respect for duty and the principle of morality can play no role at all in human actions phenomenally described and yet such actions can outwardly satisfy the requirements of morality. In fact, Kant appears to have something like the latter view in mind, for he immediately proceeds to illustrate his claim with examples of the lawlike but entirely unintended consequences of human actions, cases in which in spite of the arbitrary and self-interested character of particular human decisions "individual human beings and even entire peoples . . . are led without noticing it to the aim of nature that is even unknown to them." For instance, Kant holds, although individual decisions to marry or have children may be made entirely arbitrarily, the human species nevertheless reproduces itself with great regularity.[10] The opening claim of *Universal History* thus might appear to be intended as the premise for the conclusion that there are entirely natural mechanisms that will necessarily bring about the realization and maintenance of the morally requisite goal of perpetual peace without any human intention of doing so, *a fortiori* without any morally motivated act of freely willing to bring about this result; hence Kant states that "Because the philosopher cannot presuppose any rational *aim of his own* among human beings and their play at large, there is no alternative but for him to attempt to discover a *natural*

---

[9] As Kant was later to argue in the *Critique of Practical Reason* (see especially 5: 97–98).

[10] This theme had intrigued Kant for many years, at least since his essay *The Only Possible Basis for a Proof of the Existence of God* of 1764 (see 2:111–12). Contemporary observation in countries subject to economic uncertainty such as the former Soviet Union or Italy suggests that birthrates may be more subject to the effects of individual decision making than Kant imagined.

aim in this senseless course of human affairs" (8:18). So when Kant proceeds to argue that it is the aim of nature to bring about human happiness through the development of human reason (First through Third Propositions, 8:18–19) and, in particular, to describe how natural mechanisms will lead human beings to develop the institutions that "in the end" will be "the cause of a lawful [*gesetz-mäßigen*] order in society" (Fourth Proposition, 8:20), his claim could appear to be, not to be sure that nature inevitably calls forth the emergence of *moral* motivation and reasoning in humankind that will eventually suffice for the establishment of perpetual peace, but still that natural mechanisms will eventually produce patterns of *prudential* or *self-interested* motivation and reasoning that will unwittingly suffice for the establishment and maintenance of the perpetual peace that is, of course, a moral duty.

In both *Universal History* and *Perpetual Peace*, Kant then holds that the realization of world peace requires two institutions, namely republican constitutions in particular regions – that is, civil constitutions aimed at maintaining the condition of distributive justice by representative government with a division of powers, where those exercising sovereignty are representatives rather than proprietors of the whole state and where the exercise of legislative, judicial, and executive powers is not in the hands of the same representatives – and a *federation* among these republics rather than a single world state. *Perpetual Peace* adds to this bipartite institutional scheme, described in its "definitive articles" (8:348–60), only the transitional conditions described in its "preliminary articles" (8:343–47), that is, rules for the conduct and finance of wars that need to be obeyed even in a present state of war or readiness for war in order to remove what would otherwise be permanent incitements and inducements to future war such as the desire for revenge and the need to pay off national debts. But Kant can still seem to write as if nature, operating through prudence, must inevitably, even if only eventually, force human beings to adopt local republican constitutions and then to unite these states into an international federation, and that once these institutions have been created they will then ensure the maintenance of perpetual peace: thus, in *Universal History* he says that "human beings, who are otherwise so taken with unrestricted freedom, are forced to enter into the condition of coercion [of a civil society] by need" (Fifth Proposition, 8:22), that in turn "Nature . . . through war, through the overextended and never-remitting preparation for war, . . . finally through devastations, reversals, and even total internal exhaustion of their powers drives [even the great societies and bodies of state] into that which reason could also have dictated without so much tragic experience, namely to leave behind the lawless condition of wild animals and enter into a league of nations" (Seventh Proposition, 8:24), and finally, "partly internally through the best possible arrangement of the civil constitution[s] and partly externally through a common agreement and legislation a condition is attained, which, like a civil commonwealth, can preserve itself like an *automaton*" (8:25).

(a) In spite of any suggestion of inevitability, however, whether in *Universal History* or in *Perpetual Peace*, it is clear that, even if natural tendencies to prudence could drive human beings into an international federation of republics without an explicitly moral intention, these institutions would not be able to maintain perpetual peace "like an automaton." The most obvious problem lies in the assumption that an international federation can maintain peace without an explicitly moral decision to do so on the part of its participating nations. That is, nature alone is not merely incapable of producing a morally praiseworthy motivation for the establishment of perpetual peace; it is not in fact capable of producing and maintaining perpetual peace.

Kant's reasons for preferring a world federation of republics to a single world state seem to have been fundamentally empirical. He offers what seems to be an *a priori* argument that the idea of a world state is self-contradictory, because it would require two incompatible levels of sovereignty, the single sovereignty of a world state and the several sovereignties of individual states, which would be both subjects in relation to the world sovereign yet superiors in relation to their own subjects. This argument obviously presupposes that "peoples are to constitute different states and not be melted together into a single state," and thus that a world state would have to be added to regional states rather than preceding or replacing them (*PP*, 8:354). This presupposition, however, seems to be grounded in the empirical assumption that civil constitutions naturally arise in confined regions, and that no one of them could be extended to the whole globe without unjust conquest of other peoples already maintaining local conditions of right instead of, for instance, voluntary union. More explicitly, Kant makes the further empirical claim that, even if such a state could lawfully come into existence, a world state could not be expected to *maintain* global justice and thus fulfill our duty of securing the conditions of perpetual peace, "for with the increased domain of the regime the laws progressively lose their impact, and a soulless despotism, after rooting out the seeds of goodness, finally lapses into anarchy" (8:367). Thus Kant apparently takes it to be a law of nature that just laws could not be maintained by a single state extending over the whole globe, for even a just state naturally lapses into despotism and then anarchy when it gets too big.[11] But if there is no single sovereign in a world federation and thus, presumably, no single overwhelming force maintained within it that is capable of coercively enforcing external legislation that could suffice to enforce distributive justice throughout the globe, it is only natural to suppose that the world federation is going to have to rely upon internal incentives, that is, the moral motivation of its member states, in order to achieve its goal of perpetual peace. Perhaps Kant thought that in a world federation beneficial relations for trade and cultural exchange would arise that would have such a strong appeal to prudence as to preclude further wars, but he certainly does not argue this. Thus it would seem that even if an international federation is a necessary condition for maintaining world peace – perhaps it would offer the only forum where inevitable disputes over trade or territory could be sure to be discussed – it would hardly seem to be a sufficient condition for maintaining peace. So even if the course of nature would inevitably yield a world federation, human history would at most be compatible with the possibility of perpetual peace, but not inevitably produce it.

(b) That an international federation without overwhelming power is not sufficient to guarantee perpetual peace should be clear. What may be less clear is that the establishment of republican constitutions within individual states may also be necessary

[11] Perhaps Kant had the image of the decline and fall of the Roman Empire in mind.

but is certainly not sufficient to ensure perpetual peace unless these states are also governed by explicitly moral intentions. Yet precisely this may be the ultimate point of *Perpetual Peace*. On first glance, it might seem as if *Perpetual Peace* was intended to advance beyond *Universal History* primarily by clarifying what it means for the internal civil constitution of the member states of the world federation to be *republican*. With that clarification (and the addition of the preliminary articles for transition to peace) added, Kant's thesis might still appear to be that individual states must ultimately be driven to adopt republican constitutions by natural necessity, and that when all states have both adopted such constitutions and formed a world federation, these institutions will make the preservation of peace inevitable. However, not only does reflection on Kant's conception of a republican constitution make clear that republics will not be forced to maintain perpetual peace by natural necessity, but only by means of a moral choice on the part of the governors; Kant's appendices to *Perpetual Peace*, in which he argues that both individual republics and the world federation must be ruled not by "political moralists" but by "moral politicians" who have chosen to govern by principles that can be publicly avowed rather than kept secret, also show that he was aware of this fact and indeed may well have written *Perpetual Peace* primarily to reject any interpretation of his earlier work as suggesting that perpetual peace might be attained through anything less than an intentional moral decision on the part of all governors of mankind to comply with our ultimate duty of justice. In any case, although this may not be clear even in its own earlier sections, *Perpetual Peace* ultimately rejects any suggestion that either the internal republican constitution of states or their external federation could operate "like an automaton" to ensure world peace.

There are two fundamental elements to Kant's theory of republican government in *Perpetual Peace*: an account of the moral principles to which a civil constitution must be committed and an account of the structure of governance through which such moral principles are best realized. The moral commitments of a republican constitution, which Kant had already stated in similar fashion two years earlier in *Theory and Practice*, are "the principles of the *freedom* of the members of a society (as human beings), . . . of the *dependence* of all on a single common legislation (as subjects), and ... a constitution founded on the law of the *equality* of all (as citizens of the state)" (*PP*, 8:349–50; cf. *TP*, 8:290). These principles give expression to the moral requirement of justice that all citizens have equal standing before a single set of laws adequate to realize maximal freedom for each compatible with equal freedom for all. Such principles, Kant then holds, will best be realized by a constitution in which, first, the *form of sovereignty* or relation between the subjects or people as a whole and the concentration of power in a governing body is *representative* rather than democratic – that is, in which power is not exercised by a simple majority of all citizens, which Kant seems to suppose will inevitably degenerate into the tyranny of the majority over any minority, but rather by some subset (although not a hereditary subset) of citizens, who will be in a better position to adjudicate disputes between majorities and minorities; and in which, second, the *form of government* or the distribution of functions within the governing body is republican rather than despotic – that is, in which there is a division of powers among the governing representatives so that legislative and executive powers especially are separated, and therefore those who execute the laws will not be able to execute laws designed merely for their own advantage (*PP*, 8:351–52). Kant's conclusion, finally, is that such a constitution will lead to the avoidance of war because citizens participating in the management of their own government in these ways will not call down upon themselves the evils of war, putting their own property and lives at risk, unlike a nonrepresentative despot who can put the lives and property of his subjects at risk while continuing to enjoy unabated his own pleasures of the hunt, table, and bed (8:351).

However, while republics so conceived may well be more cautious about going to war than tyrannies because the risks of making war may be spread more widely among those making the decisions in a republic than in a tyranny, reflection not only on history but on Kant's own conception of a republican government suggests that this increased caution will by no means suffice to make the avoidance of war altogether automatic. For one thing, separation between the executive and legislative branches of the government, although it may indeed reduce many forms of injustice in a society, still leaves open the possibility that one branch (in our own recent history typically the executive branch) may undertake war (whatever euphemism is employed) without the approval of the other, in the expectation that the risk will be born by those in the other branch. Further, the fact that the legislative branch itself is supposed to function by representation rather than by the direct action of all citizens, although it might protect minorities in numerous ways, may even allow legislative approval of war to be granted with the expectation that the risk of war will fall on others than the legislators themselves. Now presumably Kant's repeated insistence that governmental offices not be hereditary[12] is meant to minimize these risks: neither legislators nor executives are supposed to be members of a particular class that is hereditarily immune from the risks of war, but instead both groups are supposed to be drawn from and return to the larger class of citizens by whom the risks of war will be born and therefore to identify with the interests of that larger class. But even with this proviso, there are ways in which those who govern can avoid some if not all of the risks of war: for instance, the maximum age for military service can be set below the minimum age for legislative or executive service, so that those who make governmental decisions will be at least personally immune from the direct risks of military service even if their fortunes or their children will not be immune from all the risks of wars. Furthermore, at least on Kant's conception of republican government, there will be persons, even if not a hereditary class of persons, who may not be guaranteed even minimal representation in the government unless those who are eligible for governmental service are moved by a universal principle of right rather than by self-interest. For Kant explicitly requires *self-sufficiency* as a condition of political participation, apparently excluding those who are socially or economically dependent on others from both suffrage and legislative, executive, or judicial service, presumably on the ground that they may be forced to vote or act as the mouthpieces of those on whom they depend rather than as autonomous agents of the general will in their own right (*TP*, 8:294–96). But he does not exclude such persons from military

---

[12] See *TP*, 8:296, and *MM*, DR General Comment following 49, §D, 6:329.

service. So again even in a Kantian republic there will be people –
indeed, history suggests, large numbers of such people – available
to bear the risks of wars voted on by others who are not themselves
at risk, even if the military service of these dependents puts the
economic well-being of their masters at some risk.

The actual history of mankind certainly suggests that even when
decision makers are averse to putting their own persons at risk –
to which, of course, because of the perceived value of military
glory and the promise of aggrandisement, they by no means always are – they are certainly not always averse to putting at risk
their workers and servants on whom their own economic well-
being may depend or even their own children. Thus, while the
republican form of government that Kant describes presumably
spreads the risks of war making among the representatives, and
might thus increase the probability of peace, it does not seem that
such a form of government by itself could make war impossible
or even always imprudent by any natural necessity. In the end, a
moral determination of the will to avoid war would have to be
added to any natural mechanisms that might only decrease the
probability of war. So just as we already saw that a global federation without an overarching sovereign may not be able to compel
peace (while a global federation with an overarching sovereign
might not be able to maintain other aspects of justice), and ultimately requires a moral rather than merely natural will for peace,
so individual republican governments also ultimately require a
moral commitment to peace and cannot be expected to attain
and maintain peace solely by mechanical means.

Now even though this conclusion would clearly be at odds
with a constitutive interpretation of Kant's conception of nature
in *Universal History* and might seem to be equally at odds with his
apparent restatement of this position in the "definitive articles" of
Perpetual Peace, it does seem to be the point of this work's appendices – which would lead one to conclude that the work must have
been intended to have a more dialectical and even ironical form
than initially seems apparent. In the first appendix, on "The Disagreement between Morals and Politics with Regard to Perpetual
Peace," Kant argues that even "the will of *all individual* human
beings to live within a lawful constitution in accordance with

principles of freedom (the *distributive* unity of the will *of all*) is not sufficient for the end" of perpetual peace, and that a "unifying cause" in the form of a powerful agent must be added to their distributive good will in order to overcome the differences among even good-willed individuals in order to transform this distributive good will – that is, individual good intentions – into a collective good will (*PP*, 8:371). But because any person or group powerful enough to accomplish this end will presumably be powerful enough to bend the distributive will of his or its subjects to a variety of ends, there will be no natural guarantee that he or it must rule for the sake of duty and justice. Only his or their *own* commitment to that end will ensure that the populace is transformed into a collective will for justice and peace. Thus Kant concludes that republican constitutions can be achieved and maintained individually and collectively only if they are established and maintained not by *political moralists* but by *moral politicians*, that is, politicians who make it their "principle that if faults are encountered in the constitution of the state or the relationship of states which could not have been avoided, then it is [their] duty, above all for heads of state, to see to it that they are improved as soon as possible and can be made suitable to natural right, as it stands as an example before us in the idea of reason" (8:372). In other words, both within any particular state as well as within any federation of states, there must be some who are more powerful than others, and they cannot be forced to bring about a condition of justice solely by natural mechanisms of prudence and self-interest, but must themselves make the decision to do so out of their own respect for morality and justice.

Kant amplifies this point in his second appendix, on the "Transcendental Concept of Public Right." This appendix stresses that political authorities must adopt public principles of government because only principles that can be publicly avowed can be presumed to be just. Kant's argument here presupposes that there is no natural bar to adopting secret and therefore unjust policies of government, and thus no natural mechanism that can compel national or international justice; nor does he claim that rulers who wish to rule only in their own behalf must keep their intentions secret, for they may in any case have enough power to compel

obedience to their unjust aims even if they are publicly acknowledged (*TP*, 8:382–83, 385). Rather, Kant's claim is that the commitment to publicity, which every principle of justice does satisfy,
must itself be a morally motivated commitment on the part of those
who govern.

2. We may now turn to the second main point of this section, which
is that this conclusion – that satisfaction of the requirements of
morality, including the requirement of justice and its limit case in
perpetual peace, can only be expected to arise from the moral will
of human beings and not from any merely natural mechanism –
is surely the only conclusion that is compatible with the position
on the freedom of the will that Kant expounded in the 1790s, above
all in the *Religion within the Boundaries of Mere Reason* (1793–94). In
Universal History, Kant might seem to have held that *natural* responses to the unsocial sociability of mankind would ultimately
compel at least outward compliance with the requirements of justice or legality if not inward moral motivation. In the *Groundwork
for the Metaphysics of Morals*, written soon after *Universal History*,
Kant did not repeat that naturalistic argument, but committed
himself to the equally problematic position that the moral law is
also the *noumenal* causal law of a rational being (*G*, 4:447, 452–53),
and thus the necessary law of our behavior insofar as we are rational beings, a thesis that left him open to the objection made famous by Henry Sidgwick a century later that if a rational agent is
necessarily a moral agent, then, by contraposition, an immoral
agent is necessarily an irrational and therefore not an imputable
agent at all.[13]

Kant did not publicly acknowledge this objection between 1785
and 1788, but his switch to the argument for the freedom of the
will on the basis of our recognition of our moral obligation through
the principle "ought implies can" in the *Critique of Practical Reason*
(5:29–31) and even more clearly in the *Religion*[14] seems intended
to avoid precisely this implication, for although *ought* implies *can*

---

[13] See "The Kantian Conception of Free Will," *Mind* 13 (1888), reprinted in *Methods of Ethics*, 7th ed. (London: Macmillan, 1907), pp. 511–16.

[14] See especially 6:47, 6:49n, 6:50, and 6:62.

it does not imply *does* and indeed always leaves open the possibility of *does not* – in other words, radical evil. Kant's mature position that compliance with the demands of morality is inevitable for us neither as natural nor as rational beings comes to clear expression in the *Religion*, for here Kant argues precisely that although we all have *natural* inclinations to goodness (6:20, 34–35, 44) as well as an inevitable consciousness of the *moral* law (6:36), we nevertheless have a radical and inscrutable capacity to choose *either* good or evil (6:44). The point of Kant's argument in *Religion* is not just that the outward legality of actions is not a proof of virtuous motivation, or that beneficent inclinations are not sufficient to guarantee morally correct action, although he does make both of these points; his deepest claim is that even if our inclinations are naturally good and we are all unavoidably aware of the moral law, we still always have the power to choose either to accept the moral law and thereby make morally good use of our naturally good inclinations or to choose to exempt ourselves from the moral law and thereby to pervert even our naturally good inclinations. As Kant says,

> The ground of . . . evil cannot be placed, as is usually done, in the *sensibility* of the human being and the inclinations that naturally arise from that. For not only do these have no direct relation to evil (rather . . . they give opportunity for virtue) . . . rather, the propensity to evil . . . insofar as it concerns the morality of the subject, is encountered in him as a freely acting being. (*Rel*, 6:34–55)

And his view is that the choice made by any individual, whether to comply with both the inclination of nature and the demand of morality, or to subvert both of these and be evil, is free, but the decision to go one way rather than the other is always inexplicable or inscrutable.

What this implies for perpetual peace, however, must be clear. No matter what opportunities for peace natural conditions offer, and no matter how readily reason may discern what institutions are necessary to achieve and preserve peace, it is as much in the power of human beings to subvert the opportunity for peace as to realize it. Even prudence itself cannot force us to behave either legally or virtuously, since even at its best prudence is merely the source of natural inclinations to goodness that we can pervert by radical evil if we so choose. Only the inscrutable choice to be virtuous, to which nature may incline but can never force us, can actually ensure that the natural opportunities for perpetual peace will be realized.

II HISTORICAL PROGRESS AS A REGULATIVE IDEAL

In the end, then, we see that Kant's conclusion could only be that nature may afford us mechanisms that we can use to advance toward our moral goal of global justice, but that these mechanisms cannot themselves guarantee the attainment of this goal unless they are supplemented by morally motivated acts of human will. But this recognition, though perhaps the most important, is not the only clarification of Kant's view of history offered in *Perpetual Peace*. In the First Supplement to the Definitive Articles of *Perpetual Peace*, where Kant reconsiders the issue of a "Guarantee of Perpetual Peace" (8:360), two other clarifications are also to be found. On the one hand, Kant actually amplifies his earlier descriptions of natural mechanisms that might work toward peace; on the other hand, Kant now makes it clearer than ever before that his account of the natural progress of mankind toward peace is to be understood as a regulative principle rather than anything else, though we may still have to turn to other works to discover precisely what this implies.

In *Perpetual Peace*, Kant does not merely repeat his earlier argument that the "unsocial sociability" that nature has implanted in us will drive us to war with each other but then teaches us the costs of war, which we will then try to avoid by instituting republican constitutions within our states and a federation among our states (8:365–67). In addition, he now specifies two further natural mechanisms that will specifically dispose us to institute the kind of international federation that is necessary for achieving and maintaining perpetual peace. These are, first, nature's creation of differences in *language* and *religion* among human beings, which lead them to form a multiplicity of independent sovereign states that can be federated with each other in a league of nations but not superseded by a single world state, which would inevitably degenerate into tyranny or anarchy (8:367); and, second, nature's creation of both a need for and a *spirit of commerce*, which will make the numerically distinct states produced by these naturally occurring linguistic and religious differences see that there is ultimately more benefit in federation than in war (8:368).

While in this way substantively expanding his earlier catalog of the natural mechanisms for world peace, however, Kant now also clarifies the epistemological status of his historiography by explicitly stating that we have a *practical* rather than *theoretical* conception of the factors naturally disposing mankind toward peace and by at least strongly if not unequivocally suggesting that this practical conception is in turn a *regulative principle* rather than a *postulate of pure practical reason*.[15] To be sure, Kant begins this dis-

---

[15] It will come as no surprise that a full range of positions on the issue of whether Kant changes from a constitutive to a regulative interpretation of his historiography has been adopted. Several writers, hold, as I previously did, that Kant makes a fundamental shift between 1784 and 1795 from a constitutive to a regulative interpretation of his historical teleology; Yirmiahu Yovel, for instance, holds that the dogmatic view of *Universal History* was already inconsistent with the mechanistic natural science of the *Critique of Pure Reason*, but that Kant did not see the possibility of a regulative interpretation of any form of teleology until the *Critique of Judgment*, after which, of course, he had to revise the historiography of *Universal History* (*Kant and the Philosophy of History*, pp. 154–57). Others have held not only that the earlier essay contained a dogmatic teleology but even that Kant never surrendered it, even though it is clearly inconsistent with his view of autonomy; thus F. C. Beiser, although he does not explicitly mention *Perpetual Peace*, holds that the Kant's "resort to Providence" in *Theory and Practice* as well as the theory of practical postulates in the second *Critique* constitutes "a betrayal of the heart of his moral philosophy, the principle of autonomy," which "requires that we make our own history" (*Enlightenment, Revolution and Romanticism: The Genesis of Modern German Political Thought* [Cambridge, Mass.: Harvard University Press, 1992], pp. 54–55). Leslie A. Mulholland also does not seem to think that there is much difference between Kant's "speculative account of history" in *Universal History* and *Perpetual Peace*, even though, he also seems to think, Kant never supposed that there was much empirical evidence for it, but rather always held that it is "Only the moral interest stemming from the categorical command to eliminate war [that] justifies anyone in accepting the speculation" ("Kant on War and International Justice,"

cussion by saying that "That which affords this *pledge* (guarantee) is nothing less that the great artist *Nature* . . . from whose mechanical course visible purposiveness shines forth." But he quickly adopts a very different tone, and says that we call this

> purposiveness in the course of the world, as the deep-seated wisdom of a higher cause directed toward the objective final end of the human race . . . *providence* . . . which, to be sure, we do not actually *cognize* in these artifices of nature, or even *infer* from them, but which (as in all relation of the form of things to ends in general) we can and must only *add in thought*, in order to make for ourselves a concept of its possibility in accord with the analogies of human artistic production, whose relationship and harmony with the (moral) end which reason immediately prescribes that we represent is an *idea*, which is certainly excessive [*überschwenglich*] in a *theoretical* context, but in a practical context (e.g., in regard to the concept of the duty *of perpetual peace* to use every mechanism of nature thereto) is dogmatic and well grounded as far as its reality is concerned. (8:360–62)

Here Kant makes it clear not only that he rejects any claim that natural mechanisms make perpetual peace inevitable as an indisputable result of natural science and accepts only the more restricted proposition that nature is at least compatible with the achievement of global justice because it affords us mechanisms that can be exploited by moral politicians with a commitment to the end of justice to achieve that end in the same spirit. He also makes it explicit that even this more qualified proposition cannot be considered as an ordinary theoretical claim of natural science but must be regarded as an idea of another sort.

Kant-Studien 78 (1987): 25–41, at p. 39). Finally, as I have previously mentioned, Reinhard Brandt holds that Kant *already* treated his historical teleology as regulative in 1784: on his view, *Universal History*, unlike Kant's anthropology lectures, "makes no pretense to categorical-conceptual cognition," but rather puts forth its ideas of history "as regulative signs for the practice of writing history and as political advice for the politics of rulers" ("Zum 'Streit der Fakultäten,'" pp. 42–43). I am now inclined to consider this the most plausible view, although it should be noted, to be sure, that the term "Idea" occurs explicitly only in the full title of *Universal History*, not in the body of the text as it does in *Perpetual Peace*.

But what sort of nontheoretical idea is this thought supposed to be? Kant's final remark that the idea of nature's purposiveness for peace is "dogmatic" with regard to the concept of perpetual peace might suggest that we should simply classify the idea as a postulate of practical reason rather than an idea of theoretical reason, thus associating the thought of perpetual peace with the practical postulates of freedom, God, and immortality as propounded in the *Critique of Practical Reason*. But there are several reasons why this would not be the best way to interpret Kant's remark. First, as I have earlier argued, we must be cautious in our interpretation of the intended force of the postulates of pure practical reason themselves.[16] Further, the postulates of God and immortality, and even that of freedom, are ideas of *noumenal* realities that may have effects in the phenomenal world of nature but are not ideas of conditions that are immediately manifested in it, whereas the claim that nature affords us mechanisms and opportunities for the achievement of perpetual peace is certainly a claim about phenomenal nature, that is, about what may actually happen within human history rather than behind or beyond it. For that reason, it would seem misleading to associate the idea of historical progress with nonnatural ideas like those of God or immortality. Finally, Kant's suggestion that there is an analogy between the idea of "human artistic production" and the history of progress and his parenthetical remark that we should conceive of this history of progress in the same way as we conceive "all relation of the form of things to ends in general" unmistakably suggest that we are to conceive of this teleology as we are directed to conceive of natural and artistic form in the *Critique of Judgment* rather than as we are directed to conceive of God and immortality in the *Critique of Practical Reason* – in other words, as a regulative principle guiding our activity in the phenomenal world, although in this case to be sure a regulative principle for political action rather than for aesthetic judgment or scientific inquiry, and not as a postulation of pure reason about noumenal realities. Moreover, such a suggestion is entirely consistent with Kant's separation of regulative ideas from the transcendent ideas of reason, with which they were orig-

---

[16] See Chapter 10.

inally associated in the *Critique of Pure Reason*, and their reassign-
ment to a faculty of reflective judgment with explicitly empirical
application, which represents one of the most fundamental inno-
vations of the *Critique of Judgment*.[17]

Indeed, one striking passage in the *Religion* suggests that morality in general would be better served by regulative principles than
by any other form of positing the realization of its goals. Kant
writes:

> In general, if we were to limit our judgment to the *regulative* pos-
> sible practical use of [practical] principles rather than *constitu-
> tive* principles of the cognition of supersensible objects, insight
> into which is in any case impossible for us, human wisdom
> would be better off in a great many ways, and there would no
> breeding of putative knowledge about that of which we funda-
> mentally know nothing . . . [which is] ultimately to the . . . dis-
> advantage of morality. (*Rel*, 6:71n)

I take it that Kant's point here is precisely that if we dogmatically
assume moral progress, whether in the individual development
of virtue or the realization of cosmopolitan peace, to be *guaranteed*,
the net result will only be that we will relax our own efforts in behalf of what duty requires of us, thus making the fulfillment of our
duty less rather than more likely. This could itself be evidence that
Kant intended the interpretation of his whole theory of practical
postulates in a regulative rather than practical-dogmatic mode.

Exactly what sort of force is to be assigned to regulative principles is one of the most difficult and least discussed issues in the
interpretation of the *Critique of Judgment* itself, so these allusions
to that vexed work tell us more about how we are not to understand the historiography of progress than about how we are to
understand it.[18] However, several passages on the possibility of
progress toward peace in Kant's other writings of the 1790s may

[17] See my "Reason and Reflective Judgment: Kant on the Significance of Systematicity," *Nous* 24 (1990): 17–43.

[18] For some general discussion of the nature of regulative principles, see my "Los
principios del juicio reflexivo" (The principles of reflective judgment), *Diánoia:
Anuario de Filosofía* 17 (1996): 1–59.

suggest how we are to understand the regulative principle of progress and perhaps even regulative principles in general.

What would seem to be the most difficult question about the
theory of regulative principles propounded in the introductions
to the *Critique of Judgment* and in its "Critique of Teleological Judgment" is this: why do we need to think of something like the systematic organization of concepts in a scientific theory or of parts
in an organism as *guaranteed* or *highly probable* as opposed to
merely *possible* when we have compelling reasons for seeking to
discover such systematicity that will make our efforts rational as
long as success is *at least* possible? In several passages, both in *Theory and Practice* two years before *Perpetual Peace* and in the *Metaphysics of Morals* two years later, Kant suggests that in the case in
which a goal is a duty all that we need to make our pursuit of it
rational is indeed that it *not be demonstrably impossible*. In *Theory
and Practice*, Kant writes:

> In tragic view not only of the evil that burdens the human race
> from natural causes but even more that which human beings do
> to each other, the spirit is yet elevated by the prospect that it can
> be better in the future: and indeed with unselfish good will,
> when we will long be in our own graves and not harvest the
> fruits which we have in part sown ourselves. Empirical evidence
> against the success of these resolves undertaken on hope does
> not count for anything here. For [the thought] that that which
> has not yet succeeded might on that account never succeed does
> not justify surrendering even a pragmatic or technical aim (like,
> e.g., flights with aerostatic balloons); even less would it justify
> surrendering a moral aim, as long as its achievement is not
> demonstrably impossible. Beyond that, many proofs may be
> given that the human race as a whole has made more progress
> toward self-improvement in our age than in all preceding ones.
> (*TP*, 8:309–10)

This suggests that when a goal is of clear value, even for merely
technical reasons, that is, as means to an end desired for reasons
of prudence or happiness, but of course even more so when it is
morally valuable and requisite, then all that is needed to make our
efforts in its behalf entirely rational is proof that reaching it is not

impossible: if the goal is of sufficient value, the benefits of attaining it will outweigh the costs of failing to reach it as long as such failure itself is not guaranteed. Kant makes a similar point in the conclusion of the "Doctrine of Right":

> If someone cannot prove that a thing is, he may try to prove that it is not. If (as often happens), he cannot succeed in either, he can still ask whether he has any *interest* in assuming the one or the other (as an hypothesis), either from a theoretical or from a practical point of view. An assumption is adopted from a theoretical point of view in order merely to explain a certain phenomenon. . . . An assumption is adopted from a practical point of view in order to achieve a certain end, which may be either a *pragmatic* (merely technical end) or a *moral* end, that is, an end the maxim to adopt which is itself a duty. – Now it is self-evident that what is here made our duty is not the *assumption* (*suppositio*) that this end can be realized, which is a merely theoretical and also problematic judgment, for that (to believe something) yields no obligation; rather, what is incumbent on us as a duty is to act in accordance with the idea of that end, even if there is not the least theoretical probability that it can be achieved, as long as its impossibility cannot be demonstrated either. (*MM*, DR, §62, 6:354)[19]

Again, Kant's claim is that if the achievement of an end is a duty, as he goes on to say the avoidance of war is, then all that is needed to make the pursuit of that end rational is not a guarantee that it can be achieved but a proof that it is not impossible to achieve it.[20] Obviously the empirical history of mankind, even if depressing rather than encouraging, can offer no demonstration of the impossibility of attaining perpetual peace, that is, the necessity of failure for our efforts in its behalf, because experience cannot prove any necessity at all. By contrast, even merely empirical evidence that nature offers mechanisms that can be exploited by a virtuous will to yield peace, and that nature is in this sense compatible with

---

[19] Gregor, *MM*, p. 160 (translation modified).

[20] As I argued in Chapter 10, much of Kant's argument for the postulates of pure practical reason does seem to assume a stronger conception of the conditions of the possibility of rational conduct than this.

the demands of morality, will be more than enough to make the pursuit of peace rational.

In the last sentence of the citation from *Theory and Practice*, however, Kant does seem to presuppose that there is value in empirical evidence that progress toward the moral end of peace is not merely *not impossible* but also *probable* and even *more probable* than ever before; and in his last published comments on progress toward peace, in the second essay of *The Conflict of the Faculties* on *An Old Question Raised Again: Is the Human Race Constantly Progressing?*, Kant also stresses that there is value not only in the proof that a desired goal is not impossible but also in empirical evidence that it is actually probable. In this essay, he asserts that "There must be some experience in the human race which, as an event, points to the disposition and capacity of the human race to be the *cause* of its own advance toward the better" (7:84),[21] and then argues that the French Revolution provides such evidence – not, it should be noted, because of the intentions of its participants, who may have been motivated by self-interest, which as we have now seen is not sufficient to guarantee progress toward peace, but because of the response of all disinterested spectators, such as those in Kant's own Germany, who manifest "such a universal yet disinterested sympathy for the players on one side against those on the other, even at the risk that this partiality could become very disadvantageous for them if discovered" (7:85).[22] Such a response, Kant argues, provides evidence for the possibility of progress toward republicanism and peace and a prediction of its eventual attainment which "*is not to be forgotten*, because it has revealed a tendency and faculty in human nature for improvement . . . which nature and freedom alone, united in the human race in conformity with inner principles of right . . . could have promised" (7:88).[23]

---

[21] Translation by Mary J. Gregor in *The Conflict of the Faculties* (New York: Abaris, 1979), p. 151.

[22] Ibid., p. 153.

[23] Ibid., p. 159. A number of authors have stressed that it is the response of the spectators of rather than the participants in the French Revolution that provides the crucial evidence of the possibility of progress; see Reinhard Brandt,

The last of these remarks confirms *Perpetual Peace*'s most important point, implying again that, although nature alone cannot bring about perpetual peace, it nevertheless has made human nature compatible with the moral decision of the human will. But how should we understand this essay's interest in adding empirical evidence of the possibility of progress toward peace to the – alleged if not actually provided – proof that it is not impossible, which is all that is required in *Theory and Practice* and the "Doctrine of Right"? Here I believe that we can only conjecture that in these works, as in so many of his other works from the *Critique of Judgment* on, Kant is responding to the mixed nature of human beings and attempting to bridge the gulf between the realms of nature and of freedom. I have elsewhere defended the view on which the deepest motivation of that inaugural work of the 1790s is to provide, in the experience of both natural beauty and natural organization, palpable representations of human freedom as the ultimate end of the existence of nature.[24] Just as in the third *Critique* Kant seems to have recognized that the mixed nature of human beings requires both rational and sensible representation

"Revolution und Fortschritt im Spätwerk Kants," in Hans Erich Bödeker and Ulrich Hermann, eds., *Aufklärung als Politisierung – Politisierung der Aufklärung* (Hamburg: Felix Meiner, 1987), pp. 209–21, at pp. 212–13; Heiner F. Klemme, in the introduction to his edition of Kant, *Über den Gemeinspruch . . . /Zum ewigen Frieden* (Hamburg: Felix Meiner, 1992), pp. xlv–xlvii; and Peter F. Nicholson, "Kant, Revolutions and History," in Howard L. Williams, ed., *Essays on Kant's Political Philosophy* (Chicago: University of Chicago Press, 1992), pp. 249–68, at pp. 260–63. The reason for emphasizing the spectators rather than participants is not, as Klemme and Nicholson (p. 261) suggest, that their approval shows the moral disposition to republicanism is universal and not just restricted to a certain group of Frenchmen; the point is rather, as Brandt and Nicholson (p. 263) suggest, that the response of the spectators is clearly disinterested and thus morally motivated in a way that the activities of the participants need not be or, indeed, given Kant's proscription of rebellion, cannot have been; but the significance of this point can be appreciated only once we have seen, as I have argued in this chapter, that it is not Kant's view in the 1790s that mere nature can produce perpetual peace through entirely self-interested behavior, but rather that the mechanisms for peace that nature affords will only lead to peace if they are put to that end by virtuous motivation.

[24] See my *Kant and the Experience of Freedom* (Cambridge: Cambridge University Press, 1993), especially the introduction and chs. 1 and 3.

of the possibility of freedom, so in his political writings of the 1790s, at least when taken together, he seems to have recognized that although the rational nature of human beings requires only a proof that the attainment of perpetual peace, which is its duty, is not impossible, the sensible nature of human beings also requires to be encouraged and fortified by some palpable evidence that such progress is actually probable.[25] In other words, Kant himself is not confused about what is an appropriate canon of rationality, sometimes suggesting that all that reason requires to motivate its pursuit of duty is proof that the fulfillment of duty is not impossible, yet at other times suggesting that reason requires more encouragement than that; rather, he recognized that human beings are complex, having not only a rational nature, for which proof that it is not impossible to do what they ought is enough to make attempting to do so rational, but also a sensible nature, which requires the encouragement of palpable and positive evidence of progress.

Considering the whole body of Kant's writings about perpetual peace in the 1790s, then, we find confirmation of two of the most fundamental conclusions of his most mature moral philosophy and moral anthropology: the view that virtue is never an inevitability but always a possibility for human beings with inscrutable freedom of the will, and the view that the possibility of freedom must be not only accessible to human reason through the consciousness of the moral law but also palpable to human sensibility through the experience of nature, artistic genius, and human history.

[25] See also Chapter 10, section II.

Index

Abbott, Thomas K., 172n1
Adickes, Erich, 69, 115n9
aesthetic experience, 369–71
agency, rational, 148–55, 162, 200, 394. *See also* freedom; freedom of the will; rational being
Allison, Henry E., 46nn33, 34, 55n42, 56n43, 135n5, 136n6, 293–4
Altmann, Alexander, 18nn2, 4, 22n8, 25n10, 26n11, 27n13, 28nn15, 16, 31n21
Ameriks, Karl, 55n41, 138n10, 230n18
antinomies of pure reason: Kant's early view of, 66–78; and highest good, 348–9. *See also* Kant, *Critique of Pure Reason*
appearances, contrasted to things in themselves, 45–6
apperception, 29–30, 50–1, 80–1, 115
Appiah, K. Anthony, 235n1
Aune, Bruce, 175n3, 193n17
Aurelius, Marcus, 31
autonomy, 1, 4, 9, 12, 96–7, 99–100, 108, 124–5, 133, 153–5, 202–4, 239–40, 242. *See also* freedom

Baron, Marcia, 290n3, 292, 324n30, 340n4
Baumgarten, Alexander, 68, 87n6, 93
beauty, 300–1, 336; as symbol of the morally good, 368
Beck, Lewis White, 18n4, 22n6, 24n8, 26n12, 29n18, 31nn20, 21, 35n23, 136n6, 172n1, 193n17
Beiser, Frederick C., 29n18, 426n15

belief: freedom of, 259–60; practical, 5–6, 43, 335–6, 361–2, 365, 367
beneficence, 149, 324, 341
benevolence, 314, 326–7, 341–2, 392
Bill of Rights, U.S., 263, 265, 266
Brandt, Reinhard, 380n7, 409n1, 427n15, 432n23

categorical imperative, 10, 40, 57, 131, 134, 137, 139–42, 151–2, 158, 382–3; deduction of, 147, 159–60, 172–206, 216–18, 221–2; definition of, 186; formulations of, 142–3, 159–61, 163, 172–206; and hypothetical imperatives, 189, 195; possibility of, 177–84, 202–6; validity of, 145–6, 154, 218–19
character, empirical and intelligible, 394, 396–7
charity, 256–8
coercion, 11, 236–8, 242–3, 276–7, 278–9, 283–5, 304–5, 314, 320–1, 323, 412–13
commerce, spirit of, 426
conscience, 299
consent, 148, 192, 249, 280–1
consequentialism, 32–3
conservatism, 235–6
constitution: republican, 411–12, 415–20; U.S., 262–3, 265
construction, in mathematics, 35–6, 44
contradiction, principle of (non-), 21, 26
corruption, 209–10
Cramer, Konrad, 218n8
Crusius, Christian August, 6n6, 18, 38–9, 132n4

435

Index

Davidson, Arnold I., 271n7
Declaration of Independence, U.S., 262–3, 265, 267
definitions: in mathematics, 34–6; in philosophy, 36–7
deontological moral theory, 132–6, 154, 156, 185n12
Descartes, René, 18, 26, 27, 28, 30; on *cogito*, Kant's critique of, 48–50
determinism, 11, 208, 213–14, 227–31, 393
dialectic: Kant's early view of transcendental, 66–84; in morals, 211–12. *See also* Kant, *Critique of Pure Reason*
difference principle, 272–4, 281
Donagan, Alan, 384n9
dualism, 365–7, 394
duties: also ends, 196–7, 313–14, 317–19; of love, 324, 384; to others, 299, 313, 316, 318, 324, 326–7, 384; perfect versus imperfect, 149, 316–17, 322, 325–6; of respect, 314–15, 384; of right, 316–17, 319; to self, 299–301, 313, 316, 318, 384; system of, 142, 148; of virtue, 303, 311–23, 340–1
duty: concept of, 190, 215; and moral feeling, 299–302; as motivation, 215–17, 290, 292, 294, 296–8, 303–11, 321–3, 327–8, 369, 378–9, 411; stringency of, 208, 227–31; of virtue, 319–23

education, moral, 175
Eisenberg, Paul, 324n30
Ellington, James, 172n1
empiricism, 19, 20, 58–9, 133, 188n13, 208
ends: contingent versus necessary, 57, 86–7, 89, 187–90; that are also duties, 311–14; harmony of, 85–9, 92–4; relation of particular to ends in themselves, 10, 57, 104–6, 144–6, 148–9, 162–3, 178, 198–200, 383; rational being as end in itself, 148–55; rational beings never act without, 143, 182–3, 187–90, 191–2, 195–7, 226, 344–5. *See also* humanity
Enlightenment, the, 1–2, 4, 32
Epicureans, 348
evil, 223–5, 231, 296–7, 350, 424–5
examples: of duty, 148, 177, 190, 196, 215; and principle of morality, 219–21, 227–8, 290–91, 340
experience, possibility of, 70

fact of reason, 136, 138
form, of moral maxims, 175, 186
formal principles in ethics, 8, 39, 42, 56, 89, 104–5, 134–5, 159, 190, 195, 223, 383
Formey, Samuel, 18
Formula of Autonomy, 173–6, 178, 180, 184, 201–6
Formula of Humanity as an End in Itself, 10, 57, 142–3, 159–61, 173–6, 178–80, 182–84, 188, 191–200, 206, 222
Formula of Kingdom of Ends, 142, 159–61, 173–6, 180–4, 201–6
Formula of Universal Law, 10, 57, 142–3, 159–61, 173–7, 179–80, 182–90, 191–3, 200, 205–6, 215, 222. *See also* categorical imperative
freedom: of action, 237, 241–4; compatibility with coercion, 236–8, 242–3, 276–9; as fundamental value, 1–2, 4–11, 13, 56–8, 96–100, 107–17, 129–31, 133, 152–3, 155–9, 162–71, 239–40; and happiness, 101–17; freedom of expression, 12, 236–7, 258–61; and merit, 119–23; and nature, 379–80, 386, 393–406; as postulate of practical reason, 85, 89–92, 333, 338, 349, 352–5; relation to virtue, 12, 308–11. *See also* freedom of the will
freedom of the will, 2–3, 5–7, 131, 135–8, 227–31, 394, 396–7; Mendelssohn on, 31, 53–4; and derivation of moral law, 54–7; and perpetual peace, 423–5. *See also* freedom
French Revolution, 432

Galston, William, 413n8
Garve, Christian, 339n3, 343–5, 391, 406
geometry: Mendelssohn on, 21–3; Kant on, 35
God: arguments for existence of, 27–30, 39, 47–8, 66; as author of nature, 343, 349, 355, 395, 399, 401; duty regarding, 370; as human idea, 403–5; as lawgiver, 402–3; and morality, Mendelssohn on, 32; postulate of existence of, 69, 85, 89–95, 118, 333–4, 338, 345, 349–51, 359–60
Goethe, Johann Wolfgang von, 289n2
good will, 139, 147, 153, 163, 166, 212, 215–17, 290, 304–5, 381
government, 419–20. *See also* constitution

Gregor, Mary J., 210n4, 250n24, 279n12, 310n19
Guyer, Paul, 46n34, 59n46, 138n10, 170n42, 181n9, 195n18, 356n15, 366n18, 370n21, 400n15, 429nn17, 18, 433n24

habit, 310–11
happiness: and freedom, 2–3, 9, 98, 108–17, 168, 378–9; inadequacy of as moral principle, 134–5, 140–1, 165, 212, 222–3; individual versus collective, 11, 98, 100–7, 119–20, 122–4, 344–5, 391–2; as object of morality, 88, 93–5, 100–7, 217–18, 339–42; relation to virtue, 97–100, 117–24, 348–9, 380. *See also* highest good
Hegel, Georg Wilhelm Friedrich, 25n10
Henrich, Dieter, 55n41, 207, 208–9, 214n6, 230n18
Henson, Richard, 291–2
Herman, Barbara, 185n12, 189n14, 196n21, 197n26, 199n27, 206n32, 291–2, 298, 340n4
heteronomy, 202
highest good, 9, 11, 12–13, 64, 93–5, 97, 99, 118, 212–13, 217–18, 225–7, 241, 333–4, 336–45, 366–7, 375–6, 380, 385–95, 397–400, 406–7. *See also* happiness
Hill, Thomas E., Jr., 192n17, 410n2
history, Kant's theory of, 11, 13, 372–407, 409–10
holiness, 352
humanity, as end in itself, 10, 57, 143, 149, 168–9, 192–200, 223, 314, 339, 410–11. *See also* Formula of Humanity as an End in Itself
Hume, David, 4, 209, 213, 221
Hutcheson, Francis, 42, 131, 221
hypotheses, 357
hypothetical imperatives, 40, 176, 189, 195, 202–3, 222

ideas, of reason, 78, 80–1, 83–4
illusion, dialectical or transcendental, 62, 68–9, 77–8, 83
immortality, postulate of, 89–92, 333–4, 338, 345, 350–2, 388–90, 398
imperatives. *See* categorical imperative; hypothetical imperatives
imputation, 120
incentives, 136, 143, 178–9, 190, 294–5

inclination, 3, 53, 88, 100, 104, 114, 136, 138, 143, 146, 172, 223–4, 287–8, 290–2, 294–5, 297–9, 302–3, 306–8, 311, 342, 382–3, 385
incorporation thesis, 293–4
interests, 201–2
internalism, 136, 139
intuition, 44–6, 160, 175

Jacobi, Friedrich Heinrich, 29, 43
Johnson, Robert N., 297n12, 309n18
judgment, moral, 175, 182, 212, 215, 219
justice, principles of, 264–6, 268–77, 285. *See also* right

Kant, Immanuel, works of:
  Conflict of the Faculties, 260, 410, 432
  Critique of (the Power of) Judgment, 20, 25n10, 64, 168–70, 361, 366, 368, 371, 405, 409, 433; on highest good, 225n14, 333–4, 389, 399–400; on postulates, 351, 353–4, 363–4, 428–30; on teleology, 279, 395, 400–2; on willing versus wishing, 347n11
  Critique of Practical Reason, 2, 5n5, 6, 53–4, 96–7, 99, 104, 121, 131–8, 139–42, 145, 154–5, 165–7, 215; on freedom of the will, 55–6, 183, 213, 229–30, 379, 394, 396–7, 423; on happiness, 222; on highest good, 118, 225n14, 339, 348–50, 366–7, 376, 386–9, 398–9; on postulates of practical reason, 337–8, 343, 346, 350–3, 361, 363, 398, 428; on self-contentment, 393; on virtue, 305
  Critique of Pure Reason, 5, 9, 30, 34, 36, 42, 44–50, 60–1, 100, 176n43, 410; Antinomy of Pure Reason, 47, 63, 65–6, 74, 393–4; Canon of Pure Reason, 225n14, 342, 361–2, 386–8; on highest good, 333, 342, 386–90; on hypotheses, 357; Ideal of Pure Reason, 65, 359–60; on noumenon, 55; outlines of, 69, 78–84; Paralogisms of Pure Reason, 48–9, 65–6, 83–4; Postulates of Empirical Thinking, 356; Principles of Judgment in, 195; on real versus logical possibility, 181–2; Refutation of Idealism, 50, 195n18; on regulative principles, 64, 429; transcendental deduction of the categories, 50–1; structure of Transcendental Dialectic, 65, 77–84
  Dreams of a Spirit-Seer, 19

Kant, Immanuel, works of (*cont.*)
  *Groundwork for the Metaphysics of
    Morals*, 2, 5n5, 10–11, 33n22, 96–7,
    99, 101, 111, 129, 133, 138–48, 153–4,
    162–4, 166, 240, 369, 374, 391; ex-
    amples in, 56, 177, 190, 196, 219–21,
    290–1, 340, 406; formulations of cat-
    egorical imperative in, 172–85,
    196–7; on freedom of the will, 54–5,
    91, 183, 230–1, 423; on moral worth,
    287–91, 298–9, 303, 304–5, 381–2;
    relations among three sections of,
    52–3, 139–40, 146–7, 176–80, 201,
    212–14, 217; strategy of, 207–31
  *Idea for a Universal History from a
    Cosmpolitan Point of View*, 13, 167–8,
    372–407, 408–9, 414–16, 423
  *Inquiry concerning the Distinctness of
    the Principles of Natural Theology and
    Morality*, 7, 18, 34–42, 58, 130–1, 195,
    239n4
  lectures on ethics and natural right, 9,
    57, 96, 129–30, 136n8, 152–3, 156–8,
    170–1, 240, 275, 305–6, 309, 314–18,
    320–1, 323–4, 328, 348
  lectures on logic, 346–8, 361–2
  *Metaphysical Foundations of Natural
    Science*, 372–3
  Metaphysics of Morals, 86, 124n15, 140,
    144n14, 240, 366; Doctrine of Right,
    240–7, 277–80, 411–12, 430–1; Doc-
    trine of Virtue, 196–7, 204, 392, 410;
    on aesthetic experience, 369–70; on
    moral feeling, 299–302; on virtue
    and duties of virtue, 303–4, 306–15,
    317–22, 340–2, 383–5
  *New Elucidation of the First Principles of
    Metaphysical Cognition*, 6
  *On the Common Saying: That Might Be
    Right in Theory but Not in Practice*,
    164, 257, 263–4, 343–5, 391–2, 410,
    418–20, 430–1, 433
  *On the Form and Principles of the Sen-
    sible and Intelligible Worlds* (inau-
    gural dissertation), 47n35, 63, 73
  *Only Possible Basis for a Demonstration
    of the Existence of God*, 18n3, 39–40,
    181, 358, 414n10
  Opus postumum, 394–5, 402–6
  Prolegomena to Any Future Metaphysics,
    194–5, 373
  *Religion within the Boundaries of Mere
    Reason*, 5n5, 20, 38, 56, 197n25,
    353n14; on evil, 223–5, 231; on free-

dom of the will, 423–4; on funda-
    mental maxims, 294–7; on highest
    good, 225–7; on regulative prin-
    ciples, 429
  Toward Perpetual Peace, 13, 408–34
  What Is Enlightenment?, 261
  What Is Orientation in Thinking?, 19,
    43, 45, 48
  *What Real Progress Has Metaphysics
    Made in Germany since the Time of
    Leibniz and Wolff?*, 333, 337, 351,
    354–5, 361–2, 364
Kersting, Wolfgang, 249n24, 279n12,
  283n13
kingdom of ends, 10, 142, 173–4, 201–6,
  340, 380. *See also* Formula of King-
  dom of Ends
Kleingeld, Pauline, 372n2, 373n3
Klemme, Heiner F., 433n23
Korsgaard, Christine M., 144n15, 150,
  169n40, 289n3, 382n8

language, 425–6
legislation, and interest in reason, 201–5
Leibniz, Gottfried Wilhelm, 6n6, 18,
  22n6, 27, 46, 209
Leibnizo-Wolffian philosophy, 6n6, 8,
  18–20, 29, 34
Lessing, Gotthold Ephraim, 29n18, 43
Levine, Andrew, 271n7
liberalism, 235–6; Kant's conception of,
  12, 236–9, 246, 258–61, 285–6
liberty, equal, 265, 268, 271–5
life, principle of, 116
Linden, Harry van der, 413n8
Locke, John, 209, 213, 267–8
love, 200
Ludwig, Bernd, 249n24, 264n1, 279n12

material principles in ethics, 8, 39, 42, 56,
  190, 195, 223
materialism, 49
mathematics: Mendelssohn on, 20–4, 36,
  44–6; Kant on, 20, 24, 34–7, 44–7
matter, of moral laws, 159–60, 175
maxims: particular, 184, 186, 225, 383;
  fundamental, 294–8, 327–8, 353
McCarty, Richard, 324n30
Mendelssohn, Moses, 7, 17–59, 130n2;
  on mathematics, 21–4, 44–6; on
  metaphysics, 24–30, 38, 47–51; on
  morality, 30–4, 41, 51–4; *Essay
  on Evidence*, 17–34, 43; *Jerusalem*,
  42; *Phaedon*, 42

merit, 98, 119, 121–3, 323–9
metaphysics, 4–5, 9, 20; Mendelssohn
    on, 24–30, 47–51; Kant on, 37–9,
    47–51, 66–8
metaphysics of morals, Kant's concep-
    tion of, 139–40, 145–7
Mill, John Stuart, 260
moral feeling, 299–302. *See also* respect
moral law, 3–5, 131–6, 139–40, 175–6,
    381–2; deduction of, 160–1; and
    ends, 145–6; and freedom of the
    will, 6, 135–6; and happiness, 100–1,
    105–7; and highest good, 337–45;
    as means to preserve and promote
    freedom, 8, 10, 155–9, 163; as mo-
    tive, 136–7, 143, 160, 289–93. *See also*
    categorical imperative
moral politicans, 421–3
moral psychology, 336–7, 361–71
moral sense, 18, 131
moral theology, 360
moral worth, 237, 287–305, 324, 327–9,
    380–5
motives, 178–9, 289–91, 344–5
Mulholland, Leslie A., 150–1, 246n18,
    250n24, 278n11, 279n12, 284n14,
    426n15
murder, 149

natural law theory of ethics, 31–2, 53
nature: and freedom, 374–8, 386, 393–
    406; as venue for human action, 3,
    378–9
Newton, Isaac, 37–8
Nicholson, Peter F., 433n23

obligation, 40–1, 56–7, 132
O'Neill, Onora, 161n34, 347n11
ontological argument: Mendelssohn on,
    20, 23, 27–8; Kant on, 20, 29–30,
    39–40, 358
opinion, 361–2
organisms, 400–1
original position, 268–71, 273

paternalism, 264, 267
Paton, Herbert James, 142n13, 144n15,
    150n19, 162n36, 172n1, 174nn2, 3,
    178nn6, 7, 191n15, 193n17, 222n11,
    289nn2, 3
peace, perpetual, 13, 336, 408–34
perfection, 8, 31, 41, 58
perfectionism, 30, 32–3; Kant's rejection
    of, 51–2, 58, 221

personality, 115, 154
Plato, *Meno*, 21–2
Platonism, 113
Pogge, Thomas W., 161n34, 174n2
possession: intelligible and sensible,
    244–6, 248, 279–81; original, 252–4
possibility, 180–4, 346, 355–60
postulates: of practical reason, 13, 43, 85,
    89–94, 333–71, 374, 426; with regard
    to property, 247, 279–80
Potter, Nelson, 290n3, 295n8, 307n17,
    382n8
primary goods, 270–3
progress, 425–34
promising, 148–9, 341, 383
property, Kant's conception of, 12,
    236–58, 279–86
prosyllogisms, 78–9
Pufendorf, Samuel, 32
purposes. *See* ends

Rashdall, Hastings, 289n2
rational being: concept of, 3, 54, 176–7,
    179–80, 182, 187, 191–2; as end in it-
    self, 145–6, 148–55, 162–71, 191–200,
    203–4; validity of moral law for all,
    143, 177, 186–7
rationalism, 19, 58
Rawls, John, 12, 144, 264–77, 281–2, 285
reason: distinction from common moral
    understanding, 207–9; distinction
    from understanding, 62–3, 74; prac-
    tical, 2–3, 8–9, 60–2, 64, 68–70, 74–5,
    84–95, 100–1, 104–7, 124, 143, 335–6,
    346–7; pure, 60–61, 71; seeks the un-
    conditioned, 76–84; unity of, 62–3,
    65, 73–4, 86–9
reciprocity thesis, 56
reflective judgment, 64, 429
regulative principles or ideals, 63–4, 169,
    171, 401–2, 409–10, 425–34
religion, 425–6
republics, 415–20
respect, 138, 154, 289–90, 297–9, 303–11,
    321–3, 343
right: innate, 278; universal principle of,
    240–1, 263–4, 279, 410–12; and coer-
    cion, 241–3
rights: innate versus acquired, 238, 244;
    property, 236–9, 244–58, 279–86;
    provisional versus conclusive, 283–4

schematism, 253–4
Schiller, Friedrich, 298, 353n14

Schilpp, Paul A., 40n28, 164n36
Schmucker, Josef, 40n28, 58n45, 108n6
Schneewind, J. B., 3n3
self-constraint, 312–14, 318, 320
self-contentment, 108–9, 111–12, 165, 393
self-deception, 385
self-interest, 220
self-knowledge, 48–51
self-love, 103, 138, 200, 226–7, 295–8, 302, 343
self-satisfaction, 118–19, 164–5
self-sufficiency, 420
sensibility, 62, 69, 113–14, 366–8
Shaftesbury, Anthony Ashley Cooper, third Earl of, 32
Sherman, Nancy, 366n18
Sidgwick, Henry, 135n5, 423
Simmons, Keith, 290n3
Sorrell, Tom, 297n11
Spinoza, Baruch (Benedictus), 28, 43, 403
Stoicism, 164, 348
Stratton-Lake, Philip, 174n3
Strawson, Peter, 118n12
sufficient reason, principle of, 28
suicide, 149, 341
Sulzer, Johann Georg, 17–18
supererogation, 324
sympathy, 301–2, 382
synthetic *a priori* propositions in moral theory, 179–80, 194–5, 348
systematicity, 61–3, 72, 76, 82, 90, 93–5, 115

talents, duty to develop, 148, 311–13, 328, 341, 383
teleological moral theory, 132–3, 139, 147, 154, 156, 166–70
teleology, 13, 224, 378

things in themselves, contrasted to appearances, 45–6
Tittel, Gottlob August, 53n39
transcendental idealism, and determinism, 229–31, 396–7
tyranny, 419

understanding, 60–3, 69, 83
universalizability, 141, 151, 184, 194, 382. *See also* Formula of Universal Law
unsocial sociability, 409, 423, 425

virtue, 3, 287, 303–23; as aim of nature, 377–8, 385, 434; duties of, 12, 303–4, 311–23; and highest good, 339–40, 348–9, 380, 385–93; and worthiness to be happy, 97–100, 110, 117–24. *See also* highest good
Vleeschauwer, Herman-Jean de, 38nn24, 25

Wallace, R. Jay, 118n12, 183n11
war, 415–17, 419
Ward, Keith, 104n5, 108n6
will: consistency in, 114–15; definition of, 191; contrast with wish, 348n11 *See also* freedom of the will, good will
Wolff, Christian, 18, 28, 30, 33, 38, 41, 58, 209, 221, 403
Wolff, Robert Paul, 150n19
Wood, Allen W., 40n27
world: federation, 416–18, 421; intellectual versus sensible, 112–14, 116
Wundt, Max, 38nn24, 25

Yovel, Yirmiahu, 377, 413n8, 426n15